An introduction to the volu

Over the last few years the complete restructuring of health and welfare provision has meant that there has been a re-evaluation of all sectors of this 'market'. For the voluntary sector, it has meant increased responsibility and accountability and a re-examination of the management of these organisations – charity and fundraising have become 'big business'.

But how can the voluntary sector respond to this pressure, who is running it and how should it be managed?

In *An Introduction to the Voluntary Sector* the editors and contributors examine key features, including its history, its present position and its future; they analyse the challenges it faces and provide practical guidance and analysis of the current issues, including its legal framework in the UK and EC, fundraising activities, management and accountability.

An Introduction to the Voluntary Sector will be invaluable reading for all students and lecturers of social policy and organisational studies as well as for professional policy-makers and voluntary sector personnel.

Justin Davis Smith is Head of Research and Information at the Volunteer Centre UK. **Colin Rochester** is a consultant, researcher and writer as well as Research Development Officer at the Centre for Voluntary Organisation at the London School of Economics. **Rodney Hedley** is Secretary to the Trustees of the Hilden Charitable Fund.

An introduction to the voluntary sector

Edited by
Justin Davis Smith, Colin Rochester
and Rodney Hedley

London and New York

First published 1995
by Routledge
11 New Fetter Lane, London EC4P 4EE

Simultaneously published in the USA and Canada
by Routledge
29 West 35th Street, New York, NY 10001

Typeset in Times by
Ponting–Green Publishing Services, Chesham, Bucks

Printed and bound in Great Britain by
Mackays of Chatham PLC, Chatham, Kent

British Library Cataloguing in Publication Data
A catalogue record for this book is available from the
British Library.

Library of Congress Cataloging in Publication Data
A catalog record for this book has been requested

ISBN   0–415–09921–8 (hbk)
ISBN   0–415–09922–6 (pbk)

Contents

Contributors

Julian Batsleer undertook research into charity administration in the early 1970s – long before it was fashionable. Since then he has worked in a variety of capacities on the borders between adult and higher education and the voluntary sector. He has taught politics and industrial relations for the Workers' Educational Association and established a management training service for Greater Manchester Council for Voluntary Service. He is currently a Lecturer in Management Development with the Open University's Business School and a member of the Voluntary Sector Management Programme.

Tim Dartington has been Head of Management Development at the National Council for Voluntary Organisations (NCVO) since 1986 and is a frequent contributor of management articles in *NCVO News*. He serviced the On Trust Working Party and set up the Trustee Services Unit at NCVO. He is a contributor to the Open University reader, *Managing Voluntary and Non-profit Organisations*. He has written extensively on management and organisation in institutional and community care, including *Family Care of Old People* (Souvenir 1980), *A Life Together* (Tavistock 1981) and *The Limits of Altruism* (King's Fund 1986).

Justin Davis Smith, previously political assistant to the Rt. Hon. Sir James Callaghan MP (now Lord Callaghan), is Head of Research and Information at The Volunteer Centre UK. He obtained a 1st class honours degree in modern history from the University of Loughborough in 1982, and a doctorate on the history of industrial relations after the Second World War in 1986. Recent research at The Volunteer Centre UK includes a major national survey of volunteering and a study on 50 plus volunteering as part of the Carnegie Enquiry into the Third Age. He is currently managing a ten-nation Pan-European study on volunteering, funded primarily by the Nuffield Foundation. He is author of *The Attlee and Churchill Administrations and Industrial Unrest 1945–55*, Pinter, 1990, and co-editor of *Volunteering and Society*, Bedford Square Press, 1992. He is co-founder of the Voluntary Action History Society.

Nicholas Deakin has been Professor of Social Policy and Administration at

Birmingham University since 1980. Previously, he worked in central and local government and at an independent research institute. At Birmingham he teaches at both undergraduate and postgraduate levels (in particular, on the department's master's degree in Social Services Management). He has held numerous research grants from research councils, government departments and independent trusts and foundations. His current research interests include the impact of recent changes in central government policies on the voluntary sector and the theory and practice of policies for the inner cities. His most recent major publications are *The Enterprise Culture and the Inner City* (with John Edwards), Routledge, 1993, and *The Costs of Welfare* (ed. with Robert Page), Avebury, 1993. A new edition of his text *The Politics of Welfare* will appear from Harvester Wheatsheaf in spring 1994.

Rodney Hedley is secretary to the Trustees of the Hilden Charitable Fund. His extensive experience of the voluntary sector includes a period as Research and Information Officer at the London-wide volunteering agency, ADVANCE. He has also worked as a Research Officer at the Centre for Policy on Ageing and the London School of Economics' Centre for Voluntary Organisation as well as as a freelance consultant and researcher. Among his many publications are *Volunteering and Society* (with Justin Davis Smith), Bedford Square Press, 1992, and *Understanding Management Committees* (with Colin Rochester), The Volunteer Centre UK, 1992.

Jeremy Kendall is a Research Fellow at the Personal Social Services Research Unit, University of Kent at Canterbury, where he has been since completing an M.Sc. in Health Economics at the University of York in 1989. His academic interests include the economics of the voluntary sector, non-profit studies in general and analysis of the evolving mixed economy of social care. He is currently involved in two major projects: an evaluation of the mixed economy of care funded by the Department of Health, and the UK leg of the Johns Hopkins Comparative Nonprofit Sector Project funded primarily by the Joseph Rowntree Foundation and the Charities Aid Foundation.

Martin Knapp is Professor of the Economics of Social Care, Personal Social Services Research Unit, University of Kent at Canterbury, and Professor of Health Economics and Director, Centre for the Economics of Mental Health, Institute of Psychiatry (University of London). His research focuses on social care, particularly the developing mixed economy, voluntary sector organisations and volunteering, and the economics of mental health care. He is co-editor of *Voluntas*. Recent jointly authored books include *Care in the Community: Challenge and Demonstration*, Ashgate, 1992, and *Social Care in a Mixed Economy*, Open University Press, 1994.

Diana Leat has been involved in research into the voluntary sector for almost twenty years. Diana has held research posts in several national voluntary organisations and has had research and teaching posts in a number of universities. She has written extensively on the voluntary sector and social policy. Her recent publications include: *Managing Across Sectors: Similarities and Differences between For-Profit and Voluntary Non-Profit Organisations*, VOLPROF, City University Business School, London, 1993; *The Development of Community Care by the Independent Sector*, Policy Studies Institute, London; *Management for Tomorrow* (with I. Bruce), VOLPROF, City University Business School, London. She is currently a Visiting Senior Research Fellow and Assistant Director at VOLPROF, City University Business School, London.

Colin Rochester has worked in the voluntary sector for twenty-five years. During this time he has acted as manager, elected officer, committee member and consultant at national and local level. He was one of the first students to take the specialist master's degree in voluntary sector organisation. Since 1989 he has combined freelance work as a consultant, researcher and writer with the part-time appointment as Research Development Officer at the Centre for Voluntary Organisation at the London School of Economics.

Jos Sheard became a volunteer in 1975 and has worked in the field of volunteering ever since. In the 1980s he worked for the London Voluntary Service Council and ADVANCE. He is currently Principal Officer (Volunteers) for the London Borough of Croydon Social Services Department. His publications include *The Politics of Volunteering*, ADVANCE, 1986.

Perri 6 is Lecturer in European Social Policy at the University of Bath, and was formerly Head of Policy Analysis and Research at the National Council for Voluntary Organisations. He is author of *What is a Voluntary Organisation?*, NCVO, 1991, and, with Jenny Fieldgrass, *Snapshots of the Voluntary Sector Today*, NCVO, 1992. His recent published journal papers include studies on the voluntary sector and European competition, European taxation policy, innovation, and a study with Eva Kuti on the implications of future membership of the European Union for the Hungarian non-profit sector. His book, *Liberty, Charity and Politics*, a twenty-four country study, written with Anita Randon, will be published by Dartmouth in 1994. His current research interests include work on institutional theory, on the relationship of social to public policy and on the concept of trust.

Introduction

THE RESURGENCE OF VOLUNTARY ACTION

In the years immediately after the Second World War the new 'welfare settlement' appeared to have rung down the curtain on the central role of voluntary action in meeting social needs. As the state assumed the major responsibility for the welfare of its citizens, the charities and other voluntary organisations which had pioneered and delivered so many services were to be displaced to the margins, to become little more than icing on the statutory cake.

The reality has turned out to be rather different. In the first place, the voluntary sector did not 'wither away' in the late 1940s and 1950s. While the welfare state displaced voluntary action in some fields – notably the direct relief of poverty and the provision of hospitals – there were many areas of welfare where the long-established voluntary organisations – such as the National Society for the Prevention of Cruelty to Children and other child care agencies and the Royal National Institutes for Deaf People and the Blind – continued to make a contribution that was much more than 'marginal'. Newer bodies – notably the Citizens Advice Bureaux and the Family Service Units – whose value had been demonstrated during wartime and in its immediate aftermath also became part of the fabric of welfare.

In the 1960s and 1970s, moreover, the sector gained fresh vitality. A new generation of volunteers founded a series of organisations to tackle a whole range of perceived inadequacies in welfare provision. Alongside the 'household names' of the period – such as SHELTER's Campaign for the Homeless, the Child Poverty Action Group, the Disablement Income Group and the National Association for the Care and Resettlement of Offenders – were many more new organisations – national and local – concerned with the welfare of people with specific disabilities, health needs or other problems. It was a period in which the tradition of self-help and mutual aid was revitalised and when advocacy and community development brought renewed variety to the local voluntary sector.

The growing self-confidence of the new voluntary sector during the 1970s was matched by a rising disenchantment with the state's welfare bureaucracies which spread across the political spectrum and was expressed in Hadley and Hatch's *Social Welfare and the Failure of the State* published in 1981. At local level the value of voluntary organisations as instruments of public policy was highlighted by major investment in sympathetic local groups by the Greater London Council and other Labour-controlled authorities. In the longer run, however, it was to be a very different model of statutory/voluntary relations that brought the sector back to the very centre of welfare provision.

The radical reforms of the third Thatcher administration encompassed the dismantling of the local government and health service bureaucracies responsible for the provision of social welfare. As well as creating self-governing health service trusts and grant-maintained 'opted-out' schools, these radical changes have propelled the voluntary sector on to centre stage. The major responsibility for social housing has been transferred from local government to the voluntary housing association movement. In similar fashion, the responsibilities of social services departments are being restricted. Increasingly, they will become 'enablers' rather than providers, relying on the purchase of services for older people, people with disabilities, children and families from the private and the voluntary sectors.

Far from retreating to the margins of welfare provision the voluntary sector finds itself at the centre of a fundamental change the full impact of which has still to be felt. It is a fairly safe prediction, however, that the sector will grow larger. And it has already reached dimensions that would have been unthinkable fifty years ago.

Voluntary action is notoriously difficult to quantify, definitions of voluntary organisations are contested, and the boundaries of the sector cannot be drawn with confidence (the complexities involved are explored by Jeremy Kendall and Martin Knapp in Chapter 3). But we can make a rough estimate of its current scale. One recent estimate provides a figure of between 230,000 and 300,000 voluntary organisations in England and Wales alone. A total of some three million voluntary committee members are responsible for a combined annual income of more than £17 billions and the employment of the equivalent of 250,000 full-time paid staff (6 and Fieldgrass 1992). A recent survey suggests that more than half the adult population of the United Kingdom – 23 million people – are involved in voluntary work, although many of these are active in the statutory and private sectors (Lynn and Davis Smith 1991).

THE GROWTH OF VOLUNTARY SECTOR STUDIES

The refusal of the voluntary sector to wither away and its resumption of a central position in the social policy landscape has been accompanied by a rapid development of academic interest. The lead has been taken by the United States which boasts a score of academic centres and several hundred university programmes of non-profit studies. But the creation of a new field of study has been a truly international development with activity in Australia and South America as well as Europe, East and West, and North America. While still small in scale if compared to more established areas of study, the field can support three specialist journals (*Nonprofit Management and Leadership*; *Nonprofit and Voluntary Sector Quarterly*; and *Voluntas*) and a fourth (*Nonprofit Studies*) is planned.

In Britain the development of voluntary sector studies was led by David Billis and his colleagues, initially at Brunel University and now at the London School of Economics. Other major contributions have been made by the Open University's Business School and by Martin Knapp and his colleagues at the University of Kent, while scholars at another dozen British universities have turned their attention to the study of the sector.

The present book is thus timely for two reasons. The growth of the voluntary sector and its return to the centre of the social policy stage has made it necessary, while the development of a body of research-based literature – both domestic and international – has made it possible.

THE APPROACH

An Introduction to the Voluntary Sector was originally conceived as a kind of 'road atlas' providing between one pair of covers as comprehensive as possible a guide to the salient features of the sector, its workings, and the main issues and problems which face voluntary organisations. There are already a number of studies on particular aspects of the sector – such as management and organisation and the role of volunteers – but, until now, no single text that provides a general overview.

It is aimed at two groups of readers. In the first place it is intended to provide a textbook for the growing number of students for whom the voluntary sector is an essential part of their course work. It is difficult to imagine a course in social policy or social administration that can ignore the sector and we aim to meet the needs of the general student at undergraduate and postgraduate level as well as of the increasing numbers who will make a special study of voluntary organisations.

Second, it is aimed at policy-makers and practitioners, those who develop public policy and those who wrestle with its implementation. The development of the sector has brought a rapid increase in the numbers of those who lead and manage voluntary agencies and those who – as agents of government or the private sector – will have dealings with them. We hope that this book will help them to orientate themselves in their new world.

In order to achieve both depth of understanding and breadth of coverage the book takes the form of a series of essays by acknowledged experts in the field. While some of the chapters will draw on previously unpublished material, the emphasis has been on reviewing existing literature and identifying the key issues arising from it. Its focus is the British voluntary sector but we do not take a narrowly parochial view of the brief: we have included a chapter which compares the British scene with other European countries and have drawn on relevant research from overseas.

THE CONTENTS

As co-founders of the Voluntary Action History Society the editors firmly believe that our understanding of the contemporary voluntary sector will be impoverished by the absence of a knowledge of its origins and history. In the first chapter Justin Davis Smith traces the roots of voluntary action in Britain some five hundred years into the past. He looks at the two central impulses informing voluntarism – philanthropy and mutual aid – and their continuing relevance, and, arguing that philanthropic good works have received an undue share of attention from previous writers, sets out to rescue self-help and mutual aid from comparative neglect.

Davis Smith takes the story up to the development of the welfare state after the Second World War, where Nicholas Deakin picks up the threads in Chapter 2 which brings the historical review of the development of the voluntary sector and its role up to the present day. In the process he examines the continuing role of the sector in the new welfare state of the immediate post-war period; the development of a new generation of voluntary organisations in the 1960s; the emergence of welfare pluralism in the 1970s; and the move towards the contract culture of the 1990s.

Chapter 3 attempts to bring clarity to the confused and complex terminology employed to define the boundaries of the sector and to classify or categorise voluntary organisations. Jeremy Kendall and Martin Knapp suggest that there is no single 'correct' definition and that the approach to be adopted should depend on the purpose for which the exercise is being undertaken. They describe criteria for a 'structural/operational definition' which has been developed for cross-national comparison and show how discussion of the application of these criteria pragmatically in the UK can help to clarify the debate about how to define and classify the sector.

In the following chapter Rodney Hedley looks at some of the features of the local and national voluntary sectors and attempts to tease out the extent to which they operate as a sector. In particular, he looks at the role of intermediary bodies and non-departmental public bodies before discussing the under-representation of certain sections of the population in voluntary action. And, finally, he looks at some theoretical models which help our understanding of the voluntary sector as an industry.

There is considerable confusion in the public mind between 'volunteering' and the 'voluntary sector'. Much voluntary action on an individual basis takes place in the statutory and private sectors and the 'voluntary' in many voluntary organisations is restricted to the unpaid contribution of the members of their governing bodies. The idea of volunteering has also been confused by the tendency to equate volunteers who give their time unpaid and freely on a more or less organised basis with unpaid carers and people on low-paid job experience schemes or community service orders. As well as teasing out these confusions in Chapter 5 Jos Sheard reviews recent government policies towards volunteers and the evidence as to the motivations of those who take up voluntary work.

Chapter 6 puts the sector in context by offering some comparative material from mainland Europe. In it Perri 6 considers first how some of the key issues faced by the sector in the United Kingdom are manifesting themselves in other European countries, concentrating on issues of definitions, identity and recognition and key areas and styles of state regulation of the sector. Second, he argues that the option of ignoring developments in Europe is one that will not remain open to British voluntary organisations. In the short run, the institutions of the European Community are increasingly involved in regulating the fields in which voluntary bodies work. Longer term he holds out the prospect of a future in which there will be a real option of working across frontiers 'not just as a luxury but as a mainstream of their strategy'. The chapter therefore concludes with a review of the prospects for policy making at the supra-national level.

The popular idea that the voluntary sector's income is derived from 'voluntary sources', such as fundraising from the public at large, is at odds with the facts: in particular, it obscures the very substantial funding received from the state on one hand or from the sale of goods and services on the other. It also obscures, as Diana Leat points out in Chapter 7, the wide variations in the amount, the sources and the types of income raised by individual organisations. Leat reviews the various sources of finance available to voluntary agencies, summarises the main advantages and drawbacks of each source and highlights some of the problems thrown up by changing patterns of funding.

Questions of funding lead rapidly to issues of accountability. In Chapter 8 Colin Rochester argues that demands for accountability pose more difficult and complex issues for voluntary agencies than are experienced by their counterparts in the statutory or private sectors. Among the demands to be balanced by voluntary sector leaders and managers are accountability to members; to users or beneficiaries; to funders; to the community; and to the public at large. The chapter looks at the various pressures involved in each area of accountability before examining critically the adequacy of the present arrangements for the regulation of voluntary action through the Charities Act and the Charity Commission.

Accountability and regulation are, at bottom, the responsibility of the unpaid governing bodies of voluntary agencies. In Chapter 9 Tim Dartington draws on recent research to examine the ways in which committee members or trustees are recruited and trained; the ways in which they define and carry out their functions; and the boundaries and relationships between governing bodies and their staff in general and their chief executives in particular.

Finally, in Chapter 10, Julian Batsleer looks at the encounter between management and the voluntary sector which followed the 1981 Handy Report on *Improving Effectiveness in Voluntary Organisations*. In Batsleer's view the 'management question' has two elements. The first is the search for a recognisable management discourse. This has involved creating a language and developing and disseminating perspectives and theories. The second element is the search for appropriate management practice which he explores in four key areas: management competences, roles and values; human resources management; resource acquisition; and organisational structures and strategic management.

LIMITATIONS

We are conscious of a number of omissions. This is to some extent inevitable: no single textbook can claim to be truly complete. There are also problems which are specific to a field of study which is at an early stage of development: we can only seek to review and crystallise the results of research that has been undertaken, and there are some notable gaps.

We are conscious of a heavy bias in the material towards organisations in the field of social welfare. There is comparatively little information about those active in the environmental, educational and cultural fields, while housing associations and non-governmental organisations concerned with aid and development have only recently become the subject of study as part of the voluntary sector (Billis *et al*. 1994; Billis and MacKeith 1993).

A second major limitation is our concentration on voluntary organisations as providers of services rather than as sources of funding. We have chosen to exclude the thousands of charitable trusts and foundations from consideration in the interest of maintaining a manageable field of study.

Third, we are aware that our coverage of the many issues involving volunteers and volunteering and the substantial literature devoted to this area is limited. We took the view that the interests of balanced coverage of our wider field meant that one chapter was the maximum we could devote to this aspect of the voluntary sector.

Finally, and most regrettably, we are concerned that we have not been able to do justice to the extent of voluntary action by black and ethnic minority communities (although we would draw the attention of readers to the section in Chapter 4 in which Rodney Hedley raises the issue). The lack of research literature here reflects the difficulties black organisations have experienced in gaining recognition and access to funding. We note that the institutions and infrastructure for the black voluntary sector have begun to emerge in the form of SIA, the National Development Agency for the Black and Minority Ethnic Voluntary Sector and the Resource Unit for Black Volunteering. (Indeed, two of us have played our part in the establishment of the latter.) We look forward to a revised version of this text in a few years' time that will be able to make good this omission.

CONCLUSION

The arrival of the voluntary sector on the centre of the public policy stage has put it under the most intense scrutiny. Under the glare of this public attention, fault-lines have been revealed in the general view that the future belongs to voluntary action. Critics in the United Kingdom (Hall 1989; Knight 1993) and in the United States, as reported in the *Philadelphia Inquirer* 1993, have questioned whether the legal and fiscal privileges enjoyed by voluntary bodies are justified. At the same time, as government policy increasingly treats voluntary agencies as mere instruments for implementing its policies, concern has been raised about the unintended organisational consequences of this approach (Billis 1993).

The need for an introduction to the voluntary sector in all its complexity has never been greater. Despite the limitations to which we have drawn attention, there has also never been so great an opportunity to bring together in one book the fruits of academic research. We believe that *An Introduction to the Voluntary Sector* will rise to the challenge by informing the actions of those who make policy and those who strive to implement it, as well as introducing students to an emerging and important new field of study.

Finally, we would like to express our gratitude to the authors of the individual chapters for their vital contributions to this important enterprise and to thank two other people who have made a substantial contribution to the book. The first of these is Eileen Mullins without whom it is highly unlikely that the manuscript would have been presented to the publisher in an acceptable form. The second is Catherine Rochester who has checked our references and compiled the bibliography which we believe will be an invaluable resource, especially for anyone coming new to the study of the sector.

Justin Davis Smith
Colin Rochester
Rodney Hedley

REFERENCES

Billis, D. (1993) *Organising Public and Voluntary Agencies*, London: Routledge.
Billis, D. and MacKeith, J. (1993) *Organising NGOs: Challenges and Trends in the Management of Overseas Aid*, London: Centre for Voluntary Organisation, London School of Economics.
Billis, D., Ashby, J., Ewart, A. and Rochester, C. (1994) *Taking Stock: The Shifting Foundations of Governance and Strategy in Housing Associations*, London: Centre for Voluntary Organisation, London School of Economics.
Hadley, R. and Hatch, S. (1981) *Social Welfare and the Failure of the State*, London: Allen & Unwin.
Hall, S. (1989) *The Voluntary Sector Under Attack?*, London: Islington Voluntary Action Council.
Knight, B. (1993) *Voluntary Action*, London: Home Office.

Lynn, P. and Davis Smith, J. (1991) *The 1991 National Survey of Voluntary Activity in the UK*, Berkhamsted: The Volunteer Centre UK.
6, P. and Fieldgrass, J. (1992) *Snapshots of the Voluntary Sector*, London: National Council for Voluntary Organisations.

1   The voluntary tradition
Philanthropy and self-help in Britain 1500–1945

Justin Davis Smith

INTRODUCTION

A French visitor to the British Isles in the mid-nineteenth century was struck by the prevalence of voluntary associations. He wrote:

> This tendency of the English to form groups through the attractions of certain pleasures, deserves our attention. . . .In France men like to meet for the sake of meeting; the Englishman is perhaps less sociable: he requires an object, a community of tastes, a peculiar tie, which draws him nearer his fellowmen. . . .The voluntary association in groups and series, is the great counterpoise of British personality.
>
> (A. Esquiros, The English at Home, 4 volumes (1861–3),
quoted in Bailey 1978)

Enthusiasm for voluntary action shows no sign of abating (although it is not, of course, suggested that such action is a peculiarly English or indeed British phenomenon). It is estimated that there are currently about 170,000 registered charities and perhaps as many as 300,000 voluntary organisations in England and Wales (NCVO 1992). A recent survey suggests that 23 million people take part in voluntary activities each year (The Volunteer Centre UK). Much has been written about voluntary action in recent years, about its size and shape and its role in relation to the state. However, with a few notable exceptions (for example, work by Owen and Harrison and more recently Finlayson and Prochaska), it has been the subject of little rigorous historical analysis. This chapter starts from the standpoint that, in order to understand the role of voluntary action in Britain today, it is necessary to adopt an historical perspective. And not only one going back to the nineteenth century – important though that period was in its development. The chapter will argue that the roots of voluntary action in Britain can be traced back at least as far as the sixteenth century, and possibly much earlier.

Any attempt to write a history of voluntary action in Britain over the past 500 years must of necessity be selective. David Owen (1964), the author of the major work in this field, was rightly criticised for focusing too heavily on the work of philanthropic organisations and individuals concerned with the relief of poverty and distress, and for ignoring whole fields of voluntary action to do with mutual aid and reform (see, for example, Harrison 1966). Trying to condense such a history into ten thousand words runs the risk of making the same mistakes as Owen, on a larger scale. It is necessary, therefore, at the outset to say both what this chapter is and what it is not.

First what it is not. The chapter is not a comprehensive review of voluntary action in Britain since 1500. Nor is it a discourse on the lives and work of the great men and women who shaped the development of the voluntary sector; in fact, with a few exceptions, it does not deal with individuals at all. The chapter is not a review of the history of the great organisations – the national societies which, springing up in the nineteenth century, came so to dominate the voluntary sector landscape. It deliberately chooses to steer clear of charity law and the system of governmental regulations covering the work of charitable institutions (although reference is made to some of the landmark legislation). Finally, the chapter is not concerned with any attempt to try and measure the size and shape of the sector at different times over the past 500 years.

So what is it about? The starting point is the now famous division made by William Beveridge in his 1948 Report between the two main impulses of voluntary action: philanthropy and mutual aid (Beveridge 1948). Eschewing the preference by Owen to focus exclusively on philanthropic good works, this review sets out to redress the balance and to give mutual aid its rightful place in the history of voluntary action in Britain. The first section focuses on the changing structures of philanthropic voluntary organisations, from the growth of foundations in the sixteenth century, to the rise in the late seventeenth century of associated philanthropy – an organisational form which was to reach its highest point of expression in the nineteenth century. It looks at the role of women in voluntary associations, explores the link between class and philanthropy, and examines relations between the state and voluntary action. The second section focuses on the development of mutual aid from the fraternities of the Middle Ages to the friendly societies and working men's clubs of the Victorian age. As with the first section a major theme of this section is the attitude of the state towards mutual aid groups. To aid readability the two sections of the essay follow a general chronological course, although the emphasis on a thematic approach means that some criss-crossing over time is unavoidable.

PHILANTHROPY

The 'origins' of philanthropy

Philanthropy of course did not begin in the sixteenth century. Along with mutual aid (as we shall see later) philanthropy has a long history in British society, and embryonic charitable organisations, especially organised around the monasteries and religious houses, can be traced back to medieval times and beyond. G. Le Bras has called the thirteenth century 'The Golden Age of small associations of piety geared much less towards the practice of sacraments than towards liturgy and good works', and in England alone some 500 voluntary hospitals were founded during the course of the twelfth and thirteenth centuries (Rubin 1988: 251). There are, however, several good reasons for taking the sixteenth century as a starting point for this study. For one thing, it was in this period that we see the emergence of one particular form of charitable structure, the charitable trust, which was to play such an important role in the history of the voluntary sector over the next 500 years. The period is also a good starting point for a history of voluntary action for the apparently contradictory reason that it was in the sixteenth century that the state for the first time in any appreciable way began to take an interest in the relief of poverty. The period saw the first airing of what are often seen as very Victorian notions of the deserving and undeserving poor and a questioning of the respective roles of charity and the state in dealing with poverty. Just as the Charity Organisation Society in the late nineteenth century was to question the advisability of unregulated charity, so too the Tudor period saw attempts (albeit unsuccessful) to outlaw the giving of alms to any but the deserving poor (Slack 1988).

The basic form of charity in Tudor England was the charitable trust – a gift or bequest made in perpetuity for charitable purposes. According to Jordan (1959, 1960, 1961), who carried out a detailed analysis of bequests made in ten counties of England, there was a large growth in charitable giving between 1480 and 1660. He estimated that over 3 million pounds was given to charity in the ten counties during this period, with a peak in endowments between 1610 and 1640. He also noted a change in the nature of charitable gifts, with a move away from religion towards poor relief and education. The reasons for this increase in charitable activity were held to be the rise in income of the newly emerging merchant class and an increase in levels of poverty which stimulated philanthropic action.

Recent scholars have challenged Jordan's findings. In particular, it is argued that his figures have failed to take account of inflation, and that, once this has been allowed for, not only was there no growth in charitable giving, there was in fact a decline in the late sixteenth century, with a recovery occurring only in the middle decades of the seventeenth century (Hadwin 1978; Bittle and Lane 1976; Feingold 1979). The attack on the monasteries and chantries was an obvious cause of this decline. As one member of Parliament commented in the 1650s, 'since Popery was abolished, charity has left the land', and, although in fact charity had recovered by this time the explanation holds true for the earlier period (Slack 1988). But, as Chesterman (1979) points out, even if the overall volume of charitable activity declined in the late Tudor period the amount of private money given for non-religious causes such as education and health increased considerably. Charity was moving away from the church and becoming increasingly secular.

Another feature of charity in the seventeenth century was the money given to found new trusts, rather than to contribute to existing institutions. The new merchant class saw an obvious attraction in the founding of personal memorials which carried the name of the benefactor for ever more. The emphasis during this century also began to move gradually away from the giving of casual doles to the 'undeserving poor' to the channelling of charity through institutions such as almshouses to the 'deserving poor'. However, it would be a mistake to conclude that all casual giving ceased. In Norwich, for example, it has been estimated that 80 per cent of all gifts to the poor by will before 1650 took the form of outright doles (Slack 1988: 166).

The sixteenth century saw the first attempts by the state to regulate charity. Acts of Parliament passed in the first half of the century had tried to outlaw the giving of casual doles. Towards the end of the century the focus shifted to the promotion of endowed charities. In 1597 the Charitable Uses Act was introduced with the aim of encouraging charity by clamping down on fraudulent activity. The Act established the first charity commissioners (the so-called roving commissioners) who were charged with investigating breaches of charitable trust on a county-wide basis. The Act was repealed by Parliament but reintroduced with its main provisions largely unaltered in 1601. The 1601 Charitable Uses Act with its famous preamble laid down a basic definition of charitable activity. This statement was refined in 1805 by Sir Samuel Romilly, who gave us the 'four heads' of charity, and again in 1891 by Lord Macnaghten but, despite the repeal of the Act itself, the preamble from the 1601 Statute still forms the legal basis of our understanding of 'charitable purpose'(see, for example, Chesterman 1979 and Williams 1989).

The rise of the voluntary association

Voluntary organisations along the lines that we know them today are most associated with the nineteenth century. And indeed the period did see an explosion of such organisations. However, their development can be traced back to the late seventeenth century and to what Owen (1964) called the rise of 'associated philanthropy'. The voluntary association differed in a number of important ways from the charitable trusts and endowments of the earlier period. It was not funded by a single individual whose name would be for ever linked with the charity, but by a group of wealthy philanthropists who combined together to support a charitable cause. According to Owen the rise of associated philanthropy can be linked to the parallel developments taking place in the commercial world with the development of the joint stock company. In place of the 'personal memorials' to wealthy benefactors this new form of philanthropy witnessed the development of a whole host of new voluntary organisations. One of the most shining testimonies to this new form of charity was the charity school movement. By 1729 there were over 1400 such schools in England catering for over 22,000 pupils, although the educational content of these institutions took second place to religious instruction. According to Owen:

> The charity school movement . . . . placed its stamp on British philanthropic methods. Despite its manifest shortcomings, this first large-scale venture in associated philanthropy offered a convincing demonstration of what could be achieved by the pooling of individual effort.
>
> (Owen 1964: 30)

The eighteenth century saw the spread of this new form of charitable organisation, an expansion which owed much to the Puritan influence or, as Owen puts it, to the 'Philanthropy of Piety'. At the same time, the period witnessed a reduction in the number of new charitable endowments created. One recent study of eighteenth-century charity suggests that there was a shift in the nature of charity during this period in line with the changing needs of the nation (Andrew 1989). Drawing on considerable primary sources Donna Andrew argues that charity in London in the period between 1680 and 1820 was characterised by three distinct phases. The first phase from 1680 to the 1740s saw charity being used primarily to promote education and employment. Between the 1740s and the 1760s there was a distinct shift in charity away from these areas towards maternity hospitals and child welfare agencies, a shift which she claims was due to growing concern about the need to boost London's labouring population and to meet the nation's increased manpower requirements for military preparedness, naval expansion and colonial settlements. The third phase between the 1770s and the 1820s was characterised by a shift towards charities supporting moral reform and discipline, and is explained by the state's growing anxiety about the threat of political unrest. Andrew's thesis that the focus of voluntary action reflects the wider political context in which it operates is not new. And the theory (often advanced) that voluntary action has been used by the state as a form of social control will be examined more fully later in the chapter.

Not all voluntary agencies in the eighteenth century were philanthropic. The latter years of the decade saw a flowering of debating societies and political clubs, like the Kit Kat Club and the Tory Loyal Brotherhood, the forerunner to the Athenaeum, as well as radical debating clubs like the London Corresponding Society and societies stirred by the example of the French Revolution (see Morris 1990; Hobsbawm 1964). The Masonic Order spread rapidly during the eighteenth century. Certainly not all voluntary agencies were espousing views which would be regarded as progressive. The Proclamation Society of 1787, under the influence of William Wilberforce, included the publishers of Tom Paine's *Age of Reason* among its targets. Some of the societies of the age appear not very different from those in existence today. The Watch and Ward Societies, for example, with their organisation of voluntary police patrols, stand out as a sort of eighteenth-century neighbourhood watch.

Much voluntary action in the eighteenth century was associated with the life of towns, and middle-class philanthropists made significant contributions to the development of museums, libraries and public gardens. Civic pride (and perhaps civic rivalry) was a major impetus to voluntary action.

The golden age of voluntary organisations

The nineteenth century can be seen as the golden age of the voluntary association and, while any attempt to put meaningful figures on the size of the voluntary sector is futile, a few statistics do help to illustrate its vitality and strength. In his famous *Charities of London* in 1861, Sampson Low put the aggregate income of 640 London charitable agencies at 2½ million pounds (quoted in Owen 1964: 169), and in 1870 Hawksley estimated the amount of money given to charities in London to be between 5½ and 7 million pounds a year (quoted in Best 1971: 159). In the 1880s *The Times* noted that the income of London charities was greater than that of several nation states, including Sweden, Denmark and Portugal, and twice that of the Swiss Confederation (quoted in Owen 1964: 469). The first major attempt at a review of the income and expenditure of charities was undertaken by Burdett in his *Hospitals and Charities*. Taking the year 1896 as his point of reference he estimated that the annual income of charities in Britain was 8 million pounds, a figure which had risen to 13 million pounds in a second analysis carried out in 1910 (quoted in Owen 1964: 476). But these figures must be seen simply as an approximation and serve only to reinforce the point that voluntary agencies were a significant feature of Victorian society (and a not insignificant feature of the Victorian economy).

How are we to explain the rapid growth of voluntary agencies in the nineteenth century? One explanation is that the growth was the direct consequence of the increased social need (or at least the increased visibility of such need) brought about by the population explosion and rapid industrialisation and urbanisation of the period. The traditional forms of voluntary action – endowed charities; casual doles and almshouses – were found to be inadequate to deal with the needs of the age. New forms of action were required. One response was for working people to develop their own mutual insurance groups (as we shall see later). Another response was for philanthropists to band together in voluntary associations. If the rapid industrialisation of society provided the context to the development of voluntary action, the ideological push was provided by the combination of economic liberalism, with its encouragement of self-help and distrust of the state, and evangelical Christianity with its emphasis on good works. Shaftesbury, himself one of the leading philanthropists of the period who was personally involved in over 200 charitable groups, had no doubt of the important role played by the evangelical movement in the development of voluntary action. He informed his biographer at the end of the century that he had worked with evangelicals constantly and was 'satisfied that most of the great philanthropic movements of this century have sprung from them' (quoted in Finlayson

1981). The history of the city missions, the visiting societies and numerous other movements bear witness to the role of evangelicalism in the spread of philanthropy in the nineteenth century. This is not to suggest that people's motives for joining voluntary agencies were wholly tied up with the desire to do good works. As studies of the motivation to volunteer in our time have shown (see Jos Sheard's chapter on volunteering), motives are rarely purely altruistic and the desire for a position in the community or simply to enjoy the convivial and social aspects of voluntary participation should be neither discounted nor frowned upon in any assessment of philanthropic action in the Victorian age. People no doubt joined voluntary groups and contributed to charities for all manner of reasons both altruistic and personal. But it is clear that the rise of evangelicalism played a part in stimulating such activity.

Not all voluntary action of this period was philanthropic. Ignoring for a moment the mutual-aid and self-help strand, there was a rich tradition of voluntary activity concerned with campaigning and political protest, so much so that a good case could have been made in this chapter for extending Beveridge's simple two-fold distinction between philanthropy and mutual aid and including campaigning activity as a third element in its own right. Voluntary groups were established to campaign for all manner of causes, from factory legislation and sanitary improvements to prison reform and observation of the sabbath. The value of voluntary action to the democratic process was noted by the great social philosopher de Tocqueville, who wrote of the importance of voluntary organisations as a bulwark against excessive state power (see Poggi 1972), and Richard Cobden (who led perhaps the most sophisticated campaign of the period to abolish the Corn Laws), who stated that there could be 'no healthy political existence' without voluntary groups (quoted in Harrison 1971: 34). Many of the techniques of campaigning and lobbying which are so familiar to contemporary pressure groups were developed during this period. Harrison has claimed that public meetings and mass publicity campaigns were invented by the anti-slavery movement of the 1830s and developed by the Anti-Corn Law League, the Temperance Movement and others (Harrison 1971). It was not only in the skills of campaigning and lobbying that nineteenth-century voluntary associations left their mark. Many of today's fundraising techniques were learnt during this period. The Victorian bazaars were the clear forerunners of charity fetes; and charity shops were in existence as early as the 1820s. Even that apparently most modern of fundraising practices, payroll giving, was being practised by Dr Barnado's at the turn of the twentieth century.

For many women in Victorian England voluntary work was an opportunity to break free from the confines of a patriarchal society (see, for example, Davidoff 1973). One contemporary estimate put the figure for the involvement of women working 'continuously' and 'semi-professionally' within charitable organisations at 500,000 which made it one of the biggest employers of women outside domestic service (quoted in Prochaska 1980: 224). The voluntary sector offered women, or at least middle-class women, a position of influence and responsibility that was otherwise denied to them in society. However, one should not exaggerate the openness of voluntary groups. Certainly there was opposition to women's involvement in charitable work from some quarters. One conservative member of the clergy warned of vain and unfeminine women, of 'amazonian women who challenge attention and put us upon our defence' (quoted in Prochaska 1980: 25), but some voluntary groups were not immune from discrimination on the grounds of gender. Many national charities had auxiliary branches especially for women members, but a number of leading organisations refused to allow women to serve as committee members or to attend annual general meetings. The Royal Society for Prevention of Cruelty to Animals, for example, allowed women on its governing body only as late as 1896. And, while voluntary groups opened up new roles for women from middle-class backgrounds, their success in attracting women from the working class was limited.

Voluntary action and class

The claim that voluntary groups were the preserve of the middle classes was one that was often heard from critics in the nineteenth century, and the spectre of Lady Bountiful doling out largess to the poor and needy became (and to some extent remains) a hate figure for the British Left. But criticism was not confined to the working-class movements. There was no more forceful critic of the charity worker than Charles Dickens. 'I've never took charity yet, nor yet has anyone belonging to me', said Betty Higden in *Our Mutual Friend* (quoted in Pope 1978). Frank Prochaska (1988, 1990) has argued that volunteers were in fact drawn from the working classes, but most of the examples he quotes are from the skilled artisan groups, the so-called labour aristocracy. As we know from surveys today, volunteering costs money and time and those on low incomes are likely to be discriminated against in their ability to volunteer, although it is also certainly the case that most surveys measure only formal volunteering and that surveys of informal activity may be more likely to reveal a greater degree of involvement from people in lower socio-economic groups. The position in nineteenth-century Britain was no doubt similar. Formal volunteering was largely the preserve of the well-to-do and the skilled working class, with the unskilled tending to get involved in less organised settings. This tendency to overlook the charitable work of the working class was criticised in 1840 by John Collins the Chartist, who commented that:

> If there was any good thing done by any of the middle classes it appeared in all the newspapers. . . .but nobody heard of the kindly sympathies of the working man, for his unfortunate brother. . . .All this was done privately, and. . .therefore there was no idea on the part of the middle classes that working men possessed any feeling or humanity.
>
> (Quoted in Harrison 1966: 369)

Much depends on our definition of voluntary action. If we define it simply in terms of philanthropic behaviour, then the above crude analysis probably holds true. But if, as I have argued in this chapter, we include mutual-aid activity and self-help in the definition then the class distinctions break down, at least to some extent. Mutual aid was the poor man's voluntary action, although even then it must be conceded that for the most part involvement in the friendly societies, the building societies and the working men's clubs tended to be primarily from the skilled working class. Attempts to involve the unskilled masses in friendly societies and other mutual-aid groups, as with philanthropic voluntary societies, met with only limited success.

There was some open working-class hostility to Victorian philanthropy. The temperance movement was seen by many as a direct attack upon the main source of working-class leisure, the public house, and the sabbatarian movement as an attack upon the one day in the week when the labouring classes could enjoy leisure activities (Stedman Jones 1971; Bailey 1978; Harrison 1971). The visiting societies were also met with a hostile reception on occasions. One critic claimed that the practice initiated by the bible societies of collecting a penny a week from households was a 'cruel and unnecessary tax upon the hard earnings of the lower classes' (quoted in Prochaska 1980: 44), and the hostility engendered in some working-class areas made it unsafe for volunteers to ply their trade. To overcome these difficulties some visiting societies, such as the Colporteurs Society in Scotland, made a deliberate attempt to recruit working-class volunteers (Checkland 1980). One of the most extreme examples of working-class hostility to voluntary activity was the Skeleton Army which conducted riots against the Salvation Army between 1878 and 1890. The first Skeleton Army was set up in Weston-super-Mare and attracted support in at least sixty towns over the next decade. Opposition to the Salvation Army was generally non-violent and consisted of nothing more than 'Rough Music' and the disruption of processions. But physical assault was not absent altogether. Most of the recruits to the Skeleton Army were from the working class, but there was support from some publicans who saw the Army proper as a threat to their livelihood (Bailey 1977).

Voluntary action as social control

To what extent can the expansion of voluntary agencies in the nineteenth century be seen as part of a conscious attempt by the establishment to impose middle-class values on the working class? The social control thesis has provoked serious disagreement among historians (see, for example, Thompson 1981; Wiener 1978; Bailey 1978; Donajgrodzki 1977). Those against the concept have argued that it is reductionist, and ignores both the fact that working people were often in the ascendancy in voluntary movements and that, even where agencies were run by the middle class, working people invariably gained much from the enterprise. Proponents of the social control thesis argue that one of the key motivations behind establishment support for voluntary agencies (both mutual aid and philanthropic) was the desire to provide a rational alternative to wasteful working-class leisure pursuits (particularly the pub) and the belief that the most certain way to reduce support for political radicalism was to provide material assistance during time of greatest hardship. The evidence is not conclusive either way. Certainly a theory which seeks to explain the growth of voluntary action in the nineteenth century purely in terms of social control is liable to come unstuck. But there is evidence that voluntary agencies were seen by some establishment figures at least as a useful antidote to working-class values and political protest. Both sides of the argument can be seen over the issue of the Sunday school movement which spread rapidly from the 1780s and which was attracting 200,000 working-class children by 1800 and 2 million by mid-century. The Sunday schools are a useful arena to test out the social control thesis as they were attended solely by children of the working class.

E.P. Thompson saw the Sunday schools as prime agents of social control, accusing them of schooling the working class in the 'time thrift' necessary in an industrial society. 'Once within the school gates', he wrote, 'the child entered the new universe of disciplined time' (Thompson 1967: 84). In Thompson's view, the schools were the tool by which the newly emerging capitalist classes would ensure that they got the disciplined labour necessary for the new factory life. Laqueur has argued against Thompson. He claims that 'the Sunday school was a part of, and not an imposition on to, popular culture' (Laqueur 1976). Sunday schools in his view were an integral part of working-class communities, providing a range of mutual benefits like sick clubs and benefit societies, in addition to education. The evidence is contradictory. Certainly the schools were dominated, at least in their early years, by middle-class teachers, and sponsors, although in later years ex-pupils drawn from the working classes took over the tutoring roles. But the schools did undoubtedly serve an important function in working-class communities. Moreover, during the period of radical ferment during the late eighteenth century, rather than supporting their establishment as a counter-weight to political radicalism, some clergy opposed the schools as being seditious. The schools were essentially local affairs, most common in the industrial districts of Lancashire and Yorkshire but not exclusively an urban phenomenon. Some supporters clearly saw them as examples of rational recreation. But gradually they became absorbed into working-class culture, even if, unlike the working men's clubs (of which we will hear more later), they were never entirely taken over by the working class themselves.

But the social control thesis cannot simply be ignored. Examples of contemporary pronouncements abound which show that support for voluntary action was seen as a good way of deflecting popular protest. For example, in the mid-nineteenth century after the Prince Consort had visited one poor household in London for the Society for Improving the Condition of the Labouring Classes, Shaftesbury is reputed to have said: 'Ay truly, this is the way to stifle Chartism' (quoted in Owen 1964: 377). In 1907 a Guild of Help was set up in Plymouth to co-ordinate voluntary activity. Sir John Gorst, a former Under-Secretary for India and Secretary to the Treasury, argued at the first public meeting that without such action being taken 'the people would try socialism as an experiment' (quoted in Scott 1982). There was undoubtedly a strand to philanthropic action which was concerned with reforming the habits of the working class rather than simply relieving poverty. The charity school movement, the mechanics' institutes, the housing programmes of Octavia Hill, the Cheap Repository Tracts of Hannah More, the Moral Reform Campaign with its attack on theatres and music halls, all contained within them an element of moral and social indoctrination which lends weight to the social control thesis, without of course proving it.

Voluntary action and the state

The voluntary sector has been ill served by historians who, where they have considered it at all, have tended to treat it as an interesting (or sometimes less than interesting) prelude to the development of the welfare state (e.g. Fraser 1973; Thane 1982). This 'Whiggish' interpretation of history has seen the inexorable growth of the state following on from the failure and decline of the voluntary response. According to this view, the state and voluntary action had little to do with each other for the better part of the nineteenth century, when the relationship between the two was characterised by a separation of spheres, or in the Webbs' famous phrase of 1912, by the theory of 'parallel bars' (Webb and Webb 1912). It was only towards the end of the century, as the failings of the voluntary principle became apparent, that the state began to assume more and more responsibility for the provision of welfare services. As the role of the state expanded, so, it is argued, the voluntary sector contracted.

While there is a good deal of truth in this thesis, it masks as much as it reveals. For one thing the state did not first *begin* to get involved with voluntary agencies in the latter years of the nineteenth century. On the contrary, there was a well-established tradition of statutory support for voluntary action going back well into the early years of the century. Second, the voluntary sector did not simply fade into oblivion with the rise of the state in the early years of the twentieth century. The social legislation of the great reforming Liberal governments after 1905 certainly eroded the influence of voluntary agencies but it did not destroy them altogether, and the sector retained for itself an important, albeit different, role in society throughout the inter-war years. In fact, the same trend can be identified in relation to the position of the voluntary sector after the Second World War. As Nicholas Deakin shows in the following chapter, the creation of the welfare state after 1945, while profoundly affecting the role of voluntary action, did not destroy it, and a revitalised voluntary sector was to emerge in the latter decades of the century.

State involvement with voluntary agencies was well developed by the middle years of the century. An example was in the field of care for poor children where, by the mid-1850s, the poor law board had certified a list of schools, reformatories and refuges which meant that they were open to government inspection and available for government grants. By the end of the century there were over 200 charitable institutions which had received government assistance to cater for poor children (Prochaska 1980: 153). Other examples of early partnerships between the state and voluntary agencies were state grants to the Magdalene Asylums to keep 'troublesome' women off the streets and grants to voluntary agencies to support discharged prisoners.

The state also got involved in regulating charities. Throughout the nineteenth century there was a debate about the degree of regulation needed to oversee the activities of charitable trusts and foundations. As the true size of the charitable sector became apparent (through such enquiries as the Brougham Commission into charitable endowments which sat from 1818 to 1835) so the pressure to regulate grew. In 1850 a Royal Commission was set up to look at the issue of charitable malpractice, and in 1853 The Charitable Trusts Act was passed, establishing the Charity Commission (which came into being in 1860) to oversee the work of charities, although the effectiveness of its work over the years was to be severely hampered by its limited powers (e.g. Williams 1989; Chesterman 1979).

Charity Organisation Society and scientific philanthropy

One of the main proponents of the principle of separate spheres between the state and the voluntary sector was the Charity Organisation Society, which was at the forefront of the movement for scientific philanthropy (on the COS see Bosanquet 1914; Fido 1988; Lewis 1993; Mowat 1961; Stedman Jones 1971; Woodroofe 1962). The philosophy of the COS, formed in 1869, was based on two interlinked beliefs. One was the idea that philanthropy had been growing in a haphazard and random fashion during the course of the century. There was held to be little relation between the presence of voluntary agencies and social need and much overlapping of effort and waste of resources. Tied in with this was the belief that the haphazard nature of charity was leading to pauperisation of many sections of society. The solution was to organise charity in a 'scientific' way which would rationalise provision and prevent pauperisation. The COS consistently argued against indiscriminate charity. During the severe manufacturing depression in London in 1879 the COS opposed the setting up of a Mansion House Relief Fund on the grounds that such a fund would 'open not a fountain but a sluice which would overwhelm the country' (quoted in Stedman Jones 1971: 278).

The basis of the COS's belief in separate spheres for charity and government was the idea that it was possible to distinguish between the deserving and the undeserving poor (a notion which, as we have seen, had its roots in the sixteenth century) and that these two different types of client should be dealt with in very different ways. It was the responsibility of the state to deal with the indigent and the undeserving and the responsibility of charity to deal with the deserving poor, those individuals who through no fault of their own had run into temporary difficulty and who, it was believed, with a little judicious assistance could be helped back on to their feet. This principle was given official backing in 1869 (the same year as the setting up of the COS) when George Goschen, President of the Poor Law in the Gladstone Government, restated, in the now famous Minute on 'The Relief of the Poor in the Metropolis', the view that the separation of spheres between the state and voluntary action existed and should be maintained. The Goschen Minute was a reaffirmation of the principles of the 1834 Poor Law which had set out to abolish outdoor relief. Experience over the half century since the New Poor Law had been passed had pointed to the fact that outdoor relief was still being provided in many areas, and that it was proving to be an increasing burden on the rates. Government support for the principle of separate spheres was motivated at least as much by the desire to reduce the burden on the rates as it was by any philosophical notion of the unique separateness of the two arms of relief.

The claim that charitable growth was uneven and haphazard was certainly borne out by the facts. There were numerous charities serving a similar function, many based around religious denominations. In 1883 there were four London organisations collecting for animal welfare, and in the 1870s five organisations were campaigning to reduce the Sunday gloom (Harrison 1966). Critics claimed that many poor households were being visited by competing organisations several times a month. Samuel Barnett, a founder member of the COS, but who was later to fall out with the Society in a most public way, said in 1874 that 'indiscriminate charity is among the curses of London' (quoted in Webb 1938).

The COS was not the first to attempt to co-ordinate charitable provision. The work of Thomas Chalmers in Glasgow pre-dates much of the work of the Society, as does the Elberfeld system of relief in Germany (see Young and Ashton 1956). In Liverpool there were earlier attempts by William Rathbone to link together the main relief agencies (Simey 1992). But the COS was the most important such co-ordinating charity, not so much for what it achieved at the time, but for the impact it had on contemporary debate on social policy and for the legacy it left for the future development of social casework and visiting.

The COS set itself up as a clearing house for charitable activity. Any application for relief, to whatever agency, was to be channelled through the local society branch. Volunteer visitors would be sent to the home of the applicant to assess the validity of the claim and, if it was felt to be appropriate, suggestion was made for relief. The main test was to be whether or not applicants could, by receiving aid, help themselves to regain their independence. Those deserving members of the poor would qualify for relief. The undeserving, who were feckless and idle and could be assumed to become merely dependent on outdoor relief, would be directed to the poor law. The COS looked favourably upon self-help. Membership of a friendly society was taken as an indicator of a level of thrift. Charles Loch, the influential secretary of the Society, said he hoped charity would 'create what in a sense might be called a great friendly society' (quoted in Fido 1977: 224). By 1886 the COS in London was dealing with 25,000 cases a year.

The COS failed in its attempt to rationalise charitable activity. For one thing, other relief organisations were unwilling to surrender their independence of action and to leave judgements of worth to the Society. For another, the COS was never very influential outside London, as Yeo has suggested with his study of voluntary action in Reading (Yeo 1976). It was also the case that, with the exception of a few London boroughs and isolated provincial areas such as Brixworth, where leading COS personnel also sat on poor law boards, there was little success in linking in the Society with the poor law. There was also opposition to the Society's approach. Shaftesbury, who agreed with its general thrust, felt it lacked a sense of mercy and humanity (Finlayson 1981). However, the main reason for failure was the mistaken assumption that it was possible in some way to draw clear distinctions between the poor in terms of the deserving and the undeserving. The distinctions simply did not stand up to close scrutiny. As one historian of the poor law has argued: 'The shiftless, able-bodied idler always seemed on closer investigation to fade into a mass of orphans, widows, sick or aged, unemployed or exploited workers' (Rose 1988: 67).

Although the COS believed vehemently in separate spheres for charity and government, it was felt to be necessary to be aware of the state's relief activities in order to avoid an overlapping of functions. However, the Organisation remained resolutely opposed to municipalisation. For the COS the supremacy of the voluntary response was an article of faith. Loch said that 'an elected corporation or municipal body could neither provide the training nor strengthen the inspiration – Associated charity could do both' (quoted in Checkland 1980: 316). The voluntary principle was to be upheld in all spheres where it was in the ascendancy. Thus the COS opposed both the 1908 Old Age Pensions Act and the 1911 National Insurance Act as being 'indiscriminate'. Fraser says of the COS that it was 'professionally pioneering but ideologically reactionary' and it is difficult to disagree (Fraser 1974: 121).

The COS remained unconvinced of the need for greater state involvement. It was not alone. Shaftesbury, who had played a leading role in the ragged school movement, was vigorously opposed to the state entering the field of education. He told an audience in 1870: 'The voluntary principle is essential to this movement. . .[it] cannot be done by the established principle; it must be done by the voluntary principle, and the voluntary principle alone' (quoted in Pope 1978: 194). Others thought differently, such as Mary

Carpenter who remained a strong advocate for state involvement in education (Manton 1976).

The rise of the state

The latter years of the nineteenth century saw calls for a greater role for the state in social welfare provision. These were led by the Fabians, the Social Democratic Federation and other socialist parties who pointed to the failure of the voluntary response to deal with the growing problems of industrial society. Owen (1964) refers to the changing social temper of the period in the 1880s and 1890s. Canon Barnett, Vicar of St Jude's, Whitechapel, published an article in the *Nineteenth Century* entitled Practical Socialism, calling for increased state action. His intervention is symbolic because Barnett was a founder member of the COS and suggests that even once-enthusiastic supporters of the voluntary principle were losing faith in its ability to cure all of society's ills. Supporters of a greater role for the state argued that the facts were on their side. They pointed to the series of famous social surveys and reports by, among others, Booth (1889–1903), Rowntree (1901) and Mearns (1883) which highlighted the extent of the poverty and deprivation in many of the industrial cities of Britain in the last quarter of the century. In the light of such evidence the notion that poverty was a moral issue rather than a structural one (a notion which was central to the separate spheres argument) began to lose its credibility. Jane Lewis (1993) has argued that the debate at this time began to shift away from the deserving/undeserving split towards a helpable/unhelpable split – which removed the moral dimension from discussions on poverty.

Nowhere was the failure of the voluntary response more apparent than in the area of housing. There had been a number of charitable attempts to provide affordable, good-quality housing for working people, including those by Octavia Hill and by the Peabody Trust, although the strict conditions imposed on tenants in these dwellings (no painting of the walls; no pictures; outside doors locked at 11pm) undermined their appeal and led to them being described as 'Poor Law bastilles' (Stedman Jones 1971: 187). Other organisations, such as the Improved Industrial Dwellings Company, approached the problem by seeking to prove that there was a profit to be made out of the building of low-cost houses for working people, but their efforts also failed to make a dent in the problem. Writing in the 1930s, Elizabeth Macadam could find 'no subject on which philanthropy has so signally failed either to do the job itself or to stimulate the state to do it adequately' (Macadam 1934: 138–9).

The Royal Commission on the Poor Laws and Relief of Distress which met between 1905 and 1909 gave voice to both supporters and detractors of the statutory response. The Majority Report called for a larger role for the voluntary sector in the provision of social welfare and (in line with the thinking behind the New Poor Law) said that state aid should be 'less agreeable' than voluntary aid (Royal Commission 1905–9). The Report recommended a scheme of voluntary aid committees to work alongside the public relief agencies.

The Minority Report, written by Beatrice Webb and George Lansbury, rejected the call for such committees and argued instead for a radical new relationship between the state and the voluntary sector. This report, the ideas of which were developed further by the Webbs in 1912, argued that in place of the separate spheres model there should be a relationship based on the model of an extension ladder. In this new model the state would provide the basic level of services and the voluntary sector would top up the provision, 'carrying onward the work of the public authorities to their finer shades of physical, moral and spiritual perfection' (Webb and Webb 1912: 252). Although this view received little support at the time, it was an idea ahead of its time. In many respects the model of relations between the state and the voluntary sector which emerged after 1945 was based along these lines. The language of the extension ladder may not have reappeared, but the accepted role for the voluntary sector (until the 1970s) was very much that of supporting and complementing the work of the state. There was criticism at the time that the Minority Report saw no role for the voluntary sector. This was refuted. The Dean of Norwich (Beatrice's only convert on the Commission) said 'what we want is the volunteer as aiding and supplementing the public authority; never as substitute or alternative' (quoted in Owen 1964: 521).

The tide was turning in the direction of the state. By the time of the Royal Commission the influence of the COS, and with it unbridled faith in the voluntarist principle, had begun to wane. In Reading in 1908–9 it was estimated that 'official bodies' already spent £27,000 on relief compared to £8,000 by voluntary bodies (Yeo 1976: 299). In 1904 the first Guild of Help was set up in Bradford and by 1917 there were eighty-three in existence. The Guilds (who adopted the motto 'not alms but a friend') were co-ordinating bodies along the lines of the COS, but in other respects they were very different, most notably in their attitude towards the state. The Guilds of Help stressed partnership with the statutory bodies and they welcomed the 1911 National Insurance Act on the grounds that it would 'broaden the outlook for the philanthropist' (Laybourn 1992).

The 1911 National Insurance Act was just one of a series of Acts passed by the great reforming Liberal governments of 1905 to 1914 which greatly expanded the role of the state in the provision of social welfare. Other legislation provided for school meals, a school medical service, old age pensions (subject to a means test) and limited unemployment insurance. Taken together, these measures represented a major enlargement of the responsibilities of the state and a corresponding reduction of the responsibilities of voluntary agencies. C.S. Loch of the COS wrote in 1913 that the social legislation 'indicates very clearly that the spirit of enterprise in social matters [had] passed from the people to the state' (quoted in Finlayson 1990:

185). G.D.H. Cole, writing in 1945 on the history of voluntary action, noted the importance of the Liberal social reforms for the role of voluntary action: 'In the long run, the entire situation as between the advocates of voluntaryism and state action was altered by the immense changes in the activities of the state which took place mainly after the advent of the Liberal Government at the end of 1905 and the election of a new Parliament in which the Labour Party appeared for the first time as a significant political group' (Cole 1945: 21). However, while it is undoubtedly the case that the role of the state was enlarged as a consequence of the Liberal reforms and that the role of voluntary agencies, particularly in the provision of financial assistance, was reduced, it does not automatically follow that voluntary action underwent a sharp and dramatic decline. On the contrary, voluntary action showed a remarkable gift for survival throughout the first half of the twentieth century, as both Prochaska (1992) and Finlayson (1990) have shown. Some voluntary agencies carried on much as before with their work quite separate from the work of the newly enlarged state. Others shifted the focus of their activity away from work which had been overtaken by the state into new areas of concern. Cole argues that voluntary agencies between the wars changed their work to meet specialised needs rather than general needs and acted to fill in the gaps in statutory provision rather than to provide an alternative form of service.

The First World War provided both a stimulus and a jolt to the voluntary sector. It gave a boost to the work of many charities, for example the Red Cross and Order of St John, which provided hospital accommodation for servicemen, helped by a grant from the War Office, and the Women's Institute, set up in 1915, which played an important role in food production with funds from the Board of Agriculture. However, it also threatened to undermine the sector's role. The experience of total war saw the state assuming a greater role *vis-à-vis* the lives of citizens than ever before and there was a feeling that relations between the state and its people would never be the same again. The building of a 'land fit for heroes' was widely felt to be too great a task to be left to the voluntary sector. Many voluntarists viewed the future with trepidation.

The new philanthropy

Fears of the decline of the voluntary sector were overstated. Relations between the state and the voluntary sector in the inter-war years were marked by increasing interdependence. Symptomatic of the developing 'partnership' was the establishment of the National Council of Social Service (now the National Council for Voluntary Organisations) in 1919. The Council owed much to the pioneering co-ordinating work of voluntary action in Hampstead and Liverpool and, of course, to the work of the COS and the Guilds of Help. The Council's main aim may have been to provide a co-ordinating role for voluntary action based around the networks of the councils of social service and the rural development councils, but a secondary aim was to develop closer ties with government. The agency role (with the voluntary sector delivering services on behalf of the state) was developed, although many voluntary groups remained immune from state funding. This was the age of the 'new philanthropy', as described by Elizabeth Macadam in the 1930s (Macadam 1934). In 1929 Liverpool charities were receiving 13 per cent of their income from public authorities as payment for services, and in Manchester 17 per cent of charity income was derived from contract payments by 1938 (Owen 1964: 530). It has been estimated that by 1934 something like 37 per cent of the total income of registered charities was being received from the state as payment for services (Braithwaithe 1938: 171). Not all voluntary agencies welcomed this developing partnership. Some argued that the sector was in danger of losing its independence (claims which have resurfaced in recent years with the spread of community care and contract funding). When in 1936–7 the Ministry of Labour granted over £100,000 to the National Council of Social Service for work with the unemployed there was criticism from some voluntary groups that, by colluding with the government over relief for the unemployed, the National Council was distracting attention from the real issue of getting people back to work (Owen 1964: 531; Harris 1990, 1991). As we will see in the following chapter, this opposition was mirrored fifty years later when parts of the voluntary sector got involved with government schemes for job creation and training.

The *extent* of the partnership between the voluntary sector and the state during the inter-war years is open to question, at least at national governmental level. As Macadam points out, there is little evidence of government policy to stimulate the sector during this period, although the 1929 Local Government Act required local authorities to consult with voluntary hospitals in the planning of services. At local authority level attempts were made to co-ordinate the activities of the public and voluntary services. In 1932 the London County Council issued a document entitled 'Co-operation with Voluntary Agencies' (probably the first such official document) and set up three pilot schemes to stimulate closer working arrangements.

There were other developments taking place in the voluntary sector between the wars which deserve a mention. The period saw the creation of a number of large new trusts and foundations modelled on (and to some extent financed by) similar bodies in the United States. Key examples were the Carnegie United Kingdom Trust (1913), the Wellcome Foundation (1924) and the Pilgrim Trust (1930). The founding of these new trusts provides a nice symmetry to this review of the history of voluntary action in Britain, and takes us back to the developments of the endowed foundations of the sixteenth and seventeenth centuries. There were also changes taking place to voluntary associations. Most notably, they were getting bigger (partly due to increased government funding) and more professional, in the sense of taking on more paid staff members. One contemporary commentator noted the trend towards increased professionalism and bureaucracy at least in the field of social services:

> The salariat of the voluntary organisations has increased very much in numbers, in status, and in efficiency. There has been a striking transformation of voluntary social service; it is conducted nowadays on a larger scale, with more science and less sentimentality, than formerly. The greater part of the administrative work is carried on by professional social workers, who tend more and more to be staffs analogous to the staffs of government departments or of local authorities.

> (Mess 1947: 204)

The Second World War, as did the First, saw the state assume increased responsibilities over the lives of the British people. Voluntary action was taken over to help with the war effort. At the outset of war the NCSS established a Standing Conference of Voluntary Organisations in Time of War, a consultative body to work with government on planning the voluntary sector's role during the hostilities. An agreement followed for financial support to voluntary organisations undertaking work required by government. Many charities contributed to the war effort. The Women's Voluntary Service, which was set up in 1938 with government financial assistance, played a valuable role throughout the conflict. The British Red Cross and the Order of St John ran the auxiliary hospitals on behalf of the Ministry of Health. Voluntary agencies played a key role in the evacuation of civilians and the Citizens Advice Bureau movement (which was established just prior to the war) was, by the end of 1942, dealing with 2½ million enquiries a year (Bourdillon 1945). Not all developments were to the voluntarists' liking. Many agencies were dislocated by the manpower shortages and many feared for their survival in the new climate of universal social welfare heralded by the Beveridge Report.

The Beveridge Report of 1942 outlined proposals for a comprehensive system of social insurance. In February 1944 the Coalition government published a White Paper on health provision which outlined proposals for a 'free' comprehensive health service, while at the same time guaranteeing the voluntary hospitals full independence and a role in joint planning. It was not the government's intention, the White Paper noted, 'to destroy or to diminish a system which is so well rooted in the good will of its supporters' (quoted in Prochaska 1992: 149). The Labour Party had also been thinking about the future of welfare arrangements after the war, and its attitude towards the voluntary sector was more problematic. A policy document on hospital provision published by the party in 1943 stated that local authorities would take over voluntary hospitals and make them conform to a 'plan'. There was a long-standing ideological objection to charity from some elements of the Labour Party. But any idea that Labour was implacably opposed to voluntary traditions should be refuted. Its leader, Clement Attlee, had been assistant secretary at Toynbee Hall (albeit only for a year) and, as president of the institution, gave his support for voluntary action: 'We shall always have alongside the great range of public services, the voluntary services which humanize our national life and bring it down from the general to the particular' (quoted in Briggs and Macartney 1984: 35–6).

Labour was returned to office in the landslide election of 1945 and set about implementing the Beveridge proposals with enthusiasm. Aneurin Bevan, the new Minister of Health, who was charged with overseeing the creation of the national health service (not directly part of the Beveridge plan), was highly critical of the voluntary hospitals, referring to them as 'a patch-quilt of local paternalisms' and an 'enemy of intelligent planning' (Prochaska 1992: 156). The National Health Service Act of 1948 brought the voluntary hospitals under state control. However, in other fields of activity the Labour administration proved more sympathetic to the voluntary sector and it looked to voluntary groups (where they existed) to deliver a range of social welfare services. Just as the voluntary sector had failed to wither away following the Liberal reforms at the beginning of the century, so the sector continued to exhibit a resilience in the years following the post-war settlement. The durability of the voluntary sector after 1945 is examined by Nicholas Deakin in the following chapter.

MUTUAL AID AND SELF-HELP

The origins of mutual aid

The second main impulse of voluntary action, as identified by Beveridge in his 1948 report, was mutual aid (or self-help) – that impulse which 'has its origin in a sense of one's own need for security against misfortune, and realisation that, since one's fellows have the same need, by undertaking to help one another all may help themselves' (Beveridge 1948). This chapter will draw no distinction between mutual aid and self-help, although it is recognised that some other authors have identified in the two terms quite different traditions and philosophies (for example, Wann 1992). Much of the confusion is due to a misreading of the high priest of self-help, Samuel Smiles and the deliberate attempt by 'New Right' political thinkers in the late twentieth century to distance self-help from the less politically acceptable notion of mutual aid with its connotations of solidarity and mutuality. Smiles himself was adamant that no such distinction should be drawn. In the preface to the 1886 version of *Self Help* he complained bitterly that the title had been taken as 'a eulogy of selfishness' and went on to say that 'the duty of helping one's self in the highest sense involves the helping of one's neighbours' (quoted in McLaurin 1988: 31). So, armed with Smiles as an ally, this chapter uses the terms self-help and mutual aid interchangeably.

Beveridge saw the nineteenth-century friendly society as the embodiment of the spirit of mutual aid and, while any analysis of the history of voluntary action must pay full attention to this important social movement, our search for the origins of self-help begins several centuries earlier with the fraternities, confraternities and religious guilds of medieval England. Some observers would argue for a richer heritage still and, as Loewenberg (1992) has shown with his pioneering studies of philanthropy in ancient Israel, mutual aid had a place in the earliest civilisations. But, as with philanthropy, the sixteenth century is taken as the starting point for this review.

The guilds of medieval England (and Europe) were essentially religious gatherings with the purpose of offering prayers to the dead. But they also had a social and welfare function which makes it legitimate to see them as early examples of mutual aid, even as prototype friendly societies. Most guilds supplied food and shelter for members in need and some of the larger ones ran schools and almshouses and, in common with the friendly societies of the nineteenth century, offered members help with the costs of funerals (Scarisbrick 1984; Black 1984).

The fraternities had basic democratic structures which mirror the later development of the voluntary association. Officers were elected to posts, usually at an annual general meeting, and subscriptions were collected from members. Unlike in virtually all other institutions of the time women were allowed to be members in their own right, and even to hold office, although in practice this tended not to happen. The democratic nature of the guilds should not be overstated. A number of organisations deliberately set their membership rates high, thereby closing themselves off from poorer sections of society, although many others retained their open character.

Counting numbers of voluntary agencies today is an inexact science. Estimating numbers of guilds 500 years ago is nigh on impossible, although records do survive to enable us to give an impression of their scope at least at local level. For example, there were well over 100 guilds in Northampton-shire alone in the early sixteenth century, and in Yorkshire the largest guild had over 70,000 members during the course of its history (Scarisbrick 1984: 28). But beyond this general impression that guilds formed an important element of civil society we cannot go. What we do know is that the guilds were decimated by the Reformation which, along with the dissolution of the monasteries, swept away chantries and religious fraternities, and, although they saw a brief revival during the restoration of the old religion under the reign of Mary, they never regained their pre-eminent position. But the legacy of the guilds, with their emphasis on mutual support and democratic control, lived on and was to re-emerge with the development of the friendly society movement in the late eighteenth century.

The friendly societies and Victorian self-help

The friendly society movement was one of the most important social movements of the Victorian age, and perhaps the most important working-class movement. Certainly in terms of sheer numbers of members it was more important than either of the other two great working-class movements, the trade unions and co-operatives. One estimate in 1872 put membership of friendly societies at 4 million, as opposed to one million for trade unions and half a million for co-operatives (quoted in Gosden 1961: 7), and even this may have been an underestimate because many societies remained unregistered. Beveridge dismissed the claim that trade unions could be seen as mutual aid societies and does not include them in his 1948 report, and, although his reasons do not stand up to close scrutiny, there are good reasons for excluding them (and the co-ops) from this review, if only for lack of space and the fact that they have received full attention elsewhere. By contrast friendly societies have received scant attention from historians.

Although some societies rightly claimed an ancestry to the medieval guilds, friendly societies as they were known to the Victorian age can be traced back to the seventeenth century. One of the earliest was the Friendly Benefit Society of Bethnal Green formed in 1687. It was during the latter half of the eighteenth century, under pressure from rapid industrialisation and urbanisation, that the growth in numbers of societies took off. In his famous *Observations on Friendly Societies* published in 1801, F.M. Eden estimated there to be over 7,000 societies with a total membership of around 650,000 (quoted in Gosden 1961: 4). Between 1815 and the Royal Commission on Friendly and Benefit Building Societies which reported in 1874 there was a four-fold increase in membership. The link between industrialisation and membership is obvious from an analysis of the geographical spread of societies. Although not exclusively an urban phenomenon, it was the industrial areas of Lancashire and Yorkshire which lay at the heart of the movement. One study has estimated that in the town of Bolton alone in 1850 there were over 200 lodges of various societies (Bailey 1978).

The societies took on a number of different forms: the Royal Commission identified no fewer than seventeen different types. However, two or three broad groupings can be discerned. At the beginning of the nineteenth century the most common type was the small local independent society, usually based around the pub, whose officers were chosen by rotation. During the course of the century these were superseded by the large affiliated societies such as the Independent Order of Oddfellows Manchester Unity (with 400,000 members by the time of the Royal Commission) and the 350,000 strong Ancient Order of Foresters, where control was less in the hands of the local members but was assumed by middle-class professionals such as doctors and businessmen. There were societies based around particular trades and societies set up with the specific purpose of providing members with a decent funeral (the goose and burial clubs).

Membership of the societies was generally restricted to men, although in some areas of the country where women's trades were important, societies emerged to cater for this new industrial class. An example was Luton where in 1872 a society for women hat workers was established with

300 members (Gosden 1961). Membership was also largely restricted to members of the better-off working class, to skilled artisans and tradesmen who could afford to pay the monthly dues. Rowntree found in York in 1901 that the 'very poor are but seldom members of friendly societies' (quoted in Green 1985). One of the major failings of the movement and that which would undermine its case against state encroachment into the sphere of sickness insurance was its inability to appeal to the unskilled working class, although some of the smaller, rural societies did attract farm labourers. Societies usually imposed a cut-off age of 40 for membership to guard against large claims for ill health, but this did not prevent a number from collapsing due to financial exhaustion.

The two main financial benefits of the societies were insurance against sickness and payment of members' funeral costs. Many societies also arranged for medical attendance. In addition, the societies had an important social function. It would be a mistake to see the friendly societies as purely insurance clubs. The convivial aspect of membership was of equal value. Most meetings took place in the local pub, there were elaborate initiation ceremonies (like the Masons') and excursions and social events were arranged during the course of the year.

The building societies

The friendly societies dwarfed other working-class societies in terms of members. But they were not the only such organisations founded on the principles of mutual aid and self-help. Mention must be made of the building society movement in any review of self-help in the nineteenth century. The building societies followed the same pattern of development as the friendly societies: initial local structures controlled by working-class members, moving towards national structures with centralised control. The early building societies were classic examples of mutual aid. Small numbers of skilled tradesmen (often no more than twenty) joined together for the purpose of helping themselves and each other to buy a house. As with the friendly societies, dues were paid to the building society at a monthly meeting, and the social side of affairs was also important. The early societies were terminating societies in that they shut down after every member had brought a house. It was estimated that there were perhaps 250 societies in existence in 1825 but the real period of growth was from the 1840s. It was from this period that the societies began to become permanent, and their nature began to change. They became less controlled by their members and were taken over by middle-class professionals, although some working-class terminating societies continued to exist as late as the 1870s. By 1875 the building societies had become virtually commercialised undertakings and· can no longer be included in our analysis of self-help (see, for example, Johnson 1985).

The working men's clubs

The development of working men's clubs is of interest because it illustrates the opposite trend of development from the friendly societies and building societies. This movement was not a working-class movement at the outset but began as part of the middle-class attempt to impose a rational recreation on the working population (see Bailey 1978; Price 1971; Taylor 1972). Its history begins in rural areas in the middle years of the century, but by the 1860s it had spread to the industrial regions of Lancashire. The Working Men's Club and Institute Union was set up by Henry Solly in 1862 to co-ordinate the development of clubs. To begin with, the growth was slow, owing largely to working-class suspicions of the motives of the middle-class founders. There was a strong temperance base to societies which threatened the working-class culture of the pub. There was a ban on political discussion, evidence of the concern among the establishment that the clubs might prove to be a subversive force. In fact the early working men's clubs, with their middle-class patrons, were more in line with the tradition of philanthropy than that of mutual aid.

But by the 1870s things had changed. The working-class members had begun to assume control of the clubs. The temperance aims had gone – ironically it was the sale of drink which provided much of the finance which enabled them to become self-sufficient. As they became more of a mutual-aid grouping so they became more attractive to the working class. By 1881 there were over 500 clubs in existence. By 1883 there were over 500,000 members. As the name suggests the clubs had a male membership only. The issue of women's membership was raised at two annual conferences in the 1870s but was received with little enthusiasm. Gradually, around the turn of the century, the focus of the clubs changed and they became geared mainly to providing entertainment.

The state and mutual aid

The attitude of the state towards friendly and other mutual aid societies fluctuated over the course of time, depending on whether they were held to be a threat or a support to the established order. The first general Act to deal with societies was in 1793 and this aimed to encourage their formation, thereby removing the burden on the poor rate, although there was some concern that societies were a cover for seditious activity in the wake of the revolutions in France. Such was the state's support for the idea of mutual insurance that in the early years of the century attempts were made to foster official societies, run by the establishment for working people. This experiment met with little success. The period 1815–30 was one of great social unrest. Friendly societies were increasingly viewed with suspicion by the state. One of the claims made was that, with the ban on trade unions under the Combination Acts of 1799, unions were organising themselves under the guise of friendly societies, and certainly there was a great deal of overlap between the functions and structures of the early trade unions and the local and trade friendly societies. In 1833 a group of agricultural labourers in Tolpuddle were prosecuted for forming an association under the name of the Friendly Society of Agricultural Labourers.

By the 1830s government attitude towards the societies had shifted, in line with the prevailing political doctrine of *laissez faire*. Rather than being actively encouraged (or discouraged) the societies were to be left alone. The Acts of Parliament relating to societies passed between 1834 and 1875 were concerned not with extending their role but with tidying up administrative procedures. However, while the state was anxious not to be seen to interfere with the free operation of the societies it was nevertheless keen that they should expand, and the strengthening of the friendly societies was one of the aims of the Poor Law Amendment Act of 1834. With its principles of less eligibility and low levels of relief it was hoped that working people would be forced to take out their own insurance, and the growth of friendly society membership during the second half of the century suggests that the aim was achieved to some extent.

By 1875 the societies had changed in character. They had become much less involved with social activities, and dominated instead by matters of insurance. Local control had largely passed to national affiliated bodies, mirroring the centralising developments which were taking place during this period in the philanthropic voluntary associations. The societies were coming under increasing attack for being unable (and unwilling) to provide insurance for members in old age. The last decades of the nineteenth century saw a public debate around the issue of a statutory national pensions scheme. The societies remained resolutely opposed to such initiatives, and to begin with were not alone. In 1891 the president of the TUC spoke out in favour of 'self-help'. But the spirit of the time was moving against the societies and in favour of a statutory response. The opposition of the societies was both principled and self-interested: it was felt that working people would be unable to afford two insurance payments, one to the state and one to the societies. Joseph Chamberlain suggested that the societies should administer the state scheme but this did not find favour either. In their opposition to a national pensions scheme the societies could count on the unflinching support of the COS. The concerns of the friendly societies were acknowledged in the Old Age Pensions Act of 1908 which, as a non-contributory scheme, posed less of a threat to their finances. In fact, the scheme actually helped the societies by removing the financial burden caused by the payment of continuous sick benefit for the elderly. But the general feeling of the societies was that the principle of self-help had been undermined fatally.

The National Insurance Act of 1911, with its scheme of compulsory contributory insurance, posed more of a threat to the friendly societies and mutual insurance groups, although historians are divided upon the extent of the body blow which this dealt to them. Certainly their influence was significantly curtailed. This was not inevitable. There was a possibility that the societies could have been used by the state as agents to administer the insurance scheme, and indeed this was Lloyd George's wish. But the idea was defeated in parliament, partly, it has been claimed, by the vested interests of the medical profession who were keen to strengthen their hold at the expense of the societies (Green 1985). Some societies did carve out a role for themselves after 1911 as 'approved institutions', which enabled them to continue to provide medical benefits to insured people subject to the approval of local insurance committees. And Gosden (1973: 282) has argued that the societies 'not only survived but apparently flourished until the 1940s and the changes which were then made in the administrative structure of the national insurance system'. But in reality their influence in the inter-war years was negligible.

What was lost with the passing of influence of the friendly societies? First, it must be said that there had not been universal support for them. Beatrice Webb and the Minority Report (although supportive of their mutual-aid function) had criticised the medical contract system, on the grounds that it kept doctors' wages unfairly low, and there was a more fundamental criticism that the societies had failed because they had been unable (or unwilling) to appeal to the people most in need of insurance, the very poor (Gosden 1973; Gilbert 1966; Webb and Webb 1912). It was also the case that friendly societies did not provide medical services to women or children of the insured members. The societies themselves were distressed at the attack on their role. The Oddfellows magazine stormed in September 1911:

> Working men are waking to the fact that this is a subtle attempt to take from the class to which they belong the administration of the great voluntary organisations which they have built up for themselves, and to hand over the future control to the paid servants of the governing class. . . .This is not liberty; this is not development of self government, but a new form of autocracy and tyranny not less but the more dangerous because it is benevolent in its intentions.
>
> (*Oddfellows Magazine* September 1911, quoted in Gosden 1961: 544)

Perhaps the greatest loss with the demise of the friendly societies was that control over medical provision was taken away from the members and passed to the medical profession, a process which was reinforced by the changes made by Bevan after the Second World War. However, by the time of the 1911 Act the societies were not the democratic societies of the past. Control by members of local societies had passed to the large affiliated societies. The real tragedy was not 1911 (as has been claimed by Green (1985) and others) but the undermining of the spirit of mutuality and members' control which had been such a key feature of the early societies.

As with philanthropy, the mutual-aid impulse refused to disappear and the 1960s saw a resurgence of self-help activity, albeit no longer geared to mutual insurance, but to single-issue concerns such as bereavement and disability. This revival of self-help is picked up by Nicholas Deakin in the following chapter.

CONCLUSION: TOWARDS 1945

What was the position of the voluntary sector at the end of the period covered by this review? We have rejected the view that the rise of the state saw the destruction of the voluntary sector. This did not happen. The voluntary sector carved out a new if altered role for itself in society. According to G.D.H. Cole:

> It is a great mistake to suppose that as the scope of state action expands, the scope of voluntary social service necessarily contracts. Its character changes in conformity both with changing views of the province of state action and with the growth of the spirit and substance of democracy.
>
> (1945: 29)

Some agencies did see their role diminished (for example, voluntary hospitals and friendly societies); some others carried on much as before, without any links with the state; still others came into closer contact with statutory bodies. The 'new philanthropy' of partnership between the state and the voluntary sector became increasingly important during the inter-war period, and contract funding became an ever larger element of total funding of the sector. The 'separate spheres' ideology had been swept away but had not yet been replaced by a coherent counter ideology, and in fact Jane Lewis (1993) has argued that the sector is still searching for its defining ideology. In place of the notion of 'separate spheres' there was growing support for the view of the voluntary sector as complementing and supplementing statutory provision. For example, Macadam had argued that the sector 'finds its most appropriate sphere' in experimental work, in work which is flexible or specialised and in acting as a watchdog on statutory services (1934: 287). Macadam was adamant what the limit of such action was. 'Any action which may postpone the performance of the duties of the state or municipality must be shunned' (1934: 289). Much the same was concluded by Mess who reviewed the performance of the voluntary social services between the wars. For him, the main role of voluntary action was to carry out tasks delegated to it by the state (one can see how the notion of contracting is not new); to carry out separate tasks according to a 'division of labour' between the statutory and voluntary services (still some element of separate spheres); and to act as critic of government (1947: 205–7). But he also stressed more positive reasons for the sector's existence. Voluntary action had a value in its own right:

> It is most important in a democratic society that active citizenship should be widespread. Whilst only a comparatively few persons can take direct part in the work of the statutory authorities, it is possible and desirable for

a much greater number to watch that work intelligently and to contribute to its efficiency.

(Mess 1947: 213)

In this statement we see the assertion (albeit not fully developed) of the importance of voluntary action as an agent of democratic participation which takes us back to de Tocqueville and Cobden and looks forward to the ideas behind the resurgence of voluntary action in the post-war period.

REFERENCES

Andrew, D. (1989) *Philanthropy and Police: London Charity in the Eighteenth Century*, Princeton, NJ: Princeton University Press.

Bailey, P. (1978) *Leisure and Class in Victorian England: Rational Recreation and the Contest for Control, 1830–1885*, London: Routledge & Kegan Paul.

Bailey, V. (1977) 'Salvation Army riots: the "Skeleton Army" and legal authority in the provincial town', in A.P. Donajgrodzki (ed.) *Social Control in Nineteenth Century Britain*, London: Croom Helm.

Best, G. (1971) *Mid Victorian Britain: 1851–1875*, London: Weidenfeld & Nicolson.

Beveridge, W. (1948) *Voluntary Action: A Report on Methods of Social Advance*, London: Allen & Unwin.

Bittle, W.G. and Lane, R.T. (1976) 'Inflation and philanthropy in England: a re-assessment of W.K. Jordan's data', *Economic History Review*, 2nd Series, XXIX: 203–10.

Black, A. (1984) *Guilds and Civil Society in European Political Thought from the Twelfth Century to the Present*, London: Methuen.

Booth, C. (1889–1903) *The Life and Labour of the People in London*, 17 volumes, London.

Bosanquet, H. (1914) *Social Work in London 1869–1912: A History of the COS*, London: John Murray.

Bourdillon, A.F.C. (ed.) (1945) *Voluntary Social Services*, London: Methuen.

Braithwaithe, C. (1938) *The Voluntary Citizen*, London.

Brenton, M. (1985) *The Voluntary Sector in British Social Services*, London: Longman.

Briggs, A. and Macartney, A. (1984) *Toynbee Hall: The First Hundred Years*, London: Routledge & Kegan Paul.

Checkland, O. (1980) *Philanthropy in Victorian Scotland: Social Welfare and the Voluntary Principle*, Edinburgh: John Donald.

Chesterman, M. (1979) *Charities, Trusts and Social Welfare*, London: Weidenfeld & Nicolson.

Cole, G.D.H. (1945) 'A retrospect of the history of voluntary social service', in A.F.C. Bourdillon (ed.) *Voluntary Social Services*, London: Methuen.

Davidoff, L. (1973) *The Best Circles: Women and Society in Victorian England*, London: Cresset Library.

Donajgrodzki, A.P. (ed.) (1977) *Social Control in Nineteenth Century Britain*, London: Croom Helm.

Feingold, M. (1979) 'Jordan revisited: patterns of charitable giving in sixteenth- and seventeenth-century England', *History of Education*, VIII: 265.

Fido, J. (1977) 'The Charity Organisation Society and social casework in London 1869–1900', in A.P. Donajgrodzki (ed.) *Social Control in Nineteenth Century Britain*, London: Croom Helm.

Finlayson, G. (1981) *The Seventh Earl of Shaftesbury, 1801–1885*, London: Eyre Methuen.
Finlayson, G. (1990) 'A moving frontier: voluntarism and the state in British social welfare 1911–1949', *Twentieth Century British History*, 1 (2): 183–206.
Fraser, D. (1973) *The Evolution of the British Welfare State*, London: Macmillan.
Gilbert, B. (1966) *The Evolution of National Insurance in Great Britain: The Origins of the Welfare State*, London: Michael Joseph.
Gosden, P.H.J.H. (1961) *The Friendly Societies in England 1815–1875*, Manchester: Manchester University Press.
Gosden, P.H.J.H. (1973) *Self Help: Voluntary Associations in Nineteenth Century Britain*, London: Batsford.
Green, D. (1985) *Working Class Patients and the Medical Establishment: Self Help in Britain from the Mid-Nineteenth Century to 1948*, Aldershot: Gower/Maurice Temple Smith.
Hadwin, J.F. (1978) 'Deflating philanthropy', *Economic History Review*, 2nd Series, XXXC.
Harris, B. (1990) 'Government and charity in the distressed mining areas of England and Wales, 1928–30', in J. Barry and C. Jones (eds) *Medicine and Charity in Western Europe before the Welfare State*, London: Routledge.
Harris, B. (1991) 'Unemployment and charity in the South Wales coalfield between the wars', unpublished paper.
Harrison, B. (1966) 'Philanthropy and the Victorians', *Victorian Studies*, IX: 353–74.
Harrison, B. (1971) *Drink and the Victorians: The Temperance Question in England 1815–1872*, London: Faber.
Hobsbawm, E. (1964) *Labouring Men*, London: Weidenfeld & Nicolson.
Johnson, P. (1985) *Saving and Spending: The Working Class Economy in Britain 1870–1939*, Oxford: Oxford University Press.
Jordan, W.K. (1959) *Philanthropy in England 1480–1660*, London: Russell Sage Foundation.
Jordan, W.K. (1960) *The Charities of London 1480–1660*, London: Allen & Unwin.
Jordan, W.K. (1961) *The Charities of Rural England 1480–1660*, London: Allen & Unwin.
Laqueur, T.W. (1976) *Religion and Respectability: Sunday Schools and Working Class Culture 1780–1850*, New Haven, CT: Yale University Press.
Laybourn, K. (1992) 'The changing face of Edwardian philanthropy: the Guild of Help Movement and the new philanthropy 1905–1919', unpublished paper presented at a meeting of *The Voluntary Action History Society*.
Lewis, J. (1993) 'The boundary between voluntary and statutory social service in the late nineteenth and early twentieth century', unpublished paper presented at a meeting of *The Voluntary Action History Society*.
Loewenberg, F. (1992) 'The roots of organised charity in the Ancient World', unpublished paper presented at a meeting of *The Voluntary Action History Society*.
Macadam, E. (1934) *The New Philanthropy*, London: Allen & Unwin.
McLaurin, A. (1988) 'Reworking "work" in some Victorian writing and visual art', in E.M. Sigsworth (ed.) *In Search of Victorian Values: Aspects of Nineteeth Century Thought and Society*, Manchester: Manchester University Press.
Manton, J. (1976) *Mary Carpenter and the Children of the Streets*, London: Heinemann Education.
Mearns, A. (1883) *The Bitter Cry of Outcast London: An Enquiry into the Conditions of the Abject Poor*, London.
Mess, H.A. (1947) *Voluntary Social Services Since 1918*, London: Kegan Paul.
Morris, R.J. (1990) 'Clubs, societies and associations', in F.M.L. Thompson (ed.) *The Cambridge Social History of England 1750–1950*, 3rd volume, Cambridge: Cambridge University Press.
Mowat, C.L. (1961) *The Charity Organisation Society 1869–1913*, London: Methuen.

National Council for Voluntary Organisations (1992) *Snapshots of the Voluntary Sector Today*, London: NCVO.

Owen, D. (1964) *English Philanthropy 1660–1960*, London: Oxford University Press.

Poggi, G. (1972) *Images of Society: Essays on the Sociological Theories of Tocqueville, Marx and Durkheim*, Oxford: Oxford University Press.

Pope, N. (1978) *Dickens and Charity*, London: Macmillan.

Price, R.N. (1971) 'The working men's club movement and Victorian social reform ideology', *Victorian Studies*, XV: 117–47.

Prochaska, F. (1980) *Women and Philanthropy in Nineteenth Century England*, Oxford: Clarendon Press.

Prochaska, F. (1988) *The Voluntary Impulse: Philanthropy in Modern Britain*, London: Faber.

Prochaska, F. (1990) 'Philanthropy', in F.M.L. Thompson (ed.) *The Cambridge Social History of England 1750–1950*, 3rd volume, Cambridge: Cambridge University Press, pp. 357–93.

Prochaska, F. (1992) *Philanthropy and the Hospitals of London: The King's Fund 1897–1990*, Oxford: Clarendon Press.

Rose, M. (1988) 'The disappearing pauper: Victorian attitudes to the relief of the poor', in E.M. Sigsworth (ed.) *In Search of Victorian Values: Aspects of Nineteenth Century Thought and Society*, Manchester: Manchester University Press.

Rowntree, B. Seebohm (1901) *Poverty: A Study of Town Life*, London.

Royal Commission on the Poor Laws and Relief of Distress, (1905–9) *Majority and Minority Reports*.

Rubin, M. (1988) *Charity and Community in Medieval Cambridge*, Cambridge: Cambridge University Press.

Scarisbrick, J.J. (1984) *The Reformation and the English People*, Oxford: Blackwell.

Scott, R. (1982) *Plymouth People: The Story of the Plymouth Guild of Community Service 1907–1982*, Plymouth: Plymouth Guild of Community Service.

Sigsworth, E.M. (ed.) (1988) *In Search of Victorian Values: Aspects of Nineteenth Century Thought and Society*, Manchester: Manchester University Press.

Simey, M.B. (1992) *Charity Rediscovered: A Study of Philanthropic Effort in Nineteenth Century Liverpool*, Liverpool: Liverpool University Press.

Slack, P. (1988) *Poverty and Policy in Tudor and Stuart England*, London: Longman.

Stedman Jones, G. (1971) *Outcast London: A Study in the Relationship between Classes in Victorian Society*, Oxford: Oxford University Press.

Taylor, J. (1972) *From Self Help to Glamour: The Working Men's Club 1860–1972*, History Workshop pamphlet.

Thane, P. (1982) *The Foundations of the Welfare State*, London: Longman.

Thompson, E.P. (1967) 'Time, work, discipline and industrial capitalism', *Past and Present*, 38.

Thompson, F.M.L. (1981) 'Social control in Victorian Britain', *Economic History Review*, 189–208.

The Volunteer Centre UK (1991) *The 1991 National Survey of Voluntary Activity in the UK*, Berkhamsted: The Volunteer Centre UK.

Wann, M. (1992) 'Self help groups: is there room for volunteers?', in R. Hedley and J. Davis Smith (eds) *Volunteering and Society: Principles and Practice*, London: Bedford Square Press.

Webb, B. (1938) *My Apprenticeship*, London: Longman.

Webb, S. and Webb, B. (1912) *The Prevention of Destitution*, London: Longman.

Wiener, M.J. (1978) 'Social control in nineteenth century Britain', *Journal of Social History*, XII: 314–21.

Williams, I. (1989) *The Alms Trade: Charities, Past, Present and Future*, London: Unwin Hyman.

Woodroofe, K. (1962) *From Charity to Social Work*, London: Routledge & Kegan Paul.

Yeo, S. (1976) *Religion and Voluntary Organisations in Crisis*, London: Croom Helm.

Young, A.F. and Ashton, E.T. (1956) *British Social Work in the Nineteenth Century*, London: Routledge & Kegan Paul.

2 The perils of partnership
The voluntary sector and the state, 1945–1992

Nicholas Deakin

VOLUNTARISM IN SEARCH OF A ROLE

In 1946, the Warden of Toynbee Hall, the original and perhaps still the most famous of all East End settlements, wrote to a number of the settlement's prominent supporters in the City of London (which lies within easy walking distance) appealing for help in putting it back on a working basis after the disruption caused by the war. The reply the Warden received from one of them was curt. The state should provide the resources because 'our present bureaucratic system under a totalitarian government is robbing the individual so that he can no longer enjoy the immense pleasure of supporting beneficent activities of this kind', he wrote (Sir R. Waley-Cohen to J.J. Mallon in Briggs and Macartney 1984: 135).

This comment encapsulates in extreme form the attitudes of some of those involved in one small – though highly visible – area of voluntary action towards the 1945–51 Labour government and what it was trying to achieve. Rather different but equally disquieting reflections troubled those responsible for organising other aspects of voluntary activity: the National Council of Social Service (NCSS) had prepared a plan for post-war action, as part of the general enthusiasm for reconstruction planning that had swept the country once it had become evident that the war was nearly won. In doing so, the Council recognised that it would have to confront a widespread belief that (in its historian's words) 'the old pioneer services had had their day and that the welfare state with its plans to care for the individual from cradle to grave, would make the work of most voluntary organisations wholly unnecessary' (Brasnett 1969: 134). Perhaps not surprisingly, this was not a view accepted by the NCSS's planning committee. Nevertheless, it reflected the evident anxieties in the voluntary sector about the attitudes and intentions of the Labour government which had just secured one of the few decisive victories to have fallen to left-wing parties this century.

In fact, despite these apprehensions, the Labour Party and its leaders were far less statist in their attitudes towards welfare than has sometimes been suggested. There was no master plan for the imposition of state control over the individual citizen; and when Winston Churchill tried to suggest as much during the 1945 election campaign in his 'Gestapo' broadcast, he was rightly regarded as having gone too far. Clement Attlee for Labour, in a cutting and effective response, had no difficulty in refuting Churchill's accusations, which he dismissed as 'merely a secondhand version of the academic views of an Austrian – Friedrich von Hayek – who is very popular just now with the Conservative party' (Harris 1982: 256). If anything, the problem was the opposite. Labour had no developed plan of its own for social policy, having participated in devising the measures put forward by the coalition government and adopted in addition the proposals in the Beveridge report, but with strong private reservations on the part of several senior figures. The manifesto for the 1945 Election (*Let Us Face the Future*) was cautious in tone and contained little evidence of a comprehensive strategy for welfare. As a result, as Jose Harris rather brutally puts it, 'the Welfare State came into being with no clearly defined conception of welfare and no coherent theory of the State' (in Smith 1986: 256). Nevertheless, it would be right to say that the wartime period had brought greater acceptance of the central, directing role of the state and (unwillingly, in some cases) a recognition that collective endeavour would continue to be the order of the day, at least for the immediate post-war period.

What place did these changed circumstances leave for the voluntary sector? In confronting the new situation, it had some assets. If the war had been a stimulus for expansion of the state sector of welfare, the voluntary sector could also claim to have 'had a good war'. In the process, it had also changed and developed. The report of the Nuffield Social Reconstruction Survey on voluntary organisations, published at the end of the war, provides a useful portrait of the voluntary sector at the end of this period of development; it also helpfully identifies a range of activities as particularly relevant for future involvement by voluntary organisations. In his introduction, G.D.H. Cole, who acted as director, dismissed the notion that all social service activities should be taken over by the state as 'one which is in the process of disappearing in many parts of the country'. This was as well, since 'it is a great mistake to suppose that as the scope of state action expands, the scope of voluntary action contracts: its character changes, in conformity both with the changing view of the province of state action and with the growth of the spirit and substance of democracy' (Bourdillon 1945: 29). It is therefore especially important to identify the right agenda and to equip workers with the right skills. Professional training undertaken in the proper spirit helps to 'form one of the vital links between the public and the voluntary spheres of society' (ibid.: 30).

What functions would this newly professionalised – and democratically accountable – voluntarism best serve? Cole and his collaborators had several proposals: child care, family welfare, youth work, adult education, advice and information. Casework could form the link between these activities and casework skills would provide the basis of collaboration between statutory and voluntary agencies. As Una Cormack argued, casework 'is a bridge between the old individualism of the past and the new community of the future and has infinite possibilities for service after the war with either voluntary societies or statutory authorities' (Bourdillon 1945: 111). Cole, however, had an important proviso: in this transformation it would be important not to lose sight of the mutual-aid organisations, with their roots in the organised working class. He comments: 'the tendency of those who are active in many fields of social service to ignore this (the social service) aspect of them often results in a singularly distorted view of the facts. It is vitally important for the future of the social services that the "voluntary agencies" and the movements based primarily on mutual aid shall come to a better understanding' (ibid.:134).

The voluntary sector therefore prepared to engage in a new relationship with an expanded state system with credentials going in some respects beyond the traditional typecasting as pioneer, supplementer of state provision and candid friend. New attitudes were developing as new skills were acquired and new tasks addressed, some of them directly generated by the expansion of state functions (Morris 1955). Wartime experience had convinced government departments of the value of their activities and demonstrated their capacity to adapt, and where necessary carry out additional functions (Land, Lowe and Whiteside 1992).

The danger in these developments (as Margaret Simey pointed out) was their instability. She commented that 'the voluntary society and voluntary worker feel that they are being constantly forced to shift their ground, though often unable to decide where to shift to' (1951: 30). Did post-war developments in the state sector help to define the role with sufficient clarity?

Completion of the welfare state

The main body of the welfare state legislation was passed with a rush in the first period of Labour government – the sequence of reforms was completed with the coming into force on the appointed day (5 July 1948) of the National Health Service Act. Most of the post-war legislative reforms were uncontroversial, in political terms. A version of the Beveridge proposals was put in place in the National Insurance Act (1946), Dalton providing the money 'with a song in his heart' (one not often heard at the Treasury!) and Attlee taking the opportunity in the debate to reflect on the changes as the completion of a long process of addressing the problem of poverty. The only significant dissenter was Beveridge himself; Tory spokesmen took the position that the argument was all over at last and good riddance (Deakin 1987: 47).

Health was the important exception. On arrival in office, Aneurin Bevan immediately overturned the cautious reform project that the coalition government had been engaged upon. He solved the problem of the management of the hospitals (deficiencies in which had been clearly exposed during war) by the bold expedient of nationalising all of them and imposing a new system of regional hospital boards. In so doing, Bevan swept into the net not just the voluntary hospitals which had been the focus for much charitable effort but also those run by local authorities, despite Herbert Morrison's fervent opposition (Campbell 1987). This could be – and was – presented as a vast expansion of the power of the state, a theme exploited by the British Medical Association in their long though ultimately unsuccessful campaign against the NHS legislation. It was echoed by the Conservative opposition which divided the House (uniquely in the welfare legislation) on both second and third reading. Bevan's solution was certainly deficient in accountability – his faith in Parliamentary control as an instrument proved all too fallible in practice. It also cut across the Cole idea of increased citizen participation as a theme for post-war social policy by reducing local voluntary involvement in the hospital sector to the marginal level of the provision of tea and sympathy for visitors.

Taken together, the effect of the Labour reforms was to change the size and shape of the space within which the voluntary sector had to operate. Most important was the end (for the meantime) of any substantial role in addressing issues of poverty in the direct sense of meeting financial need. Philanthropy in its traditional form was therefore relegated to a marginal role, certainly as long as the belief persisted that the national assistance safety net would hold, though Political and Economic Planning (PEP) was warning as early as 1952 about the inadequacies of provision, as Beveridge himself had consistently done. A second apparently moribund giant was idleness. One of the most significant features of the post-war scene was the coming to pass of Beveridge's apparently optimistic assumption about holding unemployment down. The 1944 White Paper commitment that the government would in future accept responsibility for doing so was kept; and Labour managed the potentially tricky transition of demobilisation success-fully. There was therefore no substantial role for the voluntary sector here either – which was just as well, seeing how unpopular the NCSS's involve-ment had been in the 1930s. The third substantial area where voluntary activity was no longer of major significance – as we have just seen – was the hospital (not health) service.

By way of compensation Labour was keen to stress that many other areas were open to voluntary sector activity. Herbert Morrison, who as Lord. President acted as co-ordinator of the government's social policy pro-gramme, was insistent on that point. As leader of the London County Council in the 1930s he had presided over a number of successful examples in statutory–voluntary collaboration, notably the much-admired school care committees; he was in no sense opposed to voluntary action. When, in a speech to the London Council of Voluntary Service in 1948, he praised the voluntary sector as 'the pioneers who point the way and the critics who keep us up to the mark' he meant what he said. More important, he also referred to the importance of encouraging 'the variety and freedom of voluntary associations' and identifying areas 'where statutory and voluntary effort can cooperate efficiently' (Morrison 1949).

There was every sign that the government intended to deliver on Morrisons undertakings. Morris concludes that statutory–voluntary co-operation 'had not been interrupted by the Acts of 1946 and 1948' (1955: 177). The NCSS eagerly grasped at the prospect of an expanded role in co-ordinating voluntary effort and by the end of the Labour government's period in office could conclude, in the words of the official history, that 'the importance of voluntary organisations was now definitely recognised and the authorities were prepared to regard them as important instruments of community life, not merely as useful agents' (Brasnett 1969: 175). And the official record supports this conclusion: the authors of the commentary on state papers point to the significance of the extended role performed by the voluntary sector, further expanded by the Children Act (1948) and the parallel provisions for the elderly in the National Assistance Act of the same year. As they observe, 'the expansion of voluntary effort took place despite the election of a Labour government committed to the public provision of services. Most voluntary groups were independent of government control and were therefore free to develop their own policies. However, even where organisations were tied to government departments, as was the case with the WVS, they had by the mid-1940s established so important a role that they could not easily be dismissed' (Land *et al.* 1992: 187).

After 1947, there was a general change in the political climate; the élan of the first two years was lost after the economic crisis of 1947, when the government's competence was first seriously called into question. The halo effect of the wartime period and faith in planning as a cure-all was beginning to fade. Labour captured a second wind when Stafford Cripps moved to the Treasury; but his puritanical message of austerity and sacrifice was not to everyone's taste. The association of state planning – and by extension state welfare – with uniform drabness and shortages dates from this period, which was also marked by Labour's failure to solve the housing crisis and the long drawn-out row between Bevan and the Treasury about the cost of the NHS. The impact of the Korean war and the consequent cost of rearmament cut short the incipient economic recovery that had been nurtured with such pain and sacrifice (Cairncross 1985). Meanwhile, a new criticism of state welfare was advanced, from a surprising quarter.

Beveridge rides again

In 1948 William Beveridge published his third report, *Voluntary Action.* This was intended to complement and extend the work that he had done in the first two, on social insurance and unemployment. Like the second, it was privately financed – in this case by the National Deposit Friendly Society. By this stage in his career, Beveridge no longer had any doubt about the significance of action 'outside the state'. In the introduction to his report, he wrote: 'in a totalitarian society all action outside the citizen's home, and it may be much that goes on there, is directed or controlled by the State. By contrast, vigour or abundance of Voluntary Action outside one's home, individually and in association with other citizens, for bettering one's own life and that of one's fellows, is one of the hallmarks of a free society' (Beveridge 1948: 10). The issue that he set out to explore was the form that voluntary action should take and the objectives it was best adapted to meet. Like the Nuffield Survey, Beveridge distinguished sharply between philanthropy and mutual aid as forms of voluntary action, adding to them two ancillary motives: thrift and 'the Business motive, the pursuit of a livelihood or gain for oneself in meeting the needs of one's fellow-citizens'.

The bulk of the report (and the supporting volume of research evidence) is devoted to demonstrating the continued viability of mutual aid, especially when – in combination with thrift – it produced the friendly society. But Beveridge's account can be distinguished from Cole's parallel if much briefer one in attaching a much lower priority to democracy both as a value in itself and as a means of citizen participation. Beveridge also devotes far less attention to the political expressions of mutual aid in the working class, trades unions (which he dismissed as no longer being authentic voluntary organisations) and the co-operative movement.

In assessing the tasks that remain to be discharged in the 'social service state' (his preferred term) Beveridge identifies a range of special needs (mostly those of deprived or handicapped groups) and a number of public education functions – information, adult education, 'rational' use of leisure. He concludes that these can best be discharged in co-operation between the state and voluntary agencies, with a 'Minister-guardian' of voluntary action and – rather than a Voluntary Action Grants Committee on the lines of the UGC – an independent corporation endowed by the state for subsidising social advance by voluntary action, 'where departmental interest is unlikely' (Beveridge 1948: 317). In parallel, there should be new legislation making amends for the damage that the state had done to friendly societies by withdrawing recognition from them.

Beveridge concludes by drawing a sharply limited picture of the role of the state, which is 'to do what the state alone can do: manage money' although 'in a free society it is master of very little else. The happiness or unhappiness of the society in which we live depends on ourselves as citizens, not on the instrument of political power that we call the state' (ibid.: 320). But the alternative does not lie in enlisting the fourth of the motives Beveridge identifies. 'The business motive,' he pronounces severely, 'in the field covered by this report, is seen in continual or repeated conflict with the philanthropic motive and has too often been successful . . . . The business motive is a good servant but a bad master and a society that gives itself up to the dominance of the business motive is a bad society. We do not put first things first in putting ourselves first' (ibid.: 322). The religious impulse is less powerful than it was; democracy has yet to rediscover 'the virtues of aristocracy'. Only the rediscovery of morality by all citizens can rescue us from selfishness and turn human society into 'one large friendly society'.

Beveridge's third report has been subjected to a number of different interpretations. At one extreme, it has been dismissed as a tired and dishonoured prophet's disillusioned farewell to social policy – disillusionment being caused chiefly by not being engaged on implementation of his earlier plans (Harris 1977). Alternatively, it has been seen as key to his thinking – his crowning attempt (as a 'liberal collectivist') to find a third way between state and market, and to create a 'buffer zone' in which significant voluntary action can take place (Williams and Williams 1987). However, the practicality of Beveridge's programme is open to doubt. Compared with the earlier two reports, the closing recommendations are limp; and, despite his discovery of a 'limitless field' for action, notably remoralising leisure activity, the research volume shows that the friendly societies in which he put so much faith were virtually moribund. His past eminence did at least secure for Beveridge the doubtful honour of a debate in the House of Lords on his proposals (22 June 1949) where his document was quietly buried under generalised praise both for the report itself and voluntary action in general. However, the debate did give Lord Pakenham, speaking for the Labour government, the chance to repeat once again the official position. Partnership between state and voluntary sector was endorsed, though not the notion of a single plan, as such, since 'the whole *raison d'être*' of the voluntary sector was 'its freedom from external control'. He added: 'we are convinced that voluntary associations have rendered, are rendering and must be encouraged to continue to render, great and indispensible service to the community. I hope that deliberate expression of our basic Governmental attitude will carry far and wide' (House of Lords *Hansard* 1947).

Conservatives in power

The Conservatives spent their post-war period in opposition preparing (under the guidance of R.A. Butler) for their return to power. One of the main issues which had to be confronted was what to do about the welfare state legislation. Butler's simple answer was that, rather than resist it, the Conservative line should be to claim the lion's share of the credit. But not all Conservatives (even the 'Rabians' in Central Office) were prepared to swallow Labour's welfare programme whole. There was outright opposition to the introduction of the NHS, as we have already seen. The 'One Nation group' (Angus Maude, Enoch Powell and Iain Macleod) in their influential pamphlet of that name, expressed concern with the implications of universalism, seeing no reason why the state shouldn't contemplate means testing. Concern with the impact of redistributive policies produced a touching plea for a revived philanthropy: 'Evils result from the assumption by the community of the exclusive role of Grand Almoner, which must follow from the elimination of private fortunes. . .leadership, which by its nature the state cannot exercise, depends on the existence of aggregations of wealth at the disposal of individuals' (Raison 1990: 27).

However, when the Conservatives came back to power in 1951 Churchill decided against precipitate action on the grounds that Labour's reforms needed 'time to bed in'. The issue of the cost of the health service (already exposed by Bevan's resignation) was pursued; but when the audit of expenditure by the Guillebaud Committee gave the all clear the Conservatives were prepared to let it rest. One Nation did not pursue their campaign after Macleod became Minister of Health, although he was always keen to draw a clear distinction between the welfare policies of the main parties.

Colin Clarke in his call for remoralisation of welfare by taking responsibility away from the state (1954) was therefore a voice in the wilderness. For the meantime the tide was running the other way – steady maintenance of existing welfare activity in the state sector and continued encouragement of voluntary action as junior partner in the enterprise. An audit of voluntary sector activity by Madeline Rooff published in the tenth year of the welfare state found voluntary activity well entrenched in the three areas of policy selected for review: maternity and child welfare, the mental health services and services for the blind. Summarising her evidence, Rooff concludes that a new distribution of voluntary effort was emerging as the pattern of social policy generally changed and that this was reflected 'in the changing functions of voluntary organisations, or more accurately, in the changing emphasis placed upon their various functions' which in turn depended increasingly on the priorities set by public authorities (1955: 260).

This in turn reflects the tendency towards the end of the 1950s to push on further in the direction of comprehensive plannning. On the Labour side, there was growing pressure to move on to a second stage, 'beyond Beveridge', and to restate the objectives of social policy in a more positive way. Richard Titmuss' essay on 'the social divisions of welfare' emphasised the need to see welfare provision in the round, not merely as social services provided by the state but also in terms of taxation and occupational benefits (Titmuss 1958). Parallel rethinking was taking place on the Conservative side as increased prosperity first brought the period of rationing of resources and austerity to an end and then opened up opportunities for increased individual consumption and leisure. These changes were also widely held to have brought about the Conservatives' third election victory in 1959.

Planning revisited

At the end of the 1950s a series of new developments reopened many of the issues around the provision of welfare. First, there was a renewed willingness to contemplate the application of expertise drawn from the social sciences (on the part of both government and opposition). Second, there was a revival of interest in planning, which was to be freed from the taint of failure and post-war controls by drawing on the apparently successful French model of indicative planning. Then there was a developing concern about the capacity of structures for delivery of welfare, both the machinery of central government and in a number of the key services. And finally, a further review of professional training and standards as the struggle of social work to become accepted as a full-blown profession entered a new phase (Younghusband 1978).

On the first, the key role played by Richard Crossman on Labour's side must be seen. He maintained that an opportunity had been missed by the 1945–51 government. In *Towards Socialism* he argued that the Beveridge era was now closed and the welfare system needed complete overhaul. For this purpose he gathered a group of experts based at the London School of Economics to help with the task, concentrating initially on pensions but in the expectation of being able to move away from 'the pessimistic determination to ensure that since poverty was endemic poverty must at least be fairly shared' (1965: 146). Crossman and his 'skiffle group' (his term) looked at options for change that discarded the flat-rate universalism at the centre of the Beveridge enterprise. Crossman himself was less enthusiastic about voluntary effort, presenting himself – in retropect – as a socialist technocrat with no time for charities and Brian Abel-Smith, a key player in the group, had been positively dismissive, talking of the 'long tradition of personal authoritarianism behind the voluntary charity movement' (Mackenzie 1958: 70).

But 'top–down' reform on a large scale had to wait for another Labour election victory. This came in 1964, by a far narrower margin than 1945, propelled by Harold Wilson's embracing of the 'technological revolution' of the time. The government launched out on an ambitious programme of change but ran almost at once into a series of economic setbacks. Disillusionment with a reform agenda that postponed delivery to the Greek kalends was reflected in the attitudes of the 'constituency for change' in all parties and none.

THE FORWARD MARCH OF STATE WELFARE DIVERTED?

The 1950s had been essentially a period of consolidation in the voluntary sector, underpinned by the discovery that its position was not after all seriously threatened and probably never had been. This consolidation meant that it was in better shape to confront the change of direction in state welfare being signalled by both main political parties after 1959.

The expansionist plans of the new Labour government came to a speedy halt shortly after they had come to office in 1964, a protracted economic crisis finally leading to devaluation. But the sequence of reviews by departmental committees and Royal Commissions of different aspects of welfare (some of them already set in motion or even completed before Labour came to office) continued unabated. Taken together, they made up an audit (admittedly not a wholly systematic one) of the social condition of Britain and presented a set of pressing claims for the attention of government. By the late 1960s these reviews covered virtually the whole range of welfare services as well as the machinery of central government (and were about to encompass local government as well). If adopted, they would make up a wholesale reform, funded from the 'dividend of growth' which had somehow become overdue. But despite its postponement there was still a confident assumption both that new resources would eventually appear and that they should be used for this purpose.

In these plans, there was always, as before, a place for the voluntary sector. But by now it was a different kind of voluntary sector with which governments had to deal. One of the principal changes was the appearance of a new generation of volunteers, who were entering existing organisations and creating new ones of their own. Their arrival helped to transform the reputation of voluntary action and decisively banished the past image of volunteerism. Their participation in activities funded and managed within the statutory system also raised all sorts of old questions about the distinction between professional and voluntary activity, but in a new form. The need for convincing answers to these questions became progressively greater as the move towards professionalism accelerated in the 'caring' sector of welfare – especially social work. These developments also raised issues about the location and purpose of professional training and of trained staff.

Part of this transformation came about as a spillover from a new interest in what was beginning to be called the Third World, as former British colonies moved to independence. These changes released a latent idealism about overseas development and helping to build new societies which found expression in the phenomenal expansion of Oxfam and the creation of VSO (Voluntary Service Overseas) by Alec Dickson, who later brought that approach back home with Community Service Volunteers. Some of it was the direct outcome of the identification of startling deficiencies in existing services (provision for homeless, institutional care of elderly or 'mentally handicapped', services for disabled) or gaps that had never been properly filled – nursery or kindergarten care for the under 5s, or the absence of any special services for what were then still called 'Commonweath immigrants'. In addressing these issues it was possible to draw on resources released by economic progress. In particular, much of the new activity was based on the participation of younger women – the escape of the 'captive wives' (in Hannah Gavron's phrase), overthrowing assumptions about compulsory withdrawal into childrearing; and the organisational skills learned at neighbourhood level then developing into 'second wave' feminism which in turn generated new projects and new ways of addressing them.

These developments were dramatised in a sequence of exposures – ranging from academic studies through consultancy reports, campaigning books to television programmes – which provided a counterpoint to the picture given in official reports and fed the increased appetite of the media for exposés.

They gave birth to (or provided the occasion for the evolution of) a whole group of new campaigning bodies: DIG, Aegis, Gingerbread, CPAG, Shelter, CARD. These in turn found themselves in uneasy relationship both with governments (of both parties) and with established voluntary organisations.

These organisations, having settled into co-operation with the state apparatus created at end of war as welcome (but always junior) partners now also found themselves in a new environment and having to adapt to it. Innovation had always been recognised as a legitimate function of voluntarism. But in the 'classic model' pioneering is followed by takeover and assimilation into the state sector. However, this pattern began to change. For example, when the statutory sector took over responsibility for direct care of discharged prisoners an energetic new voluntary organisation appeared in NACRO. Continuity of this kind in the involvement of the voluntary sector owed its credibility at least in part to the exposure of continuing weaknesses in statutory provision in this as in other areas.

Other large voluntary organisations coped with change by adapting from being universal providers to a new more selective and particular role, as in the case of child care organisations like Barnardo's and National Children's Homes. Others saw their particular pioneering role incorporated into the statutory setting but maintained an independent existence, stopping on the verge of assimilation (Family Service Units). Such collaborations signalled a further development in the pattern of funding relationships between voluntary organisations and the state: the appearance of all sorts of devices that implied a continuing role – grants, co-ordinating arrangements at local level, mostly through local councils of voluntary service and (very gingerly) moves towards joint planning, as in the 1962 health and welfare circular. Settlements also adapted by modifying their functions to act as 'community centres' for urban areas going through traumatic changes inflicted by clearance of unfit housing and comprehensive redevelopment of the neighbourhoods in which they were located.

However modified in form and function, these organisations had to fit in alongside the new wave of providers of services either built up from scratch (preschool playgroups associations) or clustering round the expanded circumference of state activity. Advice services had also begun to appear that were not simply adjuncts to the official machinery or interpreters of existing forms of provision but critical of them. Welfare rights' and neighbourhood law centres saw their functions as not confined to casework but including a strong campaigning role. All these new organisations were impatient with the established demarcation lines and difficult to fob off with paternalistic assumptions about the limits that should be set on voluntary action.

Successive governments confronted this changing scene and drew the conclusion that partnership would have to change in character. The state should still do more; but do it rather differently – more professionally, with better expert advice and hence more systematically, but also more responsively. Official reports of the 1960s are speckled with references to the importance of public participation, culminating in a report exclusively devoted to the topic (Skeffington 1969) and reiterations of the need for community development to sustain and supplement what is being done 'top–down'. In this new dispensation, the state would be a more understanding and flexible partner, but still very much the senior one – helped in future planning by research (the 1960s saw an exponential expansion of government social and economic research). Above all, the state would have the resources to introduce and sustain the necessary reforms, and thereby avoid the mistakes made twenty years earlier, with the introduction of the Beveridge model with its 'spartan, minimalist, safety net character' which 'increasingly clashed with the values of a more affluent and millenarian age' (Harris in Gourish and O'Day 1991: 52).

Aves and after

This was the situation that confronted the Aves committee, set up to review the role of the volunteer in the social services. The welfare system was changing rapidly and there were some instabilities in process of reform then (1969) under way. Aves set out to provide some guidelines to cover this new situation – with volunteers moving more and more into the orbit of statutory organisations when (as the committee puts it) 'we have seen a swing from maximum use of volunters to maximum use of trained staff; and now, possibly a trend back again to greater recognition of the volunteer's role' (para. 20). This higher profile of volunteering had been caused, in the committee's view, by 'a remarkable series of independent pioneering efforts, which reproduce, sometimes with equally dramatic effect, the pioneering efforts of the past. . .the pioneering tends to come from the young, from egalitarians [sic] from those who resent social dysfunctioning and individual misery and have sufficiently strong convictions to try to do something about it' (ibid.). However, the committee also detected a lack of focus in attempts to address this new situation – pointing to a 'lack of any clear policy or agreement as to what their [the volunteers'] proper function is and in what ways the services which they offer can most appropriately be used'.

The trend towards professionalisation compounded the difficulty. The committee talks about the importance of training but carefully adds a proviso about not 'blurring the distinction' between professionals and volunteers. The 'unique' contribution of volunteers must be safeguarded by not using them as substitutes for paid staff but rather to 'improve a service by adding something to what is already being done, or by opening up new possibilities' (para. 283).The mechanism for achieving these goals, the committee suggests, would be through intervention by central government: providing more funding and the creation of a new agency specifically to promote volunteer activity.

Governments – first Labour, then, after Ted Heath's unexpected 1970 election victory, Conservative – responded positively to these proposals, if not always precisely in spirit that Aves was attempting to cultivate. The context of the statutory–voluntary relationship was still changing rapidly with further progress in the overhaul of state welfare. The most important structural change was the creation of unified social services departments. This stemmed from one of the most radical of the 1960s inquiries, the Seebohm Committee – and was also linked to the creation of a new unified Department of Health and Social Security. Taken together with other changes, these developments meant that the welfare state (especially the local state) constituted a very different kind of partner for voluntary organisations.

In laying down a blueprint for the reform of social services Seebohm had made provision for the involvement of voluntary organisations and for volunteers working with and within the new social services departments. These were perceived as particularly virtuous if they promoted citizen participation (para. 495); but if they were to be supported by SSDs they needed to demonstrate that they met basic criteria of good practice in training and capacity to innovate. The merits of the 'new volunteers' were also recognised, and their potential capacity to help SSDs; but strictly in a supplementary role with proper co-ordination – the chief officer of new departments would need to have this in their already vast portfolio of responsibilities (para. 500).

Over the next few years the new departments in new authorities struggled to make some sense of these proposals, helped by government's acceptance of the Aves recommendations (the establishment of the Volunteer Centre) and by the creation within the Home Office (1972) of a new co-ordinating body, the Voluntary Services Unit (VSU) charged with co-ordinating government policy towards the voluntary sector as a whole (Watkins 1993). Direct government funding for the voluntary sector started to increase sharply and continued when Labour returned to office in 1974: at this point offical attitudes towards the sector appeared consistently benign – the last residue of any Labour hostility to voluntarism had now dissipated (Crossman in Halsey 1976).

But, on the ground, the progress was not so smooth. The British Association of Social Workers' response to Aves was a committee of inquiry set up to explore how this potentiality for co-operation could best be realised. The committee found that those social workers who had actually worked with volunteers 'have a consistently favourable view of them, while those who do not rarely express any consistent disapproval' (Holme and Maizels 1978: 171). It found a sharp contrast between probation (where the value of volunteers was well understood and acted upon) and social services. However, the report exposed a further problem. In the new SSDs – also in contrast with probation – managers from quite a junior level upwards were tending to withdraw from any direct involvement in casework. Decisions about the form of collaboration and extent of volunteer involvement were therefore tending to be settled *ad hoc* by junior staff with responsibility for cases using them as supplementary labour in those areas where staff were finding it difficult to cope – especially work with the elderly and physically handicapped.

This relegation of volunteers to a subordinate and supplementary role was not only out of phase with the mood of the times; it did not reflect the rapid changes within the voluntary sector itself as standards of training rose and professionalisation of management increased. A study of manpower resources in the voluntary sector, carried out for the official advisory body, the Personal Social Services Council (PSSC), by Adrian Webb and colleagues, showed that forty-four national voluntary organisations were employing 14,000 staff, many of them trained and that the organisations expected a steady further expansion – by 25 per cent over the next five years. In his conclusions, Webb stressed the need to clarify the sector's future role, quoting the Labour Home Secretary Roy Jenkins as telling the London Council of Social Services (LCSS): 'just as the voluntary organisations are less effective without the financial resources provided by local authorities, so the local authorities would be less effective without the labour-intensive service by voluntary organisations', and a county director of social services deploring the fragmentation of social services and the 'needless duplication and gaps [which] need to be coordinated within a master plan, which only the County are in a position to draw up' (Webb *et al.* 1976: 8).

This need for a considered review of the relationship was answered by the appearance of the report of the Wolfenden Committee (1978). This was commissioned by two large charitable foundations (Joseph Rowntree and Carnegie) as part of a search for definition of their own future role in this area; in many respects it is a rather typical 'great and good' product of the end of the consensus period. The committee's analysis was based on the view that four major sectors of activity existed (informal, state, commercial and voluntary) and what was at stake was the future relationship between them. The report signposts the new developments in the voluntary sector since the 1950s: the reorientation of much existing activity, the appearance of new organisations, emergence of mutual aid and the increased effectiveness of co-ordination. It also points to increased support for the voluntary sector by both central and local government. The report goes on to address the future role of voluntary organisations in relation to all the other sectors; and concludes (in noticeably rather different, less *dirigiste* terms than previous similar exercises) that 'in the space between the loosely structured informal system and the more strictly organised statutory system, people can use the medium of the voluntary organisation to join with others in devising means to meet their own needs or those of others they wish to help' (Wolfenden 1978: 29). The deficiencies of the statutory sector are also depicted in somewhat harsher light than in earlier reviews, with stress on the weaknesses of monopolistic bureaucracy, problems of diminished accountability to users of services and the deterring of closer public involvement (a swing of fashion is evident here too). But, as for the fourth sector, the committee are almost as dismissive as their precursor Beveridge (though without his moralising). They simply 'assume that the commercial sector as a means of providing the social needs with which we are concerned is unlikely to grow to any significant degree before the end of the century' (ibid.: 24).

Given this analysis, how can the voluntary sector best be helped to discharge its role? There are some distinctly old-fashioned elements in the recommendations: there should be a 'social plan' which will 'make the optimum and maximum use of resources' (ibid.: 193). More of those resources should be provided by government. But, principally, the means of co-ordination should be strengthened by direct funding of local development agencies – the rural community councils and councils of voluntary service. The recipe is spruced up as partnership, with a beady eye to the increasingly evident deficiencies of the statutory partner.

But the point for patching had already passed. By the time that the Wolfenden report appeared, disillusionment with state welfare was clearly evident, at every level. The critique operated at a number of different levels. First, effectiveness: nothing that the statutory welfare had set out to achieve had ever succeeded (Gladstone 1979: 40). Next, morality: state welfare had produced the ultimate dependent society and undermined the status and stability of the family, which should be the foundation stone of society (Barnett 1986). A critique of responsiveness: state welfare cannot escape weaknesses of all public bureaucracies; their size and mode of operation distances them from the clients that they are nominally trying to help. Instead, they fall victim to the 'bureau maximising' ambitions of their managers (public choice theory provided in easily digestible form by the Institute of Economic Affairs' pamphlets on welfare policy).

Added to this, there were two crucial setbacks. First, the reappearance of unemployment, which reached one million (though this figure was later amended downwards) during the Heath government, plunging the country back into a whole series of problems that were widely assumed to have been solved. Unemployment was a symptom of a second and more basic problem: the inability of successive governments to manage the economy successfully in the face of world recession following the oil price shock of 1973. After the collapse of the Barber boom, virtual national bankruptcy was declared in 1976 with the IMF coming in and imposing a record level of cuts in public expenditure. One obvious outcome was that it became quite clear that there would be no further dividend of growth; the assumption of continued expansion of state welfare (however stop-and-start) was finally falsified. The whole universe of welfare became dominated from the late 1970s onwards by 'the cuts'.

In 1979 the NCSS, shortly to become the National Council for Voluntary Organisations (NCVO), conducted its own review of options for the future, commissioning a senior member of its staff to provide a wide-ranging conspectus of the new universe in which the voluntary sector would have to operate. Shortly before his study was published, the country had elected a Conservative government; it was already clear that this would produce substantial changes in the direction of public policy but not yet what that would mean in detail. In some respects Francis Gladstone's *Voluntary Action in a Changing World* is notably more pessimistic about the prospects for voluntarism than Wolfenden had been, but in other ways its tone is almost jaunty. The era of growth in state-provided welfare may indeed be over, but that provides a real chance to look without preconditions at the opportunities now on offer. 'So far as welfare services are concerned', Gladstone writes, 'what seems to be needed is not more of the same but something different.' That something is 'radical welfare pluralism', which means dissolving the close relationship with the state and striking out in the direction of self-help and community development. Future development in the 1980s must be first and foremost 'a question of localised initiative' (ibid.: 122). This involves looking again at the institutions of mutual aid: co-operatives, credit unions and self-build housing associations. This is welfare bottom–up, directly accountable through the participation of those both providing and receiving it.

Over this restyled enterprise presides a somewhat implausible hero: William Beveridge. Gladstone takes from his third report not just the thundering peroration – 'all mankind a Friendly Society' – but the concept of a third way which does not follow the path laid down by the state (the 'master of money and nothing else' is now not even that) or business (despite Natwest sponsorship of the report – another prefiguration of the 1980s). Gladstone scrupulously observes the conventions by admitting that dependence on independent voluntary effort leaves gaps and unevennesses, but better that (he makes it clear) than the drab disabling uniformity of a state sector in decline. All that the third sector lacked to give full expression to these alternatives was a political voice. Pending that, a statement of this kind coming from the body with the recognised co-ordinating responsibility for the sector as a whole, was bound to (and did) make a substantial impact.

CHARTING A THIRD WAY

In every area of public policy the election of the Conservative government in 1979 eventually brought about important changes, but it was not immediately clear at the outset what the full implications for the voluntary sector would be. However, it was instantly evident that the government meant business (in every sense). From the outset, the declared intention was to reduce public expenditure ('at the heart of Britain's economic problems' according to the 1979 White Paper) and in the cant of the day to 'roll back the frontiers of the State'. But to whose advantage?

Certainly, these initial declarations of intent heightened the sense already developing in the voluntary sector that linkage through partnership with the statutory welfare state was equivalent to having a large stake in a bankrupt firm. Nor were shares in professionalism trading at a very high value. The new government's impatience with 'provider power' as exercised through the public sector unions had already been made evident in opposition; and it extended to the 'bureau-professionals' in the welfare area and to teachers and social workers in particular.

The first moves in this area, however, were limited and largely predictable. The government had much more challenging tasks on hand – reducing the share of GDP taken by state expenditure (an objective never actually achieved) and facing down the public sector unions. Mrs Thatcher also had to move cautiously through the early political stage when old-fashioned paternalistic Tories, unconvinced of the merits of her programme, were still in the Cabinet in substantial numbers. The declared intentions towards the voluntary sector set out in the manifesto were still at the level of benevolent cliché. Not until 1981 was any indication given of the role for which the sector was being cast. Then, Mrs Thatcher's speech to the WRVS indicated that a central place in the enterprise would be reserved for voluntaryism (by which she probably meant volunteers); one likely assignment that they might be asked to discharge would be the 'remoralisation' project to which she attached such personal significance.

But meanwhile other alternative projects were in the course of development. 'Radical Welfare Pluralism' was developing steadily from the basis laid down in Gladstone's study. This also signified a break with the post-war welfare consensus in its way as drastic as the Thatcher project. Further ripples were still spreading from the Wolfenden report: Stephen Hatch (the committee's senior research officer) published in 1980 a study on local welfare 'outside the state'. In 1981 he and Roger Hadley produced their own polemic explicitly and provocatively about 'the failure of the state', arguing for a decisive break with the post-war legacy of bureaucratic statism, especially since resources (not necessarily financial) could be found elsewhere. There had been a burgeoning of self-help groups, some organised around disease, others generic. Experiments were undertaken in decentralised service delivery, first on a single 'patch', in a term that swiftly became fashionable (Normanton); then within an entire local authority (Walsall).

By that stage, the movement had a possible political focus in the newly formed SDP, which attracted not only a substantial segment of the right wing of the Labour party but a group of libertarian 'anti-statists', most conspicuously Michael Young (purveyor-general of innovation to the left for a generation) and also Hatch himself and the then Director of the NCVO. For a brief period, it looked as if the Social Democratic Party (SDP) might (in another cliché of the day) 'break the mould' and propel its ideas to the centre of political debate. But it was not to be; after the disappointing election result of 1983, the SDP faded away into a squabbling sect.

A new conservatism in action

The government advanced cautiously into the potentially contentious area of welfare, concentrating during their first term (1979–83) on economic policy and within that context on the drastic overhaul of fiscal and labour market policies. But both had implications for voluntary action. One of the emerging issues of the late 1970s (see above) had been the return of mass unemployment. The Conservatives had been severely critical of Labour's record between 1974 and 1979; the best remembered poster from the 1979 election campaign (when unemployment was actually coming down) was the Saatchis' 'Labour isn't working'. The main instrument available to government for addressing unemployment was the Manpower Services Commission, a tripartite quango (government–employers–union) created at the fag-end of the corporatist period; during the late 1970s it had occupied itself with attempts to improve training and a cautious programme of schemes designed to get unemployed people back to work.

The Conservatives had been sceptical about the MSC in opposition. However, with unemployment rising rapidly past 2 million and the devastating impact on industry of Geoffrey Howe's counter-inflationary policy making more job losses on a huge scale inevitable, the MSC became the key focus of government policy and recipient of public funds. The consensus-minded chair, Richard O'Brien, was discarded in favour of the former property developer, David Young, who enjoyed the personal support of Margaret Thatcher. Young launched an extensive campaign, with vigorous use of advertising, modelled on the activities of the international Jewish charity Organisation for Rehabilitation and Training (ORT). But for success Young required not merely the benevolence of the philanthropic (as ORT did) but the close involvement of the voluntary sector in implementation of a new series of schemes which would bypass existing formal structures. The most important of these was the Community Programme.

The initial reaction of the voluntary sector was suspicious. Unemployment was a highly visible political issue and they were being invited to participate in a controversial programme which critics portrayed as addressing symptoms, not causes. Two factors combined to beat down resistance. The intermediate bodies to whom MSC was especially looking were under increasingly strong financial pressure as cuts bit into other sources of revenue, especially funding from local government. MSC funds came with strings attached (explicitly non-political objectives, so no campaigning was allowed), but they were copious. Second, there was simply a sense that 'something had to be done' (to repeat the Prince of Wales' celebrated remark in the 1930s).

So MSC officials, in David Young's words, were set to 'work unceasingly to overcome the hostility and suspicion of the voluntary sector. They spoke at meetings up and down the land, often seven days a week. They were so successful that in the end the voluntary sector adopted the programme as their own and would not be parted from it' (1990: 88). This is not the whole story (see Addy and Scott 1988). What was at stake once organisations had swallowed their anxieties was continuity in policy and funding. First at the MSC then on promotion to ministerial office, Young was juggling with schemes – and, critics at the time suspected, fiddling with the figures;

renaming and remarketing new schemes was the name of his game. The 'solutions' he brought to the Prime Minister (for which she so highly esteemed him, to the intense annoyance of his colleagues) hinged on achieving the public sector equivalents of increased sales figures – a reduction in unemployment statistics, eventually achieved after it had risen to over 3 million.

Voluntary organisations were also juggling but with sharply reduced budgets and vastly increased pressure of needs. The level of their developing dependency on the MSC was illustrated by the extent of their involvement in the Community Programme, in which voluntary agencies were supplying over half the projects when it closed in 1988. At this point the MSC was providing 20 per cent of all government funding going to the whole sector; and 72 per cent of this was attributable to the Community Programme (Waine in Manning and Page 1992: 78). Switches of rules and content of schemes at short notice proved fatal to some of the most vulnerable organisations. The pill was not sweetened by subsequent revelations from one of the junior ministers involved (Alan Clark) that voluntary sector suspicions of the government's basic motivation were largely justified. As Barbara Waine comments, they had found themselves 'providing low skilled part-time employment as part of a programme with a definite political bias' (ibid.: 79).

The other area of direct government intervention was more positive in its impact: the effect of changing fiscal policy. Tax concessions of some kind affecting charities and charitable giving were introduced in every budget from 1980 onwards; but achieved most momentum in the Lawson Chancellorship. One of the declared objectives of lightening the burden of direct taxation was to free the better off to make choices about the use of their money – among which, it was hoped, philanthropic giving would feature more prominently. These hopes were not immediately realised; more specific measures were subsequently introduced – for example, 'payroll giving' in 1987. Results in terms of level of donations remained disappointing; but the attempt was symbolic of the government's wider intentions to secure greater involvement by individuals in responsibility for welfare.

The local state strikes back

The main impact of government action on the voluntary sector in their first two terms, however, was indirect and resulted from the other half of the conservative project: diminishing the state's role and in particular that of local government. Local authorities initially attracted disapproval for 'Treasury' reasons – they represented an element in public policy which risked escaping from central government control and compromising their intention to reduce both public expenditure and the range of public functions. Local government soon gave other and more immediate causes for disapproval. What became known as the 'municipal socialist' authorities introduced a distinctive new set of policies – economic development, equal opportunities pursued through the creation of women's committees and race relations units, restructured housing departments, and measures for decentralisation of services and 'contract compliance'. The new left-wing leaderships reached out to the voluntary sector for both ideas and political support, and particularly to the community groups in which many of them had learned their politics. This led to the construction of what became known as the 'rainbow coalition', in which politically acceptable voluntary bodies were supported by generous funding but with strings attached: local authority conditions of employment and trades union membership. Black groups, their needs often overlooked in earlier collaborations between statutory and voluntary sectors, were among the conspicuous beneficiaries of these new policies.

The government had no time for any of this. They set themselves to grind the life out of the enterprise, by a range of measures: cuts in resources; limitations on powers to raise money and spend it (capping); new forms of inspection and review (the Audit Commission); and eventually abolition of the Greater London Council (seen as the main offender) and the metropolitan counties. The local authorities fought back and in so doing sought to enlist their client voluntary organisations in the campaign. This created a difficult situation, especially for co-ordinating bodies, both nationally and locally. Cross-memberships as well as financial ties made taking an independent line extremely difficult; several organisations collapsed into internal turmoil (Knight 1993).

By the end of their second term (1987) the Conservative government had in substance won their battle with local authorities. This helped to give further impetus to proceed with more drastic structural reforms. These too had important implications for voluntary organisations who were now expected to take on a more active role as agencies for the delivery of welfare. By this stage, the government had a clearer notion of what the voluntary sector could do and some ideas about the restrictions on its capacity to act.

A new agenda?

The initial confusion of voluntary action with volunteering had been tempered with experience of closer involvement. Three objectives can be distinguished in the programmes put in place: first, the need to revive philanthropy – and encourage more involvement of business and businessmen; second, the importance of improving standards of management; third, the need to remotivate individuals (beyond fiscal measures already described) to take responsibility.

The revival of philanthropy was intimately linked to the 'enterprise culture' mission which was the cornerstone of the 1978 documents prepared for the party's general election campaign (Ridley 1992). From the point of neo-liberal capture of the party in 1975 it was always regarded as clear that values would have to be changed if economic revival was to be achieved. To revive the enterprise culture in a truly enterprising way individuals would need rewards but also to be reminded of their reponsibilities. This is where 'Victorian values' came in: a sense of common purpose, strong local loyalties and classes perceived as not separated geographically but linked in the Victorian city. All these themes come together in Conservative inner-city policy. Inner cities were portrayed as the site of desolation and dependency (Young 1990) and the exemplification of the destructiveness of the welfare state (Ridley 1992). This perception was intensified after the inner-city 'disturbances' of 1981 in Toxteth and Brixton.

But dependency is not inevitable; enterprise can be released. This was Michael Heseltine's mission (1987). He abandoned the 'corporatist' solutions of his Labour (and Conservative) predecessors and drew on American models to mount a private sector-led attack on inner-city dereliction, in which business was to be the prime mover. But not solely for profit. Rather, he sought to promote the notion of 'socially responsible' business; the government organised 'Business in the Community' to act as a pressure group and set in motion whole series of business-led philanthropic initiatives. Socially responsible business was also to be involved in less high-profile ways: schemes for giving (IBM, Marks and Spencer); secondments; skills exchanges mediated by the Action Resource Centre. The tide of activity rose as rising levels of prosperity in the second half of the 1980s launched a new round of tax cuts. Philanthropy appeared to have been successfully relaunched.

The second element was the issue of standards of management in the voluntary sector. Were voluntary organisations fit to perform the more ambitious role for which they were being auditioned? Here, the crucial role had been that of the national intermediary bodies and the new generation of chief executives (as they now like to be called) of voluntary organisations – the so-called 'moving spirits'. This is professionalisation in a sense quite different from the acquisition of casework skills in the 1950s and 1960s.

There were two ways in which this could be achieved: first, to draw and apply lessons from the general approach in the private sector: what is often called the 'new managerialism' and the changing of the corporate culture that was simultaneously under way (Peters and Waterman 1982); and, second, the use of networking to sell the product throughout the voluntary sector, with NCVO taking a lead role. Hence the Handy report on *Improving Effectiveness in the Voluntary Sector* (NCVO 1981) and the funding of management development by NatWest; the dissemination of values by movement at senior staff level (the 'roundabout' of agencies exchanging chief executives) and closer involvement of senior businessmen in advisory capacities. This period also saw the implantation of management teaching into social science faculties of polytechnics and universities – and the eventual emergence of specialist courses in training voluntary sector management. By the mid-1980s, this element in the project was well advanced, with the benevolent support of central government both financially and through the Voluntary Service Unit (Watkins 1993).

The 'selling' of management as a key element in changing the profile of the voluntary sector was in itself an important enterprise; as Barry Knight observes, 'resistance to management was deep rooted' (1993: 47), not least because it appeared to cut across many of the core values of voluntarism. By the end of the decade, the position had changed substantially; but a senior industrialist (Alex Reed) was still driven to comment censoriously on the lack of sound 'business management' that he had encountered in charities (Knight 1993: 46).

The third element in the government's programme was the remotivation of individuals – otherwise known as the 'Active Citizen' enterprise. This argument is based in part on striking a balance between rights and responsibilities. To escape from the dependency induced by over-reliance on state welfare, the citizen has to accept ultimate responsibility for the welfare of himself and his family. If he does so, the state will recognise his entitlements as a citizen. But it is both more rewarding and more reinforcing of character if the citizen exercises these entitlements through his own efforts (and pays for them). Hence, one reason for the importance of using public money for sustaining and expanding the private sector in housing, education, health and (in the second half of the 1980s) pensions. Cuts in direct taxation further widen the range of those enabled to do so. But responsibility implies a duty to invest in sustaining the social fabric: voluntary work – fundraising, bringing professional expertise to management of voluntary organisations – is the obvious way of paying this debt and ensuring that stability is preserved. The rapid expansion of different methods of fundraising, originally triggered by Bob Geldorf's 'Band Aid' concerts for Third World famine relief but extending into telethons and special fundraising exercises (sponsored marathons, 'Red Nose' days) provided what appear to be pain-free ways of achieving some of these objectives.

Implementing a new partnership

Having left welfare issues largely on one side during the first two terms (the exception being social security; but that was driven by the economic agenda), the Conservatives, once re-elected for a third term in 1987, cast aside all inhibitions. The reform agenda of the following year led David Willetts to describe it as an 'annus mirabilis' for social policy. Education, health, children, community care were all involved. There are several common themes, the most important of which is the fundamental change in the role of the state. Direct service delivery is no longer to be the responsibility of public bureaucracies. Services are either to be hived off altogether into the private sector (on the model of the privatisation of nationalised industries and public utilities) or to be delivered through 'quasi-markets', with the state retaining the role of purchasing on behalf of the consumer but from providers either already outside the public sector proper or consigned there (NHS trusts, grant-maintained schools). Another general theme has been the maximum decentralisation of responsibility for service delivery, but centralisation of control over direction of policy and provision of (semi) independent scrutiny of outcomes by regulatory agencies and inspectorates.

This has meant the breakup of most public sector intermediate organisations and in particular a very much diminished role (with the partial exception of community care) for the voluntary sector's one-time 'natural' partners in local government. By way of compensation, voluntary bodies have received a substantial increase in direct funding from government and the opportunity to compete for new service delivery tasks. But in doing so, they are entering a new universe with very different rules of engagement: in shorthand, the 'contract culture'. Some are well equipped to cope with it. Most large voluntary agencies have taken on board the lessons of the management revolution of the 1980s and kitted themselves out with all the paraphernalia of the enterprise culture: mission statements, logos, personal identification with tasks, 'passion' (even obsession) for excellence. Others resisted but have recognised that survival has meant being able to play the game according to the new rules. Others are still simply bewildered or hardly aware of what the rules are – 'generic' organisations operating at community level and many ethnic and women's groups. Others still have been deliberately excluded because their objectives do not mesh with the project: these are the deplorable 'pressure groups' – mainly advocacy and campaigning bodies.

The voluntary sector goes to market

It is far too early to pronounce on the success of this enterprise. But we can point to some milestones on the road. The new philanthropy proved soluble when dampened by the recession after 1989 – the 'city fathers' mostly decided that their paternal responsibilities were to their own firms and jobs, not the common good. This part of the enterprise lost momentum when Mrs Thatcher, who had invested much personal attention in it, left Downing Street. The new management has rolled on, however. By the early 1990s, large voluntary organisations, with the help of foundations, were confident enough to export their expertise to the newly emancipated former eastern bloc countries trying to construct civil society from scratch.

Part of the pressure to keep adapting was brought about by further changes in central government, in both structure and values. Relations with other agencies were also changing as a result – Whitehall became more aware of other sets of values and other ways of doing things. Relations with the voluntary sector were comprehensively reviewed in the Home Office's *Efficiency Scrutiny* (1990); some of the crudities of the MSC era had been eliminated but there was still an evident desire to 'manage' the voluntary sector and its activities, despite the usual hat-tipping to the importance of innovation. A year later, the Labour party's own committee gave a final quietus to notions of the 'withering away' of voluntarism but placed more emphasis on local co-ordination on the basis of the central directing role of the local authority (a case of catching yesterday's bandwagon).

Meanwhile, the new Conservative government of John Major (1990–) was placing more emphasis on empowerment of the individual, codified in his much-derided 'Citizen's Charter' (1991). This was designed to provide the individual with a full account of his claims on the public sector, as a consumer of public services, and ways in which he can obtain satisfaction if these claims are not met. There is a useful summing up of the government's position just before the beginning of their new term of office in their White Paper *The Individual and the Community* (1992). In his introduction, the Prime Minister calls for 'more volunteering, more charitable giving and more business involvement in the community'. The uniqueness of the UK voluntary sector is stressed, the little battalions (this time) paraded alongside the companies, and assurances given that in seeking to involve the voluntary sector more closely in service delivery the intention is not 'to provide cheap alternatives to public services'. Often, however, voluntary organisations are 'pursuing objectives that accord with or complement government goals, in whole or in part'. After accounting for the increase in government spending and the improvements in building effective relations brought about by the implementation of the scrutiny recommendations, the document looks forward to continued voluntary sector involvement to meet government objectives of improved flexibility and choice.

Finally, the White Paper sketches out the familiar theme of a 'third force', 'operating dynamically and effectively between those areas that are properly the responsibility of government and those that are properly the responsibility of the individual' (1992: 36). But in so doing the third force has a new member: 'active corporate citizens'; or, as they are more often known, businesses. A long way from Beveridge, indeed; but then, as Margaret Thatcher once observed, the whole point about the good Samaritan was not that he stopped but that he had the money.

CONCLUSION

It would be a gross oversimplification to portray the evolution of the voluntary sector over the post-war period as being merely one consequence of the advance and subsequent retreat of the state. Certainly, developments in the role of the state – especially in the field of welfare – have been one of the major determining factors in defining the tasks that voluntary agencies have carried out. The Webbs' image of the sector as the extension ladder still has considerable force, although the terrain on which the bottom rungs have been planted has grown increasingly shaky over this period as a whole.

However, other developments have been almost as influential as the growth (and subsequent shrinkage) in the circumference of the state's sphere of action. Changing values, for one: attitude shifts in the 1960s, influenced by a sense of increased national prosperity, followed by reactions produced by the opposite perception a decade later have had consequences that cut across the artificial boundaries between the statutory and voluntary sectors. The rise and fall of professionalism in welfare, in which many hopes were invested in both sectors, has been another phenomenon with wider implications. It will be interesting to see whether the heavy investment in managerial reform that has been a key characteristic of the last decade in both sectors leads in due course to similar outcomes.

External influences have also been a significant factor in promoting change. The impact of developments in the Third World, especially in the area of community development, is often underplayed. The lessons from America, by contrast, have been eagerly learnt and applied, especially in the area of management development. Overshadowing all of these, however, has been the constant pressure of economic circumstances. To the extent that there has been a consistent theme in government attitudes towards the voluntary sector it has been the utility of voluntary provision in reducing the costs of provision – 'value for money', in 1980s terms. Other agendas have come and gone: this one is eternal, like its parent, the Treasury.

REFERENCES

Addy, T. and Scott, D. (1988) *Fatal Impacts? The MSC and Voluntary Action*, Manchester: William Temple Foundation.
Aves Committee (1969) *The Voluntary Worker in the Social Services*, London: Allen & Unwin.
Barnett, C. (1986) *The Audit of War*: London: Macmillan.
Beveridge, W. (1948) *Voluntary Action*, London: Allen & Unwin.
Bourdillon, A.F.C. (ed.) (1945) *Voluntary Social Services: Their Place in the Modern State*, London: Methuen.
Brasnett, M. (1969) *Voluntary Social Action*, London: Bedford Square Press.
Briggs, A. and Macartney, A (1984) *Toynbee Hall: The First Hundred Years*, London: Routledge & Kegan Paul.
Cairncross, A. (1985) *Years of Recovery*, London: Methuen.
Campbell, J. (1987) *Nye Bevan and the Mirage of British Socialism*, London: Weidenfeld & Nicolson.
Crossman, R.H.S. (1965) *Towards Socialism*, London: Fontana.
Deakin, N. (1987) *The Politics of Welfare*, London: Methuen.
Gladstone, F. (1979) *Voluntary Action in a Changing World*, London: Bedford Square Press.
Gourish, T. and O'Day, A. (eds) (1991) *Britain since 1945*, London: Macmillan.
Halsey, A.H. (ed.) (1976) *Traditions of Social Policy*, Oxford: Blackwell.
Harris, J. (1977) *William Beveridge: A Biography*, Oxford: Clarendon Press.
Harris, K. (1982) *Attlee*, London: Weidenfeld & Nicolson.
Heseltine, M. (1987) *Where there's a Will*, London: Hutchinson.
Holme, A. and Maizels, J. (1978) *Social Workers and Volunteers*, London: Allen & Unwin.
Home Office (1990) *Efficiency Scrutiny of Government Funding of the Voluntary Sector*, London: HMSO.
Home Office (1992) *The Individual and the Community*, London: HMSO.
Knight, B. (1993) *Voluntary Action*, London: Home Office.

Land, A., Lowe, R. and Whiteside, N. (1992) *The Development of the Welfare State, 1939–1951*, London: HMSO.

Mackenzie, N. (1958) *Conviction*, London: Macgibbon & Kee.

Manning, N. and Page, R. (1992) *Social Policy Review 4*, Kent: Social Policy Association.

Morris, M. (1955) *Voluntary Organisations and Social Progress*, London: Gollancz.

Morris, M (1969) *Voluntary Work in the Welfare State*, London: Routledge & Kegan Paul.

Morrison, H. (1949) *The Peaceful Revolution*, London: Allen & Unwin.

NCVO (1981) *Improving Effectiveness in Voluntary Organisations*, London: National Council for Voluntary Organisations.

Peters, T. and Waterman, R. (1982) *In Search of Excellence*, New York: Harper & Row.

Raison, T. (1990) *The Conservatives and the Welfare State*, Basingstoke: Macmillan.

Ridley, N. (1992) *My Style of Government*, London: Fontana.

Rooff, M. (1955) *A Hundred Years of Family Welfare*, London: Michael Joseph.

Simey, M. (1951) *Charitable Effort in Liverpool in the Nineteenth Century*, Liverpool: Liverpool University Press.

Skeffington, A. (1969) *People and Planning*, London: HMSO.

Smith, H.L. (ed.) (1986) *War and Social Change*, Manchester: Manchester University Press.

Titmuss, R. (1958) *Essays on the Welfare State*, London: Unwin University Books.

Watkins, R. (1993) *The Origins of the Voluntary Service Unit*, paper prepared for the Voluntary Action History Society (TS).

Webb, A. *et al.* (1976) *Voluntary Social Services: Management Resources*, London: Personal Social Services Council.

Williams, K. and Williams, J. (eds) (1987) *A Beveridge Reader*, London: Allen & Unwin.

Wolfenden Committee (1978) *The Future for Voluntary Organisations*, London: Croom Helm.

Young, D. (1990) *The Enterprise Years*, London: Headline.

Younghusband, E. (1978) *Social Work in Britain 1950–1975*, London: Allen & Unwin.

3 A loose and baggy monster

Boundaries, definitions and typologies

Jeremy Kendall and Martin Knapp

INTRODUCTION

The extent and nature of the voluntary sector's contributions to the UK economy and society often remain unremarked or are discussed confusedly because of a lack of clarity on the terminology, definitions and classifications being (often implicitly) employed. Indeed, observers and analysts of the sector most often begin their accounts by remarking that the voluntary sector contains a bewildering array of organisational forms, activities, motivations and ideologies. In spite of these difficulties, this chapter aims to show that important insights into the nature of the sector can be gained by explicitly addressing this issue, while noting that the preferred approach will depend on the purpose for which the categorisations are required (Johnson 1981; 6 1991). There is no single 'correct' definition which can or should be uniquely applied in all circumstances.

A useful way into this inherently messy topic is to start at the rather general level of setting the sector in its societal context by considering the functions that it fulfils, and how organisations in it may be resourced and controlled. This constitutes the start of the first section, which also attempts to give a broad summary of some of the motivations, norms and values that various writers have especially linked with the voluntary sector. The following section is rather more specific, with the focus shifted on to particular fields of activity or 'industries' in which voluntary bodies are engaged. Included here are some summary statistics to give some indication of the relative size and significance of selected key areas.

Armed with these complementary overviews of the organisational terrain,[1] the third section steps back to pose the question of what this startling diversity of bodies may have in common: i.e. what criteria must an entity meet to be regarded as being part of 'the voluntary sector'? We describe key characteristics identified by UK researchers and outline in more detail the components of a 'structural/operational definition'. This is being employed for purposes of cross-national comparison, and seems to have a comparative advantage over the use of legal, economic/financial or functional definitions for this particular purpose (Salamon and Anheier 1993). However, these criteria are not absolute, but may be met to varying degrees, so that the boundaries around the sector are best thought of as blurred rather than neatly defined. We describe how this approach can be applied pragmatically in the UK, and note how some of the debates about the appropriate definition and treatment of the sector can be thought of as either implying different interpretations of these criteria or introducing new criteria to partition its components.

MAJOR TYPES OF ORGANISATION

Societal functions of voluntary organisations

In order to highlight the niche occupied by these organisations in UK society, we can categorise them by primary *function*, even though most voluntary bodies would characterise themselves as *multi-functional*. The following set of functions for voluntary sector organisations has often been identified (Brenton 1985; see also Murray 1969; Wolfenden 1978; Johnson 1981; Handy 1988; Nathan 1990; Gutch *et al*. 1990).

- The *service-providing function* 'typifies those voluntary agencies which supply a direct service to people, in kind or in the form of information, advice and support' (Brenton 1985: 11). In the social services field, agencies are active in the provision of the full range of residential, respite, domiciliary and day care services to individual and multiple client groups. Nursing homes, hospices and hospitals in health care and schools in education are further prominent examples. Law centres, citizens' advice bureaux and independent advice centres are legal service providers, while environmental groups running bird reserves, cleaning canals and preserving buildings, for example, could also fit into this category. A large amount of voluntary action in this area has historically been characterised as 'pioneering', catalytic and demonstrative (Nathan 1952; Knapp *et al*. 1990).
- The *mutual-aid function* is 'about self-help and exchange around a common need or interest' (Brenton 1985: 12), and has 'developed worldwide into a major social phenomenon. . .developing primarily around psychosocial and medical problems' (Hasenfield and Gidron 1993: 217). It is the main feature of organisations like Cruse (for widows), Alcoholics Anonymous, gay and lesbian support groups and a whole range of local community-based organisations in education, health and recreation.
- A third function identified by Brenton is policy advocacy or campaigning. Brenton describes this as the *pressure-group function*, 'the marshalling of information around some specific cause or group interest and the application of this to some public arena through direct action, campaigning, lobbying and advocacy to achieve a desired change' (1985: 12). It involves 'the production of pressure on decision-makers in any sector to change policy and practices usually on behalf of some identifiable groups' (Kendall

and 6 1994). The Child Poverty Action group, Liberty (formerly the National Council for Civil Liberties) and Oxfam are three well-known campaigning or pressure groups.

- Fourth, it is worth separately identifying *individual* advocacy, although for Brenton this is presumably submerged under other headings. This involves presenting a case on behalf of individuals to receive goods and services so there is some overlap with the information providers we identified above. This is particularly important in the fields of health and social services. For example, in mental health it covers: professional support from MIND, a national charity for people with mental health problems, at Mental Health Review Tribunals; citizen advocacy, in which advocates are ordinary people involved in one-to-one relationships with vulnerable individuals, acting on their behalf to identify needs, represent interests and stand up for their rights; and self-advocacy involving user control and combining individual, personal and public advocacy.
- Finally, we have what Brenton terms the *resource* and *co-ordinating functions*, which typically involve blending service provision to other voluntary sector bodies, often in particular industries, acting as 'a central catalyst or repository of expertise, information, research etc., on a specialist subject', with 'represent[ing] a membership of other voluntary bodies and seek[ing] to liaise between them and coordinat[ing] their activities, their public relations or their connections with government' (1985: 12). Involved in this liaison and representation work are generalist sector-wide national and local *intermediaries* (Wolfenden 1978) such as the National Council for Voluntary Organisations, the Charities Aid Foundation, the Volunteer Centre, Local Development Agencies (Councils for Voluntary Service, Rural Community Councils, Volunteer Bureaux and similar bodies), together with industry-specific bodies such as the National Youth Agency and the National Federation of Housing Associations.

Types of voluntary organisation distinguished by resourcing and control

Another way to categorise the voluntary sector, perhaps in conjunction with the functional approach, is to identify different structural types, depending on the *arrangements for control* and/or *method of resourcing* (human and financial). Elements of the former have already informed our distinction between service provision and mutual aid, and different types of individual advocacy, and Gutch *et al.* (1990: 58) point out that for some purposes it may be useful to make the distinction between *democratic* and *oligarchic* bodies, whose trustees (see Chapter 8) are elected and appointed respectively. Stephen Hatch (1980: 35–8), in the follow-up locality research undertaken after the Wolfenden Committee's deliberations (see Chapter 2), makes 'the basic distinction between organisations dependent mainly on voluntary effort, and organisations dependent mainly on paid staff'. He then goes on to distinguish in the former sector between beneficiary-controlled or 'mutual-aid associations' (overlapping with the second function identified by Brenton as described above), which pursue members' interests, and 'volunteer organisations' oriented towards helping non-members. In the latter sector, he distinguishes between bodies according to whether they are funded 'predominantly' from statutory or from non-statutory sources (Hatch 1980: 35–8).

The recent government-sponsored review of links between statutory bodies and the voluntary sector and the Community Development Foundation have both made distinctions similar to those made by Hatch (Home Office 1990; Chanan 1991; see also Ball 1989). One type distinguished would be the intermediary bodies identified by the Wolfenden Committee (1978) and Brenton (1985). Using Chanan's approach and terminology (which are not in common currency, but useful), another three varieties can be distinguished. *Professional non-profit organisations* are providers of professional services – employing paid staff at national and local level – where the national organisations directly run the local offices and raise funds for local work. *Voluntary service organisations* have professionally organised national head-quarters, but autonomous local groups which raise their own funds and use volunteers (and sometimes also paid staff). This arrangement is often described as 'federated', reflecting a looseness of structure to be contrasted with the more centralised operation associated with professional non-profit organisations (Ball 1989: 8). Here it is generally the case that 'the number of conditions that a local branch has to meet in order to be admitted into membership of [the] national federation is small' (Wolfenden 1978: 38). *Independent local community groups*, finally, are 'self-standing bodies with no head office to provide support' (Home Office 1990: 3); their overwhelmingly important resources are their volunteer members' unpaid labour. In common with the (local) mutual-aid and pressure group functional varieties in Brenton's taxonomy, the essence of the 'output' of many of the latter groups will be participative community development, rather than direct service provision. This activity can involve 'organising and developing institutional links within a geographical area or community of interest' (Kendall and 6 1994). Such bodies are notoriously difficult to classify in terms of an 'industry' or market since, by their very nature, conventional distinctions – between demand and supply sides, user and volunteer or process and output, for example – often conflict with underlying ideologies and operating principles.

> Development functions have a different and socially more complex pattern [than service delivery functions]. These are where the primary purpose is for people *to get together with others to solve a problem*. The problem might be post-natal depression, housing conditions, employment opportunities, care for the disabled, poor public transport, or a threat to the local environment. . . .A main benefit is the participation itself because this is

what enables people to emerge from their isolation, gain a greater sense of independence and interdependence, gain social contacts, pick up information and intervene actively in decisions affecting the whole locality.

(Chanan 1991: 11)

In further work, the Community Development Foundation has gone on to define the 'autonomy' implicit in their description of these bodies as 'independent'. 'Autonomous' local voluntary organisations are described as those which are controlled 'predominantly' by local resident users, members or volunteers, while in 'externally-led' groups, public authorities, national (voluntary) bodies or external funders 'decide what really happens' (Chanan 1993).[2] Hasenfield and Gidron (1993) have offered further refinements. They distinguish between 'self help groups' and '[professional] human service organisations' on the basis of external resource dependency, the position of clients/members, breadth of 'domain and mission' and service technology (1993: 222, Table 1). The two groups are contrasted in that:

A self-help group can be defined as a group of individuals who experience a common problem, who share their personal stories and knowledge to help one another cope with their situation, and who simultaneously help and are helped. In addition, the group emphasises face-to-face interactions and informal and interchangeable roles. In contrast, human service organisations are characterised by career-oriented staff members who need not personally experience the problems they address, distinct staff and client roles, a professionally based body of knowledge, and formal division of labor.

(Hasenfield and Gidron 1993: 218)

None of these categorisations would claim to be exhaustive, and, to make further progress, we really need to look more specifically at the sector's spread in terms of industry or field of activity. However, there are some further additions we should make at this stage if we are concerned with financial structures. *Nationally affiliated local fundraising groups* do not really fit well into any of the categories described above. Here, local groups, most often active in the field of specific diseases and medical conditions, exist partly to fundraise for a national body through a three-tier structure of local branches and regional and national offices (Deans 1989: 147) and partly to retain some funds for local mutual-support activities of the type referred to above. Ball (1989: 10) somewhat confusingly refers to these as 'Self-help organisations'.

It is also worth mentioning that voluntary bodies are often categorised on the basis of whether they carry out their activities *internally* or *exist primarily to make external grants* to other organisations or to individuals. Most of the structures and types we have discussed above will be of the former variety, although there will of course be transfers of resources made from national to local level, in the case of voluntary service or federated organisations, and in the other direction in the case of nationally affiliated local fundraising groups (whose national headquarters will often themselves be grant-makers). 'Trust' or 'foundation' is often used as short-hand for a grant-making organisation, and this is indeed often the appropriate legal structure for this type of organisation, although service-providing voluntary organisations often also describe themselves as trusts, even if this is not their technical legal status. These organisations are sometimes further subdivided according to their sources of income. If this is derived primarily from income earned on an endowment or other capital resource, they may be referred to as *endowed (grant-making) trusts*. However, other charitable grant-making bodies also operate whose income is derived primarily from other sources. These include bodies heavily dependent on statutory sources and hence often regarded as quangos, such as the Arts Council, the Regional Arts Boards and the Independent Living Fund, and consortia of voluntary groups, such as Opportunities for Volunteering and UK 2000, to which responsibility for allocating grants has been devolved by central government departments in various spheres of interest. An example of a single organisation acting in this way is the Royal Society (one of the best-known learned societies), which has devolved responsibility for allocating governmental research funds alongside its numerous other activities.

In addition, two further groups of major grant-making bodies can be identified whose income is derived from donative sources: first, *multiple-purpose grant-making fundraising bodies*, or 'federated fundraising bodies' to borrow from American usage, which often work through the media at national and local level. Prominent examples are Telethon, Children in Need and various appeal trusts and funds established by radio stations (Leat 1989; Davis 1993). Second, there are *single-purpose grant-making locally oriented fundraising groups*, which are separate entities existing primarily to provide in kind, time or cash support to particular service providers which may themselves be voluntary or public agencies. This category includes leagues of hospital friends and parent–teacher associations. These can be contrasted with nationally affiliated local fundraising organisations already described by the fact that their causes are specifically local, rather than operating through a national network (although leagues of friends and parent–teacher associations do have confederations representing them at national level).

Values, norms and motivations

Several commentators have gone further in describing the sector by explicitly alluding to what are seen as distinctive motivations, norms or values determining behaviour. In the American and other international literature on the sector, it has been suggested that it provides a vehicle for the pursuit of status, political power, prestige, control over output quality and religious or ideological goals (James and Rose-Ackerman 1986; James 1987). Jeavons (1992) suggests the sector is distinctive from government and the private (for-profit) sector in its 'value expressive' function, in that it 'has usually come into being and exist[s] primarily to give expression to the social, philosophical, moral, or religious values of their founders and supporters'. At the level of the individual, for paid workers, Mirvis (1992) and Onyx (1993) cite survey evidence that employees in the voluntary sector in the US and Australia are less cynical and gain more satisfaction than their counterparts in the private and government sectors. However, the evidence of a commitment differential between the sectors can be ambiguous and these sorts of comparisons are notoriously difficult to make. On unpaid work, Clary *et al.* (1992) report that volunteering not only performs a 'values function', but also provides social and career opportunities, enhances understanding and self-esteem, and has a protective function (including the relief of guilt and a way of dealing with personal problems).

At a broader level, an attempt has been made to link motives to particular subsets of the sector. In the UK, Beveridge (1948) characterised the sector as being underpinned by two broad impulses, the philanthropic motive and the mutual aid motive, associated with middle-class and working-class voluntary action respectively. David Gerard, a left-wing critic of charity law (see 'Conclusion' below), argued in the early 1980s that 'voluntary action is essentially value based. It consists of giving practical effect to personal and group values, sometimes through the medium of association. . .it is rooted in a general disposition to co-operate' (1983: 34). Following Gouldner, he identifies two relevant norms which provide guidelines for individuals' behaviour: *beneficence* – governing personal responsibilities to those in need; and *reciprocity*, sustaining mutually beneficial exchanges. In addition, Gerard suggests an additional norm is needed to 'account for participation in voluntary work' – *solidarity*.[3] This is contrasted with beneficence which:

> is related to notions of hierarchy and dependence; stresses moral and religious obligations and carries dangers of complacency, stigma, and the freezing of inequalities. Solidarity, on the other hand, involves identifying with and sharing the reality of life of the poor in some demonstrable sense, is related to notions of equality and self-determination and emphasises social and political action. It carries dangers, however, of 'cognitive imperialism' (ie the imposition of the activist's perception and methods of evaluation and action on the target group) and attempts at utopian social engineering.
>
> (Gerard 1983: 36–7)

If organisational norms are thought of as determining actual behaviour within different parts of the sector, then the norm of beneficence can be matched with Beveridge's philanthropic agencies and the norm of reciprocity with the sector's mutual-aid wing. Gerard suggests that we need to consider a third type of agency, 'devoted to social change' as a means of giving 'institutional expression' to the norm of solidarity, and he attempts to categorise a sample of voluntary bodies as either 'old-style charities', emphasising social order and recognised and sustained by charity law, or 'new-style' groups with a social change orientation, which are not so favoured (see also Kendall and Knapp 1995). While he admits that it is difficult to categorise many organisations in this way given their mixed motivational characteristics, and it is necessary to make some rather heroic assumptions, he does posit a number of features associated with each of these ideal types. 'Old-style' organisations involve adherence to moral and spiritual values, conservatism, stability and service to those in need, whereas 'new-style' ones are associated with secular and material values, radicalism, change and identification with those in need. His study found the former to be far more prevalent than the latter.

This approach does present serious methodological problems when motivations and values within organisations inevitably vary considerably, and because the extent and nature of the various stakeholders' power, influence and control within organisations inevitably shift over time. Similar problems are encountered when trying to distinguish between 'self-help' and 'professional' organisations in some of the distinctions that were made earlier. However, as with those typologies, these distinctions are still useful as a descriptive starting point.

Nevertheless, it should always be recognised that voluntary agencies are operating within a mixed and increasingly blurred economy of voluntary, private and government providers, so distinctions of this sort may become increasingly hard to maintain (Taylor *et al.* 1994). The voluntary sector is unlikely to have a monopoly on the values and motivations identified above, or indeed any others. For example, we noted that control over output quality and a sense of commitment have been identified by some as characteristics or motives of individuals in the voluntary sector. Yet these are also key features of many private 'for-profit' sector organisations, particularly in the partnership, small business and family-run end of the sector (Scase and Goffee 1982; Judge and Knapp 1984), and there is also considerable individual mobility between sectors (Young 1989).

Partly prompted by the confusion represented by this mix, Paton (1991) has suggested two dimensions as particularly important in categorising organisations: their size and degree of institutionalisation and bureaucratisation; and their underlying organisational purpose and way in which activities are legitimated.

Paton's schema is shown in Figure 3.1, and, although some voluntary and charitable bodies are excluded or borderline to what is described as the 'social economy' (some examples are given at the foot of the diagram), many are located at the core of the box shown in the centre of the right-hand column as:

> small or medium-sized value-based organisation[s] founded on commitment (arising from devotion, compassion, enthusiasm, solidarity, defiance, etc) and working for a common or public benefit.
>
> (Paton 1991: 7)

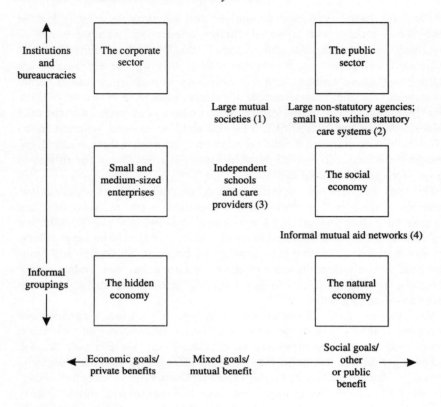

Figure 3.1 Types of organisation in and around the social economy
Source: Paton 1991: 8

This is particularly useful because it reminds us that characteristics can be shared between sectors as much as within them. For example, a body affiliated to a voluntary service organisation providing residential services located towards the south of the schema may have more in common with a private residential home run by a husband and wife as partners than the branch of a professional non-profit organisation, which in turn may operate more like a local authority-run facility, located towards the north.

The distinction made between social and private goals, embracing 'public benefit' and mutual aid, and profit orientation respectively, is of course not clear-cut for the reasons we have discussed. Paton's dimensions clearly overlap with some of the contrasts made above, and we return to the theme that these distinctions may be hard to make in practice in the concluding section.

INDUSTRIES AND FIELDS OF ACTIVITY

The startling diversity of the sector can also usefully be framed by identifying the primary fields of activity in which the sector is engaged. Figure 3.2 shows the International Classification of Non-profit Organisations (ICNPO) which has been specifically developed to capture and categorise key areas of voluntary sector involvement and at the same time be compatible with classification systems used within other sectors or across all sectors (see Salamon and Anheier 1993).

This is complementary to the categorisations discussed in the previous sections: many of the industries identified will have the full range of functions described above being performed by voluntary organisations within them, and these may be cross-cut with some or even all of the structures, patterns of control, values and motivations identified in previous sections. Because it has been developed for purposes of cross-national comparison, the ICNPO inevitably represents a compromise between different national experiences, and cannot be expected to be fully tailored to the individual idiosyncrasies of participating countries. However, it does appear to work reasonably well in the UK, and gives a very helpful way of differentiating between parts of the sector both for the purposes of statistical mapping and for analysis of its historical development, links with government and other policy issues (see Kendall and Knapp 1995). In this section, we consider briefly just five of these key fields of activity: social services, health, international activities, education and research, and environmental organisations.

The profile of the sector is perhaps highest in the public mind in the delivery of *social services (ICNPO group 4)*, where it has also been most thoroughly researched by social policy analysts and historians, for example. The sector is a key player in the provision of services for people with physical and sensory disabilities, children and families, people with learning difficulties and the elderly, as well as providing support for carers, and in the delivery of services specifically targeted on ethnic minorities and women. Social service organisations include large, long-established and highly respected charities, such as Barnardo's in the child-care field, Age Concern for the elderly and the Spastics Society for people with learning difficulties. These have incomes in the millons or tens of millions pounds brackets, and employ several thousand full-time and part-time paid staff alongside volunteers nationally and locally in the provision of both mainstream and pioneering services. Across all client groups and services there are considerable variations in the degree of autonomy exercised by local branches and facilities, ranging from the 'tight' professional non-profit to the 'loose' federated structures we described earlier. Many of these larger agencies or

Figure 3.2 The International Classification of Nonprofit Organisations

Group 1: Culture and Recreation
Organisations and activities in general and specialised fields of culture and recreation.

1 100 Culture
Media and Communications
Visual Arts, Architecture, Ceramic Art
Performing Arts
Historical, Literary and Humanistic Societies
Museums
Zoos and Aquariums

1 200 Recreation
Sports Clubs
Recreation and Social Clubs

1 300 Service Clubs

Group 2: Education and Research
Organisations and activities administering, providing, promoting, conducting, supporting and servicing education and research.

2 100 Primary and Secondary Education
Elementary, Primary and Secondary Education

2 200 Higher Education
Higher Education (university level)

2 300 Other Education
Vocational/Technical Schools
Adult/Continuing Education

2 400 Research
Medical Research
Science and technology
Social Sciences, Policy Studies

Group 3: Health
Organisations that engage in health-related activities, providing health care, both general and specialised services, administration of health care services, and health support services.

3 100 Hospitals and Rehabilitation
Hospitals
Rehabilitation

3 200 Nursing Homes
Nursing Homes

3 300 Mental Health and Crisis Intervention
Psychiatric Hospitals
Mental Health Treatment
Crisis Intervention

3 400 Other Health Services
Public Health and Wellness Education
Health Treatment, Primarily Outpatient
Rehabilitative Medical Services
Emergency Medical Services

Group 4: Social Services
Organisations and institutions providing human and social services to a community or target population.

4 100 Social Services
Child Welfare, Child Services, Day Care
Youth Services and Youth Welfare
Family Services
Services for the Handicapped
Services for the Elderly
Self-Help and other Personal Social Services

4 200 Emergency and Relief
Disaster/Emergency Prevention and Control
Temporary Shelters
Refugee Assistance

Figure 3.2 (continued)

4 300 Income Support and Maintenance
Income Support and Maintenance
Material Assistance

Group 5: Environment
Organisations promoting and providing services in environmental conservation, pollution control and prevention, environmental education and health, and animal protection.

5 100 Environment
Pollution Abatement and Control
Natural Resources
Conservation and Protection
Environmental Beautification and Open Spaces

5 200 Animals
Animal Protection and Welfare
Wildlife Preservation and Protection
Veterinary Services

Group 6: Development and Housing
Organisations promoting programmes and providing services to help improve communities and the economic and social wellbeing of society.

6 100 Economic, Social & Community Development
Community and Neighbourhood Organisations
Economic Development
Social Development

6 200 Housing
Housing Association
Housing Assistance

6 300 Employment and Training
Job Training Programmes
Vocational Counselling and Guidance
Vocational Rehabilitation and Sheltered Workshops

Group 7: Law, Advocacy, and Politics
Organisations and groups that work to protect and promote civil and other rights, or advocate the social and political interests of general or special constituencies, offer legal services and promote public safety.

7 100 Civic and Advocacy Organisation
Advocacy Organisation
Civil Rights Association
Ethnic Association
Civic Associations

7 200 Law and Legal Services
Legal Services
Crime Prevention and Public Safety
Rehabilitation of Offenders
Victim Support
Consumer Protection Associations

7 300 Political Organisations*
Political Parties and Organisations

Group 8: Philanthropic Intermediaries and Voluntarism Promotion
Philanthropic organisations and organisations promoting charity and charitable activities.

8 100 Philanthropic Intermediaries and Voluntarism Promotion
Grantmaking Foundations
Voluntarism Promotion and Support
Fund-Raising Organisations

Figure 3.2 (continued)

Group 9: International Activities
Organisations promoting greater
intercultural understanding
between peoples of different
countries and historical
backgrounds and also those
providing relief during
emergencies and promoting
development and welfare abroad.

   9 100 International Activities
   Exchange/Friendship/Cultural
   Programmes
   Development Assistance
   Associations
   International Disaster and
   Relief Organisations
   International Human Rights &
   Peace Organisations

Group 10: Religion*
Organisations promoting religious
beliefs and administering
religious services and rituals;
includes churches, mosques,
synagogues, temples, shrines,
seminaries, monasteries, and
similar religious institutions, in
addition to related associations
and auxiliaries of such
organisations.

   *10 100 Religious
   Congregations and
   Associations*
   Congregations
   Associations of Congregations

*Group 11: Business, Professional
Associations and Unions*
Organisations promoting, regulating
and safeguarding business,
professional and labour interests.

   *11 100 Business, Professional
   Associations and Unions*
   Business Associations
   Professional Associations
   Labour Unions

*Group 12: (Not Elsewhere
Classified)*

   12 100 NEC

* Included for some purposes only.
Source: Salamon and Anheier 1993: 190–1

federations operate residential care facilities, alongside the delivery of domiciliary, day care, respite and meals services, as well as a wide range of advocacy, self-help and intermediary activities. The social care sector also comprises financially medium-sized and small groups. These may be either entirely self-help groups as described by Hasenfield and Gidron (1993), perhaps with no paid staff or public funding and not involved at all in conventional service delivery. Alternatively, many operate a single or very small number of mainstream facilities often utilising statutory support of various kinds to enable them to employ paid staff.

Many of the voluntary social services bodies – particularly the 'brand name' charities of the type we mentioned above – have intimate links with local and central government arising partly through substantial inputs of finance in the form of grants, service level agreements and contracts. If expenditure by local education authorities on maintained voluntary schools is disregarded (see below), social services departments are the largest single spending department of local government, with their expenditure accounting for around 40 per cent of all local government expenditure on the sector (Taylor *et al.* 1993). Central government also makes significant contributions both directly through grants and contracts and indirectly in the form of user subsidies, most prominently in the late 1980s and early 1990s through income support payments in residential care for the elderly (Forder and Knapp 1993). Links between the voluntary social services sector and local government have also developed through the participation of voluntary bodies' representatives in formal planning procedures and consultation mechanisms, and the involvement of large numbers of local authority officers and members in the internal decision-making structures of many voluntary bodies.

Also included in group 4 for the purposes of classification is the vast *youth development sector*. This includes the uniformed groups, such as the scouts, guides, brownies, sea cadet corps, and lads and girls brigades, denominational groupings, such as the YMCA and Jewish, Methodist, Catholic and Church of England-based bodies, and others, including young farmers' clubs, boys' clubs and Gateway clubs. Membership of the seventy-five national organisations has been estimated at well over 5 million young people in England alone, with over half a million volunteers involved at various levels, but an enormous range of fragmented and entirely local activity without a supporting national infrastructure also exists. Further, the voluntary *pre-school playgroup* movement has expanded rapidly, and now involves around 1.4 million volunteers and nearly 50,000 paid staff in playgroups, parent and toddlers and under-5s groups. This may be given further stimulus if suggestions that pre-school activity be expanded through the adoption of a voucher system are adopted by the government. In addition, *emergency and relief organisations* and *income maintenance* bodies come under this head. The former are characterised by large, national organisations (including the Royal National Lifeboat Institute and the Refugee Council) dominating the sector financially and existing alongside much smaller, local groups. The latter are similarly diverse, ranging from several benevolent societies for particular occupational or professional groups with turnovers of several millions of pounds down to an estimated 19,000 parochial endowed charities providing for the relief of poverty, often by making grants to individuals, with a combined income of up to £79 million (Simpson 1987: Appendix 2).

Medicine and health are perceived by the public to be the most important of charitable fields (Charities Aid Foundation 1992: 48). Yet *Health, ICNPO group 3* is also an area where there would at first appear to be much less room for voluntary endeavour than social services because of the universalist coverage of the National Health Service (NHS). Since most of the pre-World War Two voluntary hospitals were fully integrated into the NHS, the sector's contribution to mainstream acute hospital care has been minor and declining compared to the public and even the private sector – the number of beds fell from 4,775 in eighty-eight charitable hospitals in 1979 to 4,423 in eighty-three hospitals in 1990, compared to 133 private hospitals with 6,483 beds and 1,300 NHS hospitals with 200,000 beds (Kendall *et al.* 1992). However, the sector is still prominent in numerous other health-related fields. Many of the nationally affiliated fundraising groups we identified earlier are *medical research charities* funding research undertaken in the statutory and voluntary sectors (including hospitals and universities), and these account for a high proportion of charity shops, door to door collections and street collections. These fund research alongside a small number of endowed grant-making medical research charities, including the massive Wellcome trust, holding investments, shares and loans worth in excess of £5 billion in 1991 and spending some £92 million on grants in 1991/2 (Henderson Administration Group 1993: 480; Charities Aid Foundation 1993: 90). In that year, medical research charities as a whole were funding medical research valued at around one quarter of a billion pounds (Cabinet Office 1992: 76), exceeding expenditure by the government's Medical Research Council, having first matched this funding source in the mid-1980s (Deans 1989).

The sector also fulfils the various societal functions identified above in health as it does in social care. It is particularly prominent as a supplementer of statutory and, to a lesser extent, private provision in certain *areas of long-term care that merge into social care*, such as nursing homes, convalescence and support for people with mental health problems, HIV, drug and alcohol problems. It receives statutory support in varying combinations from user subsidies (including income support), district health authorities, social services departments and joint funding arrangements between the latter (Lehmann 1991). It also provides key inputs into National Health policy communities and sub-communities (Ham 1992: 131–4). In the area of *hospice-related care for the terminally ill* it has emerged as the primary provider alongside the NHS, supported through a combination of donative income and NHS funding. By 1990, it is estimated, the voluntary hospice sector's total income was in the region of £150 million and it was employing over 7,000 paid staff. The sector is also particularly prominent in *emergency medical services, health promotion and education and alternative or complementary medicine*. For example, in emergency medical services alone there were nearly 6,000 groups, corps and divisions linked to 145 Red Cross, St Andrew's Ambulance and St John's Ambulance in 1990 involving over 100,000 volunteers, funded through a combination of local private donative, private nondonative and local government resources.

International voluntary agencies (ICNPO group 9), often known now as nongovernmental organisations or NGOs, also rank very highly in the public's awareness of the voluntary sector because of some organisations' high-profile involvement in global relief and development efforts (Howard 1993). Oxfam and Save the Children, for example, are household names, although when people are asked to rank charities in terms of the importance of their specific aims, international aid comes a fair way down the list (Charities Aid Foundation 1992: 48). The vast bulk of this activity is performed by over 300 large national organisations: the fragmented character of large amounts of voluntary social services activity is not evident in this field, with most local activity being through branches of national agencies. Unlike their counterparts in the US and other European countries, the aid sector still relies primarily on private donative rather than statutory income (Robinson 1994), although government funding is increasing from a very low base. Total expenditure by the Overseas Development Administration on the sector has increased dramatically from only £13 million in 1982/3 to £110 million in 1991/2 at constant (1989/90) prices (Kendall and 6 1994).

Also, in contrast to some segments of the social services described above (and the housing and education field described below), although 'some are keen to exercise influence upon the executive and legislature, most are watchful of any development that might imply close relationships' (Burnell 1989: 115). NGOs, in addition to being susceptible to the well-rehearsed fears about the adverse effects of government funding,[4] have a further problem: Foreign governments and NGOs have tended to regard government-funded NGOs with particular suspicion as potential instruments for 'external political intervention' (Burnell 1989: 124–6).

The largest 'industry' in terms of total income and paid employment is in fact none of the activities so far described, but *ICNPO group 2, Education and research*. This comprises schools, colleges, universities and polytechnics/new universities and other education and research establishments. Total income across all these establishments, dominated by the universities, polytechnics/new universities and maintained voluntary and independent schools, was in excess of £10 billion in 1990, with well over 300,000 paid employees. Large chunks of this field are often largely overlooked in descriptions of the sector, or two different sets of institutions are explicitly excluded for two very different reasons, in spite of the fact that many are registered, excepted or exempted charities (Kendall and Knapp 1995; Chapter 8 of this volume). First, the universities, as participants in a *national system* of higher education

First, the universities, as participants in a *national system* of higher education in partnership with the state at the *central* level (and with government effectively taking funding responsibility between the mid-1960s and early 1980s), have sometimes been regarded as public bodies despite their legal status and self-governance (Shattock 1989). Similarly, large numbers of schools, although founded as voluntary bodies over the past 400 years, have entered into such close relationships with *local* government – including full funding of their running costs – that, as partners in the 'dual system' providing free at the point of use ('maintained') education, they have been regarded as effectively incorporated into the state sector.[5] This is in spite of the fact that, unlike the vast majority of voluntary hospitals which were fully absorbed into the state in terms of governance in the social legislation of the 1940s (although teaching hospitals initially retained considerable autonomy), the governors of voluntary aided and special agreement schools (dominated by appointees of the founding trust) retained ultimate control of admissions, staffing policy and use of buildings.

Second, many observers from the left and centre of the political spectrum have criticised the charitable status of many independent schools in general and the 'public schools' in particular (see also 'Conclusion' below). This same line of argument could be employed to exclude them from the wider voluntary sector. The 'independent' and 'maintained' schools field is perhaps the one where the role of religion is still most prominent today. The relative size of the denominational shares in both sectors – dominated by Church of England and Catholic and, to a lesser extent, Methodist schools in England – is an interesting reflection of the relative strength of different faiths historically (although the influence of religion still looms large across many other industries, particularly those that we have already discussed).

If these institutions are not included as part of the voluntary sector in this industry (although they *do* need to be included for purposes of consistent cross-national comparison), a much smaller education voluntary sector emerges, but one which is nevertheless significant and one with a very specific 'market niche'. With annual incomes often in excess of £1 million, over 150 nonmaintained, grant-aided and independent voluntary special schools cater for nearly 10,000 pupils with statements of often very particular special educational needs, and are funded almost entirely (but not directly controlled) by local education authorities across the UK (Kendall 1993). Within local government, education departments are second only to social services departments in funding the sector (although this ordering would be reversed if maintained voluntary schools were included), and some three-quarters of these funds are fee payments for specific pupils to special schools predominantly in the voluntary sector (some are also run as private commercial bodies). Also located in the voluntary education sector are such diverse organisations as the Workers' Educational Association, Women's Institutes, cultural education groups for ethnic and other minorities, and learned societies, independent research institutes, associations, many of which receive significant amounts of funding from central government departments and the various statutory research councils.

ICNPO group 6, Development and housing is also an industry, part of whose growth has been facilitated by the availability of statutory resources, but in this case from central government chanelled through quangos. In subgroup 6100, some 2,400 *housing associations* were employing well over 45,000 paid staff and involving over 12,000 people on voluntary management committees in England alone in 1990. These voluntary bodies (most of which are not charitable) saw their 'market share' in housing (including owner-occupied properties) increase three-fold to 2.7 per cent of dwellings between 1971 and 1988, representing 8 per cent of the rented sector in that year (with the remainder provided by local authorities and private landlords). By 1990, housing associations across the UK were providing over 670,000 housing units, and by 1991/2 housing quango support across the UK was worth £2.5 billion, compared to £1.2 billion in 1988/9 (at constant 1989/90 prices). This huge investment of public money was in addition to indirect public support via housing benefit payments, which are claimed by some 54 per cent of housing association tenants (NFHA 1991). Housing is usually targeted at special needs tenants, including those with low incomes, disabilities or age-related needs.

The exponential growth of the sector's delivery of government-funded *voluntary training projects* (part of subgroup 6300, Employment and training) had peaked at over three-quarters of a billion pounds in 1987/8 (constant 1989/90 prices), and outweighed *all* local authority support for the sector combined in that and the preceding two years (if spending in the maintained voluntary education sector is not included). However, unlike for housing associations, government support for training projects in the sector has not continued to grow into the 1990s, but had slumped dramatically to £139 million in 1990/1, the latest year for which figures are available.

Although in both of the subgroups described above large resource inputs are derived from government alongside smaller amounts from donations and commercial sources, the remaining subgroup of group 6, Economic, social and community development, exhibits a staggering array of diversity in its funding sources, and in the balance between paid and unpaid activities. The 'loose and baggy monster' is particularly messy and untidy here! The economic development wing of this subgroup ranges from local enterprise agencies and trusts offering advice and support to conventional small businesses, through co-operative development agencies and technical aid centres, to community transport intitiatives and non-profit-distributing businesses trading for the benefit of local geographical or ethnic communities. We saw above that 'community development' is a particularly slippery concept to deal with, and many community-based groups can best be categorised as fulfilling a mutual-aid or community development function within one particular industry. However, large numbers of organisations are fulfilling this function across a range of ICNPO categories, and can best be included here, including over 6,000 *multi-purpose charitable village halls* in English rural areas, as many as 5,000 *voluntary community centres* run by geographically or ethnically based community associations in urban areas, and around sixty *settlements and social action centres*. Many of these are entirely reliant on volunteers, and those that do have paid staff often have a total of only one or two full- or part-time workers. They rely on varying combinations of fees charged to the voluntary organisations that use them, grants, primarily from local authorities including those directed from central government through the Urban Programme (in the case of facilities appropriately located for eligibility), and other private donative and nondonative resources. Other groups which should be mentioned here are the network of race equality councils, multi-purpose neighbourhood councils and committees, and an unknown but certainly vast number of residents' and tenants' associations which do not operate community hall facilities.

Finally, we consider *Group 5, Environmental organisations*, which is defined to include voluntary bodies active in such diverse fields as the conservation and protection of natural resources, those concerned with land space and the use of buildings (including amenity and civic societies), pollution control, and environmental health and education, as well as those promoting animal protection and welfare, and the conservation of wildlife and its habitats. Focusing only on *registered* charities and disregarding the charitable Arts Council and British Council as quangos, the National Trust, with total income of £132 million and net assets worth £355 million in 1992 (Charities Aid Foundation 1993: 7), has consistently been the largest organisation as measured by total income in recent years. Membership of this and other leading national environmental voluntary groups, such as the World Wide Fund for Nature and Friends of the Earth, grew rapidly during the 1980s (Central Statistical Office 1991). However, most voluntary environmental groups are relatively small, with annual incomes of less than £10,000, and do not have any paid staff. Indeed, many have incomes of less than £1,000, lack a formal legal structure and do not have charitable status. The environment category as a whole had an income of just under £680 million in 1990, incurred expenditure of £629 million with some 17,000 paid staff and the involvement of at least 393,000 volunteers. Its key sources of income are membership subscriptions and donations although this is perceived to be inadequate – and only 19 per cent of total income (£120 million) originates from central and local government. The level of grass-roots support for the sector appears to be increasing, while there is an overwhelming view within the sector that the government has not allocated sufficient resources to the implementation of environmental policy. It is regarded as having shown a lack of commitment to the sector by failing to provide adequate funding or to involve the sector sufficiently in policy formation and review (Pinner *et al.* 1993).

This description gives some idea of the range of activities undertaken in just selected parts of the sector. Constraints on length mean that our description of the sector's involvement by 'industry' has been brief and limited to five fields of activity. The four or five industries shown in Figure 3.2 which have not been covered are all substantial in the UK and contain as much variety between and within them as the industries described above. For a complete description of the sector across its full range of activities in terms of its financial and human resources and levels of activity, see Kendall and Knapp (1995).

DEFINING THE VOLUNTARY SECTOR

The first two sections have illustrated that voluntary organisations perform a large number of functions in society, contain a huge variety of organisational forms and are active across a wide range of industries. We have not considered legal structures and the issue of charitable status here, but, as Chapter 8 demonstrates, this adds a further layer of complexity to the institutional landscape. The sector has evolved in response to a variety of needs, buffeted, encouraged and influenced by government action and other exogenous decisions. Confronted with this diversity, it has been common for UK researchers either to concentrate on registered charities (for example, see Posnett 1993) or to build up a definition from component criteria which organisations should satisfy before being labelled as 'voluntary'. For example, Hatch (1980) identified three conditions for an entity to be in the voluntary sector – formal, independent of government and not profit-distributing – and Brenton (1985) included these same three conditions, plus self-governing (private) and public benefit. Johnson's (1981) four factors were independence from government, self-governing (private), not profit-distributing and receiving some of its income from voluntary donations. Knapp *et al.* (1987) and 6 (1991) have suggest longer lists. Thus, there appears to be a consensus that the identification of appropriate criteria is virtually obligatory if progress is to be made towards the description and analysis of a meaningful construct.

Five criteria have recently been identified as relevant for the purposes of cross-national comparison of the sector, overlapping to various degrees with those described above, with two additional criteria applicable to narrow the definition as required. This 'structural/operational definition' appears to perform better than the alternative options – including the legal approach, the economic/financial approach and the functional approach – on the evaluative criteria of economic significance and explanatory power (Salamon and Anheier 1993). In this section, we discuss each of these in turn, identifying their relevance and interpretation in the UK context. The five core criteria are that an organisation should be formal, self-governing, independent of government, not profit-distributing (and primarily non-business) and voluntary.[6]

Formal organisation

All of the entities discussed in this section have formal character as organisations, ruling out of the study the huge set of informal (household, neighbour-support) activities or links which are so important in some fields, particularly community development and social welfare. If it could be reliably measured, we would find that the informal sector was far larger than the three formal sectors combined in these fields. Public policy in the UK has recently paid more attention to this informal sector, for example in the *1990 National Health Service and Community Care Act*. Our research interest here, however, is in formal, structured entities, with a charter, constitution or set of rules (thus including charitable trusts and unincorporated associations), perhaps formally registered with a public body (including the tax authorities) or with a local or national voluntary sector intermediary, and possibly (though not necessarily) incorporated under company law.

Independent of government and self-governing

The second and third requirements of the core definition are that a voluntary organisation should be constitutionally or institutionally independent of government and self-governing, that is with its own internal decision-making structures and not controlled by a private (for-profit) firm or by government. A grey area that emerges here is that organisations which are legally independent of government may nevertheless be subject to a good deal of direct or indirect government control and influence, either in their formation or in their subsequent arrangements for governance and operation. Several charitable bodies exist which have been formed or incorporated by Acts of Parliament, and/or for whom many of the trustees are government appointees, and/or are fully funded by, or heavily reliant on, public money. Some of these agencies are consequently widely seen as government sector public bodies, although their assets are independently owned and legally protected from government. We came across some of these agencies in the first two sections, including several significant quangos and voluntary schools in the 'maintained' sector. While many would regard these as effectively public sector agencies, or self-governing bodies within the public sector, despite their legal statuses, some bodies similarly reliant on statutory funding *are* commonly regarded as voluntary. Included in this category are many intermediary bodies, the Women's Royal Voluntary Service, law centres and citizens' advice bureaux.

More generally and across the sector as a whole Brenton (1985), Wolch (1990) and Beckford (1991) are among the many commentators who have expressed concern over the extent of state control over or 'penetration of' the voluntary sector, and questioned its capacity to operate in a meaningfully independent and autonomous fashion. Wolch characterises the sector as evolving into the 'Shadow State', a 'para-state apparatus. . . .administered outside of traditional democratic politics' (1990: 4), and utilised as a strategic weapon in the struggle between central and local tiers of government. The empirical question is where to draw the line between independence and dependence. Ideally, we might examine the extent to which each borderline organisation controls its own constitution (6 1991) and examine carefully the interactions between the various actors involved in resource allocation decisions. More pragmatically, we can start by assuming that all bodies initially identified as 'voluntary' by our other criteria are independent of government unless otherwise proven. In discussing the scale of the sector, remaining 'borderline' groups of organisations such as those identified above can then be deducted from the total if required.

Not profit-distributing and primarily non-business

The non-distribution constraint, to use Hansmann's (1980) terminology, is fundamental to most but not all definitions of the voluntary or non-profit sector: it bars a voluntary organisation 'from distributing its net earnings, if any, to individuals who exercise control over it, such as members, officers, directors, or trustees' (Hansmann 1980: 838). There can be no shareholders as such: profits can be earned, but must be ploughed back into the organisation for investment purposes, to enable cross-subsidisation or to effect transfers to 'noncontrolling persons' (Hansmann 1987: 27). The trustees of charitable bodies must remain disinterested and, under the legal restriction operating in the UK, this generally means unpaid.[7] The non-distribution constraint rules out most co-operatives (including, for example, workers' co-operatives and agricultural co-operatives). In as much as the 'primarily nonbusiness' dimension of this criterion embraces the general orientation of organisations, it excludes most mutual benefit financial intermediaries, including some which have historically been regarded as part of the sector (such as building societies and some friendly societies), but whose commercial orientation is now so marked that they are virtually indistinguishable to users from private, for-profit bodies (Beveridge 1948; Wolfenden 1978). It also excludes the Automobile Association, the Royal Automobile Club and other smaller mutual non-profit motoring organisations. Borderline cases included in the UK context are the rapidly growing community-based credit union movement, housing co-operatives and community businesses which combine trading activities with social purposes. The non-distribution and primarily non-business criterion does not exclude 'professional non-profits' from the sector although, as we have seen, this may be a useful subcategory *within* it. Nor does it prevent an organisation ploughing profits back into the improvement of conditions of employment, inflated salaries, opulent offices and other generous fringe benefits, but the limited evidence for the UK voluntary sector suggests this is uncommon (see, for example, Reward 1992).

Voluntarism

To be regarded as part of the voluntary sector, the structural operational definition requires that an organisation benefits to a meaningful degree from philanthropy or voluntary citizen involvement. Even if 100 per cent of an organisation's income came from government or from fees paid by clients, there might still be voluntarism in the form of gifts in kind or of time from volunteers, either in the labour force or on the management committee. We have seen above that the latter is mandatory in the case of charitable bodies. Voluntarism is, of course, not the preserve of the voluntary sector, but the voluntary nature of organisations' governance is perhaps the single most important defining characteristic of the sector (Prashar 1991). It is also a key ingredient in nurturing trust and preserving the public's goodwill towards it (Nathan 1990). In the labour force, although volunteering is often thought of as services provided in return for no pay, or expenses only, anyone willingly accepting a wage below the market clearing rate is 'volunteering' strictly speaking.[8]

For the purposes of our definition, it is not necessary to require that voluntarism be motivated solely by the legal interpretation of altruism (see Chesterman 1979: Chapters 14, 17). Enlightened self-interest, reciprocity and solidarity, moral duty and other motivations which underpin both charitable and non-charitable voluntary activity and which we touched on above will do just as well. It need hardly be said that, once again, we have a criterion which can be met (or violated) to varying degrees. Choosing the 'right' degree is not straightforward. Where the voluntarism condition is clearly violated (but other criteria hold) and most of an organisation's income comes from government or private nondonative sources, an organisation is not regarded as part of the sector. For example, we would not consider the newly emerging bodies sometimes known as *not-for-profit agencies* in the UK, which are especially active in the social care area, to be part of the sector. For the present, at least, they appear to satisfy all criteria except voluntarism (and perhaps, by extension, the non-distribution constraint), for members of management boards are paid and/or receive monetary payments linked to the health of the organisation, and they receive few or no other voluntary resources. If significant time or money donations were to be secured by these bodies at some point in the future, however, then they would fall within the core definition of the sector.

CONCLUSION

The preceding sections have sought to capture some of the diversity across the enormous panorama of voluntary sector activity existing in the UK today, in terms of societal functions, structural characteristics, fields of activity and values and motivations. It has been only partial in some regards (particularly concerning fields of activities, values and motivations), but should hopefully give the reader a flavour of the range of organisations and relationships that exist 'out there' in the voluntary sector.

The five criteria referred to in the previous section, taken together, generate a structural operational definition of the voluntary sector as being used for cross-national comparative purposes. Figure 3.3 shows the implications of these for coverage of the sector in the UK, with the additional exclusions of political parties and sacramental religious bodies also shown (see note 6). The area covered by the bold line, relating to registered charities, is contrasted with the shaded area, relating to all bodies covered when our core criteria are applied. With the exception of purely religious trusts, all bodies that are charitable in law are covered by our definition, whether registered, exempted or excepted, or for some other reason unregistered. Other, non-charitable bodies which appear to meet all our criteria to a meaningful degree are also included for our purposes, and some economically significant examples are given at the foot of the figure. Also included in our definition but non-charitable are bodies 'too political' to be regarded as charitable in law; 'exclusive' self-help or mutual-aid groups across the industries which have been denied charitable status; and any voluntary bodies which have either made a conscious decision not to be officially sanctioned as charitable bodies because the advantages (see Chapter 8) are thought to be outweighed by the concomitant constraints, responsibilities and costs, or because they are unaware of their eligibility for charitable status. (Technically, some of the organisations in the last category may legally be charitable without realising it.)

We have seen that the *extent* to which some of our criteria apply is itself a controversial issue. In other words, the boundaries of the sector are and always have been somewhat blurred or fuzzy, although it could be argued that they are becoming *increasingly* unclear as a result of government policies, particularly in the social services and education industries (see Kendall and Knapp 1995). In reality, most of these criteria are characterised by a continuum rather than being simply met or not met in their entirety.

A potential criterion which we have not discussed, but whose controversial interpretation underpins the legal 'definition' of charity (see Chapter 8 in this volume), the approach of some researchers and perhaps the 'popular concept' or 'street definition' of the voluntary sector, is the notion of 'public benefit'. Some commentators see this as the key characteristic of the voluntary sector. For example, Beveridge (1948) talked of 'voluntary action for a public purpose – for social advance', Robin Guthrie, the former Chief Charity Commissioner, has argued that *charity* is 'best defined as an action or gift of benefit to others' (1988: 17), and we noted in the second section that Paton uses the concept in his schema. Moreover, economic theorists have often conceptualised the sector as a complementary mechanism alongside government for the independent production of goods and services which are public, quasi-public or produce external benefits (e.g. Weisbrod 1988). However, the 'public benefit' criterion was not included or discussed in the previous section

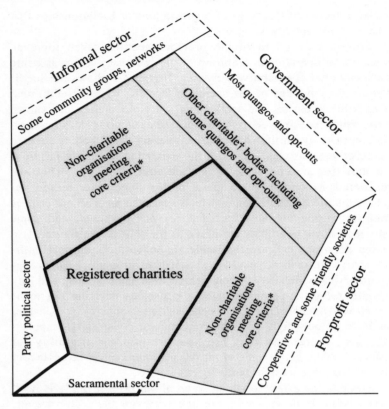

Figure 3.3 UK coverage of structural/operational definition
† Includes exempted and excepted charities
* Includes most housing associations, tenants' and residents' associations; trade unions, and professional, trade and business-support agencies; most recreational organisations; and community business (except Scotland)

since it is arguably even harder to apply in practice than the criteria we did discuss. Even within the legal framework, Lord Simonds in the *Inland Revenue Commissioners v Baddeley Case* (1955) referred to the public benefit purpose as 'the most difficult of the many difficult problems in this branch of the law'. What is more, the legal 'definition' of public benefit in the context of the entire *status quo* has been vehemently criticised by numerous commentators, particularly from both the Marxist and centre left, as defining public benefit inappropriately, in a way often linked to its evolution away from its original 'unifying purpose' of relieving poverty traceable back to the 1601 preamble and before (see Chapter 1). In particular, the charitable status afforded to fee-paying schools, health centres, hospitals and professional associations, variously described as socially exclusive, élitist and inaccessible through prohibitively high fees have been regarded by these observers as conferring 'unfair' tax privileges and ideological support on these establishments. At the same time, the denial of this status to self-help and pressure group activities is interpreted as inequitable and inegalitarian, and a deliberate constraint by 'the establishment' and vested interests on the sector's role as a catalyst for social change (Chesterman 1979; Gladstone 1982; Brenton 1985; Wolch 1990; Beckford 1991).

Thus, the dividing line between primarily member-serving or mutual aid and primarily public benefit or altruistic organisations is an extremely controversial one, and is likely to remain so. We noted earlier that some have regarded organisations in the sector as differentiated from other groups though their stakeholders' high levels of commitment, benevolence, altruism or beneficence and solidarity (concepts linked intimately to the notion of 'public benefit'). Yet involvement in the sector is clearly not the only avenue for the expression of these or other values. Further, this approach may run the danger of overemphasising the weaknesses or failures of other sectors, while not recognising the limitations of voluntary organisations as a group. The latter arise both in terms of the 'voluntary failures' of 'genuine' voluntary organisations – paternalism, amateurism, insufficiency and particularism (Salamon 1987) – and through the possibility of the existence in the sector of opportunistic 'for-profits in disguise' because the non-distribution constraint is imperfectly policed. A more useful comparative approach might involve looking at the *relative* importance of mixtures of values and motivations between and within sectors, while tracking the movements of individuals between them.

NOTES

Much of the work reported in this chapter was made possible by the authors' involvement in the UK leg of the Johns Hopkins Comparative Nonprofit Sector Project. A full account of this study is given in Kendall and Knapp (1995). The financial assistance of the Joseph Rowntree Foundation is gratefully acknowledged.

1 Elsewhere one of us has argued that the cross-classification of the sector by industry and societal function may be a particularly fruitful way of thinking about relations between the sector and government in terms of direct and indirect funding and other resource relationships, regulation and responses to pressure (Kendall and 6 1994).

2 This research found the former outnumbered the latter (and an intermediate 'semi-autonomous' category) in seven European locales in 1990, including Thamesmead in the UK (Chanan 1993). This contrasts with the findings of the Wolfenden Committee in the late 1970s that 'although there are a fair number of purely local organisations, the proportion of local voluntary organisations that are not linked to national organisations in any way is small' (Wolfenden 1978: 38).

3 Interestingly, this is regarded as one of the 'basic principles' underpinning *l'économie sociale* in France (Archambault 1993), a concept which has also been

adopted in Belgium (Defourny 1992), Spain and Directorate Generale XXIII of the European Commission (Kendall and Knapp 1992; Chapter 6 of this volume).

4 These include the loss of autonomy, the undermining of such characteristics as flexibility, cost-effectiveness and the capacity to innovate and encourage participation, which may have prompted government funding in the first place (Knapp *et al.* 1990), and the 'crowding out' of nonstatutory sources of income (Steinberg 1993; Forder and Kendall 1993). See also the discussion of the 'independence from government' criterion in the 'Conclusion'.

5 Recent additional entrants into the sector, or statutory/independent hybrids, include the city technology colleges and schools which opt out of local government control to become grant maintained by the Department for Education, which are both eligible for exempted charitable status. Similarly hybrid, but *local* government-funded 'not for profit' trusts have emerged in social services.

6 Two further optional criteria are being used to parameterise the sector for purposes of the Johns Hopkins Comparative Nonprofit Sector Project (Kendall and Knapp 1995). Party political organisations and purely sacramental activity are excluded for purposes of statistical comparison, although they can be retained in the sector if required for broader purposes (Figure 3.2 shows that they can be allocated to ICNPO subgroup 7300 and ICNPO group 10 respectively). The exclusion of the latter alone probably reduces the total income of the sector by an amount well in excess of £1 billion. The Archbishop of Canterbury, in suggesting to the Charity Directors' Network in 1992 that the Church of England 'is one of the oldest and largest voluntary organisations of all', was certainly accurate in terms of the Church's total income, which stood at some £550 million in 1991 (and with assets worth some £2.2 billion) despite disastrous speculation on the property markets (Central Board of Finance of the Church of England 1992; *The Independent* 23 June 1993).

7 Charitable trustees can be compensated for legitimate expenses incurred while carrying out their duties. In addition, in a small number of cases the document originating or controlling a charity specifically authorises payments over and above legitimate expenses.

8 There is some evidence of this variety of 'worker voluntarism' in the Australian voluntary sector. Onyx (1993) suggests that her sample of workers in the 'community sector' 'to a certain extent seem[ed] to be prepared to forgo higher salary for the sake of doing worthwhile work ("it feels good to work not only for the pay packet"). The desire to work for social change was the biggest single discriminator between community sector and private sector employees' (p. 15).

REFERENCES

Archambault, E. (1993) 'Defining the nonprofit sector: France', Johns Hopkins Comparative Nonprofit Sector Project Working Paper No. 7, Johns Hopkins University Institute of Policy Studies, Baltimore.

Ball, M. (1989) *Multiple Funding in the Voluntary Sector*, London: Voluntary Services Unit, Home Office.

Beckford, J. (1991) 'Great Britain: voluntarism and sectional interests', in R. Wuthnow (ed.) *Between States and Markets: The Voluntary Sector in Comparative Perspective*, New Jersey: Princeton University Press.

Lord Beveridge (1948) *Voluntary Action: A Report on Methods of Social Advance*, London: Allen & Unwin.

Brenton, M. (1985) *The Voluntary Sector in British Social Services*, Harlow: Longman.

Burnell, P. (1989) 'Charity that begins abroad: issues in government funding', in A. Ware (ed.) *Charities and Government*, Manchester: Manchester University Press.

Cabinet Office (1992) *Annual Review of Government Funded Research & Development*, London: Cabinet Office of Public Service and Science Office of Science and Technology, HMSO.

Central Board of Finance of the Church of England (1992) *Still Giving in Faith? A Report on the Church's Finances 1989–1995*, London: General Synod of the Church of England.

Central Statistical Office (1991) *Social Trends*, London: HMSO.

Chanan, G. (1991) *Taken for Granted: Community Activity and the Crisis of the Voluntary Sector*, London: Community Development Foundation Publications.

Chanan, G. (1993) 'Local voluntary sectors: the hidden dynamic', in S. Saxon-Harrold and J. Kendall (eds) *Researching the Voluntary Sector*, Vol. 1, Tonbridge: Charities Aid Foundation, pp. 143–56.

Charities Aid Foundation (1992) *Individual Giving and Volunteering in Britain*, Tonbridge: Charities Aid Foundation.

Charities Aid Foundation (1993) *Charity Trends 1993*, Tonbridge: Charities Aid Foundation.

Chesterman, M. (1979) *Charities, Trusts and Social Welfare*, London: Weidenfeld & Nicolson.

Clary, E., Snyder, M. and Ridge, R. (1992) 'Volunteers' motivations: a functional strategy for the recruitment, placement, and retention of volunteers', *Nonprofit Management & Leadership*, 2 (4): 333–50.

Davis, B. (1993) 'Broadcast appeals', in Charities Aid Foundation *Charity Trends 1993*, Tonbridge: Charities Aid Foundation.

Deans, T. (1989) 'Organising medical research: the role of charities and the state', in A. Ware (ed.) *Charities and Government*, Manchester: Manchester University Press.

Defourny, J. (1992) 'The sector of "social economy" in Belgium', in J. Defourny and J.L. Monzon Campos (eds) *The Third Sector Cooperative, Mutual and Nonprofit Organizations*, Brussels: De Boeck Université.

Forder, J. and Kendall, J. (1993) 'The economics of voluntary and non-profit organisations in the UK: achievements and prospects', paper presented at NCVO symposium, Researching Voluntary and Non-profit Organisations in the UK: The State of the Art, April, South Bank University.

Forder, J. and Knapp, M. (1993) 'Social care markets: the voluntary sector and residential care for elderly people in England', in S. Saxon-Harrold and J. Kendall (eds) *Researching the Voluntary Sector*, Vol. 1, Tonbridge: Charities Aid Foundation.

Gerard, D. (1983) *Charities in Britain: Conservatism or Change?*, London: Bedford Square Press.

Gladstone, F. (1982) *Charity Law and Social Justice*, London: Bedford Square Press.

Gutch, R., Kunz, C. and Spencer, K. (1990) *Partners or Agents?*, London: National Council for Voluntary Organisations.

Guthrie, R. (1988) *Charity and the Nation*, London: Charities Aid Foundation.

Ham, C. (1992) *Health Policy in Britain*, Basingstoke: Macmillan.

Handy, C. (1988) *Understanding Voluntary Organisations*, Harmondsworth: Penguin.

Hansmann, H. (1980) 'The role of nonprofit enterprise', *Yale Law Journal*, 89: 835–901.

Hansmann, H. (1987) 'Economic theories of nonprofit organisation', in W.W. Powell (ed.) *The Nonprofit Sector: A Research Handbook*, New Haven, CT: Yale University Press.

Hasenfield, Y. and Gidron, B. (1993) 'Self-help groups and human service organisations: an interorganisational perspective', *Social Services Review*, June: 217–36.

Hatch, S. (1980) *Outside the State*, London: Croom Helm.

Henderson Administration Group (1993) *The Henderson Top 1000 Charities 1993: A Guide to UK Charities*, London: Hemmington Scott Publishing.

Home Office (1990) *Efficiency Scrutiny of Government Funding of the Voluntary Sector*, London: HMSO.

Howard, R. (1993) 'A call to alms', *The Observer*, Life: 18–19.

James, E. (1987) 'The nonprofit sector in comparative perspective', in W.W. Powell (ed.) *The Nonprofit Sector: A Research Handbook*, New Haven, CT: Yale University Press.

James, E. and Rose-Ackerman, S. (1986) *The Nonprofit Enterprise in Market Economies, Fundamentals of Pure and Applied Economics*, Vol. 9: London: Harwood Academic.

Jeavons, T. (1992) 'When the management is the message: relating values to management practice in nonprofit organisations', *Nonprofit Management & Leadership*, 2 (4): 403–18.

Johnson, N. (1981) *Voluntary Social Services*, Oxford: Martin Robertson.

Judge, K. and Knapp, M. (1984) 'Efficiency in the production of welfare', in R. Klein and M. O'Higgins (eds) *The Future of Welfare*, Oxford: Blackwell.

Kendall, J. (1993) 'Voluntary special schools in the UK', Discussion Paper 1,006, Canterbury: Personal Social Services Research Unit, University of Kent at Canterbury.

Kendall, J. and Knapp, M. (1992) *Charity Statistics in a European Context*, Research and Statistics Unit Occasional Paper No. 2, Tonbridge: Charities Aid Foundation.

Kendall. J. and Knapp, M. (1995) *The UK Voluntary Sector*, Manchester: Manchester University Press, forthcoming.

Kendall, J. and 6, P. (1994) 'Government and the voluntary sector', in S. Saxon-Harrold and J. Kendall (eds) *Researching the Voluntary Sector*, Vol. 2, Tonbridge: Charities Aid Foundation.

Kendall, J., Knapp, M., Paton, R. and Thomas, A. (1992) 'The "social economy" in the UK', in J. Defourny and J.L. Monzon Campos (eds) *The Third Sector Cooperative, Mutual and Nonprofit Organizations*, Brussels: De Boeck Université.

Knapp, M., Robertson, E. and Thomason, C. (1987) 'Public money, voluntary action', Discussion Paper 500, unpublished report to the Home Office, Canterbury: Personal Social Services Research Unit, University of Kent at Canterbury.

Knapp, M., Robertson, E. and Thomason. C. (1990) 'Public money, voluntary action: whose welfare?', in H. Anheier and W. Seibel (eds) *The Third Sector: Comparative Studies of Non-profit Organizations*, Berlin: de Gruyter.

Leat, D. (1989) *Fundraising and Grant Making: A Case Study of ITV Telethon '88*, Tonbridge: Charities Aid Foundation.

Lehmann, M. (1991) 'Health authority support for charities and voluntary organisations', in Charities Aid Foundation *Charity Trends 1991*, Tonbridge: Charities Aid Foundation.

Mirvis, P. (1992) 'The quality of employment in the non-profit sector: an update of employee attitudes in non-profits versus business and government', *Nonprofit Management & Leadership*, 3 (1): 23–42.

Murray, G. (1969) *Voluntary Organisations and Social Welfare*, Glasgow: Oliver & Boyd.

Nathan Committee (1952) *Report to the Committee on Law and Practice Relating to Charitable Trusts*, Cmd 8710, London: HMSO.

Lord Nathan (1990) *Effectiveness and the Voluntary Sector*, London: NCVO.

NCVO (1992) *On Trust: Increasing the Effectiveness of Charity Trustees and Management Committees*, London: National Council for Voluntary Organisations.

NFHA (1991) *Of Little Benefit: Housing Benefit and Housing Association Tenants*, London: National Federation of Housing Associations.

Onyx, J. (1993) 'Career paths in the third sector: implications for human resource management', Queensland University of Technology Working Paper No. 30, Sydney: Queensland University of Technology.

Paton, R. (1990) 'The emerging social economy', *Management Issues*, 3: 2–7.

Paton, R. (1991) 'The social economy: value-based organisations in the wider society', in J. Batsleer, C. Cornforth and R. Paton (eds) *Issues in Voluntary and Nonprofit Management*, Wokingham: Addison-Wesley.

Pinner, J., Fenyo, A., Kendall, J., Knapp, M. and 6, P. (1993) *The Voluntary Sector and the Environment: Scope, Contributions, Issues*, RSU Occasional Paper Number 5, Tonbridge: Charities Aid Foundation.

Posnett, J. (1993) 'The resources of registered charities in England and Wales – 1990/91', in S. Saxon-Harrold and J. Kendall (eds) *Researching the Voluntary Sector*, Vol. 1, Tonbridge: Charities Aid Foundation.

Prashar, U. (1991) 'Introduction', *The Voluntary Agencies Directory*, London: Bedford Square Press.

The Reward Group (1992) *Charities 1991/92*, Stone, Staffordshire: The Reward Group.

Robinson, M. (1994) 'International aid charities in Britain', in S. Saxon-Harrold and J. Kendall (eds) *Researching the Voluntary Sector*, Vol. 2, Tonbridge: Charities Aid Foundation.

Salamon, L. (1987) 'Partners in public service: the scope and theory of government–nonprofit relations', in W.W. Powell (ed.) *The Nonprofit Sector: A Research Handbook*, New Haven, CT: Yale University Press.

Salamon, L. and Anheier, H. (1993) 'A comparative study of the non-profit sector: purposes, methodology, definition and classification', in S. Saxon-Harrold and J. Kendall (eds) *Researching the Voluntary Sector*, Vol. 1, Tonbridge: Charities Aid Foundation.

Scase, R. and Goffee, R. (1982) *The Entrepreneurial Middle Class*, London: Croom Helm.

Shattock, M. (1989) 'The universities as charities: private giving and the role of the state in the advancement of learning', in A. Ware (ed.) *Charities and Government*, Manchester: Manchester University Press.

Simpson, D. (1987) *Information Systems for the Voluntary Sector Project Report 1985 to 1988*, Devizes: Community Council for Wiltshire.

Steinberg, R. (1993) 'Does government spending crowd out donations? Interpreting the evidence', in A. Ben-Ner and B. Gui (eds) *The Nonprofit Sector in the Mixed Economy*, Michigan: University of Michigan Press.

Taylor, M., Kendall, J. and Fenyo, A. (1993) 'The survey of local authority payments to voluntary and charitable organisations', in Charities Aid Foundation, *Charity Trends 1993*, Tonbridge: Charities Aid Foundation.

Taylor, M., Langan, J. and Hoggett, P. (1994) 'Independent organisations in community care', in S. Saxon-Harrold and J. Kendall (eds) *Researching the Voluntary Sector*, Vol. 2, Tonbridge: Charities Aid Foundation.

Weisbrod, B. (1988) *The Nonprofit Economy*, London: Harvard University Press.

Wolch, J. (1990) *The Shadow State: Government and Voluntary Sector in Transition*, New York: The Foundation Center.

Wolfenden Committee (1978) *The Future of Voluntary Organisations: Report of the Wolfenden Committee*, London: Croom Helm.

Young, D. (1989) 'Beyond tax exemption: a focus on organizational performance versus legal status', in V. Hodgkinson, R.W. Lyman, and Associates *The Future of the Nonprofit Sector*, London: Jossey-Bass.

6, P. (1991) *What is a Voluntary Organisation? Defining the Voluntary and Non-profit Sectors*, London: National Council for Voluntary Organisations.

4   Inside the voluntary sector

Rodney Hedley

In the previous chapter Martin Knapp and Jeremy Kendall reviewed a number of conceptual models which seek to define and classify voluntary organisations. In this chapter I shall attempt to tease out how voluntary organisations as a 'sector' function. I shall begin by discussing features of both the local and national voluntary sectors and will draw out some of the apparent tensions in the way voluntary organisations are responsive to their constituencies. I will then look at the role of the so-called intermediary bodies; consider briefly non-departmental public bodies; and then discuss the under-representation of certain sections of the population in voluntary action. Finally I will review a number of theoretical models which help our understanding of the voluntary sector as an industry.

SOME NUMBERS

To start with some numbers. While Knapp and Kendall reveal the problematic nature of classifying voluntary organisations, we do need a ready reckoner of the numbers of voluntary agencies working today in the United Kingdom. Work carried out in 1992 by Perri 6 and Jenny Fieldgrass has probably produced the best summary data we have (6 and Fieldgrass 1992), and below I quote their estimates:

Type of voluntary agency	Estimated number
Charities registered in England and Wales:	166,503
Charities in Scotland:	15,000
Charities in Northern Ireland:	5,000
Charities *exempted* from registration – universities; museums; industrial and provident societies:	11,243
Charities *excepted* from registration – voluntary aided schools; some schools; scout and guide troops:	30,000
Friendly societies:	5,122
Sports clubs:	150,000
Professional associations:	400
Trades unions:	319

These were the types of voluntary organisation from which 6 and Fieldgrass *felt* they could obtain some reliable statistics. They could not begin to count all the 'small' groups operating at local level.

THE LOCAL VOLUNTARY SECTOR

So let us start by trying to get some view of the local voluntary sector. In the post-war period a number of studies have been carried out in this area, notably the Mass Observation Survey work quoted in Beveridge (Beveridge 1948); Madeline Rooff's narrower brief on organisations working with the mentally ill and handicapped in 1955 (Rooff 1955); and Stacey's work on organ-isations working in Banbury in 1959 and 1968 (Stacey 1962, 1973). However, it is fair to say that it was not until the Wolfenden Report of 1977 that a more focused view of voluntary organisations as a 'sector' was established (Wolfenden 1978; see also Hatch 1980).

Research carried out for the Wolfenden Report looked at voluntary activity in a range of local settings. The Senior Research Officer, Stephen Hatch, did not find enormous numbers of voluntary agencies in the areas reviewed, a criticism of his approach being that he perhaps concentrated too much on voluntary organisations which were in the 'orbit' of the councils for voluntary service in each location. He found the local voluntary sector innovatory in its approach. He said:

> The pioneering role remains an important one for the voluntary sector. Specialist agencies, financially dependent upon grants and working with stigmatised and unpopular groups were often to be found in this role. More widely, voluntary organizations are the instruments through which a host of independent initiatives are brought into effect, *only a few of which would from a national perspective be thought of as pioneering*.
>
> (Hatch 1980, my emphasis)

Hatch produced evidence which showed that, while there was a welfare bias, voluntary agencies tended to have a *generalist* approach in the range of activities they offered, and indeed, although he did not use the concepts of *mutual aid* and *philanthropy* as postulated by Beveridge (and dis-cussed at length in Davis Smith's chapter), he talked of their mutual-aid function, noting participation and self-help with the breaking down of 'helper' and 'helped'.

The main worry for Hatch, also proclaimed loudly in the Wolfenden Report, was the lack of planned and co-ordinated support for this growing and innovative sector. (He found that over half the voluntary organisations in the study had been formed since 1960.)

This worry was explored by a number of commentators in the early 1980s: from government-sponsored research (Abrams *et al.* 1980) to those from the radical community work tradition who had witnessed a range of community work interventions withering away at local level because of the lack of structured funding and on-going development of expertise and professionalism (Henderson and Thomas 1981).

Hatch's solution was to see greater co-ordination through the use of what he called intermediary bodies (see below), and more joint planning and funding through the state at either local or national level. However, co-ordination, and a close relationship with the state, was clearly problematic for many voluntary agencies, proud of their independence. Abrams commented at length on the control or 'colonisation' of voluntary action by dominant state *and* large professional voluntary organisations (Abrams *et al.* 1990).

Developments in the 1980s saw dramatic growth in the funding for the local voluntary sector, particularly in inner-city areas, and through the Manpower Services Commission (although the figures we have from Charity Trends show a plateau in funding after 1988); the ending of MSC funding (in the same year) caused severe upheavals (CAF 1991; Addy and Scott 1986). The real change was that many local voluntary sectors found themselves with an infrastructure of paid professionals for the first time.

So what does the local voluntary sector look like in the 1990s?

The most recent – and probably most comprehensive – research we have on the nature of modern voluntary action is from Barry Knight and his research team at CENTRIS.

While Knight's work has been heavily criticised, most notably for his conclusions, it is probably the best summary data we have of the shaping of the local voluntary sector (Mocroft 1993). The statistics which follow are taken from Chapters 6 and 7 of *Voluntary Action* (Knight 1993).

Knight and his research team looked at voluntary activity in fourteen localities in the UK, in a variety of contrasting contexts – inner-city, rural and so on. Knight's team took an approach similar to Hatch's in their definition of voluntary activity – thus, independent schools, trades unions, professional associations, sports clubs and churches were excluded.

In the fourteen districts Knight found 3,691 agencies serving a combined population of 946,000 people. While the overall ratio of organisations to population was one organisation to every 256 people, this varied from one to 165 people in a Scottish town, to one to 361 people in an inner-city area.

The evidence dovetails nicely with previous work by Hatch (Hatch 1980) and Abrams' extensive survey of 1980 (Abrams *et al.* 1981) in showing that there was more voluntary action in areas where there was apparently less overt need – as measured by deprivation factors. So, crudely put, voluntary action is supplied in inverse relation to need.

Knight found that around 43 per cent of local voluntary groups were registered charities. He then looked at whether they were legally incorporated (for a discussion on what incorporation means see Kendall and Knapp in the previous chapter). He called these organisations 'institutions'. He contrasted these with 'loose associations' and those which had characteristics of both, which he called 'hybrids'.

Reviewing 201 local agencies he found:

40 per cent were institutions
37 per cent were associations
23 per cent were hybrids.

He found that institutions were more prevalent in affluent areas; and associations were more prevalent in less affluent areas. This evidence reinforces the middle-class nature of voluntary organisations, most notably shown in data on volunteering (Lynn and Davis Smith 1991) and highlights how working-class and black informal networks can often be ignored or bypassed by the 'organised' voluntary sector (Obaze 1992). Similar findings were made in the 1970s with the Home's Office's Community development experiments, and the Home Office Local Development Fund programme of the early 1980s (Henderson and Taylor 1982; Henderson and Thomas 1981; Jackson 1983). In these 'experiments' resources were targeted into voluntary organisations working in deprived areas (mostly inner-city areas) with the expectation that voluntary sector agencies would generate their own structures: in the outcome they did not, or could survive only with extensive government funding. (It is interesting to note that the new inner-city initiatives concentrate on 'competition' and commercial enterprise, with an emphasis on individual mobility rather than the creation of community networks.)

Knight found that 'social welfare' in its broadest sense was the most frequent activity of local voluntary groups – around a quarter of those surveyed had this aim. The social welfare function was followed by advice and information; education and training; recreation; and campaigning. These findings echo those of Hatch. Knight found it difficult to tie down the nature of local voluntary agencies' work in a simple framework – most agencies *provided a range of services and activities*, the main differences stemming from types of beneficiaries – the elderly, children and so on, although even then it was difficult to be categorical (with groups helping carers for example). It was striking that in eleven of the fourteen areas studied the researchers could identify not one voluntary organisation targeting ethnic minorities.

Knight teased out the representative nature of voluntary organisations by measuring whether they were 'philanthropic' in nature or whether they were more about 'social solidarity'.

Knight found 81 per cent of local voluntary agencies in affluent areas were philanthropic as opposed to 44 per cent of those in poor areas. Knight said:

One interpretation of these statistics would be that in poor areas, voluntary organizations tended to be made up of poor people trying to do something about their poverty; in richer areas, voluntary organizations tended to be more likely about non poor people trying to do something about the poverty of others.

(Knight 1993: 86)

Overall Knight found that 40 per cent of local organisations had paid staff – with inner-city areas making greater use of staff.

An argument put by Hatch (Hatch 1980) was that there should be greater partnership between local voluntary agencies and local authorities. In twelve of the fourteen areas looked at Knight found that there was little co-ordination or joint planning. Knight's findings sum up nicely a whole raft of (rather dreary) research literature showing how poor the joint work between the statutory and voluntary sectors has been – even where there *is a legal requirement for such planning* (Wistow, Hardy and Turrell 1990).

Looking more closely at the work of councils for voluntary service Knight found that there was little confidence expressed in them by local voluntary groups – or by local statutory funders.

To get another flavour of the local voluntary sector we can quote research sponsored by the Department of Employment in 1990. The Department was conscious of the problems it had encountered with the voluntary sector in implementing the range of Manpower Services Commission employment measures over the 1980s (see Deakin in Chapter 2), and was keen to gauge how there could be 'better consultation' with 'local voluntary sectors' and the newly created Training and Enterprise Councils (TECs). This is how the researchers summed up the local voluntary sectors (Hedley, Keeley-Huggett and Rochester 1992):

Local voluntary groups felt a strong attachment to their local areas of operation. Many of these were very small indeed: data from Lambeth showed that 70 per cent of groups operated within their local ward area while we were told that community groups could be defined as narrowly as one housing estate. We found local rivalries and suspicions – in Wearside the groups in the new town area of Washington believed Sunderland 'creamed off' resources. Sunderland groups felt the opposite! Similarly groups in Lewisham thought that a disproportionate amount of funding was concentrated on Deptford. During the mapping exercise in Oldham, we noticed strong local identities. In sorting the type of beneficiary organizations which served a particular local area or neighbourhood topped the list of beneficiary types. In Trafford, groups commented they lost volunteers to Manchester City, because voluntary groups tended to be based there. Groups in Trafford felt they were tainted by Trafford middle class image, whereas, in fact there was much urban deprivation. Groups commented on the way that local and central government initiatives defined areas, one respondent, in Moss Side, Manchester said: 'For many initiatives we're lumped in with Hume, but for City Challenge we weren't I don't suppose anyone asked the people . . .'. The ethnic minority population was significant in three of the TEC areas and was concentrated in particular neighbourhoods. The groups tended to be under-resourced and not linked in with local umbrella bodies.

THE NATIONAL VOLUNTARY SECTOR

As a ready reckoner on the health of national voluntary agencies we can take the NCVO *Voluntary Agencies Directory* – which has around 2,500 entries, mostly for England (NCVO 1993). The smallness of this number can be contrasted to the figures with which we opened the chapter – notably the figure of 166,000 charities.

A major methodological failure of the Wolfenden Report was the lack of a sophisticated (or perhaps sensitive) approach to the nature of national voluntary agencies. Hatch defined national voluntary agencies as either *independent intermediary bodies* or *generalist independent national intermediary bodies*.

The invention (or adoption) of the word intermediary was perhaps an uncritical acceptance of the so-called virtues of those national bodies which gave evidence and which clearly emphasised their role in acting on behalf of their members in respect of the 'powers that be' – the government. Hatch's research appears to have considered their *expressed* function, not their real function. The Wolfenden Committee also made, as Deakin explores in his chapter, what appear in hindsight to have been naive assumptions about the future role of the welfare state.

Questions about the role of national voluntary agencies came to the fore in the 1980s. Gladstone's work raised the whole rationale of voluntary action in the welfare state, and Gerrard's thorough, if difficult to read, research showed up tensions in the way voluntary agencies were organised, emphasising the conflicting ideologies from professionals and constituents (Gladstone 1980; Gerrard 1983). Meantime Hatch, with Roger Hadley, produced, in effect, a manifesto for local voluntary action – the virtues of 'bottom–up' against the vices of hierarchy and 'top–down' rampant in the welfare state bureaucracies whether statutory *or* voluntary (Hadley and Hatch 1982). As a contrast, bland acceptance of the harmonious nature of the voluntary sector was shown in the work of the American academic Ralph Kramer who, in reviewing the work of leading social welfare charities in the UK, hardly considered the role of local voluntary action or the relationship of national bodies to their affiliates, members or branches (Kramer 1990).

We have had to wait until 1993 for a comprehensive profile of the national voluntary sector, considered again by Knight in *Voluntary Action*. Knight and his colleagues surveyed 1,173 national voluntary agencies across the UK.

Knight found that 24 per cent of national voluntary organisations had been formed in the period 1601–1944; 24 per cent had been formed in the period 1949–69; 24 per cent in the period 1970 to 1979; and 23 per cent in the period 1980 to 1992. Thus, half the agencies had been formed in the last twenty years. (These results fit with those of other surveys such as Hedley 1993.)

While a quarter of the national agencies surveyed served all the countries of the UK, 29 per cent served only one UK country.

The most typical annual income of a national voluntary agency – about a third of the agencies – was between £100,000 and £250,000 but the income ranged from six agencies with income of less than £1,000 to thirty-seven having an income of over £10 million.

Knight found that *the longest established agencies were the most successful in raising income* – organisations dealing with equal opportunities and human rights tended to be poorer; agencies in Northern Ireland and Wales tended to be poorer than those in England.

Half the national voluntary agencies were based in London, Knight thus confirming a criticism long levelled by radical commentators such as Bob Holman who has seen the dominance of the capital as a great disservice to representative and responsive community and voluntary action (Holman 1991).

While just under 10 per cent of organisations had no staff members, around half had up to twenty members of staff.

Knight looked at how the national agencies were organised. He differentiated between agencies which were 'flat' and 'associative' in how they were organised, those that were 'hierarchical' and 'bureaucratic' and those that were a cross between the two – hybrids.

Around 37 per cent were found to be associative; 24 per cent were hybrid and, of the rest, 40 per cent were bureaucratic. These tended to be the richer organisations.

Just over half, 52 per cent, were, surprisingly, unincorporated. Just over half, 54 per cent, had branches, implying *direct control over the local organisations*. Three-quarters of the agencies, 76 per cent, used volunteers.

As with local voluntary agencies Knight contrasted 'philanthropic' orientated agencies with 'social solidarity' agencies. Service philanthropy tended to be performed by richer organisations with bureaucratic managements and with, relatively, low membership figures. Social solidarity agencies were poorer in income, had associative managements and higher levels of membership. He noted that independent *generalist* intermediary bodies – and actually only a handful of such agencies were identified – tended to be richer, with institutional management and average memberships.

We can add to Knight's review some recent work by Ralph Kramer who studied twenty national social welfare organisations in 1989 (Kramer 1990). Interesting here are some trend figures. He found that, over the period 1976 to 1987, staff rose from 6,727 in 1976 to 10,245 in 1988, a 61 per cent increase – reflecting the growth in the sector as a response to state retrenchment. Kramer noted that the dominant governance style was still through self-perpetuating committees – and he comments on problems that governing boards had with changing senior staff. He noticed that there was some attempt by these major bodies to draw in 'consumer' and 'user' views, perhaps reflecting demands from their constituencies – as Kramer does not tell us we do not know. A somewhat disconcerting finding of his was that women, as members of governing bodies, actually declined in number over the period from around a third of board members to 20 per cent.

A CLOSER LOOK AT THE NOTION OF INTERMEDIARY BODIES

We now return to the notion of intermediary bodies. Hatch, the lead researcher on Wolfenden, suggested that intermediary bodies exhibited the following characteristics – they were organisations which:

- were likely to support organisations (rather than a client group or people directly – however, some bodies might pilot projects or have direct control over fieldwork;
- were likely to have a co-ordinating function or indirect control of the activities of their members;
- were likely to have a resource function, administering funds or other resources such as professional worker support;
- were likely to have a research, policy and development function;
- were likely to have a regulatory function, promoting good practice either by encouragement or by sanction – ineligibility for membership;
- were likely to be involved in the professionalism and career development of their members' staff and volunteers.

Hatch contrasted *independent intermediary bodies* with *generalist independent national intermediary bodies*.

An example of an independent intermediary body would be Crossroads Care, the Association of Crossroads Care Attendant Schemes, a charity which in 1991 was an umbrella body for 215 independently registered Crossroads charities working on a local basis. Crossroads schemes in membership of the national association subscribe to model rules as laid down by the national body and have the *opportunity* to take support and guidance from – but are not controlled by – Crossroad's national and regional staff (Hedley and Rochester 1991). Age Concern England follows a similar model. Age Concern groups in membership are encouraged to abide by national guidelines, but local independent Age Concern groups are likely to tell you how independent they are!

The best example of a generalist independent national intermediary body is the National Council for Voluntary Organisations (NCVO). As it says in its promotional literature:

Established in 1919 as the representative body for the voluntary sector in England, NCVO now gives voice to some 600 national organizations – from large household name charities to small self help groups.

(NCVO 1992)

Hatch used the word *independent* to contrast organisations such as Crossroads and NCVO with those which were, in effect, organs of government – once known as QUANGOs, now known as Non-Departmental Public Bodies. (For a tirade against these bodies see the essay by Theresa Gorman and her colleagues (Gorman *et al.* 1986)). These bodies, while they may often have charitable status, are agents of government, with their governing committees dependent on government nomination. While in the technical legal sense they may appear to have a good deal of freedom, the (almost) yearly ritual of conflict the Arts Council goes through perhaps highlights the problems engendered by the guiding hand of the state (*Guardian* 1993).

Hatch was a keen advocate of *generalist* intermediary bodies. Here is what Wolfenden concluded:

> We are convinced there is a strong case for the generalist independent intermediary bodies in each of the four parts of the UK and that their role in the future is likely to be more important than ever. If they are to concentrate on the type of function we have suggested it follows that a substantial amount of their income must be from government. It is not a high price to pay for the services they engender.
>
> (Wolfenden 1978)

Such was the case in 1978/9 that the National Council for Social Service (as the National Council for Voluntary Organisations used to be called) found itself in political hot water with its membership after making an aborted bid to control and channel central government funding to local intermediary bodies. As a result, two of its major constituents, the Councils for Voluntary Service National Association and the Association of Rural Community Councils, were given the impetus to break free from NCVO and become independent organisations in their own right (for an amusing article on this see Turner (1978)).

Knight's review of national intermediary bodies (generalist or not) and of *generalist* intermediary bodies at local level was critical. He felt that they were unresponsive to the real needs of their constituents. At local level we can add the findings of the previously cited TEC study:

> In all the areas under review, save Lambeth, there were councils for voluntary service (CVS). While agreeing that CVSs were important for information, voluntary organizations were adamant in saying that these were not *reflective* of the voluntary sector in terms of membership, or *representative* in the sense of having a mandate to speak on behalf of voluntary groups in matters of policy. CVSs were seen as one channel of communication – however groups realised that the 'powers that be' saw these agencies as the official channel of communication and policy. Voluntary agencies tended to give priority to their 'own' networks. Hence in Wearside advice centres' staff met regularly; and women's groups regularly liaised. Respondents commented that funders felt that the lack of a common voice was perceived as a weakness of the sector – whereas its diversity was its strength.
>
> (Hedley, Keeley-Huggett and Rochester 1992)

We can add a historical dimension with similar debates over how far the CVSs, and guild movement, from the 1900s to the Second World War saw themselves as direct service providers or co-ordinators of service. Similar debates were raised by Lansley in the 1970s, with feasibility studies on the role of local voluntary sectors in the light of local government reorganisation (Lansley 1976); and Leat and her colleagues in the 1980s who highlighted how major local voluntary agencies could – effectively – cream off resources (Leat, Tester and Unell 1986).

Knight also attacked in particular the paid professionals of national agencies who, he found, were more concerned with internal politics, their own salary scales and status. He felt that they were not interested in change and innovation – the hallmarks of real voluntary action. Knight echoes views from the community work and self-help movement (Henderson and Thomas 1982; Wann 1992) and from academic commentators such as Maria Brenton who, when examining the supposed innovative nature of voluntary agencies, drew attention to evidence that innovation came with the creation of new voluntary bodies rather than from initiatives from those already well established (Brenton 1985). However, it still has to be accepted that, while intermediary bodies cream off resources, leaving them in a dominant position, they do have to rely on the active support of their members: *there is a demand for them, and many are heavily reliant on fee income from their members* (CAF 1991; Kramer 1990).

IN DEFENCE OF INTERMEDIARY BODIES

So what do voluntary agencies receive from intermediary bodies? An interesting study was carried out by NCVO in 1992 on the advice needs of national and local voluntary agencies – *Voluntary Organizations, Their Size and Advice Needs* (NCVO 1992). In a market research exercise by Social and Community Planning 1,115 voluntary agencies were interviewed. Four-fifths (82 per cent) were national. Asked in 1992 what advice they used to carry out their work the following table was obtained:

% taking advice in last 12 months on the following issues	All 1,115	NCVO 416	Non-NCVO 498	Local 201
Fundraising	72	83	59	81
New technology	72	83	61	74
Legal	70	81	60	74
Communications/marketing	70	73	60	71
Financial management	66	76	56	70
Personnel	62	78	44	76
General	60	71	46	73
Training	62	62	37	70
Office management	50	59	38	60
Organisation management	27	33	17	36
Lobbying	24	29	18	26
Partnership	15	16	8	32

Source: NCVO (1992: 47)

Noteworthy from the table is the similar pattern of need for both local and national voluntary agencies. For what we might call direct work – lobbying and organisational management – clearly national and voluntary groups felt better advised elsewhere. A similar exercise by the Volunteer Centre UK (*Volunteers Magazine* 1993) showed that the majority of organisations were adequately informed about 'bread and butter issues' in volunteering but felt least informed about technical issues such as contracts, National Vocational Qualification (NVQ) and charity law. Sixty per cent said they relied on information from local and national voluntary agencies.

Training is another important area. A major function of national voluntary agencies is to ensure that acquired competencies are added to traditional professional standards – in social work and teaching, and latterly in management and accountancy (see Batsleer's chapter). Encouragement of 'good practice standards' is encouraged by the carrot approach – mostly through subsidised training. The move to accreditation in education standards through National Vocational Qualifications has helped to give the voluntary sector a greater voice in determining standards, and this could increase the *power and influence of national bodies over their members*. It is interesting to note that the recent Volunteer Centre UK survey found that 78 per cent of respondents said there should be a professional volunteer organiser qualification (there is not one at present), but felt that if it was established it might create problems if funders demanded the qualification as this would discriminate against groups that organised volunteers with workers (or volunteers) who did not have such qualifications (*Volunteers Magazine* 1993).

The move to the 'contract culture' where the state looks to provide social services with the use of the independent sector (voluntary and statutory agencies) on a contract basis – as opposed to grant aid (see chapters by Deakin and Leat) – may change the role of intermediary bodies in how they promote standards. The evidence we have on the effects of contracts is still sketchy. Currently funders – purchasers – appear to be more concerned about outputs than inputs, and are not very much worried about the way voluntary agencies arrange their affairs. If anything, local intermediary bodies are under threat because their services – information and support – are not tangible things for the state to buy. A fear is that if the UK follows the American model it is likely that established voluntary agencies will become yet more established and will crowd out innovative projects which will simply not be backed. Indeed, while national bodies prefer – and can only encourage – standards, a number are exploring franchise-type arrangements where local groups will have to, in effect, make bids and be regularly inspected in order to carry a *national brand name* (Davis Smith and Hedley 1994).

But intermediary bodies such as CVSs are channels, and are still a focus for voluntary action. Recent work by Rochester (Rochester 1993), in a London borough which did not have a CVS and had a very underdeveloped voluntary sector (in small numbers, if by no other measure), saw the vital importance of creating a CVS to ensure that there was a voice for the sector.

Finally, we should quote a recommendation from a report by the Association of Charitable Foundations, Charities Aid Foundation and Corporate Responsibility Groups, *Resourcing the Voluntary Sector, The Funders Perspective* (Hazell and Whybrew 1993). They recommended:

> The role of national and development agencies which provide support, information and representation for the sector should be recognised in funding decisions.

NON-DEPARTMENTAL BODIES

Another concern for any student of the voluntary sector is the role of what are now called Non-Departmental Bodies. The major government review of funding for the voluntary sector, *Efficiency Scrutiny of Government Funding of the Voluntary Sector* (Home Office 1990), showed the importance of such bodies. Its analysis of spending for 1988/9 is given below:

Government grants made in 1988/9

Method of payment	Number of schemes	Sum spent 000s	% of total sum
Payment through:			
NDPBs	22	1,162,629	55.0
Voluntary organisations	16	11,350	0.5
Local authorities	12	87,412	4.1
Health authorities	2	1,131	0.1
Joint funding/LA/HA and voluntary organisations	1	56	
Total paid through agents	53	1,262,578	59.4
Direct grants	165	862,360	40.6
TOTAL	218	2,142,938	

Source: Home Office (1990: 97)

This table shows that over half of central government funding for the voluntary sector was made through NDPs – 55 per cent; whereas 165 voluntary agencies received grants direct. And sixteen voluntary agencies acted as agents for government funds, taking on some regulatory function in doing so.

In 1988/9 the NDPs quoted included the Rural Development Commission; the Nature Conservancy Council; the Sports Council; the Countryside Commission; the Housing Corporation; and the Commission for Racial Equality. Included as voluntary organisations were: the Local Development Agencies Fund (via NCVO); Opportunities for Volunteering (via a number of national voluntary agencies); UK 2000; and the National Advisory Unit for Community Transport.

The *Scrutiny* report recommended greater co-ordination, more use of contracting, and saw a greater role for broker agencies. With the move to market testing (Kunz *et al.* 1989) in central and local government there is likely to be a more extensive use of NDPs which will have a role in contracting services to voluntary agencies.

THE VOLUNTARY SECTOR – REPRESENTATIVE OF THE POPULATION?

From the local studies quoted we know that voluntary action does appear to be provided inversely to need. A battery of sociological information shows the way that the black community has been denied equality of opportunity in its access to education, training, job opportunities and welfare services. Studies have shown similar under-representation of sections of the working class. This being so we might not expect the voluntary sector to be any more 'fair'. Indeed, such evidence as we have shows that until recently voluntary agencies by their very selective nature have ignored black needs (Liverpool University 1990; MacLeod 1988). As the research report *Black People and Volunteering* succinctly put it:

> The black voluntary sector is booming – but this is because black people have had to create their own organisations. . . .White voluntary agencies have not responded to black needs because for the best of reasons black people are seen as marginal because of their small numbers, or for the worst of reasons because there is real prejudice and racism.
>
> (Black Perspectives in Volunteering Group 1988)

Black organisations, while numerous, appear to be outside the 'conventional white' voluntary sector. A number of studies have shown that black groups tend not to attract the funding resources that white groups obtain. Similar patterns have been shown for working-class organisations in urban areas, as Abrams' study of mining communities showed (Abrams *et al.* 1990). Further, a number of black commentators have shown that, in addition to white agencies attracting the resources, there is a tendency for black groups to be 'set up to fail': funders giving targets which cannot be met without resources allocated (Wenham 1993). A further factor is that black groups tend to be generalist – holistic – so that they cannot meet the specific service aims of funders (London Boroughs Grant Committee 1993; ITV Thames Telethon 1993). To quote Hazell and Whybrew again:

> the difficulty of funding projects with multiple benefits but which are seen as the responsibility of a single statutory agency. . .the contract culture tends to squeeze out the small community based groups often placed to service disadvantaged or minority groups.
>
> (Hazell and Whybrew 1993: 6)

What can be said of black groups can be said of other marginalised groups.

The 1980s has seen a drift to 'user participation' in the sector as a recognition of how voluntary agencies drift away from their self-help roots. But it is a long haul. User participation is different from governance – as a recent survey in *Third Sector* magazine showed, black involvement in the governing bodies of national voluntary agencies is barely more than tokenism (*Third Sector* 1993).

Tackling equal opportunities will be a major issue for the sector in the next ten years. Otherwise, as Obaze has speculated, black and marginalised groups will become a rump or an under-class to the mainstream voluntary sector: ignored and under-resourced (Obaze 1993).

UNDERSTANDING THE FUNDAMENTAL TENSION IN THE VOLUNTARY SECTOR

We have sketched out some features of the local and national voluntary sector. Anyone involved in the voluntary sector has to cope with the political tensions that growth will bring in moving organisations away from direct voluntary action (what Knight (1993) calls first force organisation) into more service provision (what Knight calls third force organisation). The state is asking for voluntary agencies to take on an extended role, perhaps pushing them into that 'third' force status.

Knight, already critical of the way larger bureaucratic voluntary bodies work, recommends that the sector should be honest and that groups accepting government money should be clear about what they are:

An organization must be either a first force organization or a third force organization. It cannot be both.

(Knight 1993)

To make the situation more honest Knight proposes that third force voluntary organisations should receive tax advantages only if they perform well in their contractual relations with government. Meantime, first force organisations will have no tax advantage, and should not expect to receive government monies. The point Knight misses, and which is covered in Davis Smith's and Deakin's chapters is that there can be no quick fix. By their very nature voluntary agencies have to live with compromise and work out their relationship with the state and other funders. Their diversity is their strength. And voluntary agencies appear to be well able to combine philanthropy with mutual aid; and can combine service provision with campaigning. Research by Loughborough University on public perception of the work of voluntary organisations and the media coverage shows that the general public do perceive voluntary agencies as agencies that challenge the status quo, and that indeed on most of the occasions when voluntary agencies are quoted in the media it is to raise the political issue of needs (Goulding *et al.* 1993). To enforce a split in the sector would have adverse effects. To take the example of black groups again – all the evidence shows that they need more of an infrastructure. If Knight's recommendations became policy these groups would not have the opportunity to rise to third force status – white agencies would continue to set the black agenda. A situation would be perpetuated which Knight apparently abhors!

What is needed is some understanding of the tendency in voluntary agencies to become more formal and bureaucratic. In the 1920s the political theorist Michaels drew attention to how political parties and trades unions became dominated by 'oligarchies', so much so that he saw the process as inevitable and the phrase the 'Iron Law of Oligarchies' was coined (quoted in James 1987). However it was not until 1955 that the American sociologists Chaplin and Tsouderos saw more subtle processes going on in voluntary organisations (Chaplin and Tsouderos 1956).

In their seminal essay on 'The formalization process in voluntary association', which was based on a study of ninety-one voluntary agencies, they saw:

> A sequential, stage by stage development of voluntary associations over time; an increasing complexity in the social structure, a progressive prescription and standardization of social relationships, and finally, an increasing bureaucratization of organization.

Expressed in plainer English they found that, as membership of voluntary agencies increased, the percentage of active volunteers involved in the running of the organisation decreased. Further, when paid staff were employed, membership did not increase, if anything it levelled off. The number of board meetings and membership meetings became less frequent.

The literature on formalisation is extensive, and coping with the tensions it generates is shown in a number of management approaches which are described in the chapters by Julian Batsleer and Tim Dartington. Management approaches can be described as taking a 'micro' perspective. It is necessary to take a macro perspective and look at the voluntary sector as a whole – as an industry.

Here we can take the lead from other American sociologists, DiMaggio and Powell, both of whom offer an interesting conceptual model of how the voluntary sector evolves and creates its own infrastructure (DiMaggio and Powell 1983).

DiMaggio and Powell were interested in the growth of arts organisations in the USA in the 1960s and 1970s. They were intrigued to see how a new industry came into existence and developed. The evidence they quote is impressive. Reviewing federal support to arts organisations they noted how, following a major funding programme in 1961, arts agencies were developed where none had been before; how existing arts organisations followed the models of the newly created agencies; how they then developed their own state networks of organisation which soon bred their own secretariats; then how they set up their own umbrella bodies, at the same time setting up their own career structures and professional standards. As the *coup de grâce*, they note how they became, in effect, semi-regulatory bodies with funding functions of their own.

In the last ten years we can see the creation of new national voluntary concerns – or industries – the national networks covering victim support schemes; home start; volunteer bureaux; and the recent growth of organisations for AIDS sufferers (Citron 1989; Ridley 1991). DiMaggio and Powell use the term 'isomorphism' to describe the process whereby organisations within the same field took on 'the same shape'. They identified three ingredients of this process:

- *coercive isomorphism*: where agencies are forced to adopt similar structures in order to take advantage of funding programmes, legal protection or financial advantages;
- *mimetic isomorphism*: where organisations entering a field copy or adapt the models existing in order to be accepted;
- *normative isomorphism*: where common standards are established, notably by professionals, on how organisations should operate.

DiMaggio and Powells' framework is plausible. Voluntary agencies in the UK which are charities have to adopt a particular financial and legal regime (even down to accounting practice – see Colin Rochester's chapter). Mimetic and normative isomorphism is shown in what is seen as 'good practice'. While we may accept that organisations within fields of the voluntary sector are broadly similar – it is another thing to say that there is harmony. Within a given field organisations will be competing for resources, and organisations may opt to create their own approach. In recent years there has been major dissent within national networks – councils for voluntary services were divided over their support for the Manpower Services Commission (Sheard 1986). More recently within child welfare, agencies have fallen out of line over their approach to secure units (*Third Sector* 1993). In 1989 three major national mental health charities were publicly arguing over policy approaches – drawing much national media attention (*Community Care* 1989). But this is the main point: the real strength of the voluntary sector is its actual diversity, and its role must be one of dissent.

REFERENCES

Abrams, P., Abrams, S., Humphrey, R. and Snaith, R. (1981) *Action for Care*, Berkhamsted: The Volunteer Centre UK.
Abrams, P., Abrams, S., Humphrey, R. and Snaith, R. (1990) *Neighbourhood Care and Social Policy*, London: HMSO.
Addy, P. and Scott, M. (1986) *Fatal Impacts: MSC and the Voluntary Sector*, Manchester: Manchester University Press.
Beveridge, W. (1948) *Voluntary Action*, London: Allen & Unwin (see Vol. 2 for the Mass Observation Reports).
Black Perspectives in Volunteering Group and ADVANCE (1988) *Black People and Volunteering*, London: ADVANCE.
Brenton, M. (1985) *The Voluntary Sector in British Social Services*, London: Longman.
Chaplin, F.S. and Tsouderos, J.E. (1956) 'The formalization process in voluntary associations', *Social Forces*, 34.

Charities Aid Foundation (1991) *Charity Trends 1991*, Tonbridge: Charities Aid Foundation.
Citron, J. (1989) *The Citizens Advice Bureaux: For the Community by the Community*, London: Pluto Press.
Community Care (1989) see issues over May and June.
Davis Smith, J. and Hedley, R. (1994) *Volunteers and the Contract Culture*, Berkhamsted: The Volunteer Centre UK.
DiMaggio, P. and Powell, W.W. (1983) 'The iron cage revisited: institutional isomorphism and collective rationality', *American Sociological Review*, 48.
Gerrard, D. (1983) *Charities in Britain: Conservatism or Change?* London: Bedford Square Press.
Gladstone, F. (1980) *Voluntary Action in a Changing World*, London: Bedford Square Press.
Gorman, T., Robson, B., Sharper B. and Taylor, C. (1986) *Quangos Just Grow: Political Bodies in Voluntary Clothing*, London: Centre for Policy Studies.
Goulding, P., Fenton, N. and Radley, A. (1993) *Charities, Media and Public Opinion: A Research Report*, Loughborough University.
Guardian (1993), articles over the period 13–20 December.
Hadley, R. and Hatch, S. (1982) *Social Welfare*, London: Allen & Unwin.
Hatch, S. (1980) *Outside the State*, London: Croom Helm.
Hazell, R. and Whybrew, T. (1993) *Resourcing the Voluntary Sector*, Association of Charitable Foundations, Charities Aid Foundation and Corporate Responsibility Group.
Hedley, R. (1993) 'On the creation of charities', unpublished paper.
Hedley, R., and Rochester, C. (1991) *Contracts at the Crossroads*, Crossroads National Association.
Hedley, R., Keeley-Huggett, B. and Rochester, C. (1992) *Making A Connection: TEC's Consultative Arrangements with the Voluntary Sector*, London: Department of Employment.
Henderson, P. and Taylor, P. (1992) *Voluntarism: A Practitioner View*, ACW.
Henderson, P. and Thomas, D. (1982) *Readings in Community Work*, London: Allen & Unwin.
Holman, B. (1991) *Good Old George*, London: Lyon Press.
Home Office (1990) *Efficiency Scrutiny of Government Funding of the Voluntary Sector*, London: HMSO.
ITV Thames Telethon (1993) *Black Perspectives*, London: Thames Telethon/LVSC.
Jackson, H. (1983) *Developing Local Voluntary Action: Four Experimental Small Grants Schemes*, Home Office Research Bulletin, 16.
James, E. (1987) 'The non-profit sector in comparative perspective', in W.W. Powell (ed.) *The Nonprofit Sector: A Research Handbook*, New Haven, CT: Yale University Press.
Knight, B. (1993) *Voluntary Action*, CENTRIS.
Kramer, R. (1990) 'Change and continuity in British voluntary organisations, 1976 to 1988', *Voluntas*, 1(2): 33–60.
Kunz, C. *et al.* (1989) *Bidding for Change?* Birmingham: The Birmingham Settlement.
Lansley, J. (1976) *Voluntary Organisations Facing Change*, Calouste Gulbenkian Foundation and Joseph Rowntree Memorial Trust.
Leat, D., Tester, S. and Unell, J. (1986) *A Price Worth Paying? A Study of the Effects of Government Grant Aid to Voluntary Organisations*, London: Policy Studies Institute.
Liverpool University (1990) *Voluntary Organisations and the Black Community in Liverpool*, Liverpool University Press.
London Boroughs Grant Committee (1993) *Black and Asian Groups, A Sectorial Review*, London: London Boroughs Grant Committee.

Lynn, P. and Davis Smith, J. (1991) *The 1991 National Survey of Voluntary Activity in the UK*, Berkhamsted: The Volunteer Centre UK.

MacLeod, L. (1988) *Irrespective of Race, Colour or Creed? Voluntary Organisations and Ethnic Minority Groups in Scotland*, Scottish Council for Voluntary Organisations.

Mocroft, I. (1993) article in *Third Sector*, November.

National Council for Voluntary Organisations (1992) *Voluntary Organisations – Their Size and Advice Needs, NCVO's Mapping Exercise for England*, London: NCVO.

National Council for Voluntary Organisations (1993) *The Voluntary Agencies Directory*, London: NCVO.

Obaze, D. (1992) 'Black people and volunteering', in R. Hedley and J. Davis Smith (eds) (1992) *Volunteering and Society*, London: Bedford Square Press.

Obaze, D. (1993) 'Racism in the voluntary sector', *Third Sector*, September.

Ridley, A. (1991) *The Eighth Arnold Goodman Charity Lecture*, 8 June.

Rochester, C. (1993) 'The voluntary sector in one London borough: the size and significance of voluntary organisations in Havering', in S. Saxon-Harrold and J. Kendall (eds) *Researching the Voluntary Sector*, Tonbridge: Charities Aid Foundation.

Rooff, M. (1955) *Voluntary Societies and Social Policy*, London: Routledge & Kegan Paul.

Sheard, J. (1986) *The Politics of Volunteering*, London: ADVANCE.

Stacey, M. (1962) *Continuity and Change in an English Town, Banbury*, London: Allen & Unwin.

Stacey, M. (1973) *Continuity and Change in an English Town, Banbury Ten Years On*, London: Allen & Unwin.

Third Sector (1993), issues in August.

Turner, J. (1978) 'Voluntary rations', *New Society*, 8 November.

Volunteers Magazine (1993) 'Preparing for the next five years', November.

Wann, M. (1992) 'Self-help groups: is there room for volunteers?', in R. Hedley and J. Davis Smith (eds) (1992) *Volunteering and Society*, London: Bedford Square Press.

Wenham, M. (1993) *Funded To Fail*, African Caribbean Community Development Unit, LVSC.

Wistow, G., Hardy, B. and Turrell, A. (1990) *Collaboration Under Financial Contraint*, London: Allen & Unwin.

Wolfenden, Lord (1978) *The Future of Voluntary Organisations*, London: Croom Helm.

6, P. and Fieldgrass, J. (1992) *Snapshots of the Voluntary Sector*, London: National Council for Voluntary Organisations.

5   From lady bountiful to active citizen

Volunteering and the voluntary sector

Jos Sheard

> Without volunteers, the Welfare state would have collapsed many years
> ago. There are an estimated six million carers looking after elderly or
> disabled relatives, neighbours and friends. Five years ago, these carers
> were estimated to be saving the health and social services some £25 billion.
> Over and above these six million 'volunteers', seventeen million other
> people are estimated to do some voluntary work.

This is an extract from a *Guardian* editorial published on 5 April 1993, under
the title 'Volunteering to help the carers', and timed to coincide with the full
implementation of the Community Care legislation. The article makes the
point, all too often overlooked by policy-makers and public-sector managers,
that volunteers make a major input to the welfare state; and therefore, at a
time of intense debate about the future of the welfare state, that it is important
to define a clear policy on the role of volunteers, rather than merely allowing
them to be sucked into whatever vacuum is left by the 'rolling back' of state
provision. At the same time, however, by conflating volunteers with informal
carers, the article also illustrates the sort of confused thinking about volunteers which is one of the major obstacles to the development of clear policy.

The *Guardian* returned to this theme the following month (26 May 1993)
with an article linked to UK Volunteers' Week which, under the title 'Props
for the welfare state', invited readers 'to consider the plight of carers forced
to shore up the social services'. The story focused on a young woman caring
for her disabled mother-in-law and elderly mother, as well as two young
children. 'As a carer', we are told, '[she] is one of a growing army of
"informal volunteers". . .[who] are at the sharpest end of Britain's burgeoning voluntary sector.'

Once again, the confusion is all too obvious: 'volunteers' equals 'carers'
equals 'the voluntary sector'. In failing to distinguish properly between these
concepts, the *Guardian* does a grave disservice to all three, as well as
seriously undermining its own analysis. But the aim in quoting these articles
is not to show up the *Guardian* as particularly bad in this respect. Quite the
reverse: the *Guardian* is arguably the best informed of the national dailies on
social policy issues. Yet even here, discussion of volunteering is char-

acterised by a woeful lack of precision in terminology and of clarity in thinking.

Over the last few years, as various commentators have pointed out, the waters have become even more muddied by the arrival on the scene of various 'paid volunteering' schemes, 'volunteer' initiatives in the school and workplace, Community Service Orders in the justice system and moves towards American-style 'workfare' systems for the unemployed (Hedley and Davis Smith 1992). The combined effect of these is to blur still further the boundaries of volunteering. Therefore the first challenge for anyone writing about volunteers and voluntary work is to define what they mean by these terms.

Traditional definitions have focused on the three most commonly perceived elements: the gift of time; the element of free choice; and the lack of payment (Hedley and Davis Smith 1992). These are reflected, for example, in the Volunteer Centre UK's definition of volunteering:

> Work undertaken on behalf of self or others outside the immediate family; not directly in return for wages; undertaken by free choice; not required by the state or its agencies.
>
> (Volunteer Centre 1983)

Similarly, the national surveys of volunteering carried out by Social and Community Planning Research on behalf of the Volunteer Centre UK in 1981 and 1991 spoke of:

> Any activity which involves spending time, unpaid, doing something which aims to benefit someone (individuals or groups), other than or in addition to close relatives, or to benefit the environment.
>
> (Field and Hedges 1984; Lynn and Davis Smith 1991)

Each of these definitions seems to me to have its own strengths and weaknesses. The Volunteer Centre definition refers to 'free choice', which I think is an omission in the SCPR version. On the other hand, I feel uneasy with the Volunteer Centre's equivocal phrase about 'not directly in return for wages', as it appears to open the door to the concept of 'paid volunteering', which in my view is a contradiction in terms.

For my own working definition, I would extract the four elements which in my view are essential to volunteering. Each of these is important, not only for what it says that volunteering *is*, but also for what it says it is *not*. Thus:

Volunteering *is*:	Volunteering *is not*:
• Unpaid (except for out of pocket expenses)	• Paid work (including low- or semi-paid work, e.g. employment training)
• Freely chosen	• Compulsory or coerced (e.g. Community Service Orders)

- Done through the medium of an organisation or agency
- For the benefit of others or the environment as well as oneself

- Informal help between friends, family, neighbours
- Self-help, religious and leisure activities

It should be obvious to readers of this book that, despite statements such as those quoted earlier, volunteers are not synonymous with the voluntary sector. Clearly, a book on the voluntary sector would not be complete without a section on volunteers, since volunteers have played, and continue to play, a key role in the development and activities of most voluntary organisations. Indeed, the modern voluntary sector could be said to owe its existence largely to those archetypal volunteers, the reformers and philanthropists of the nineteenth and early twentieth centuries. However, these days many voluntary organisations employ paid staff, and some have little or no volunteer involvement. This trend has gained pace in recent years, in the context of the 'contract culture', and the increasing professionalism and 'new managerialism' spreading through the voluntary sector.

Conversely, there is widespread volunteer activity within the public sector, and some also in the private sector (currently a growing trend with increasing private sector involvement in residential and community care). Volunteering in the statutory services – the health service, social services, probation and education – grew considerably during the 1970s and 1980s, as many statutory authorities appointed their own volunteer co-ordinators to complement paid service provision. However, current evidence is pointing to the beginning of a decline in volunteer involvement in the public sector, as resource constraints force authorities to concentrate on 'core' services, and legislation pushes them away from direct service provision and into purchasing, commissioning or enabling roles (Presland 1993; CSV 1993). This is a subject I will return to later in the chapter.

Volunteering in the 1990s is facing something of an identity problem. Partly because the concept of volunteering is often so poorly understood or ill-defined, it is at risk of being hijacked by a variety of interest groups seeking to project their own particular agendas on to it. This, however, is nothing new. At least since the 1960s, the development of volunteering in Britain has been strongly influenced by the attitudes of the government of the day, which in turn were conditioned by government perceptions of the prevailing social problems and concerns. In fact, one might almost say that successive governments have seen in volunteering a panacea for whatever society's current ills happen to be.

Thus, in the 1960s, the Establishment, alarmed by the new youth culture, and the various manifestations of the 'generation gap' – Mods and Rockers, hippies, student revolt and so on – turned to voluntary work as a safe and constructive outlet for the otherwise potentially destructive energies of the young. A multitude of 'young volunteer' organisations was created, the best known perhaps being Community Service Volunteers, Task Force and Young Volunteer Force Foundation. The Queen spoke in her 1965 Christmas message of 'youth on the march', and the *Daily Mirror* in 1966 launched a crusade for 'youth in action'. This great surge of activity has been described as a 'Volunteer Boom' (Dartington 1971).

However, as the 1960s' alternative youth culture ran out of steam, some of the unrealistic expectations and inherent contradictions of the 'young volunteer' movement became apparent. On the one hand, there was a growing dissatisfaction stemming from the perception that these young volunteers were simply 'papering over the cracks' of social services, without addressing the root causes of isolation, poverty, deprivation, etc. On the other hand, there was a feeling that recruiting large numbers of inexperienced young people was not a particularly effective way even of papering over the cracks; that, if volunteers are to be successful in relieving social problems, both they and those supporting them require a certain level of skill and competence, as well as energy and enthusiasm.

These perceptions were crystallised in the Aves report on *The Voluntary Worker in the Social Services* (Aves 1969). Following hard on the heels of the Seebohm report, which set the blueprint for the modern social services departments, Aves presented volunteering as a valid and effective means of service delivery within this context, complementary to the work of professional staff, and requiring professional support and management. Aves laid the infrastructural foundations for an effective volunteering movement in this country; her recommendations led to the establishment of the Voluntary Services Unit in the Home Office, the Volunteer Centre UK and a national network of volunteer bureaux, as well as the creation of hundreds of paid volunteer organiser posts in statutory and voluntary organisations throughout Britain.

The 1970s can therefore be characterised as a period of professionalisation, and to some extent bureaucratisation, of the volunteering movement. This was aided by the continuing consensus on welfare, coupled with the ongoing expansion of state provision. However, the assumptions underpinning this were shaken by the beginning of public spending cuts imposed by the IMF in 1976, and the increasing industrial unrest faced by the Labour government from 1977 onwards, culminating in the Winter of Discontent.

These developments threw into sharper relief the underlying tensions between volunteers and paid workers; the situation was exacerbated when David Ennals, then Secretary of State for Social Services in the Labour government, authorised health authorities in 1979 to call for volunteers to maintain essential services during the industrial action. Subsequent research has shown that, in practical terms, the impact of volunteers on the 1979 Health Service strikes was minimal (Davis Smith 1992). In most cases, confrontation was avoided by volunteer organisers, Health Service managers and trade unions agreeing locally to work within the so-called 'Drain

Guidelines'. These guidelines, the product in a sense of the bureaucratisation of volunteering referred to earlier, had been published by the Volunteer Centre UK in 1975. Produced by a working party of statutory sector and voluntary sector representatives and trade unionists, chaired by Geoffrey Drain, General Secretary of NALGO, they offered advice on relationships between volunteers and 'Paid Non-Professional Workers', with particular reference to avoiding the use of volunteers as strike-breakers. However, the publicity given to alleged instances of volunteers being involved in confrontations with strikers, and picket-line violence, certainly helped to polarise the situation, and contributed to a decidedly frosty relationship between the volunteer movement and the trade union movement throughout the early 1980s.

If the Labour government of the late 1970s was seen to be giving reluctant encouragement to volunteering, there was no such reluctance about the pro-volunteer rhetoric of the incoming Conservative government of 1979. Mrs Thatcher was elected on the platform of curbing trade union power and rolling back the frontiers of the state, and she and a number of her senior colleagues left no doubt that they saw volunteers as natural allies in this battle, in a series of speeches both leading up to and after the election (Sheard 1986, 1992). As Mrs Thatcher put it in a speech to the WRVS in 1981:

> The volunteer movement is at the heart of all our social welfare provision . . . . The willingness of men and women to give service is one of freedom's greatest safeguards. It ensures that caring remains free from political control. It leaves men and women independent enough to meet needs as they see them, and not only as the state provides.

This rhetoric was backed up with action a few months after the election when Patrick Jenkin, the Secretary of State for Health and Social Services, issued a health service circular calling on health authorities to formulate plans for the use of volunteers in any future industrial action. This deliberately cut across the consensus-based approach of the Drain Guidelines, and provoked still greater suspicion of volunteers on the part of trade unions.

In the event, subsequent outbreaks of industrial unrest in the public sector throughout the 1980s were few and far between, and instances of volunteers being used as strike-breakers were rare (Davis Smith 1992). This could be taken as evidence of the government's success in its stated aim of curbing the unions. If so, however, this had arguably little to do with volunteers, but a good deal more to do with the huge rise in unemployment which followed the Conservative election victory.

Just as in the 1960s the government had promoted volunteering as a way of protecting society from the threat of disaffected youth; and just as in the late 1970s the government had called on volunteers to protect society from the threat of union power; so, in the 1980s, the government turned to volunteering to protect society from the threats associated with the return of mass unemployment.

In the summer of 1981, a series of riots erupted in inner-city areas of

London, Bristol and Liverpool. Subsequent political and media comment linked these riots with the dramatic increase in unemployment which these areas had experienced over the previous couple of years. Shortly afterwards, as part of a package of measures in response to the riots, the Prime Minister announced two new programmes aimed at encouraging unemployed people to do voluntary work. These became known as 'Opportunities for Volunteering' (administered by the DHSS) and the 'Voluntary Projects Programme' (administered by the Manpower Services Commission).

As a result of these programmes and their successors, many of those in the volunteering movement spent much of the 1980s grappling with the philosophical, political and practical implications of linking volunteering with unemployment. Indeed, for a few years around the middle of the decade, it appeared that large swathes of the voluntary sector had been co-opted as delivery agents for the Manpower Services Commission's ever-changing array of 'Special Employment Measures'. This was hardly surprising, since the ever-tightening public spending regime meant that this was one of the few sources of public funding still available.

However, as the decade wore on, the heat gradually went out of the debate about unemployment and volunteering. This was perhaps partly because, through experience, there grew a greater realism about what could be achieved. A number of studies showed that, although voluntary work can have a very beneficial effect for a small proportion of unemployed people, it is on the whole irrelevant to the majority (Gay and Hatch 1983; Ford 1985; Mocroft and Doyle 1987). But perhaps more importantly, unemployment levels fell around the mid-1980s, and when they started to rise again towards the end of the decade, unemployment was no longer the spectre it had been ten years earlier. We had been here before, and British society had proved that it could live with 3 million unemployed.

So, by the beginning of the 1990s, unemployment had dropped off the agenda, to be replaced by – what? The key social and political factors facing volunteering in the 1990s include the development of community care, a political consensus around the new welfare pluralism, the contract culture and a government committed to 'active citizenship' and the further rolling back of the state. On the face of it these factors, taken together, would appear to offer considerable opportunities for the development and growth of volunteering. However, these opportunities need to be set in the context of increasing competition for resources at both a national and a local level. I shall be looking more closely at the implications of these later in the chapter. First, however, I think it might be helpful to move from the abstract to the concrete for a while, and give some facts and figures on the scale and range of volunteering in Britain today.

The most comprehensive and up to date source of information is the national survey carried out by Social and Community Planning Research for the Volunteer Centre UK in 1991 (Lynn and Davis Smith 1991). Since this survey used the same methodology as the previous SCPR/Volunteer Centre survey undertaken in 1981 (Field and Hedges 1984), it is possible to make comparisons in order to identify changes and trends in volunteering over the intervening decade.

According to the SCPR/Volunteer Centre research, about half of the UK population undertake some voluntary work in any given year. The average time spent volunteering is 2.7 hours per week. On this basis, it can be estimated that volunteers in Britain work a total of some 62 million hours per week, which is equivalent to just over 7 per cent of the total hours spent in paid employment (Hedley and Davis Smith 1992). In aggregate, therefore, the impact of volunteering can be seen as significant in relation to the total economy.

Of the 50 per cent of the population who are involved in voluntary work, about two-thirds volunteer at least once a month and two-fifths are active every week. A quarter of all volunteers (5.5 million people) spend at least four hours per week doing voluntary work.

Comparison of the figures for 1991 with those from 1981 shows that there has been an increase in the proportion of the population taking part in voluntary work (up from 44 to 51 per cent). The percentage of people volunteering on a weekly or monthly basis has also risen, and there has been a slight increase in the average number of hours per week spent volunteering.

Clearly, not all of this voluntary work takes place in what is normally regarded as the voluntary sector. Volunteers are active in the public and private sectors, in trade unions, churches, political parties, sports and leisure associations, and many other settings. Unfortunately, the surveys do not permit us to quantify the level of volunteer involvement on a sector by sector basis.

The typical stereotype of a volunteer is that of a middle-aged, middle-class, white female; but the research does not really bear this out. Overall levels of participation are about the same for both men and women; although there is something of a gender bias in the types of work undertaken, with women tending to be more involved in health and social welfare services, fund-raising, church- and school-related activities, while men tend to gravitate to committee work, sports, hobbies, advice work and transport.

The peak ages for involvement in voluntary work are from the mid-20s to the mid-50s. However, while the proportion active in volunteering declines after the age of 55, older people tend to spend more hours per week in voluntary work than younger people.

There are clear correlations between volunteering and socio-economic grouping. Higher rates of participation are associated with:

- higher income levels;
- being in paid employment;
- higher levels of skills and education;
- owner-occupiers;
- having access to a car and telephone.

The level of volunteering by people from black and ethnic minority communities appears to be similar to that for the general population. However, evidence suggests that black and ethnic minority people are more likely to be involved in informal voluntary activity, and are under-represented in formal 'white' voluntary organisations (Advance 1988; Hedley and Rampersad 1992).

As far as the tasks performed by volunteers are concerned, those most commonly undertaken are raising and handling money, followed by providing direct services, committee work and transport. Other areas include representation, visiting people, advice and information, and secretarial/administrative work. Growth areas since 1981 include representation and transport work, and participation in groups concerned with the environment, sports and exercise, and the elderly. The areas showing the biggest decline are committee work and secretarial/administrative work.

What motivates people to volunteer? There are probably as many answers to this question as there are volunteers, but, putting together the evidence of a number of research studies, we can identify about half a dozen main reasons why people volunteer (Field and Hedges 1984; Hatch 1983; CAF 1990):

- altruism (mentioned by up to 50 per cent of volunteers);
- having a personal interest in an activity (mentioned by between a third and a quarter of volunteers);
- responding to a direct request for help (about 10 per cent);
- religious concerns (about 10 per cent);
- filling in spare time (between 5 and 10 per cent);
- gaining work experience (about 2 per cent according to the surveys, but probably a much larger figure at times of recession and high unemployment).

Perhaps equally relevant to organisations wishing to recruit, and retain, volunteers are the reasons why people do not volunteer and the reasons why people stop volunteering. The survey evidence suggests the following (SCPR 1990):

Reasons for not volunteering:

- too busy/inconvenient;
- might cost money;
- don't want to have to raise/ask people for money;
- don't want to go out at night;
- anxiety about getting over-involved;
- feeling that money raised might not be properly used;
- concern about exploitation of volunteers;
- 'not that sort of person';
- 'nobody ever asked me'.

Reasons for stopping volunteering:

- change in personal circumstances (moved house, job, etc.);
- becoming over-involved;
- disenchantment;
- poor organisation, inadequate support/back-up, etc.

Volunteering clearly taps into a natural urge which people have to help their fellow citizens. At the same time, it enables individuals to place boundaries around their involvement, and thus provides a 'safe' and structured outlet for their altruism and social concern. By volunteering through an organisation, rather than helping on an individual basis, they feel that they will be protected from over-involvement and abuse, will be supported and encouraged in their role, and can reduce or withdraw their commitment if necessary.

Organisations seeking to involve volunteers, therefore, need to take account of these motivations and concerns. They need to maximise those factors which positively motivate people – the feeling of achieving something worthwhile, sense of belonging, etc. – while minimising those factors which, by either their presence or their absence, can put people off (the so-called 'Hygiene Factors') (Herzberg 1966). Thus, a checklist of items to be addressed by any organisation wishing to develop an effective strategy for volunteer recruitment and retention might read as follows:

- selection/screening;
- equal opportunities;
- job descriptions/guidelines;
- training and information;
- regular support and supervision;
- someone to talk to about any problems or queries;
- out of pocket expenses;
- health and safety (including provision for safe transport);
- insurance cover.

Having considered the question of why people volunteer, it seems appropriate to turn to another question which is less frequently addressed, but, I think, equally important: why do organisations involve volunteers? For many organisations, were they to give the matter any thought, the answer would probably be some combination of 'because we've always done it', 'because we can't afford to pay staff' and just 'because they're there'. However, I would argue that there are more positive reasons than this for involving volunteers, and that organisations which adopt a more positive rationale will on the whole be more successful and effective in their work with volunteers.

An example of such a positive rationale can be found in Croydon's 1992 Community Care Plan. This states that:

The involvement of volunteers can:-

- extend the resources available, and thus the level and range of services;
- add an informal and personal touch, making services more 'user friendly';
- provide links with local community resources and networks;
- help in the process of 'normalisation' (as professional services can sometimes stigmatise users);
- improve the cost effectiveness of services by freeing staff to concentrate on professional tasks;
- provide an extra dimension of flexibility in developing innovative services;
- offer wider choice to the service user. (London Borough of Croydon 1992)

Inevitably, there tends to exist a degree of tension between the role of volunteers and that of paid staff, and it is understandable that there is a long-standing suspicion of volunteers on the part of the trade union movement. Some of the history of this relationship was referred to earlier, though the origins go back much further, to the 1926 General Strike and beyond (Davis Smith 1992). The 'Drain Guidelines' on relationships between volunteers and paid staff were also referred to earlier, and these were updated by the Volunteer Centre UK in 1990. These remain the standard guidance on how to avoid confrontation between volunteers and trade unions, and have proved their worth over the years.

However, perhaps the best way of avoiding conflict between volunteers and paid workers is to have a clear and positive set of organisational values about the role of volunteers. Volunteers should not be seen as a substitute for paid staff, but as a complement or a positive alternative. Indeed, one can think of a number of roles which are arguably more appropriately and effectively played by volunteers than by paid staff: befriending and advocacy spring to mind as two obvious examples. It is interesting that the two most significant recent pieces of legislation in the health and social welfare field, the Children Act and the Community Care and National Health Service Act, each put this type of role on a statutory footing, in their respective provisions for 'Lay Visitors' in residential care and 'Independent Visitors' for children.

What of the future for volunteering? As ever, the signs at the moment are contradictory. As the national surveys quoted earlier have shown, by the beginning of the 1990s, more people were spending more time volunteering than ever before. At the same time, however, many organisations were complaining of a shortage of volunteers (Lynn and Davis Smith 1991).

This may be at least partly explained by the fact that, while the number of volunteers has grown, the demand for services has grown even more quickly. This is true particularly in the health and social welfare sector, where demand is increasing rapidly because of the ageing population and the development of community care; whereas much of the recent growth in volunteering has taken place in other fields, such as sports, leisure and environmental work.

On the face of it, the political environment for volunteering has been favourable over the last decade and a half, as the promotion of 'voluntarism' has been a consistent strand in Conservative policy. In the late 1980s and early 1990s, a succession of government ministers, including Douglas Hurd, John MacGregor, John Patten and Margaret Thatcher, made a number of high-profile speeches advocating the value of voluntary work, for which they coined the expression 'active citizenship'. Government policy on this was summarised in a 1992 Home Office paper, *The Individual and the Community: The Role of the Voluntary Sector*, which stated that:

> The Government will. . .aim to increase awareness of the opportunities for volunteering. Its leaflets will stress the benefits of volunteering, and encourage participation. The Government will stress how enjoyable and satisfying volunteering can be in its own right. The Government believes there is much scope to encourage more people of all ages and from all sections of society to volunteer time and skills to benefit the community.
>
> (Home Office 1992)

Shortly before this, the Home Office's *Efficiency Scrutiny of Government Funding of the Voluntary Sector* had recommended that priority be given to funding organisations which 'promote the recruitment and use of volunteers', arguing that volunteering 'is a desirable activity in its own right, and. . .a very cost-effective way of providing desirable services' (Home Office 1990).

John Major himself has thrown his weight behind the 'Active Citizenship' idea, and it can perhaps be seen as complementing the Citizen's Charters which he has made very much a personal crusade. If the various 'Charters' represent the citizen as consumer, and are concerned with rights, then 'Active Citizenship' is about the citizen as participant, and is concerned with responsibilities. In a speech to business organisations involved in charity in October 1993, Mr Major urged a return to:

> instinctive values of neighbourliness, decency and consideration for others . . . .People want a more responsible society – a less selfish society. I want you to come with us as partners as we spread the message of social responsibility and of responsible capitalism.

However, this government support for volunteering has brought with it certain problems. On the one hand, the attempt to co-opt the concept of voluntary work on behalf of Tory ideology is something to which many people, including many of those active in the voluntary sector, take exception. On the other hand, the rhetoric tends to be contradicted by the reality, as successive rounds of public spending cuts reduce still further the resources available to support volunteering at a local level, and the tightening up of benefit rules make it more difficult for some sections of the community to volunteer.

At the local level, too, there is something of a gap between expectation and reality. The introduction of community care implies a new approach to the delivery of health and social care, which is more flexible, more innovative, more local and more responsive to the individual needs of users. At the same time, financial and political constraints on the statutory authorities mean that services are increasingly contracted-out to the private and voluntary sectors. In principle, one would expect both of these factors to lead to an increase in opportunities for volunteer involvement. One might expect social services departments, as the bodies with the lead responsibility for commissioning and providing community care, to be in the forefront of developing these opportunities. But, on the contrary, evidence from surveys of social services departments carried out by both the Volunteer Centre UK and Community Service Volunteers points to a widespread lack of awareness of, and indifference to, the role of volunteers, accompanied by an alarming decline in the resources provided for volunteering at local level (Presland 1993; CSV 1993).

This reflects two different facets of the contract culture. On the one hand, statutory authorities are being forced to reduce their direct service provision and concentrate on the purchasing/enabling role. Volunteer co-ordinator posts are thus lost as departments retrench back to their core services. In London borough social services departments, for example, the number of specialist volunteering posts dropped from forty-seven in 1989 to fifteen in 1993.

At the same time, there is evidence to suggest that the contracting process may be having the effect within the voluntary sector of encouraging voluntary organisations to develop services based on paid staff in preference to involving volunteers. If funding is made available to provide a specified service at a given level of quality to a given number of users, there is clearly an incentive for voluntary sector managers to opt for the relative pre-dictability and control of employing paid staff, as against volunteers. Thus, there is a tendency for volunteer involvement to be squeezed out of voluntary sector as well as statutory sector services. And in this scenario, if the decision is taken to involve volunteers, it is at least as likely to be because they are perceived to be cheaper as because they are seen as offering a qualitatively different service.

However, voluntary work has survived many changes in the social, political and economic environment in the past, and doubtless will continue to do so in the future. It is clearly a positive sign that the number of people volunteering today is, as far as we can tell, greater than ever before. But perhaps the most encouraging factor is that the concept of voluntary work has overwhelming public support, from both volunteers and non-volunteers alike. The Volunteer Centre UK's national survey of 1991 (Lynn and Davis Smith 1991) asked its representative sample whether they agreed or disagreed with four statements about the role of volunteers in society. The results were as follows:

- over 90 per cent agreed that 'a society with voluntary workers is a caring society';

- three out of four people agreed that 'voluntary workers offer something different that could never be provided by the state system';
- only a half felt that 'if the Government fulfilled all its responsibilities there would be no need for voluntary workers';
- less than one in seven agreed that 'on the whole voluntary workers are less efficient than paid workers'.

In other words, in spite of (or perhaps because of) the materialistic age in which we live, there is something which is generally felt to be uniquely valuable about what R.M. Titmuss, in his famous study of volunteer blood donors, called 'the Gift Relationship' (Titmuss 1973). Or, to quote Ivan Illich:

> What people do or make but will not or cannot put up for sale is as immeasurable and invaluable for the economy as the oxygen they breathe.
>
> (Illich 1978)

REFERENCES

Advance (1988) *Black People and Volunteering*, London: Advance.

Aves, G. M. (1969) *The Voluntary Worker in the Social Services*, London: Allen & Unwin.

CAF (1990) *Charity Household Survey*, London: Charities Aid Foundation.

Community Service Volunteers (1993) *Volunteers: A Forgotten Resource?*, London: Community Service Volunteers.

Dartington, T. (1971) *Task Force*, London: Mitchell Beazley.

Davis Smith, J. (1992) 'An uneasy alliance', in R. Hedley and J. Davis Smith (eds) *Volunteering and Society: Principles and Practice*, London: Bedford Square Press.

DHSS (1979) *Health Services Management if Industrial Relations Break Down* HC(79)20, London: HMSO.

Field, J. and Hedges, B. (1984), *A National Survey of Volunteering*, London: Social & Community Planning Research.

Ford, K. (1985) *A Matter of Choice* Project VBx.

Gay, P. and Hatch, S. (1983) *Voluntary Work and Unemployment*, London: Manpower Services Commission.

Hatch, S. (1983) *Volunteers: Patterns, Meanings & Motives*, Berkhamsted: The Volunteer Centre UK.

Hedley, R. and Davis Smith, J. (eds) (1992) *Volunteering and Society: Principles and Practice*, London: Bedford Square Press.

Hedley, R. and Rampersad, G. (1992) *Making it Happen! Involving Black Volunteers*, London: Resource Unit to Promote Black Volunteering; Berkhamsted: The Volunteer Centre UK.

Herzberg, F. (1966) *Work and the Nature of Man*, Manchester: World Publishing.

Home Office (1990) *Profiting from Partnership: Efficiency Scrutiny of Government Funding of the Voluntary Sector*, London: HMSO.

Home Office (1992) *The Individual and the Community: The Role of the Voluntary Sector*, London: HMSO.

Illich, I. (1978) *The Right to Useful Employment – and its Professional Enemies*, London: Marion Boyars.

London Borough of Croydon (1992) *Croydon Community Care Plan 1992/92*, London Borough of Croydon.

Lynn, P. and Davis Smith, J. (1991) *The 1991 National Survey of Voluntary Activity in the UK*, Berkhamsted: The Volunteer Centre UK.

Mocroft, I. and Doyle, M. (1987) *Volunteers at Work*, Berkhamsted: The Volunteer Centre UK.

Presland, T. (1993) *Resourcing of Volunteering by Social Services Departments in England*, Berkhamsted: The Volunteer Centre UK.

SCPR (1990) *On Volunteering: A Qualitative Research Study of Images, Motivations and Experiences*, Berkhamsted: The Volunteer Centre UK.

Sheard, J. (1986) *The Politics of Volunteering*, London: ADVANCE.

Sheard, J. (1992) 'Volunteering and society, 1960–1990', in R. Hedley and J. Davis Smith (eds) *Volunteering and Society: Principles and Practice*, London: Bedford Square Press.

Titmuss, R. M. (1973) *The Gift Relationship*, London: Penguin.

Volunteer Centre UK (1975) (revised 1990) *Guidelines for Relationships between Volunteers and Paid Workers in the Health and Personal Social Services*, Berkhamsted: The Volunteer Centre UK.

Volunteer Centre UK (1983) *Charter for Volunteers: A Proposal*, Berkhamsted: The Volunteer Centre UK.

6 The voluntary and non-profit sectors in continental Europe

Perri 6

INTRODUCTION

This article does not aim to describe in detail the nature of the voluntary sector in other European countries: the literature on this is already too large, even in English, for such a review, and the development of quantitative studies is too rapid at present for any survey to be anything other than out of date by the time it reaches the press. A bibliography is provided at the end of the chapter listing suggested further reading, but is limited to works in English that are reasonably readily available.

This article will not present statistical material on the number of non-profit organisations in continental Europe, their income, expenditure, assets or employment, numbers of members, etc. These kinds of data are collected infrequently, usually on a cross-sectional basis, by different types of agency for different purposes in each country, and they are invariably not collected on a comparable basis. For example, Anheier (1992) presents secondary analysis of data produced by the German Central Statistical Office for the former West German *Länder*. The definitions on which the *Statisches Bundesamt* (SBA) collects data bear little relationship to the ones used to enable, say, Defourny's (1993b) secondary analysis of official Belgian data or Archambault's (1990) re-analysis of the SIRENE files. The result is that any aggregation of such data would be misleading and impossible to interpret at best. At some point during 1994, we can expect the findings of the Johns Hopkins Comparative Nonprofit Sector Project for the year 1990 to be published, and that research is looking at four continental European countries (France, Germany, Italy, Hungary) although a number of scholars in other countries hope to produce data for the same year on a comparable basis (e.g. Switzerland, Sweden). This occasion will be the first time that data have been produced on a comparable basis for continental European countries, using consistent definitions and classifications (see Salamon and Anheier 1992a, 1992b).

In the meantime, therefore, the reader interested in statistical measurements must use existing research with these caveats in mind. The references and the bibliography to this chapter contain a number of works which are marked with an asterisk. This indicates that the work contains some quantitative information about the sector's size in income, expenditure or employment, scope and market share, or other statistical information for one or more European countries.

There is space here to consider only some of the issues which are discussed in other papers in this volume as they arise in continental European countries, concentrating on definitions, identity and recognition; a survey of key areas of styles of state regulation of the sector; and finally a review of some of the prospects for future policy-making at the supra-national level, focusing on the institutions of the European Community. The main purpose of the present article is to introduce the novice reader to the existing literature in English (with occasional references to material in French) and to underline the importance of some of the emerging themes.

WHY DOES EUROPE MATTER?

Most of the papers in this volume are concerned with the voluntary sector in Britain, its definition, size and scope, history, management strategies and future. Someone might ask, therefore, why a reader with that interest should care about the voluntary sector in other European countries. The sceptic will say, 'Surely, this field is a matter for domestic concern. The imperative "export or die!" has no urgency for most British voluntary organisations struggling on volunteer labour and hand-to-mouth donations or local government funding, or battling with peculiarly local problems. At best, looking overseas may be an interesting source of ideas for good practice, or a good way of getting paid to go off on trips, but has no immediate practical relevance. Anyway, if we have to look elsewhere, shouldn't we look at countries like the United States and Canada which have a similar legal structure to the United Kingdom, and talk about things we understand like charity law. This European craze is just the self-indulgence of researchers.'

In my view, these sceptics are quite wrong and hopelessly out of date. The coming of the single market in the western half of Europe and the collapse of communism in the central and eastern regions have transformed the world in which the European voluntary sector operates.[1] The institutions of the European Community have come to play a major role in regulating the industries in which voluntary bodies work (Baine, Benington and Russell 1992): environmental policy, policy on equality between the sexes, policy on the position of migrants, vocational and professional education and training, and a vast range of other areas are the subject of EC directives, regulations and guidance. The Structural Funds of the EC are already major sources of funding for voluntary organisations in a wide range of areas of activity. The lobbying power of the voluntary sector has been built up in Brussels to tackle issues such as recent EC directives on the licensing requirements affecting volunteer drivers, on control of direct mailing as it affects charity fundraising and on the future of zero-rating for VAT provided in countries such as the

UK for some charities. British voluntary organisations are heavily involved in networking with other bodies in other member states, and using such networks for joint lobbying of the institutions of the Community. Already it is difficult to find an area of the sector's activity which is not the subject of some European network (Harvey 1992).

More fundamentally, the prospect is on the horizon that voluntary bodies will in future at least have a real option of working across frontiers, not just as a luxury but as a mainstream of their strategy, and therefore they will encounter voluntary and non-profit bodies from other member states doing the same thing. The Commission has presented an initiative to provide a legal basis for transnational voluntary bodies to operate (Commission of the European Communities 1991). It is quite probable that, sooner or later, European Community competition law will have to be applied to the voluntary sector (6 1992a). The consequences of this for policy on the development and possible convergence of tax treatments will have to be worked out (6 1992b). A recent survey of 533 national voluntary organisations based in England carried out by the National Council for Voluntary Organisations in March 1993 (6 1993a) aimed to find some information about the mission-critical work of English voluntary organisations in other member states of the EC; mission-critical work includes work within the charitable objectives, and is contrasted with, for example, trading in unrelated activity which is undertaken solely to secure profits to cross-subsidise mission-critical work. It elicited responses from 285 organisations; 115 of these organisations were either already actively working across frontiers within the territory of the Community or else had plans to be. Of these 115, 29 had sought a contract from a public authority in another member state; 36 planned to; 39 were providing a service for fees in another member state; 42 planned to; 48 had sought donations from the public or companies in another member state; 76 planned to; 32 had established a branch or a subsidiary organisation in another member state and 16 planned to. The skew towards seeking or planning to seek donations is very marked, and even more so in the subset of organisations which were active in or planned to be active in just one area. This skew is less surprising when it is recalled that the sample was of national bodies only; locally based bodies are both less likely to be interested in working across frontiers and less likely to attract donations to the point at which they become a significant element of total income.

There is already debate about just how much this mission-critical trade by voluntary organisations might grow. Some commentators have argued that, although there probably are limits to growth, there is reason to think that this transnational activity will be at significant levels (6 and Forder 1993). Gradually, internationalisation of the sector will transform strategic planning, conceptions of its identity, culture and perhaps donors' views.

This means that changes at national level in western Europe will influence the voluntary sector far beyond the national borders where they take place. The slow emergence of contracting out by public authorities of the delivery of welfare services to non-profit and voluntary bodies will alter the shape of a market for contracts which may, during the 1990s and the early years of the new century, look increasingly like a European market. National styles of management and objective setting will determine the extent to which non-profit bodies seek to work across frontiers, and, in the process, bring competition to donations and contracts markets that, hitherto, have been relatively quiet. For example, some people think that the large and well-developed Dutch housing association movement might be in a position in the coming few years to expand its operations into other countries (see, e.g. Doling and Symon 1993).

Policy change at the national level may in fact produce some limited convergence in the ways in which states regulate the voluntary sectors. While the sector is unlikely to bring sufficient investment and employment for states to have reasons to bid up the tax incentives for voluntary organisations to locate in their territory, other rationales are possible. One risk of the single market is that fraudulent fundraising could occur across frontiers, and that the least honest fundraisers will gravitate to the least regulated member state in order to protect themselves. This may bring about pressure from the better-regulated member states on the less so to upgrade their laws and to adopt models which converge with those of other states in order to avoid loopholes. At the level of particular industries, policy-makers may try to emulate practices from other member states which are seen as successful; comparative policy studies are becoming steadily more important in practical policy-making, as anyone following the debate about training in the UK will know.

The end of the communist regimes in central and eastern Europe has enabled voluntary activity to mushroom on a scale that no one could have predicted prior to 1988, and many links with the western European sector are already being established. The Charity Know-How Fund has financed a number of links aimed at skill transfer. The involvement of large US-based foundations has facilitated extensive links (Siegal and Yancey 1992; Flaherty 1992), and some of the training initiatives set up by agencies such as the Institute for Policy Studies at the Johns Hopkins University Baltimore have used western European trainers. A number of long-term collaborative ventures have been established, among the best-known being that between the Spastics Society in the UK and the Peto Institute in Budapest. There is already a debate about the impact on the sector both in the west and in some of these countries of future membership of the EC, when they may be exposed to direct competition from western European non-profit agencies in the single market (6 and Kuti 1992).

Convergence between the systems of regulation in the centre and east with those in the west is an explicit objective on both sides. Many policy-makers in these states hope that convergence will both give a signal to the EC that they are serious about seeking membership and also reduce the shock of adjustment to their economies when they are admitted. This rationale is also being applied in the design of non-profit laws (6 and Kuti 1992). From the western side, many lawyers are involved in advising governments on the design of laws governing the legal form of non-profit bodies, and are basing their advice on western systems, not least British and American charity law (Hopkins and Moore 1992; Flaherty 1992).

This article is based upon the presumption that there will be a slow but steady process of 'Europeanisation' of the sector, and that, already, an understanding of voluntary action in the UK which treats it as subject only to domestic forces is misleading and anachronistic.

DEFINITION, IDENTITY, RECOGNITION

Definition

Debating the definition and boundaries of the sector, discussing the relative merits of such terms as 'voluntary', 'charitable', 'third', 'philanthropic', 'non-profit', 'not-for-profit', 'association', 'foundation', and such cognates as 'sans but lucratif', has been the delight and the bane of researchers, lawyers and practitioners in this field for decades – by turns, to the boredom, fury and exhaustion of those who prefer to debate more empirical matters. The fascination with the minutiae of definition and terminology may be easier to recognise across frontiers than the actual organisations which are put under this semantic microscope.

The literature on definitions is, of course, huge. The best-known recently developed definition is that adopted by the Comparative Nonprofit Sector Project, described by Kendall and Knapp in their chapter in this volume, and set out in an international context in Salamon and Anheier (1992a). Salamon and Anheier argue that their definition of a non-profit organisation is relevant in a wide variety of countries. Some scholars would, however, contest the relevance of some its components in some European countries, although it is generally accepted now that their method of definition (which they call 'structural-operational') is probably sensible. One sticking point, for some commentators, is that Salamon and Anheier require non-profit bodies to be voluntary, 'that is, involving some meaningful degree of voluntary participation, either in the actual conduct of the agency's activities or in the management of its affairs'. The problem with limiting the scope of the non-profit sector in this way is that it becomes very difficult to handle non-profit co-operatives. In the UK, their main importance may be in the field of collectively managed rented housing, but in Sweden and Italy their importance in health and welfare services cannot be underestimated (Stryjan 1993; Borzaga 1991). Clearly, a non-profit co-operative may have salaried managers. The question is whether remuneration of the governing body at all is compatible with the non-distribution constraint.

The present author has argued that it can be, and has offered the following general framework for generating definitions of 'voluntary organisation', as a subset of non-profit organisations, according to the purposes for which definitions are required (6 1993b). The method is, like Salamon and Anheier's, 'structural-operational'.

A voluntary organisation is (6, 1993b):

1 an organisation *formally constituted* (whether or not incorporated, registered or regulated) other than by public statute or order of some statutory authority under some public Act of Parliament, but *having some control over its own governing instrument* (eg constitution, or memorandum and articles of association). The criterion is restricted to establishment by public Acts (some care is needed here, because, in England and Wales, a charity or indeed any other private body may be created and incorporated by a private Act of Parliament); and

2 *a non profit organisation*, subject to specific *constraints against unrestricted distribution of net earnings* either to its board members or to the members of the organisation (This would not preclude some restricted remunerations, or grant making to members, since grants are restricted in size by the terms of the grant making scheme. However, it rules out the issue of a dividend on a share or a debenture on a bond); and

3 more than (2), an organisation subject to an *absolute* constraint against any distribution of net earnings either to its board members or to the members of the organisation; and is

4 an organisation which is *not* a political party, university, Training and Enterprise Council, trades union, sports club or society, trade association, professional association, nor the worship activity or dimension of an organisation such as a church.

It is worth asking whether this definition corresponds to anything which might be treated as having any recognisable legal or social identity in a few other European states. To begin from the wrong end, the fourth limb of this definition has very little purchase outside the UK, and was never intended or expected to. The British concept of a voluntary organisation, as a subset of non-profit organisations, changes over time: in the nineteenth century, professional bodies might well have been included and, in the inter-war years, trades unions almost certainly would have been. In France, sports and recreational associations are among the largest category of associations. The legal status of political parties in Germany is not so very different from that of associations. Countries vary enormously in the way in which churches are regarded, and it is not uncommon to find researchers from the same country disagreeing on this question.

The first three limbs of the definition were designed, not for the kinds of organisation theoretic or management purposes which inspired approaches to boundaries such as Paton (1990), but to be sufficiently precise and focused on structural matters to be suitable for analysing laws, and, therefore, a test of the workability of these limbs should focus on law.

Law, structure and status, and the non-distribution constraint

The first limb begins from the concept of being an organisation at all. English law on the sector distinguishes between legal structure and legal status. A wide variety of legal structures are open to non-profit bodies: they may be unincorporated associations, trusts, friendly societies, industrial and provident societies, companies limited by guarantee. The question of status is rather simpler: the purposes of the body are either charitable or they are not; exemption from corporate income tax and eligibility to receive donations where the donors may offset part of the donation against their personal income tax are consequent upon charitable status. Whie being non-profit is necessary for charitable status, it is not sufficient. Moreover, charitable status applies directly to the funds to which the purposes attach, and only secondarily and by implication to the organisation in which the funds and purposes are invested. Not all of the various legal structures which govern the character of the organisation are open only to non-profit bodies; that is, it is not a necessary condition of using the structure.

The distinction between structure and status is found in many other European countries; in French legal *argot*, the legal structure is given by the *régime juridique* ('governing juridical scheme') and the legal status by the *régime fiscal*. In most countries, two legal structures are used: the association and the foundation. The theoretical difference, in most countries, is that an association is supposed to be the legal instrument by which a group of individual people (or legal persons) come together for some purpose, and a foundation is the means by which an asset (sum of money, land, etc.) is dedicated exclusively to some purpose. In practice, of course, both usually require the creation of an organisation, as soon as operations of any size are envisaged, and so many of the same problems and issues are raised in each branch of the *régime juridique*. This legal distinction between association and foundation is found in many civil law countries, and has persisted despite these difficulties; for comprehensive comparative surveys of laws in this field, see Hondius and van der Ploeg (1992) and Hemström (1992).

By contrast with English charity law (Chesterman 1979), the legal status is usually a direct creation of the tax law, rather than being a pre-existing notion onto which tax considerations were bolted rather late in its life.

It is more common for the non-distribution constraint (limbs 2 and 3 above) to be an express requirement of using the legal structure. The *régime juridique* in Belgian law of 27 June 1921 on associations, for example, expressly requires that they be non-profit, and as such, are called '*associations sans but lucratif*' (ASBL: an association, the objective of which is not to make [distribute] profits): the ASBL is one which 'ne se livre pas des opérations industrielles ou commercielles, ou qui ne cherche pas à procurer à ses membres un gain matériel' ('does not undertake commercial or industrial operations, and does not seek to provide its members with any material gain') (Article 1, paragraph 2) (Alfandari and Nardone 1990).[2] The

French law of 1 July 1901 has an essentially equivalent requirement as part of its definition of an association that 'L'association est la convention par laquelle deux ou plusieurs personnes mettent en commun d'une façon permanente leurs connaissance ou leur activité dans un *but autre que partager des bénéfices*.' ('An association is that legal instrument by which two or more people pool, by a permanent instrument, their knowledge or activities for a purpose other than that of dividing the benefits from that knowledge or activity between them') (Article 1, sentence 1) (Alfandari and Nardone 1990). Similar requirements are found for foundations, but, in some cases, the requirement is more explicit in the law on status than on structure. Again French law will serve as an example. The law of 23 July 1987 finally gave some legal definition to foundations and required that they have 'une oeuvre générale' ('a general function') and be 'à but non lucratif' ('a purpose other than making [distributing] profit') (Alfandari and Nardone 1990). However, this law is essentially tax law rather than naturally part of the *régime juridique*, since its basic task is amending Article 238 of the Tax Code; it is generally assumed that it is following implicit law in the *régime juridique*, on which there are some dicta (Baron and Delsol 1992).

In almost every country, the same worries are found in the law about where the boundaries of the non-distribution constraint are to be placed. Rules are found limiting 'economic activity' or devious and disguised ways of syphoning off the surplus of the organisation to members of the board or of the organisation (Alfandari and Nardone 1990; Sousi and Mayaud 1992). Thus the issue of the degree of latitude between limbs 2 and 3 of the definition is a major issue almost everywhere.

Another important difference between English and most continental European law is that it is conventional for the provisions concerning legal structure as either a foundation or an association in continental European countries automatically to grant legal personality to qualifying bodies. That is, the right of the organisation acting in its own name to hold property, open a bank account, to employ staff, to sue and be sued, is usually granted with the legal structure. Under English law, only incorporated bodies have legal personality. Correspondingly, where, in most European countries, obtaining legal personality is a necessary condition of securing tax-exempt status, this is not the case in English charity law.

It is *de rigueur* in discussions such as this one to dwell upon the difference between the English common law system and the variety of continental civil law systems, drawing attention to the importance of codification as the basis for legal authority in civil law. Some scholars have elevated the distinction into one of fundamental importance not just for the legal treatment of the non-profit sector, but for the whole character of its relationship to society. Anheier and Seibel (1990a) make the following large claims:

> Although to some degree dependent on the degree of centralisation, civil
> law countries developed a *state-oriented third sector*. Organisations in the

third sector tend to resemble state agencies more closely than for-profit firms. Public provision is emphasised over voluntarism. In common law countries, the third sector is more *market-oriented*.

This seems to me to be over-stated, for several reasons. First, their description of the sector in civil law countries could stand perfectly well for much of the English sector until very recently. Second, Scotland is in part a civil law country. Third, the importance of contracting with the state has been shown to be significant to the sector in the US. Finally, most of the same issues about how to mark off the sector from for-profit behaviour seem to occur as much in civil law treatments of the sector as in English and US law. Whatever the difficulties that lawyers from different traditions have in talking to one another, it seems to the present author that the practical and theoretical importance of the difference between the charity and civil law traditions has been exaggerated. What the systems have in common is much more remarkable than wherein they differ.

Identities

Moving beyond the narrow legal questions to issues of the sector's identity, however, interesting differences emerge not only with the UK but also within continental Europe.

Since the election of the socialist President Mitterand in 1981, the concept of the *économie sociale* (literally, 'social economy') has been revived in France and, to a lesser degree, in the Benelux countries, to pick out non-profit bodies, co-operatives and mutual organisations (Defourny 1993b). Mutual organisations are found all over Europe in financial services; co-operatives are very important in some countries in agriculture, and of widespread importance in housing and consumer goods retailing. There are official French bodies charged with the responsibility of mediating between the state and the *économie sociale*. The idea has some resonance in other countries where the culture of co-operatives and non-profit bodies is very close. However, there is a lively debate about the real significance of the term *économie sociale* even in France. While some regard it as a cultural identity of common interest and self-perception present in a long tradition and belatedly recognised by government, others regard it as little better than the rhetoric of the socialists in their attempt to use for essentially political and ideological ends the *tissu associatif* ('the fabric of associational life') (defined by Seibel 1992: 63, as 'the network of reputational and power elites, sociologically belonging to the middle class, with the associations as its structural basis'), and argue that other interventions such as the decentralisation of governmental organisation in France have been much more significant. Certainly, some people have argued that the only way to understand the yoking together of such disparate organisational forms is in order to contrast them with for-profit firms and the ideological commitment to them which is characteristic of pro-capitalist politics.

One might expect that Italy would be a country where the concept of the *économie sociale* would have some relevance, because, since their invention in the late 1970s, those non-profit co-operatives known as 'social solidarity co-operatives' have become major providers of publicly contracted educational, cultural and social services in many cities (Borzaga 1991: 705–6). The role of non-profit co-operatives in the provision of welfare services has become important also in Sweden (Stryjan 1993), where some commentators are happy now to speak of a 'third sector' in ways reminiscent of the concept of the *économie sociale*. The Italian sector has, however, a more complex identity. The term *volontariato* is widely used, particularly in social Catholic circles, to denote 'volunteer-using organisations', such as the Red Cross, but is also used in a wider sense, to mean all non-profit bodies, including foundations and purely the sector of voluntary associations (*associazismo sociale*). The growing importance of social movements in Italy during the 1980s led to a quite different non-profit culture not always regarded as part of the *volontariato*, when the word is used in a cultural rather than a legal sense: Perlmutter (1991: 181) reports suspicion among social movements of the voluntary sector as a body broadly within the establishment. Some similar trends can be found in Germany, where, Anheier (1991) has argued, there is an important 'counter-cultural' non-profit sector linked to social movements: in cities such as Berlin, there are also close social movement community businesses, co-operatives and for-profit firms with as clear a common identity as the large established welfare sector (MacFarlane, Laville and Ruether-Greaves 1992).

The social and cultural identity of the Dutch sector is quite distinctive, because, for many purposes, the statutory welfare purposes have always been delivered by the non-profit sector (Aquina 1992), not under contract, but as part of the long-standing religious 'pillarisation' of Dutch society and polity (Therborn 1989). There appears to be no single legal or other rubric under which all Dutch voluntary organisations would recognise themselves.

In the renascent democracies of eastern and central Europe, it is probably premature to speak of a clear identity under which non-profit bodies are recognised. The *économie sociale* concept seems unlikely to find many takers, perhaps because of its socialist political resonance. In Hungary, the English term 'nonprofit' (in the American unhyphenated spelling!) is in widespread use, but the term 'third sector' is also used in the American sense to denote the non-profit sector rather than in the western European sense where it is often used as a synonym for the *économie sociale* (Defourny and Monzón Campos 1992).

Other identities for the sector in Europe have been proposed, mainly from academic standpoints. For example, Hood and Schuppert (1988) argued that much of the sector should be seen as simply one component of a wider mix of organisations outside the mainstream, directly government-managed bureaucracy for the delivery of public services, together treated as 'para-government'. Those not interested primarily in public administration have not taken up the idea very extensively. The inclusion of the well-known and very controversial article by Wilson and Butler (1985) in the collection edited by Streeck and Schmitter (1985) on *private interest government* attempted to situate the sector in the same terrain from the standpoint of political science, and this may have some connections with Salamon's (1987) concept of the non-profit sector as a central component in *third party government*, which has been used by Anheier (1992: 50–4) to explain the situation of the German non-profit sector. However, few practitioners in Europe tend to think in such terms.

Independence and politics

The rhetoric of non-profit practitioners in countries such as the UK and the US, and the language of definitions such as the one given above, is sometimes read as if it suggested that, because the sector can be picked out, defined, and recognised, it follows that in some way it must be (or, at any rate, ought to be) independent, not merely in formal respects, but in substantive behaviour from the state, for-profit firms and political parties. The definition given above requires formal, but not behavioural independence. Various criteria for formal independence have been proposed: Billis (1992) recently proposed one whereby the test would be whether the organisation can decide, without seeking the permission of a state body, whether or not to come into or go out of existence; see 6 (1993b) for a discussion of the merits of various such criteria.

The *non sequitur* that where there is formal, there must be behavioural independence – which, perhaps, we might call 'the definitional illusion' – has its adherents almost everywhere, although few serious scholars give it much credence (for a comprehensive debunking from an American perspective, see Hall (1992)). The heavy financial dependence of non-profit bodies on the state is generally recognised throughout Europe; by contrast, its 'discovery' in the US by Salamon and Abrahamson (1981) came as a surprise to many there. Of course, in every country individual personnel working in the sector or on boards are frequently members of the political parties, and it is generally considered undemocratic to restrict their liberty to join such parties or even hold office in them: even the 1986 Widdicombe report and subsequent 1989 local government legislation in the UK did not propose to restrict office holding in political parties for persons involved in voluntary organisations funded by local authorities, although there was talk of it in some circles at the time.

Some scholars claim that connections between political parties and non-profit bodies are very close in particular countries. 6 and Randon (1994, forthcoming) show that, in continental Europe, there are few if any significant restrictions on the liberty of political speech by non-profit bodies of the kind found in English charity law or North American charity and tax law. In Germany, it is generally accepted that the *Vereine* and *Stiftungen* forms are legitimate means of democratic political expression, and the fact that some foundations are closely allied to particular political parties does not excite the kind of anxiety which London and Washington periodically undergo about the partisan links of the 'think tanks'. Against this background of greater political liberty, the arguments of commentators such as Seibel (1992) that, in France and Germany, party patronage and clientelism are common features of resource allocation in the non-profit sector can be understood. Similar views have been advanced about the Italian non-profit sector (Perlmutter 1991). However, one might wonder whether the situation is much different in the for-profit sector: many firms have relations of clientelism and patronage with political parties in the UK whereby they may make donations, personnel may make their careers by movement between government when a particular party is in office and the for-profit sector, and particular firms or whole industries may be the beneficiaries of the policies of particular parties.

REGULATION, SUBSIDY AND PURCHASING: RELATIONS WITH STATES

Non-profit organisations have formal relations with the states in Europe at a number of levels and, for each, there may be regulatory objectives. In most countries, the tax authorities have a central supervisory role (6 and Randon 1994, forthcoming). First, the systems of constitutional law often grant liberty of association. Second, the civil law systems or codes may spell out the conditions under which a non-profit organisation may have legal personality. Third, tax laws may provide for relief from corporate income tax, or (in the case of the UK and Portugal) in some small measure from VAT, or from local taxes, or for relief for donors against their personal income tax for donations; such laws may also lay down conditions under which non-profit bodies which satisfy the civil law requirements of legal structure may obtain these benefits, and to what extent donors may dispose of their wealth to non-profit bodies without incurring tax penalties. Fourth, public law may grant specific public authorities the powers to make grants or subsidies to non-profit agencies for a widely specified range of tasks (the agreements may be 'public law contracts' as in Germany (Loges 1992) or non-enforceable private law donations) or to enter into private law contracts with them. Fifth, public law (for example in France) may grant rights to receive donations, which would not automatically (as in the UK) apply to any organisation.[3]

In many countries, and not only in the UK, contracting by public authorities with non-profit bodies has become an important means of the delivery of public services. In Italy, contracting with non-profit bodies in personal social services and in some areas of health care has been a mainstream form of provision since the 1970s (Ascoli 1992; Pasquinelli 1992; Bassi 1993), and, at local level, it is becoming more significant in France, although recent research has not yet distinguished between flows of resources from French local authorities under contract and flows under grants (Mizrahi-Tchernonog 1992a, 1992b).

Patterns of regulation in law vary widely between countries. 6 and Randon (1994, forthcoming) show that, in general, continental European countries have none of the restrictions on freedom of political speech for non-profit organisations which are common in the charity law countries. Palmer and Finlayson (1993) show that few countries adopt the kinds of detailed requirements concerning accounting standards specific to the sector which are set out in the British *Statement of Recommended Practice No 2*, although a number of countries have sector-specific standards.

Much regulation in Germany appears to be done informally through the peak associations (Anheier 1991, 1992), and through the social insurance agencies which typically have non-enforceable public law-based agreements (not private law contracts) with the main six welfare associations at *Land* level. Although the legal basis of the German system in the concept of subsidiarity is more formalised than in many countries, the concept of subsidiarity is widely recognised to govern regulatory relations between states and non-profit bodies (cf. van der Ploeg 1992 on the Netherlands). Although many commentators have described the German system as neo-corporatist by analogy with the neo-corporatist systems of wage bargaining used in West Germany from the 1950s until the 1980s, the degree of centralisation and multi-party bargaining there appears to be changing.

TOWARD CONVERGENCE? THE EC AS POLICY MAKER

Like most areas of policy in which the Commission of the European Communities has ever expressed even the faintest interest, the field of non-profit activity in Europe is subject to occasional fits of moral panic, in which 'faceless Eurocrats' play the role of folk devils. For reasons that have never become clear, in the late 1980s, lawyers in the UK and elsewhere appeared to break out in a cold sweat over the rumour that the Commission proposed to 'harmonise' (whatever that might mean in this context) the national systems of law governing charities, associations, foundations and the like. In Britain and Germany, there was a brief moral panic over the possibility of a reinterpretation of Article 58 (2) of the Treaty of Rome (see 6 (1992a) for a review). 1992–3 has seen another such moment of legal and policy *angst*, when some people have begun to suggest that the delphic clause in the Treaty of Maastricht which enshrines a principle of subsidiarity would result in the export to all member states of the German system of legally governed allocation of responsibilities between national and local governments, and between the state and the non-profit sector. By comparison with these moments of dire certainty of the Approach of an Awful Doom,[4] the spasmodic attempts of the Commission to make policy and introduce legislation in this area have been so modest, so undemanding, and so frankly prosaic as to be almost boring. If it were not for the fact that much wider forces are at work in Europe to increase the encounter of non-profit bodies from different countries with one another, a dispassionate observer of the Commission (an animal presumed to be extinct in the UK) could be forgiven for wondering what all the fuss has been about.

The sum total of the Commission's exertions to date are to be found in one document and one proposed law (Commission of the European Communities 1989, 1991). The first declared in ringing terms that non-profit bodies ought to benefit from the opportunities presented by the single market, and be subject to the rules on competition, in much the same way as anyone else. The second proposed the creation of an entirely optional legal status of European Association for bodies wanting a means of securing legal personality in every member state at a single stroke. The latter has passed through the European Parliament, and is now left to the tender mercies of the Council of Ministers; it is expected that the German and Danish opposition and the lukewarm British position may leave it in the condition of limbo into which feebly favoured European initiatives are consigned for their peculiar torment.

Beyond this, Directorate-General XXIII, which has responsibility for the *économie sociale* for those countries that recognise it and for associations, foundations, co-operatives and mutuals for those that do not, has proposed that it will at some unspecified date in late 1993 or 1994, bring forward a new policy document, or *livre blanc*. This is expected to review the issues of competition policy and taxation policy which relate to the sector, but no one seriously expects radical initiatives. More importantly, it will consider whether measures can be proposed which will limit the capacity of the least scrupulous fundraisers to gravitate to the least regulated member state and to use the facility of the freedom of movement of capital to engage in cross-frontier fraud; however, it is not thought likely that bold and far-reaching legislative measures will be proposed. It may also deal with a number of more practical proposals concerning payments.

If we are to expect convergence in the identity, regulation or policy treatment of the sector, it seems that we need not look with either fear or relish to the Commission for its delivery. If the sectors and their legal and policy treatments are to become more alike, it can only be as a result of increased fundraising and service provision across frontiers (there are reasons to think that growth here will be steady, but not rapid; see 6 and Forder 1993), or else from the mutual mimesis of governments, which has rarely been a rapid process in any field of public policy.

Does this, then, vindicate after all the sceptical argument put at the beginning of the paper? Hardly. Clearly, transnationalisation of the sector's fundraising and service provision has begun, and trends in state policy such as contracting are spreading across frontiers. Sooner or later, the Community will have to confront the problem of fraud. No doubt, it must proceed with caution, and react to events rather than anticipate them, for fear of provoking more of the Europhobia of the sort that dominated the headlines in 1992–3. None the less, a single market requires common rules and common standards of their enforcement, if it is not to produce outcomes which are, in the long run, worse than autarchy, and the risks of transnational fundraising fraudsters being able to crawl through the loopholes and rents in the legal systems of the member states is a real one. As non-profit bodies increase their operations across frontiers, political pressure from their lobbyists will mount on the tax system, with demands for some sort of convergence, and at least the elimination of double taxation will be pressed (Kidd 1992; Wheeler 1992; 6 1992b). National and regional differences will remain; complete iso-morphism is unlikely, because there are as many pressures for variation in style, identity, definition and market share, as there are for convergence in some aspects of regulation. However, the policy agenda for the non-profit sectors will continue to be recast in the next decade by growing Euro-peanisation, and the UK sector can expect that its encounter with its continental European sisters will only deepen.

NOTES

1 Randon (1992), in a small-scale attitudinal survey of about 600 national voluntary organisations in membership of NCVO, conducted in 1992, found that the number of bodies concerned to develop networks and links in continental Europe and concerned about the policy environment for that work (49 per cent) exceeded the number placing fundraising as the top of their list of concerns (46 per cent).
2 It is generally thought that the two halves of the clause are genuine alternatives; it is not that they are supposed to mean the same thing. A body may satisfy either in order to qualify (Soumeryn-Kestemont and Afschrift 1991).
3 Remarkably, English law permits this to charitable trusts which have no legal personality by way of incorporation or otherwise. This charity law tradition is not followed in most civil law countries.
4 The phrase, is of course, Hilaire Belloc's, from an essay of that title, in which he failed to be convinced by political panics of the 1920s and early 1930s that civilisation was about to collapse as a consequence of the fires of the class struggle.

REFERENCES

Alfandari, E. and Nardone, A. (eds) (1990) *Les Associations et les fondations en Europe: régime juridique et fiscal*, Lyon: Éditions Juris Service.
Anheier, H.K. (1991) 'West Germany: the ambiguities of peak associations', in R. Wuthnow (ed.) *Between States and Markets*, Princeton, NJ: Princeton University Press, p. 64–93. *
Anheier, H.K. (1992) 'An elaborate network: profiling the third sector in Germany', in Gidron *et al.* (eds) *Government and the Third Sector*, San Francisco: Jossey-Bass, pp. 31–56 *
Anheier, H.K. and Seibel, W. (1990a) 'The third sector in comparative perspective: four propositions', in H.K. Anheier and W. Seibel (eds) *The Third Sector*, Berlin and New York: de Gruyter, pp. 379–87.
Anheier, H.K. and Seibel, W. (1990b) *The Third Sector: Comparative Studies of Nonprofit Organisations*, Berlin and New York: de Gruyter.
Aquina, H.J. (1992) 'A partnership between government and voluntary organisations: changing relationships in Dutch society', in B. Gidron *et al.* (eds) *Government and the Third Sector*, San Francisco: Jossey-Bass, pp. 57–74.
Archambault, E. (1990) 'Public authorities and the nonprofit sector in France', in H.K.

Anheier and W. Seibel (eds) *The Third Sector*, Berlin and New York: de Gruyter, pp. 293–302.*

Ascoli, U. (1992) 'Towards a partnership between statutory sector and voluntary sector? Italian welfare pluralism', in S. Kuhnle and P. Selle (eds) *Government and Voluntary Organisations*, Aldershot: Avebury, pp. 136–56.

Baine, S., Benington, J. and Russell, J. (1992) *Changing Europe: Challenges Facing the Voluntary and Community Sectors in the 1990s*, London: National Council for Voluntary Organisations/Community Development Foundation.

Baron, E. and Delsol, X. (1992) *Les fondations reconnues d'utilité publique et d'entreprise: régime juridique et fiscal*, Lyon: Editions Juris Service.

Bassi, A. (1993) 'Ten years of contracting with non-profits: the case of Ravenna', paper given at the NCVO/South Bank University conference, *Contracting – selling or shrinking?*, 20–2 July 1993, London.

Billis, D. (1992) 'The shifting boundaries of the non-profit sector', paper given at the *Third International Conference on Research on Voluntary and Non-Profit Organisations*, Indiana University – Purdue University, Indianapolis, 11–13 March 1992.

Borzaga, C. (1991) 'The Italian nonprofit sector: an overview of an undervalued reality', *Annals of Public and Cooperative Economics*, 62(4): 695–710.*

Castles, F.G. (ed.) (1989) *The Comparative History of Public Policy*, Cambridge: Polity Press.

Chesterman, M. (1979) *Charities, Trusts and Social Welfare*, London: Weidenfeld & Nicolson.

Commission of the European Communities, DG XXIII (1989) *Businesses in the 'Économie Sociale' Sector: Europe's Frontier Free Market*, SEC (89) 2187, 18 December 1989, Brussels: Commission of the European Communities.

Commission of the European Communities (1991) *Statute for a European Association: Explanatory Memorandum, and Proposal for a Council Regulation (EEC) on the Statute for a European Association*, COM (91), 273, Brussels: Commission of the European Communities.

Defourny, J. (1993a) 'Les associations en Belgique: une analyse economique à la croisée des traditions francophones et anglo-saxonnes', paper given at the conference, *Well-being in Europe by Strengthening the Third Sector*, 27–9 May 1993, Barcelona.*

Defourny, J. (1993b) 'The "économie sociale" approach of the third sector: a survey', paper given at the conference, *Well-being in Europe by Strengthening the Third Sector*, 27–9 May 1993, Barcelona.

Defourny, J. and Monzón Campos, J. (eds) (1992) *The Third Sector – Économie Sociale*, Liège: CIRIEC; Brussels: de Broeck. *

Doling, J. and Symon, P. (1993) 'The non-profit provision of housing in Europe: some consequences of moving toward the market', paper given at the conference, *Well-being in Europe by Strengthening the Third Sector*, 27–9 May 1993, Barcelona. *

Flaherty, S.L.Q. (1992) 'Philanthropy without borders: US foundation activity in Eastern Europe', *Voluntas*, 3(3): 335–50.

Hall, P.D. (1992) 'Reflections on the nonprofit sector in the postliberal era', in *Inventing the Nonprofit Sector and Other Essays on Philanthropy, Voluntarism and Nonprofit Organisations*, Baltimore: Johns Hopkins University Press, pp. 85–114.

Harvey, B. (1992) *Networking in Europe: A Guide to European Voluntary Organisations*, London: National Council for Voluntary Organisations.

Hemström, C. (1992) 'The law governing organisations other than foundations', *The International Encyclopaedia of Comparative Law*, XIII: Ch. 9b.

Hondius, F.W. and van der Ploeg, T. (1992) 'Foundations', *The International Encyclopaedia of Comparative Law*, XIII: Ch 9a.

Hood, C. and Schuppert, G.F. (1988) *Delivering Public Services in Western Europe: Sharing Western European Experience of Para-Government Organisation*, London: Sage.*

Hopkins, B.R. and Moore, C.L. (1992) 'Using the lessons learned from US and English law to create a regulatory framework for charities in evolving democracies', *Voluntas*, 3(2): 194–214.

Kidd, H. (1992) 'Article 7 of the Treaty of Rome: fiscal discrimination between NGOs', in *Charity Law and Practice*, 1/2, London: Key Haven Publications, pp. 95–100.

Kuhnle, S. and Selle, P. (eds) (1992) *Government and Voluntary Organisations: A Relational Perspective*, Aldershot: Avebury.

Loges, F. (1992) 'Financial and taxation framework conditions of charitable organisations in the Federal Republic of Germany', mimeo, Bundesarbeitsgemeinschaft der Freien Wohlfahrtspflege, e.V., Bonn.

MacFarlane, R. and Laville, J-L. (1992) *Developing Community Partnerships in Europe: New Ways of Meeting Social Needs in Europe*, London: Directory of Social Change and Calouste Gulbenkian Foundation (UK Branch).

MacFarlane, R., Laville, J-L. and Ruether-Greaves, R. (1992) 'The alternative movement in Germany', in R. MacFarlane and J-L. Laville (eds) *Developing Community Partnerships in Europe*, London: Directory of Social Change and Calouste Gulbenkian Foundation (UK Branch), pp. 71–80.

Mizrahi-Tchernonog, V. (1992a) 'Building welfare systems through local associations in France', in B. Gidron *et al.* (eds) *Government and the Third Sector*, San Francisco: Jossey-Bass, pp. 215–38.*

Mizrahi-Tchernonog, V. (1992b), 'Municipal subsidies to French associations', *Voluntas*, 3(3): 351–64.*

Palmer, P. and Finlayson, N. (1993) 'Accounting treatments of the third sector', paper given at the conference, *Well-being in Europe by Strengthening the Third Sector*, 27–9 May 1993, Barcelona.

Pasquinelli, S. (1992) 'Voluntary and public social services in Italy', in B. Gidron *et al.* (eds) *Government and the Third Sector*, San Francisco: Jossey-Bass, pp. 196–214.

Paton, R. (1990) 'The emerging social economy', *Management Issues*, Spring, The Management Centre, Newcastle-upon-Tyne.

Perlmutter, T. (1991) 'Italy: why no voluntary sector?', in R. Wuthnow (ed.) *Between States and Markets*, Princeton, NJ: Princeton University Press, pp. 157–88.*

Powell, W.W. (ed.) (1987) *The Nonprofit Sector: A Research Handbook*, New Haven, CT: Yale University Press.

Randon, A. (1992) *Charities for Change: A Survey of Voluntary Organisations' Priorities*, mimeo, London: National Council for Voluntary Organisations.

Salamon, L.M. (1987) 'Partners in public service: the scope and theory of government–non-profit relations', in W.W. Powell (ed.) *The Nonprofit Sector*, New Haven, CT: Yale University Press, pp. 99–117.

Salamon, L.M. and Abrahamson, A. (1981) *The Federal Budget and the Nonprofit Sector*, Washington, DC: Urban Institute.

Salamon, L.M. and Anheier, H.K. (1992a) 'In search of the non-profit sector I: the question of definitions', *Voluntas*, 3(2): 125–52.

Salamon, L.M. and Anheier, H.K. (1992b) 'In search of the non-profit sector II: the problem of classification', *Voluntas*, 3(3): 267–310.

Seibel, W. (1992) 'Government–nonprofit relationship: styles and linkage patterns in France and Germany', in S. Kuhnle and P. Selle (eds) *Government and Voluntary Organisations*, Aldershot: Avebury, pp. 34–52.

Siegal, D. and Yancey, J. (1992) *The Rebirth of Civil Society: The Development of the Nonprofit Sector in East Central Europe and the Role of Western Assistance*, New York: Rockefeller Brothers Fund.

Soumeryn-Kestemont, M. and Afschrift, T. (1991) *Vade mecum des associations sans but lucratif*, Brussels: CREADIF.

Sousi, G. and Mayaud, Y. (eds) (1992) *Le Droit des associations: Vol 1: Belgique, France, Italie, Luxembourg, Pays-Bas, Statut de l'Association Européene*, Brussels: Commission of the European Communities in association with Éditions Lamy.

Streeck, W. and Schmitter, P.C. (eds) (1985) *Private Interest Government*, London: Sage.

Stryjan, Y. (1993) 'Co-operatives on the welfare market: the Swedish case', paper given at the conference, *Well-being in Europe by Strengthening the Third Sector*, 27–9 May 1993, Barcelona.

Therborn, G. (1989) '"Pillarisation" and "popular movements": two variants of welfare state capitalism: the Netherlands and Sweden', in F.G. Castles (ed.) *The Comparative History of Public Policy*, Cambridge: Polity Press. pp. 192–241.

van der Ploeg, T. (1992) 'Changing relationships between private nonprofit organisations and government in the Netherlands', in K.D. McCarthy *et al.* (eds) *The Nonprofit Sector in the Global Community*, San Francisco: Jossey-Bass for Independent Sector, pp. 190–204.

Wheeler, J. (1992) 'The international tax treatment of non-profit organisations', paper given at the ECAS/NCVO/DoSC conference, *Associations and Foundations in the European Community*, 24–5 November 1992.

Wilson, D.C. and Butler, R.J. (1985) 'Corporatism in the British voluntary sector', in W. Streeck and P.C. Schmitter (eds) *Private Interest Government*, London: Sage.

Wuthnow, R. (ed.) (1991) *Between States and Markets: The Voluntary Sector in Comparative Perspective*, Princeton, NJ: Princeton University Press.

6, P. (1992a) 'European competition law and the non-profit sector', *Voluntas*, 3(2): 215–46.

6, P. (1992b) 'Taxation policy and non-profit bodies in Europe', paper given at NCVO symposium, *Europe and the Voluntary Sector: What are the Policy Issues for the European Commission?*, 27 April 1992, London.

6, P. (1993a) 'English national voluntary organisations working across frontiers in the single European market', paper given at a meeting of the UK Government – Voluntary Sector Forum on European issues, 7 June 1993, NCVO, London.

6, P. (1993b) *What is a Voluntary Organisation? Defining the Voluntary and Non-profit Sectors*, London: NCVO, first published in 1991.

6, P. and Forder, J.E. (1993) 'Non-profit trade in the European single market', paper given at the conference, *Well-being in Europe by Strengthening the Third Sector*, 27–9 May 1993, Barcelona.

6, P. and Kuti, É. (1992) 'Into the European Community: impacts of future membership on Hungary's non-profit sector', *Journal of European Social Policy*, 3(4): 273–95; published in Hungarian as 6, P. and Kuti, É. (1993) 'A közös piac veszélyei és kihívásai a Magyar non-profit szektor számára' ('The challenges and dangers of the Common market for the Hungarian nonprofit sector'), *Közgazdasági Szemle*, XL(2): 110–24; and, abridged, as 6, P. (1992) 'Útban az Európai Közösség felé: a közös piaci tagság várható hatásai Magyarország non-profit szektorára', in Kuti, É. (ed.) (1992) *A nonprofit szektor Magyarországon: tanulmányok*, Nonprofit Kutatocsopsort, Budapest, pp. 46–67; forthcoming in *Journal of European Social Policy*, November 1993.

6, P. and Randon, A. (1994, forthcoming) *Liberty, Charity and Politics*, Aldershot: Dartmouth Publishing.

BIBLIOGRAPHY

The purpose of the present bibliography is not to provide a comprehensive survey of all the available literature on the non-profit sector in each relevant language, but the more modest one of listing for the student the main texts which are relatively available, at least in libraries, either in the UK or in the USA. The selection criteria have had to be flexible: essentially, I have tried to concentrate on material which is mainly about voluntary organisations or volunteering for voluntary organisations (as opposed to volunteering for state agencies). Inevitably, some papers concerned with broader patterns of changes in the welfare mix or patterns of governance in public management have crept into this listing, if they happen also to be particularly illuminating about the voluntary and non-profit sectors. An asterisk indicates that the work contains some quantitative statistical information about the sector's size in income, expenditure or employment, scope and market share, or other statistical information for one or more European countries.

Western Europe generally

Alfandari, E. and Nardone, A. (eds) (1990) *Les Associations et les fondations en Europe: régime juridique et fiscal*, Lyon: Éditions Juris Service.

Allen, D. (1992a) *Tax and Giving in the European Community*, London: Directory of Social Change.

Allen, D. (1992b) *VAT and Voluntary Organisations in the European Community*, London: Directory of Social Change.

Anheier, H.K. and Seibel, W. (eds) (1990) *The Third Sector: Comparative Studies of Nonprofit Organisations*, Berlin and New York: de Gruyter.

Anheier, H.K., Knapp, M.R.J. and Salamon, L.M. (1993) 'No numbers, no policy: can EUROSTAT count the non-profit sector', in S.K.E. Saxon-Harrold and J. Kendall (eds) (1993) *Researching the Voluntary Sector: A National, Local and International Perspective*, London and Tonbridge: Charities Aid Foundation, pp. 197–206.*

Baine, S., Benington, J. and Russell, J. (1992) *Changing Europe: Challenges Facing the Voluntary and Community Sectors in the 1990s*, London: National Council for Voluntary Organisations/Community Development Foundation.

Baldock. J. (1993) 'Patterns of change in the delivery of welfare in Europe', in P. Taylor-Gooby and R. Lawson (eds) (1993) *Markets and Managers: New Issues in the Delivery of Welfare*, Buckingham: Open University Press, pp. 24–37.

Baldock, J. and Evers, A. (1991) 'Citizenship and frail elderly people: changing patterns of provision in Europe', in N. Manning (ed.) (1991) *Social Policy Review 1990–91*, Harlow: Longman.

Baldock, J. and Evers, A. (1992) 'Innovations and care of the elderly: the cutting edge of change for social welfare systems', *Ageing and Society*, 12(3): 289–312.

Benington, J., Baine, S. and Russell, J. (1992) 'The impact of the single European market on regional and local development and on the voluntary and community sectors', in L. Hantrais, S. Mangen and M. O'Brien (eds) *The Mixed Economy of Welfare*, Cross-National Research Papers, New Series, *The Implications of 1992 for Social Policy*, No 6, The Cross-National Research Group, University of Loughborough, pp. 23–42.

CEDAG (Comité Européenne des Associations d'Intérêt Générale) (1991) *Europe: A Chance for Associations?*, Brussels and Paris: CEDAG.

Chanan, G. (1992) *Out of the Shadows: Local Community Action and the European Community*, Dublin: European Foundation for the Improvement of Living and Working Conditions.*

Commission of the European Communities (1986) *The Extent and Kind of Voluntary Work in the EEC: Question Surrounding the Relationship Between Volunteering and Employment*, Luxembourg: Commission of the European Communities.

Commission of the European Communities, DG XXIII (1989) *Businesses in the*

'Économie Sociale' Sector: Europe's Frontier Free Market, SEC (89) 2187, 18 December 1989, Brussels: Commission of the European Communities.

Commission of the European Communities (1991) *Statute for a European Association: Explanatory Memorandum, and Proposal for a Council Regulation (EEC) on the Statute for a European Association*, COM (91), 273, Brussels: Commission of the European Communities.

Davis Smith, J. (1993) *Volunteering in Europe: Opportunities and Challenges for the 1990s*, Voluntary Action Research Paper, Second Series, No 4, The Volunteer Centre UK.

Defourny, J. and Monzón Campos, J. (eds) (1992) *The Third Sector – Économie Sociale*, Liège: CIRIEC; Brussels: de Broeck. *

Demoustier, D. and Grange, A. (1993) 'Repositionnements associatifs: identités regionales and Européennes', paper given at the conference, *Well-being in Europe by Strengthening the Third Sector*, 27–9 May 1993, Barcelona.

Ely, P. (1992) 'Democracy, voluntary action and the social welfare sector in mainland Europe', in R. Hedley and J. Davis Smith (eds) (1992) *Volunteering and Society: Principles and Practice*, London: Bedford Square Press/NCVO.

Evers, A. (1992) 'Welfare pluralism and the voluntary sector in Europe: some counter-intuitive arguments', in K. Chapman (ed.) *Welfare Pluralism, the Voluntary Sector and Elderly People: East and West*, International Federation on Ageing, papers presented at the Round Table during the Second European Congress of Gerontology, Madrid, September 1991.

Gidron, B., Kramer, R.M. and Salamon, L.M. (eds) (1992) *Government and the Third Sector: Emerging Relationships in Welfare States*, San Francisco: Jossey-Bass.*

Griffiths, J. (1992) 'Company giving in Europe: what are the policy issues for the European Commission?', *Voluntas*, 3(3): 375–82.

Halfpenny, P. (1993) 'The 1991 international survey of giving', in S.K.E. Saxon-Harrold and J. Kendall (eds) (1993) *Researching the Voluntary Sector: A National, Local and International Perspective*, London and Tonbridge: Charities Aid Foundation, pp. 207–18.

Harvey, B. (1992) *Networking in Europe: A Guide to European Voluntary Organisations*, London: NCVO.

Harvey, B. (1993) 'Lobbying in Europe: the experience of voluntary organisations', in S. Mazey and J. Richardson (eds) (1993) *Lobbying in the European Community*, Oxford: Oxford University Press, pp. 188–200.

Hemström, C. (1992) 'The law governing organisations other than foundations', *The International Encyclopaedia of Comparative Law*, XIII: Ch. 9b.

Holly, K. (ed.) *Associations and Foundations in the European Community: Legal, Structural and Fiscal Issues*, London: Directory of Social Change.

Hondius, F.W. and van der Ploeg, T. (1992) 'Foundations', *The International Encyclopaedia of Comparative Law*, XIII: Ch. 9a.

Hood, C. and Schuppert, G.F. (1988) *Delivering Public Services in Western Europe: Sharing Western European Experience of Para-Government Organisation*, London: Sage.*

James, E. (ed.) (1989) *The Nonprofit Sector in International Perspective: Studies in Comparative Culture and Policy*, New York: Oxford University Press.

Katus, J. (1992) 'Networking in Europe: the ESVA case', paper given at the *Third International Conference on Research on Voluntary and Nonprofit Organisations*, Indiana University – Purdue University, Indianapolis, 11–13 March 1992.

Kendall, J. and Knapp, M.R.J. (1992) *Charity Statistics in a European Context*, Tonbridge and London: Charities Aid Foundation.

Kidd, H. (1992) 'Article 7 of the Treaty of Rome: fiscal discrimination between NGOs', in *Charity Law and Practice*, 1/2, London: Key Haven Publications, pp. 95–100.

Kramer, R.M. (1981) *Voluntary Agencies in the Welfare State*, Berkeley: University of California Press.*

Kramer, R.M. (1992a) 'Privatisation in the personal social services in the United Kingdom, Netherlands and Italy' in K.D. McCarthy *et al.* (eds) *The Nonprofit Sector in the Global Community*, San Francisco: Jossey-Bass for Independent Sector, pp. 90–107.

Kramer, R.M. (1992b) 'The roles of voluntary social service organisations in four European states: policies and trends in England, the Netherlands, Italy and Norway', in S. Kuhnle and P. Selle (eds) *Government and Voluntary Organisations*, Aldershot: Avebury, pp. 34–53.

Kuhnle, S. and Selle, P. (eds) (1992) *Government and Voluntary Organisations: A Relational Perspective*, Aldershot: Avebury.

Langley, J. (ed.) (1992) *Voluntary Organisations in Europe*, Wivenhoe: ARVAC (Association for Researchers into Voluntary Action and Community Involvement).

McCarthy, K.D. Hodgkinson, V.A. and Sumariwalla, R.D. (eds) (1992) *The Nonprofit Sector in the Global Community: Voices from Many Nations*, San Francisco: Jossey-Bass for Independent Sector.

McConnell, C. (1991) 'Community development in five European countries', *Community Development Journal*, 26(2): 103–11.

MacFarlane, R. and Laville, J-L. (1992) *Developing Community Partnerships in Europe: New Ways of Meeting Social Needs in Europe*, London: Directory of Social Change and Calouste Gulbenkian Foundation (UK Branch).

McLean, S.A., Kluger, R. and Henrey, R. in collaboration with the member firms of Coopers and Lybrand (International) (1990) *Charitable Contributions in the OECD: A Tax Study*, Yalding: Interphil.

Munday, B. (1992) *Social Services in the Member States of the European Community: A Handbook of Information and Data*, Canterbury: University of Kent.

Neuhoff, K. (1993) 'Recent developments in foundation law: institutional forms and legal types', paper given at the *Voluntas* symposium, *Foundations*, 21–3 October 1993, Paris.

Organisation for Economic Co-operation and Development and the Commission of the European Communities (1992) *Social Welfare Services Delivered by the Private Sectors*, Study Series Occasional Papers, no 10, *Innovation and Employment*, November, Brussels: Commission of the European Communities.

Palmer, P. and Finlayson, N. (1993) 'Accounting treatments of the third sector', paper given at the conference, *Well-being in Europe by Strengthening the Third Sector*, 27–9 May 1993, Barcelona.

Preite, O. (1992) 'Different laws for different functions of nonprofits: a comparative approach', paper given at the *Third International Conference on Research on Voluntary and Nonprofit Organisations*, Indiana University–Purdue University, Indianapolis, 11–13 March 1992.

Robbins, D. (1990) 'Voluntary organisations and the social state in the European Community', *Voluntas*, 1(2): 98–128.

Room, G. (1993a) *Anti-poverty Action in Europe*, Bristol: School for Advanced Urban Studies, University of Bristol.

Room, G. (1993b) 'The future of the European welfare state: welfare regimes and the third sector', paper given at the conference, *Well-being in Europe by Strengthening the Third Sector*, 27–9 May 1993, Barcelona.

Room, G. in collaboration with Berghman, J., Bouget, D., Cabrero, G.R., Hansen, F., Hartmann-Hirsch, C., Karantinos, D., Kortmann, K., O'Cinneide, S., Pereirinha, J., Robbins, D., Saraceno, C. and Vranken, J. (1993c) *Social Services and Social Exclusion: Report of the European Community Observatory on National Policies to Combat Social Exclusion*, Brussels: Commission of the European Communities, Directorate-General V (Employment, Social Affairs and Industrial Relations).

Schuster, J.M.D. (1993) 'The search for new sources of revenue for the third sector: issues in funding the arts and culture through state lotteries', paper given at the conference, *Well-being in Europe by Strengthening the Third Sector*, 27–9 May 1993, Barcelona.

Sousi, G. and Mayaud, Y. (eds) (1992) *Le Droit des associations: Vol 1: Belgique, France, Italie, Luxembourg, Pays-Bas, Statut de l'Association Européene*, Brussels: Commission of the European Communities in association with Éditions Lamy.

van der Ploeg, T. (1992a) 'The legal tradition concerning voluntary organisations: an obstacle for European integration of law on voluntary organisations?', paper given at the *Third International Conference on Research on Voluntary and Nonprofit Organisations*, Indiana University – Purdue University, Indianapolis, 11–13 March 1992.

van der Ploeg, T. (1993) 'A comparative analysis of foundation law', paper given at the *Voluntas* symposium, *Foundations*, 21–3 October 1993, Paris.

Wann, M. (1991) 'Supporting self-help groups in Europe', *Community Development Journal*, 26(2): 153–4.

Weber, N. (1993) 'Philanthropic developments in the USA, Canada, Holland, Japan and Hungary', in S.K.E. Saxon-Harrold and J. Kendall (eds) (1993) *Researching the Voluntary sector: A National, Local and International Perspective*, London and Tonbridge: Charities Aid Foundation, pp. 219–30. *

Weisbrod, B.A. and Mauser, E. (1992a) 'Tax policy toward nonprofit organisations: a ten country survey', in K.D. McCarthy *et al.* (eds) *The Nonprofit Sector in the Global Community*, San Francisco: Jossey-Bass for Independent Sector, pp. 29–50.

Weisman, N. (1993) 'The role of volunteering in Europe: a view from the European Commission', in J. Davis Smith *Volunteering in Europe*, The Volunteer Centre UK, pp. 154–6.

Wheeler, J. (1992) 'The international tax treatment of non-profit organisations', paper given at the ECAS/NCVO/DoSC conference, *Associations and Foundations in the European Community*, 24–5 November 1992.

Wuthnow, R. (ed.) (1991) *Between States and Markets: The Voluntary Sector in Comparative Perspective*, Princeton, NJ: Princeton University Press.

6, P. (1992a) 'European competition law and the non-profit sector', *Voluntas*, 3(2): 215–46.

6, P. (1992b) 'Taxation policy and non-profit bodies in Europe', paper given at NCVO symposium, *Europe and the Voluntary Sector: What are the Policy Issues for the European Commission?*, 27 April 1992, London.

6, P. (1993a) 'English national voluntary organisations working across frontiers in the single European market', paper given at a meeting of the UK Government – Voluntary Sector Forum on European issues, 7 June 1993, NCVO, London.

6, P. (1993b) 'Foundations: cross-national policy issues', paper given at the *Voluntas* symposium, *Foundations*, 21–3 October 1993, Paris.

6, P. and Forder, J.E. (1993) 'Non-profit trade in the European single market', paper given at the conference, *Well-being in Europe by Strengthening the Third Sector*, 27–9 May 1993, Barcelona.

6, P. and Randon, A. (1994, forthcoming) *Liberty, Charity and Politics*, Aldershot: Dartmouth Publishing.

Ireland

Delany, V.T.H. (1955) 'The development of the law of charities in Ireland', *International and Comparative Law Quarterly*, 4: 30–45.

Hayes, T. (1990) 'The church and the voluntary sector in Ireland: brief history and current impact', in Association of Voluntary Action Scholars (AVAS, now

ARNOVA) *Towards the 21st Century: Challenges for the Voluntary Sector: Proceedings of the Conference of the Association of Voluntary Action Scholars*, Vol. 1., London: London School of Economics.

O'Cearbhaill, D. (1991) 'Help or hindrance towards 1992: the impact of local administrative and political structures on neighbourhood development in Ireland', *Community Development Journal*, 26(2): 139–46.

Ruddle, H. and O'Connor, J. (1993) 'Volunteering in the Republic of Ireland', in J. Davis Smith *Volunteering in Europe*, The Volunteer Centre UK, pp.91–104.

France

Archambault, E. (1990) 'Public authorities and the nonprofit sector in France', in H.K. Anheier and W. Seibel (eds) *The Third Sector*, Berlin and New York: de Gruyter, pp. 293–302.*

Ferrand-Bechman, D. (1992) 'The missions, purposes, and functions of nonprofit organisations in France', in K.D. McCarthy *et al.* (eds) *The Nonprofit Sector in the Global Community*, San Francisco: Jossey-Bass for Independent Sector, pp. 230–9.

Ferrand-Bechman, D. (1993) 'Volunteering in France', in J. Davis Smith *Volunteering in Europe*, The Volunteer Centre UK, pp. 117–20.

Mizrahi-Tchernonog, V. (1992a) 'Building welfare systems through local associations in France', in B. Gidron *et al.* (eds) *Government and the Third Sector*, San Francisco: Jossey-Bass, pp. 215–38.*

Mizrahi-Tchernonog, V. (1992b) 'Municipal subsidies to French associations', *Voluntas*, 3(3): 351–64.*

Veugelers, J. and Lamont, M. (1991) 'France: alternative locations for public debate', in R. Wuthnow (ed.) *Between States and Markets*, Princeton, NJ: Princeton University Press, pp. 125–56.

Germany

Anheier, H.K. (1990) 'A profile of the third sector in Germany', in H.K. Anheier and W. Seibel (eds) *The Third Sector*, Berlin and New York: de Gruyter, pp. 313–32.*

Anheier, H.K. (1991a) 'Employment and earnings in the West German nonprofit sector: structures and trends 1970–1987', *Annals of Public and Cooperative Economics*, 62(4): pp. 673–94.*

Anheier, H.K. (1991b) 'West Germany: the ambiguities of peak associations', in R. Wuthnow (ed.) *Between States and Markets*, Princeton, NJ: Princeton University Press, pp. 64–93.*

Anheier, H.K. (1992) 'An elaborate network: profiling the third sector in Germany', in B. Gidron *et al.* (eds) *Government and the Third Sector*, San Francisco: Jossey-Bass, pp. 31–56. *.

Anheier, H.K. and Priller, E. (1991) 'The non-profit sector in East Germany: before and after unification', *Voluntas*, 2(1): 78–94.*

Anheier, H.K. and Romo, F.P. (1993) 'Foundations in Germany and the United States: a comparative analysis of size, scope and variations', paper given at the *Voluntas* symposium, *Foundations*, 21–3 October 1993, Paris. *

Bauer, R. (1990) 'Voluntary welfare associations in Germany and the United States: theses on the historical development of intermediary systems', *Voluntas*, 1(1): 97–111.

Beyer, H. and Nutzinger, H.G. (1993) 'Hierarchy or co-operation? Labour–management relations in Church institutions', *Voluntas*, 4(1): 55–72.

Dechamps, A. (1993) 'Volunteering in Germany', in J. Davis Smith *Volunteering in Europe*, The Volunteer Centre UK, pp. 81–90.

Evers, A., Ostner, I. and Wiesenthal, W. (1990) 'Cash and care: different conceptions of work and employment and their impact on innovations in the field of care', in A. Evers and H. Wintersberger (eds) *Shifts in the Welfare Mix: Their Impact on Work, Social Services and Welfare Policies*, Boulder and San Francisco: Westview Press.

Freeman, R. (1992) 'Governing the voluntary sector response to AIDS: a comparative study of the UK and Germany', *Voluntas*, 3(1): pp. 29–47; revised and reprinted with the same title in S. Kuhnle and P. Selle (eds) *Government and Voluntary Organisations*, Aldershot: Avebury, pp. 71–86.*

Jarré, D. (1991) 'Subsidiarity in social services provision in Germany', *Social Policy and Administration*, 25(3).

Loges, F. (1992) 'Financial and taxation framework conditions of charitable organisations in the Federal Republic of Germany', mimeo, Bundesarbeitsgemeinschaft der Freien Wohlfahrtspflege, e.V., Bonn.

Matzdat, J. (1989) 'On support for self-help groups at the local level', in S. Humble and J. Unell (eds) (1989) *Self-help in Health and Social Welfare: England and West Germany*, London: Routledge.

Oldfield, C. (1985) 'Volunteering in West Germany', *Youth Action*, May.

Seibel, W. (1989) 'The function of mellow weakness: nonprofit organisations as problem nonsolvers in Germany', in E. James (ed.) *The Nonprofit Sector in International Perspective*, New York: Oxford University Press, pp. 177–92.

Seibel, W. (1990) 'Government/third sector relationship in a comparative perspective: the cases of France and West Germany', *Voluntas*, 1(1): 42–61; revised and reprinted as Seibel, W. (1992) 'Government–nonprofit relationship: styles and linkage patterns in France and Germany', in S. Kuhnle and P. Selle (eds) *Government and Voluntary Organisations*, Aldershot: Avebury, pp. 34–52.

Netherlands

Aquina, H.J. (1992) 'A partnership between government and voluntary organisations: changing relationships in Dutch society', in B. Gidron *et al.*, *Government and the Third Sector*, San Francisco: Jossey-Bass, pp. 57–74.

Aquina, H. and Bekke, H. (1993) 'Governance in interaction: public tasks and private organisations', in J. Kooiman (ed.) (1993) *Modern Governance: New Government–Society Interactions*, London: Sage, pp. 159–70.

James, E. (1989) 'The private provision of public services: a comparison of Sweden and Holland', in E. James (ed.) *The Nonprofit Sector in International Perspective*, New York: Oxford University Press, pp. 31–60.*

Melief, W. (1992) 'Dutch voluntary organisations in transition', paper given at the *Third International Conference on Research on Voluntary and Non-Profit Organisations*, Indiana University – Purdue University, Indianapolis, 11–13 March 1992.

van Daal, H.J. and Willems, L. (1993) 'Volunteering in the Netherlands', in J. Davis Smith *Volunteering in Europe*, The Volunteer Centre UK, pp. 57–80.

van der Ploeg, T. (1992b) 'Changing relationships between private nonprofit organisations and government in the Netherlands', in K.D. McCarthy *et al.* (eds) *The Nonprofit Sector in the Global Community*, San Francisco: Jossey-Bass for Independent Sector, pp. 190–204.

Belgium

Bouckaert, G. (1993) 'Governance between legitimacy and efficiency: citizen participation in the Belgian fire service', in J. Kooiman (ed.) *Modern Governance: New Government–Society Interactions*, London: Sage, pp. 145–58.

Defourny, J. (1990) 'L'économie sociale en Wallonie: sources et identité d'un troisième grand secteur', *Travaux de recherches du CIRIEC*, 90/03, Université de Liège.

Defourny, J. (1993) 'Les associations en Belgique: une analyse economique à la croisée des traditions francophones et anglo-saxonnes', paper given at the conference, *Well-being in Europe by Strengthening the Third Sector*, 27–9 May 1993, Barcelona. *

Greece

Daoutopolos, G. A. (1991) 'Community development in Greece', *Community Development Journal*, 26(2): 131–8.

Giannuli, D. (1992) 'The Near East Relief/Near East Foundation in Greece, 1992–1955: a mission among the greek refugees in Asia Minor', paper given at the *Third International Conference on Research on Voluntary and Nonprofit Organisations*, Indiana University – Purdue University, Indianapolis, 11–13 March 1992.

Italy

Ascoli, U. (1992) 'Towards a partnership between statutory sector and voluntary sector? Italian welfare pluralism', in S. Kuhnle and P. Selle (eds) *Government and Voluntary Organisations*, Aldershot: Avebury, pp. 136–56.*

Borzaga, C. (1991) 'The Italian nonprofit sector: an overview of an undervalued reality', *Annals of Public and Cooperative Economics*, 62(4): 695–710.*

Brilliant, E. (9193) 'Theory and reality in the vision of Adriano Olivetti', *Voluntas*, 4(1): 95–114.

Milanesi, G. and Piccinelli, C. (1993) 'Volunteering in Italy', in J. Davis Smith *Volunteering in Europe*, Volunteer Centre UK, pp. 32–56.

Pasquinelli, S. (1989) 'Voluntary action in the welfare state: the Italian case', *Nonprofit and Voluntary Sector Quarterly*, 18(4).

Pasquinelli, S. (1992a) 'Voluntary and public social services in Italy', in B. Gidron *et al.* (eds) *Government and the Third Sector*, San Francisco: Jossey-Bass, pp. 196–214.*

Pasquinelli, S. (1992b) 'Background paper: Italy', paper given at OECD Experts' meeting on social welfare services provided by the private sectors', Paris, 6 November 1992; republished in OECD (1992), *Innovation and Employment*, Study Series, Occasional Papers, no. 10, pp. 16–17.

Perlmutter, T. (1991) 'Italy: why no voluntary sector?', in R. Wuthnow (ed.) *Between States and Markets*, Princeton, NJ: Princeton University Press, pp. 157–88.

Ranci, C. (1993) 'The role of the third sector in welfare policies in Italy', paper given at the conference, *Well-being in Europe by Strengthening the Third Sector*, 27–9 May 1993, Barcelona.

Spain

Fenyo, A., Knapp, M.R.J. and Montserrat, J. (1990) 'Inter-sectoral and international contracting-out of long-term care: evidence on comparative costs and efficiency from Britain and Spain', in L. Hantrais, S. Mangen and M. O'Brien (eds) (1990) *Caring and the Welfare State in the 1990s*, Cross-National Research Papers, New Series, *The Implications of 1992 for Social Policy*, No 2, The Cross-National Research Group, University of Loughborough, pp. 46–73.

Garvia, R. (1992) 'Mutual dependence between government and private service monopoly: the case of the Spanish blind', in S. Kuhnle and P. Selle (eds) *Government and Voluntary Organisations*, Aldershot: Avebury, pp. 108–35.

Luque, A., (1993), 'Volunteering in Spain', in J. Davis Smith *Volunteering in Europe*, The Volunteer Centre UK, pp. 121–8.

Montserrat, J. (1990) 'The role of the non-profit organisations in Spain: trends in contracting-out', in Association of Voluntary Action Scholars (AVAS, now ARNOVA) *Towards the 21st Century: Challenges for the Voluntary Sector: Proceedings of the Conference of the Association of Voluntary Action Scholars*, Vol. 2., London: London School of Economics.

Rovira, J. (1990) 'The role of nonprofit organisations in the Spanish health care market', in H.K. Anheier and W. Seibel (eds) *The Third Sector*, Berlin and New York: de Gruyter, pp. 333–46.

Denmark

Habermann, U. (1989) *Voluntary Work in a Nordic Welfare State*, Kobnhavn: Socialministeriet.

Habermann, U. (1993) 'Volunteering in Denmark', in J. Davis Smith *Volunteering in Europe*, The Volunteer Centre UK, pp. 128–34.

Norway

Grindheim, J-E. and Selle, P. (1990) 'The role of voluntary social welfare organisations in Norway: a democratic alternative to a bureaucratic welfare state?', *Voluntas*, 1(1): 62–76.*

Kuhnle, S. and Selle, P. (1992a) 'The historical precedent for government–nonprofit cooperation in Norway', in B. Gidron *et al.* (eds) *Government and the Third Sector*, San Francisco: Jossey-Bass, pp. 75–99.

Kuhnle, S. and Selle, P. (1992b) 'Governmental understanding of voluntary organisations: policy implications of conceptual change in post-war Norway', in S. Kuhnle and P. Selle (eds) *Government and Voluntary Organisations*, Aldershot: Avebury, pp. 157–84.

Olsen, B.C.R. (1993) 'Volunteering in Norway', in J. Davis Smith *Volunteering in Europe*, The Volunteer Centre UK, pp. 134–40.

Selle, P. (1993) 'Voluntary organisations and the welfare state: the case of Norway', *Voluntas*, 4(1): 1–15.

Sweden

Blennberger, E., Jeppsson-Grassman, E. and Svedberg, L. (1993) 'Volunteering in Sweden', in J. Davis Smith *Volunteering in Europe*, The Volunteer Centre UK, pp. 144–5.

Boli, J. (1991) 'Sweden: Is there a viable third sector?', in R. Wuthnow (ed.) *Between States and Markets*, Princeton, NJ: Princeton University Press. pp. 94–124.

Boli, J. (1992) 'The ties that bind: the nonprofit sector and the state in Sweden', in K.D. McCarthy *et al.* (eds) *The Nonprofit Sector in the Global Community*, San Francisco: Jossey-Bass for Independent Sector, pp. 240–3.

Pestoff, V. (1990) 'Nonprofit organisations and consumer policy: the Swedish model', in H.K. Anheier and W. Seibel (eds) *The Third Sector*, Berlin and New York: de Gruyter, pp. 77–92.

Finland

Hatunen, H. (1991) 'The role of voluntary social welfare organisations in Finnish society', Helsinki: Finnish Federation for Social Welfare.

Hemström, C. (1990) 'Law governing the associations, structures, legal systems', paper given at the *Conference on Non-governmental Organisations in a Democratic State*, Warsaw, 16–18 December 1990.

Austria

Badelt, C. (1989) 'Government versus private provision of social services: the case of Austria' in E. James (ed.) *The Nonprofit Sector on International Perspective*, New York: Oxford University Press, pp. 162–76. *

Badelt, C. (1992) 'Voluntary organisations in the welfare state: equity versus efficiency issues in institutional choice', paper given at the *Third International Conference on Research on Voluntary and Nonprofit Organisations*, Indiana University – Purdue University, Indianapolis, 11–13 March 1992.

Badelt, C. and Weiss, P. (1990), 'Non-profit, for-profit and government organisations in social service provision: comparision of behavioural patterns for Austria', *Voluntas*, 1(1): 77–96.*

Holzmann, A. (1993) 'Between welfare state and civil society: a case study on local community service centres in the Austrian province of Tyrol', paper given at the conference, *Well-being in Europe by Strengthening the Third Sector*, 27–9 May 1993, Barcelona.

Switzerland

Wagner, A. (1990) 'The nonprofit sector in Switzerland: taxonomy and dimensions', in H.K. Anheier and W. Seibel (eds) *The Third Sector*, Berlin and New York: de Gruyter, pp. 303–12.*

Wagner, A. (1992) 'The interrelationship between the public and the voluntary sectors in Switzerland: unmixing the mixed-up economy', in B. Gidron *et al.* (eds) *Government and the Third Sector*, San Francisco: Jossey-Bass, pp. 100–19.*

Wagner, A. (1993) 'The significance and function of welfare associations in Switzerland', paper given at the conference, *Well-being in Europe by Strengthening the Third Sector*, 27–9 May 1993, Barcelona. *

Central and Eastern Europe generally

Flaherty, S.L.Q. (1992) 'Philanthropy without borders: US foundation activity in Eastern Europe', *Voluntas*, 3(3): 335–50.

Ruzica, M. (1992) 'Transition, civil society, voluntary sector: focus on East Central Europe and Yugoslavia', paper given at the *Third International Conference on Research on Voluntary and Nonprofit Organisations*, Indiana University – Purdue University, Indianapolis, 11–13 March 1992.

Siegal, D. and Yancey, J. (1992) *The Rebirth of Civil Society: The Development of the Nonprofit Sector in East Central Europe and the Role of Western Assistance*, New York: Rockefeller Brothers Fund.

Hungary

Hegyesi, G. (1992) 'The revival of the non-profit sector in Hungary', in K.D. McCarthy *et al.* (eds) *The Nonprofit Sector in the Global Community*, San

Francisco: Jossey-Bass for Independent Sector, pp. 309–22.

Kuti, É. (1990) 'The possible role of the nonprofit sector in Hungary', *Voluntas*, 1(1): 26–41.

Kuti, É. (1992a) 'Scylla and Charybdis in the Hungarian nonprofit sector', in S. Kuhnle and P. Selle (eds) *Government and Voluntary Organisations*, Aldershot: Avebury, pp. 185–97.

Kuti, É. (1992b) 'Social, political and economic roles of the nonprofit sector in Hungary in the period of transition', paper given at the *Third International Conference on Research on Voluntary and Nonprofit Organisations*, Indiana University – Purdue University at Indianapolis, 11–13 March 1992.*

Marschall, M. (1990) 'The nonprofit sector in a centrally planned economy', in H.K. Anheier and W. Seibel (eds) *The Third Sector*, Berlin and New York: de Gruyter, pp. 277–92.*

Research Project on Hungarian Nonprofit Organisations (1992) 'Comment on Stephen M. Wunker, The promise of non-profits in Poland and Hungary: an analysis of third sector renaissance', *Voluntas*, 3(1): 89–98.

6, P. and Kuti, É. (1992) 'Into the European Community: impacts of future membership on Hungary's non-profit sector', *Journal of European Social Policy*, 3(4): 273–95; published in Hungarian as 6. P. and Kuti, É. (1993) 'A közös piac veszélyei és kihívásai a Magyar non-profit szektor számára' ('The challenges and dangers of the Common market for the Hungarian nonprofit sector'), *Közgazdasági Szemle*, XL(2): 110–24; and, abridged, as 6, P. (1992) 'Útban az Európai Közösség felé: a közös piaci tagság várható hatásai Magyarország non-profit szektorára', in Kuti, É. (ed.) (1992) *A nonprofit szektor Magyarországon: tanulmányok*, Budapest: Non-profit Kutatocsopsort, pp. 46–67; forthcoming in *Journal of European Social Policy*, November 1993.

Czech republic

Kostálová, K., Stein, R., Daniel, D. and Demes, P. (1993) 'Volunteering in the Czech and Slovak Republics' in J. Davis Smith *Volunteering in Europe*, The Volunteer Centre UK, pp. 105–11.

Poland

Kapiszewski, A. (1992) 'The independent sector in Poland: past and present', in K.D. McCarthy *et al.* (eds) *The Nonprofit Sector in the Global Community*, San Francisco: Jossey-Bass for Independent Sector, pp. 323–32.

Kietlinska, K. (1992a) 'The charities in Poland: an example of Church institutions: Caritas', paper given at the *Third International Conference on Research on Voluntary and Nonprofit Organisations*, Indiana University – Purdue University, Indianapolis, 11–13 March 1992.

Kietlinska, K. (1992b) 'Comment on Stephen M. Wunker, The promise of non-profits in Poland and Hungary: an analysis of third sector renaissance', *Voluntas*, 3(3): 365–75.

Kietlinska, K. (1993) 'Competition or cooperation between church and secular nonprofit organisations and the government', paper given at the conference, *Well-being in Europe by Strengthening the Third Sector*, 27–9 May 1993, Barcelona.

Wunker, S. (1991) 'The promise of non-profits in Poland and Hungary: an analysis of third sector renaissance', *Voluntas*, 2(2): 89–107.

Wygnanski, J. (1993) 'Volunteering in Poland', in J. Davis Smith *Volunteering in Europe*, The Volunteer Centre UK, pp. 112–16.

Romania

Cooperrider, D., Tolstobrach, N. and Young, D.R. (1992) 'The nonprofit sector in Romania', paper given at the *Third International Conference on Research on Voluntary and Nonprofit Organisations*, Indiana University – Purdue University, Indianapolis, 11–13 March 1992.

Johnson, A., Ourvan, L. and Young, D.R. (1993) 'The emergence of nongovernmental organisations in Romania', paper given at the conference, *Well-being in Europe by Strengthening the Third Sector*, 27–9 May 1993, Barcelona.

Bulgaria

Nikolov, S.E. (1992) 'The emerging nonprofit sector in Bulgaria', in K.D. McCarthy *et al.* (eds) *The Nonprofit Sector in the Global Community*, San Francisco: Jossey-Bass for Independent Sector, pp. 333–48.

Slovenia

Svetlik, I. (1992) 'The voluntary sector in a post-communist country: the case of Slovenia', in S. Kuhnle and P. Selle (eds) *Government and Voluntary Organisations*, Aldershot: Avebury, pp. 198–210.

Russia

Belyaeva, N. (1992) 'The independent sector in the USSR: formation, purposes, effects', in K.D. McCarthy *et al.* (eds) *The Nonprofit Sector in the Global Community*, San Francisco: Jossey-Bass for Independent Sector, pp. 349–71.

Brody, D.A. and Boris, E.T. (1992) 'Philanthropy and charity in the Soviet Union', in K.D. McCarthy *et al.* (eds) *The Nonprofit Sector in the Global Community*, San Francisco: Jossey-Bass for Independent Sector, pp. 372–84.

Gassler, R.S. (1991) 'Non-profit enterprise and Soviet economic reform', *Voluntas*, 2(1): 95–109.

Jakobsen, L. (1993) 'The emergence of the third sector in Russia', paper given at the conference, *Well-being in Europe by Strengthening the Third Sector*, 27–9 May 1993, Barcelona.

Khodekhina, I. (1993) 'Volunteering in Russia', in J. Davis Smith *Volunteering in Europe*, The Volunteer Centre UK, pp. 141–3.

Lithuania

Martinaiyte, E. (1993) 'The role of non-profit and non-government organisations of Lithuania in unstable environmental conditions', paper given at the conference, *Well-being in Europe by Strengthening the Third Sector*, 27–9 May 1993, Barcelona.

7 Funding matters
Diana Leat

INTRODUCTION

A number of general features of voluntary sector income can be identified, namely that income is unevenly distributed between organisations, that different industries or subsectors command different proportions of total sector income, and that organisations within the same size band may derive their income from different sources. The popular notion that voluntary sector income comes from voluntary sources – such as fundraising from the general public – does not accord with reality. A significant proportion of income, especially for larger organisations, comes from the state and from the sale of goods and services, with a wide variation between organisations even within the same size band.

Size, sources and types of funding raise a number of issues for individual organisations and for the sector as a whole. These issues will differ between organisations with different structures, values, sources and mixes of funding. These resource issues will be examined in this chapter. First, however, it is necessary to look briefly at the policy context within which voluntary agencies operate.

THE POLICY CONTEXT

Analysis of current and past sources of voluntary sector funding may be a poor guide to the future. In the 1990s the voluntary sector is embarking upon a major new phase in its history. Perhaps most significantly, its relationship with the state is changing and is likely to change further in the rest of this decade. Some aspects of this wider policy context have already been discussed in Nicholas Deakin's chapter. Here I shall deal only with those aspects of the policy context which will have an influence on the funding of voluntary organisations.

The wider policy context may affect the resourcing of voluntary organisations in three main ways. First, it may directly or indirectly increase demands upon voluntary organisations. Increased demand is likely to create pressures either for more resources to meet demand or for ways of containing or reducing demand by, for example, tighter eligibility criteria or a narrower definition of goals. In addition, organisations facing an increase in demand for their services, but without more resources, may try to find ways of doing more with the same amount of income, for example by introducing new, tighter forms of financial management or by drawing on reserves.

Second, the wider policy context may reduce the financial or labour resources available to voluntary organisations. If this should occur alongside an increase in demand on voluntary organisations this will double the pressure on organisations as they attempt to do more with less or find their efforts to secure extra resources thwarted.

Third, wider policies may increase the resources available to voluntary organisations, either overall or for particular areas of work or under certain conditions. These policies may present some, but not necessarily all, voluntary organisations with the prospect of increased resources but, depending on the conditions attached, they may also significantly affect the organisations' activities and their style and structure.

Increasing demand: changes in benefits to individuals

Various changes in the benefit system have been made in recent years. Social Fund loans have replaced grants for clothing, furniture and other equipment for some of the poorest in society. Income support has been withdrawn from most 16–17-year-olds. Board and lodging payments have been replaced by basic income support and housing benefit. In addition, many benefits, including those for residential care, have been frozen or at best have not kept pace with rising costs. More recently, the allocation of benefits for residential care has been transferred from central government to local authorities. The voluntary and private sectors are now expected to provide the bulk of residential (and domiciliary) care on contract to local authorities.

These changes in the benefit system have a double effect on voluntary organisations. First, they increase demand on organisations as people previously provided for by the state turn to voluntary organisations for support or to top up no longer adequate levels of benefit. Second, they reduce the level of income some organisations derive from providing, for example, accommodation and help to the young homeless or the elderly in residential care. In addition, changes in the benefit system inevitably create administrative and financial problems, not only for recipients but also for those voluntary organisations for whom they are a major source of income (Leat 1993a).

Reducing resources

Successive Conservative administrations have emphasised their commitment to encouraging the voluntary sector to stand on its own feet. The aim has been to wean voluntary organisations off dependence on statutory grant aid and to encourage funding from other sources:

Such a philosophy assumes that support of the voluntary sector is seen as very much a concern of the community at large rather than a primary concern of government via the traditional grant-making process. Responsibility for voluntary sector support is now laid firmly at the door of both commercial organisations and individual private givers.

(Wilson 1989: 63)

In reality this approach has had limited success, not least because government support to the sector has continued to rise (Hazel 1991), although in real terms central government support for the voluntary sector has increased relatively little.

More significant has been the loss in funding the voluntary sector has experienced from the demise of the Manpower Services Commission and the reduction in funding from the Urban Programme. In addition, there have been cuts in local authority expenditure on the voluntary sector. These have varied between areas and their effects in particular localities are somewhat concealed in aggregate data showing overall local authority support. More generally, spending limits on central government departments and in local authorities have meant that many voluntary organisations have experienced a real cut in the value of their resources from statutory sources.

Some increases in funding from government have had a nasty habit of turning into reductions in a relatively short period of time. In recent years several government departments have favoured short-term demonstration projects designed to stimulate, innovate and demonstrate. The assumption is that, once they have stimulated new voluntary sector activity, someone else will come forward to pick up the longer-term bill. In some cases this assumption is justified, in others it is not and a significant proportion of voluntary projects fail to survive (Hills 1991; Haffenden 1991; Mocroft and Doyle 1991).

Other reductions in resources have been even less direct. For example, some unemployment benefit offices have actively applied the requirement that recipients should be able to show that they are 'actively seeking work' and have queried whether undertaking, say, twenty hours of voluntary work is compatible with this requirement (Leat 1993c). In some areas and for some types of organisation this may effectively have reduced the availability of volunteers.

Reductions in resources must, of course, be set in the context of economic recession which affects voluntary, statutory and commercial organisations alike (CAF 1993).

Increases in funds – and conditions

Of perhaps greater importance than the reduction in resources available from government have been the increasing conditions attached to government grant aid. In the field of housing, for example, there have been increases in available resources but at the same time housing associations have been expected to raise more money from rents and to compete on equal terms in the finance market. As a result, some fear that they will be forced to compromise their mission to provide housing for the least well-off (Leat 1989b; Taylor 1991).

More generally, the Government Efficiency Scrutiny of funding of voluntary organisations has raised questions about:

> The diversity of organisations funded in particular fields and the need for rationalisation and better targeting. The Voluntary Services Unit at the Home Office has reviewed its funding to national intermediary bodies and expressed concern about duplication. Government departments are looking for more control over the management of the organisations they fund.
>
> (Taylor 1991: 28; see also Wolch 1990)

The watchwords of current government policy on funding the voluntary sector are efficiency and value-for-money – the problem is that these are concepts which the voluntary sector might define rather differently from government. Furthermore, the government's new emphasis on short-term, targeted innovative/demonstration funding duplicates the preferences and policies of many trusts and corporate givers but leaves a yawning gap in on-going funding. As a result many voluntary organisations may be forced constantly to re-package their activities as new and innovative in order to secure yet another dose of short-term funding.

SOURCES OF FUNDING AND THEIR IMPLICATIONS

Voluntary organisations are funded on different terms (e.g. for services rendered and for grant aid) and from different sources. There is a view that much of how an organisation is structured and behaves is determined by its resource dependencies:

> Resource dependence theory argues, organisations are not capable of internally generating all the resources and services they require to survive. Consequently, they engage in transactions with parties in the external environment to satisfy unfulfilled needs. Dependencies, sometimes problematic, are often created as a result of this process. These dependencies, in turn, can influence the organisation's goals, structures and the decision-making of its executives.
>
> (Romo 1993: 30; see also Aldrich and Pfeffer 1976;
> Pfeffer and Salanick 1978)

It has been suggested that heterogeneity of resource dependencies creates uncertainty for organisations which they may attempt to deal with by the establishment and use of boundary-spanning roles. These boundary-spanning roles – performed by such people as development officers, fundraisers, media officers and so on – channel information into and out of the organisation, ensuring effective transactions between the organisation and its environment (Bielefeld 1992).

Institutional theory challenges some of the assumptions and assertions of resource dependency theory, though the former is newer and less well-developed than the latter. Institutional theory sees organisations operating in environments which may be non-institutionalised or institutionalised. Non-institutionalised environments are 'characterised by rational calculi and emergent structures based on not-yet shared definitions and meanings'. Institutionalised situations are characterised by 'a stable structure of inter-action and definition of the situation, not necessarily based on rational or instrumental considerations' (Bielefeld 1992: 52).

Many voluntary organisations operate in environments where technologies are not well understood, where efficiency and effectiveness are difficult to define and measure or are considered less important than other values, but in which there are institutionalised views of what non-profit organisations should look like and how they should behave. In order to maintain credibility and legitimacy, and to secure resources, organisations need to fulfil these institutionalised expectations:

> Institutional theory, therefore, is more concerned with how and why meanings, forms and procedures come to be taken for granted and what the consequences of this are. Attention is focused on political and normative arenas and the quest for legitimacy.
>
> (Bielefeld 1992: 52)

Whereas resource dependency theory sees organisations as engaging in specific strategies related to resource flows, institutional theory suggests that organisations will engage in more general activities designed to enhance their reputations as reliable and effective fund recipients. For example, it has been argued that the 'enterprise culture' and the growth of managerialism has had a greater effect on what is expected of voluntary organisations than changes related to resource dependencies (Wilson 1992; Kramer 1992).

A detailed exposition and critique of institutional and resource dependency theories is beyond the scope of this chapter. However, it should be noted that neither theory, taken alone and applied to all organisations in all environments, is entirely satisfactory (Powell 1991; Scott 1991; Bielefeld 1992).

In what follows I shall consider some implications of, and issues raised by, different types and sources of funding. The suggestion is not that particular sources and types of funding necessarily imply certain effects on recipient organisations, nor that resource dependencies are the only influences within organisations. The assumption is simply that, in general and other things being equal (which of course they never are), certain issues are likely to be raised by receipt of certain types and sources of funding. These issues are related to types and sources of funding but they, and the organisation's responses to them, are also shaped and constrained by the organisation's political and normative environments.

INCOME FROM FEES AND CHARGES

Distribution of income from fees and charges

The voluntary sector as a whole is heavily dependent upon fees and charges as a source of income. But this is not true for all parts of the sector. Housing associations, educational, arts and cultural charities commanded 98 per cent of the sector's total income from fees and charges in 1985 (Posnett 1987). For the vast majority of voluntary organisations fees and charges probably represent only a tiny fraction of their total income, and many organisations receive nothing from this source.

A small local study undertaken by the Charities Aid Foundation found that arts organisations, housing associations, organisations providing education and residential care for children and adults, organisations providing transport services and various forms of training and consultancy are more likely than other organisations to generate income from fees and charges (Leat 1989a). The study also suggested that it is important not merely to distinguish between types of organisation but to disaggregate income *within* organisations. A particular area of work may be totally dependent upon fees and charges but the organisation as a whole may derive little income from this source.

The trend towards fees and charges

Income from fees and charges appears to be growing largely as a result of the broader changes in social policy outlined above. There are three main factors encouraging the trend towards charging by voluntary organisations. First, there are needs-led factors – the need for additional income to cover rising costs, new demands and developments, or to replace funding lost from other sources. Second, there are funder demand-led factors – the move away from general grants towards payments for carefully specified outputs. Contracting by social services departments is one example of this type and is discussed in more detail below. Third, there are factors to do with changing structures and social values – for example, the entry of commercial players into the social care market and, more generally, the notion that everything has a price (Leat 1989a, 1989b).

Problems of definition

The definition of income from fees and charges is surrounded by ambiguity and confusion. In particular, there is a large grey area in which income from fees and charges shades into grants and vice versa. Some part of the growth in fees and charges may be semantic:

The definition of 'grant' and 'agency payment' varied across authorities. One reason given for no use of grant aid but heavy use of agency and per capita fees by one authority was simply that grants had to go to the committee for a decision, thereby raising the political temperature, but agency payments could be approved by the directorate(!)

(Mocroft 1989: 81)

If the trends towards transformation of grants into agency payments were nothing more than semantic then it would be interesting but of itself of little consequence. What matters is not what funding is called but its terms and conditions and the relationships it entails.

Constraints on income from fees and charges

Is income from fees and charges an option for all voluntary organisations? The ability to generate income from fees and charges depends upon having something to sell that customers can afford to buy. 'Saleable' items within the voluntary sector include: membership, information and advice, training and consultancy, charges for use of facilities and capital resources by other organisations, administration, management and direct service provision to individuals. In general, the ability to generate fee income requires specialist expertise or capital resources, or both. Possession of these saleable resources is not evenly distributed throughout the sector. Thus, any move towards dependence upon fees and charges as a major source of income will significantly disadvantage some organisations with nothing to sell.

Generation of fee income in the voluntary sector is further restricted by the fact that ability to pay and need are central considerations for many charities. If people or organisations are not prepared, or cannot afford, to pay there is no market – no sale. Many of the people charities exist to serve cannot afford to pay and there is no organisation prepared to pay for them. Indeed, many charities exist precisely to provide services for those groups for which there is no commercial or statutory sector provision. Many charities, if they are to fulfil their objectives, must ensure that their services are available to certain groups regardless of their ability to pay. Prices must be set at levels which are affordable and certain services must be provided regardless of the recipient's ability to pay.

Some of the income charities derive from fees and charges is provided not by the consumer but by a third party – government, for example – funding purchase of goods and services for those who cannot afford to pay. The way in which organisations price goods and services, and the degree of control they have over pricing are inseparable from the question 'who pays?'. Some services will have to be provided free of charge because the recipient cannot afford to pay and no-one is prepared to pay for them. Other services will be provided, to those who cannot afford to pay, for a fee provided by a third party purchaser – but this fee may be set by the purchaser and may bear little relation to the real costs of provision. Yet other services will be provided to those who can afford to pay at a price equal to, or above, the real costs to the voluntary organisation.

Thus charges are more likely and are likely to be higher where a third-party customer is willing to pay and where customer-recipients are among the least needy and can afford to meet the cost directly. Charges may also exist among organisations which provide a mix of goods and services because charges on one service will generate a surplus for subsidy of other services within the organisation.

Greater reliance on fees and charges as a source of income raises a number of issues for individual voluntary organisations and for the sector in general.

Income from fees and charges: issues and implications

The move from grant aid to contract funding, with the tighter specification of what is paid for, is likely to affect the availability of core funding and the structure, management and control of the organisation. The loss of loosely specified funding may reduce the organisation's scope for creative risk-taking and innovation. Funding and activity may be concentrated on producing specified, predetermined outputs and there may be little time or money for anything else.

Where organisations are dependent upon fees paid by a third-party customer at a price determined by the customer, voluntary organisations may find themselves on the receiving end of changes and trade-offs which have nothing to do with the sector *per se*. For example, changes in benefit levels or eligibility may reduce the amount of money voluntary organisations raise in fees and charges.

Dependence upon fees and charges as a source of income may encourage voluntary organisations to concentrate their services on those who can afford to pay, or to redirect their activities towards those which are more saleable and capable of generating higher levels of fee income. Activities and recipient groups which do not produce fee income may be neglected or dropped altogether. And in relationships with others:

> When asked to join a co-ordinating or planning meeting, a voluntary organisation's first thought will no longer be concerned with the opportunity it presents to work with others, but with who will pay.
>
> (Taylor 1991: 46)

More subtly, increased dependence upon fees and charges may discourage organisations from sharing resources and skills as they compete with each other for customers. Fees and charges may increase the costs of organisations. There will be increased administrative and transaction costs and services previously provided free by others may now have to be paid for:

> Fees and charges do not reduce costs they merely move around the

responsibility for meeting them. And some costs may move full circle to end up back in the in-tray of those who instigated the initial move.

(Leat 1989b: 31)

The effects of charging on volunteer support and charitable giving also require consideration. Will volunteers and donors be prepared to give their time and money when the organisation is charging for its services? If voluntary organisations lost the subsidy of volunteers and donations their cost advantage over statutory and commercially provided services could disappear.

Dependence upon fees and charges is also likely to affect the way in which the work of voluntary organisations is monitored. Fees and charges, as opposed to grants, necessarily imply some return to the customer or purchaser. But, as James points out:

One problem is that quantity can be more easily monitored than quality. Fee finance then risks the danger that quality will be disregarded in favour of quantity. If quantity and quality can be monitored, then it seems we could rely on for-profits as well as non-profits, so there is no need of special treatment of 'charities'.

(James 1989: 71; see also Weisbrod 1988; Ware 1989)

As organisations spend more time on people or activities capable of generating income from fees and charges, they may jeopardise their charitable mission and ultimately their charitable status. Loss of charitable status would entail loss of the tax advantages which go with that status. 'If charities rely more on fee-finance they will be doing things that for-profits could do – and may incur hostility of for-profits for "unfair competition" due to tax advantages, as in the USA' (James 1989: 71; see also Rose-Ackerman 1990).

TRADING

A growing number of larger charities derive some part of their income from trading. Trading by charities raises complex legal issues but there are a variety of ways in which charities may legally receive, directly and indirectly, income from trading.

One important and growing form of trading is the charity shop. Charity shops contributed only around 3 per cent of the income of the top 400 charities in 1991. But this aggregate figure conceals wide variation between charities in income derived from shops. Oxfam, for example, has an estimated net income of £21 million per annum from its shops and this constitutes 45 per cent of its voluntary income. Preliminary research on charity shops suggests that running a successful operation (i.e. one which brings a maximum net income) requires careful planning, management and the right mix and location of staff and volunteers. Successful operation appears to be 'characterised by strong central direction and regional bases, combined with devolvement to, and consultation with, the local level' (St Leger 1993: 49). One advantage of income from trading may be that it is free from strings and dependencies, but the above analysis suggests that a successful operation requires management skills and time as well as particular organisational arrangements. In other words, income from trading is neither cost free nor free of structural implications.

CONTRACTING WITH LOCAL AUTHORITIES

Contracting is in one sense a necessary part of generating income from fees and charges. Fees and charges imply a contractual relationship between purchaser and recipient. In this context, however, the term 'contracting' usually refers to the provision of goods and services by a voluntary organisation under contract to a local authority. The move away from grants to more closely specified contracts has occurred in a number of fields of provision of which one of the most important for the voluntary sector is residential and domiciliary care.

The voluntary sector has been involved in the provision of residential care for centuries but in the last decade its share of the market for residential care has declined, largely due to the entry of the for-profit sector into the residential care market (Parker 1990; Forder and Knapp 1993). It is not altogether clear why voluntary sector residential care did not expand in the 1980s on the same scale as private sector care. Contributory reasons may have been the costs of residential care expansion, the voluntary sector's restricted access to capital and the decision-making structures of some organisations. Another reason may have been its commitment to community, as opposed to residential, care (Parker 1990).

Under the NHS and Community Care Act residential care is supposed to decline, with domiciliary care becoming the preferred option. Although, in theory, the voluntary sector is committed to provision of domiciliary care, it is not clear that such provision is very well developed in the sector. Before looking at the implications of contracting for social care provision it is important to highlight some of the changes brought about by the NHS and Community Care Act.

First, control of a large part of the fee income earned by voluntary social care organisations is now returned to local authorities. Second, contracting by local authorities requires competition between voluntary, statutory and for-profit organisations; competition between suppliers is intended to increase choice and give purchasers the ability to drive hard bargains, thus promoting better value-for-money. Third, one of the main aims of the Act is to increase consumer choice but, because of lack of resources and the costs of choice, this is likely to be a long-term goal, at best. Fourth, the resources available to local authorities are, many argue, inadequate and it is likely that this will mean more targeting and tighter eligibility criteria for receipt of services. In addition, local authorities will be encouraged to charge for services provided.

Evidence to date suggests that many local authorities are reluctant to contract out social care (Wistow *et al.* 1992). Local authorities are, however, required to spend 85 per cent of the money transferred to them in the voluntary and private sectors and there is evidence that many would prefer to work with the voluntary, rather than the private sector (Wistow *et al.* 1992).

Implications of contracting for voluntary organisations

At present we do not know what the real effects of contracting will be. The following points are largely informed speculation.

Financial uncertainties

The first implication of contracting is that many voluntary organisations will have to learn to live with financial uncertainty. At one level financial uncertainty for suppliers is built into the contracting process via the emphasis on competition and flexibility for purchasers. This may present problems for both large and small voluntary organisations. Small organisations live on a shoe-string and may be unable to survive with uncertainty. Large voluntary organisations may also have difficulties coping with uncertainty in so far as the stakes are higher for them and their more bureaucratic and formal planning systems may make it more difficult for them to switch to other activities. On the other hand, larger voluntary organisations may have other sources of funding, and reserves to fall back on to keep them going through the early stages and to cover start-up costs and low periods.

Financial uncertainty may be increased by concerns about the size of the market. Residential care markets may contract due to the 'new' emphasis on domiciliary care. Alternatively, or additionally, local authorities may decide to purchase from other types of organisation. If this happens, voluntary organisations providing residential care will have two broad choices. One will be to diversify into other areas (e.g. domiciliary care). The other will be to serve privately funded clients. This could then create the dilemmas and knock-on effects noted above, when ability to pay becomes more important than need.

But the size of the market from the viewpoint of any one supplier is not merely a matter of total demand. It is also a matter of the number of voluntary or private competitors within the market. Will there be enough business for financial viability and for how many organisations? The more energetic and successful the local authority is in stimulating voluntary and private sector suppliers the greater these uncertainties will be, especially if total demand remains uncertain.

Further uncertainty may stem from lack of clarity regarding costs to be covered and contract terms. Davies and Edwards' account of twelve contracts with voluntary organisations highlights some of these uncertainties concerning costs and terms (Davies and Edwards 1990). For example, who will cover infrastructure costs, who will meet rising costs due to higher standards, regulation, inflation, pay rises and more demanding or deteriorating clients?

Several of the examples presented by Davies and Edwards illustrate the compromises voluntary organisations have had to make given the money on offer from the local authority. In one case (an organisation of and for Asian women), the contract included no money to pay volunteers' expenses and required a cut in staff salaries – both accepted by the organisation in the face of closure. One commentator has argued:

> Contracts, particularly with voluntary organisations, provide purchasers with a mechanism for reducing costs, while appearing to maintain services. In the USA, voluntary sector salaries have been depressed by between 15 and 20 per cent and charitable funds are being used to substitute for government funding.
>
> (Gutch 1993: v)

In another case an organisation accepted a 4 per cent agency fee, only later realising that 10 per cent would have been more realistic. Even when the project subsequently recouped £50,000 in benefits for the authority, its request for funding for an extra worker to manage the larger number of staff and growing workload was refused (Davies and Edwards 1990).

The type of contract adopted by the purchaser will affect the degree of financial uncertainty for the voluntary organisation supplier. Longer-term, block contracts will provide more certainty than spot contracts, but may also reduce flexibility for the purchaser and consumer and discourage voluntary organisations from entering the market (see below). Fixed-price contracts may be attractive to purchasers but less attractive to voluntary organisations unless they can secure a premium (over expected costs) to cover the risk of rising costs. Cost-plus contracts may be more attractive to suppliers but much will obviously depend on the definition of costs and the size of the 'plus'.

Evidence to date suggests that some voluntary organisations will lose money from contracting if the direct and indirect effects of transaction costs are taken into account. Hedley and Rochester suggest that in the Crossroads schemes studied the amount of time and energy required to secure a relatively small contract was high; at the same time, the double pressure of the contractual process and the work involved in fulfilling the contract reduced the time available for fundraising (Hedley and Rochester 1992). Similarly, Davies and Edwards highlight the work required from organisations if they are to secure a contract. One contract went through six drafts and took the better part of a year to finalise.

Mocroft and Thomason draw parallels between local authority contracting and the Opportunities for Volunteering Scheme which has a strict 5 per cent limit for administration. National agents in the scheme complained that this figure barely covered paperwork and office costs, and did not cover the cost of managing and supporting small, local projects. They comment:

There is a tendency for specification to concentrate on the immediate, identifiable cost of a service without any element for supporting the organisation as a whole. In the UK the voluntary sector has not had the experience of identifying and loading all costs into a service agreement, while the single local authority has the power of the monopsonist to resist this should it happen.

(Mocroft and Thomason 1993: 107)

In the United States the real costs of contracting and the effects on the voluntary sector are increasingly an important issue; some argue that 'contracting is bleeding the sector dry' (quoted in Gutch 1992).

For some larger voluntary organisations these uncertainties may be off-set by varying degrees of 'organisational slack' which enable them to cover uncertainties with funds from other sources or from reserves. Substantial reserves may also enable voluntary organisations to subsidise costs, keeping the price to the local authority purchaser low and under-cutting potential voluntary and private sector competitors (Tuckman and Chang 1993). But running reserves too low, even in a good cause, is not a sensible policy for any organisation, especially in a competitive and uncertain market.

Voluntary organisations may face other financial uncertainties. What, for example, will be the effect of contracting on the willingness of volunteers to contribute their labour for nothing, and on the willingness of the general public, trusts and corporate donors to contribute money to the organisation's activities? Will both volunteers and donors come to see their gifts as indirectly subsidising local authorities? Evidence from the US suggests that the effect on donors will vary depending on the type of spending and area of activity (Knapp and Kendall 1991). Evidence in Britain is sparse, but one study has suggested that 'the insignificance of government grants. . .in explaining differences in donations offers no support for crowding out' (Posnett and Sandler 1988).

The question here, however, is somewhat different from that relating to government grants in that it concerns the perceived subsidy to services purchased by local authorities. In addition, it is important to consider whether volunteers will be prepared to commit themselves to, or be seen as suitable for, the demands of contractual tasks in more regulated, bureaucratic organisations (Leat 1989b, 1992). Again the question here is different from that of the effect of government spending on volunteering (on the latter question see, for example, Weisbrod 1988; Menchik and Weisbrod 1987; James 1989). Quite apart from any government spending effect, the growth of contracting may change what is required of the volunteer, making the volunteer 'arrangement' inadequate for some tasks and reducing the attractions of volunteering. Volunteer-using providers also need to take into account the high costs of insurance not only for people and property but also for legal costs and liabilities.

Market risks

All voluntary organisations will face costs, and risk, in entering the market. Large and small voluntary organisations will incur direct and opportunity costs in the time spent in planning and negotiating within the organisation and with purchasers, as well as in acquiring the information and developing the skills to engage in those activities. Lack of information, understanding and skills is likely to be an obstacle to greater involvement for many organisations. For larger organisations and those which are part of a wider network these deficiencies are likely to be less of a barrier than for smaller or isolated organisations. Organisations will also incur costs in buying in specialist skills such as those required for pricing and for legal matters. For larger organisations and those which are part of a wider network these costs of entry into the market may be lower than for more isolated organisations. The risk, of course, is that these costs will not bear dividends in successfully securing a contract.

One of the difficulties in increasing the range of suppliers in any market is that choice of suppliers requires trust on the part of purchasers and trust is established by a proven track record. New entrants therefore face a double problem: they need to enter the market to establish a track record and engender trust but at the same time they need some guarantees of business before it is worthwhile incurring the costs of entry. Trust is likely to be an especially important factor in the award of social care contracts (Wistow *et al*. 1992; Common and Flynn 1992; on the importance of trust more generally in relation to the role of the voluntary sector see, for example, Weisbrod 1988). The significance attached to trust will favour voluntary over private sector providers but it may also advantage voluntary organisations with an already established relationship with the local authority over newer, lesser-known organisations (Forder and Knapp 1993). Trust, combined with trans-action costs, makes it likely that those organisations which secure contracts early on will keep them, thus reducing the chances of new entrants.

Entry costs and risk will also be affected by the types of contract adopted. Longer-term, block contracts with larger or established organisations will obviously go some way towards reducing financial uncertainty for those who secure them but will do little to encourage entry of new suppliers. Indeed, block contracts, attractive to local authorities not least as a means of reducing transaction costs, may lead to the collapse of smaller agencies often providing more flexible and specialised services, as well as organisations catering for particular client groups. Given that catering for particular groups is one of the characteristics of the voluntary sector, this may make it difficult for many organisations, large and small, to secure contracts without changing their fundamental goals (Smith 1992; Forder and Knapp 1993).

Spot contracts may appear more encouraging to voluntary organisations wanting to secure a contract for the first time. In reality, however, spot contracts may do little to encourage new entrants because such organisations are unlikely to have access to start-up money and unlikely to have the reserves to bear uncertainty and losses while they become established.

Regulation

Voluntary organisations will have to consider the effects of contracting on the regulation of care and organisational practice in the provision of care. Some organisations may fear the effects of current, and future, regulation.

The Joint Advisory Group of Domiciliary Care Associations has issued guidelines for the registration of domiciliary care agencies. The guidelines are stringent and apply to all agencies running services which provide personal care and practical support to vulnerable people living in their own homes (JAGDCA 1993). The issues now emerging from the Warner inquiry into the staffing of children's homes may prompt local authority social service departments to take a closer look at the regulation of both residential and domiciliary care provision for all groups by private and voluntary agencies, especially those which do not directly employ staff (Marchant 1993; Leat 1993c). If voluntary organisations supplying care on contract were forced to employ directly all of those providing care this would entail significant legal, financial and administrative responsibilities. Many small voluntary organisations might collapse, or choose to leave the market.

With or without greater regulation or registration, all organisations involved in contracting are likely to incur greater costs in the form of increased paperwork reporting requirements. As Gutch (1993) reports in the United States, these reporting requirements may be considerable. One American commentator has graphically described the 'game' in which voluntary organisations and funders try to outwit each other in monitoring and accountability requirements (Bernstein 1991).

The administrative costs of contracting, as well as the need for more highly qualified staff to meet the required standards may increase bureaucracy and professionalisation in voluntary organisations. This may have various effects. First, greater bureaucracy and professionalisation may further increase costs, possibly to a point at which voluntary organisations lose their cost advantage relative to for-profit suppliers (Forder and Knapp 1993). Second, greater bureaucracy and professionalisation may change the composition, management style and ethos of the organisation. Volunteer involvement and the participative, flexible organisational practices, providing a high degree of personal autonomy valued by staff and volunteers, may be eroded. This in turn may have effects on the ability of voluntary organisations to recruit volunteers and paid staff at current salary levels. Another cost of contracting, inherent in contract regulation/compliance, will be greater legal liability, greater risk of legal action and higher insurance costs to cover these.

Contracting and charitable mission

Contracting generally requires the supply of services to persons or groups designated by the local authority purchaser. Voluntary organisations will want to exercise some control over the selection of clients if only for cost purposes. In addition, voluntary organisations registered as charities will need to ensure that those they serve fit their charitable mission. As noted above, some voluntary organisations exist to serve particular groups of persons which may be very different from those likely to be the focus of local authority concern. Thus, some charities may be constrained in their involvement in contracting not merely by organisational preferences but by legal barriers stemming from their charitable deeds.

The likely growing need for rationing, due to inadequate resources for social care, may complicate matters further for some voluntary organisations. If the new arrangements lead to provision of service for some and withdrawal from others, should a voluntary organisation purporting to serve all in a specified group become involved in contracting or should it rather concentrate its efforts on those who are excluded? Historically the role of charities has been to help those who fall through the state safety-net. As pressure on local authority resources increases, eligibility criteria are likely to become more tightly drawn. This not only raises issues about client vulnerability and thus costs for the supplier, but also heightens the moral dilemmas for charities. How will voluntary organisations meet the needs of increasing numbers of people ineligible for statutory help?

There will also be issues of self-interest. If voluntary organisations become the major providers of services will they have laid at their door the failures previously laid at the door of the local authority? These may include failure to provide for some, as well as inadequacies and mistakes in service provision. If this happens, what would be the effects on the reputation of the voluntary sector and on the public's willingness to give time and money?

The Association of Metropolitan Authorities has recommended that 'contracts for social care should allow voluntary organisations to supplement/extend service provision under the contract by obtaining funding from other sources (subject to consultation with the local authority)' (AMA 1990: 19). The 'other sources' in one contract described by Davies and Edwards were charges (Davies and Edwards 1990). But for many charities charging is simply not an option they are prepared to consider given that this would in effect deny a service to those who need it most. Some voluntary organisations not only refuse to consider charging themselves but are also opposed to charging by local authorities. Will charities be prepared to collaborate with local authorities in supplying contracted services for which charges are made? Some voluntary organisations may feel unable on principle to enter into contracts which involve charging; others may be prepared to do so if they are not directly implicated in charging, e.g. by responsibility for collecting charges from consumers.

Contracting and independence

Some voluntary organisations fear that involvement in local authority purchased provision will, via regulation or financial dependence, compromise their position of independence from the state. Whether all voluntary organisations are currently 'independent' of the state, what 'independence' means, and whether for some there is any real alternative to some sort of dependence on local authority funding, are debatable issues – but the fear of loss of independence may nevertheless be an important consideration in contracting.

Some voluntary organisations will be reluctant to give up control over selection of users and (non) charging policies. Voluntary and private organisations may also fear intervention in staffing and wider management practices. 'Coercive isomorphism' may occur:

> Voluntary organisations' working methods and service delivery patterns are so tightly constrained by the terms of their contracts, and local authorities are so anxious about the dangers of service failure, that voluntary sector providers increasingly come to resemble their funders.
>
> (Forder and Knapp 1993)

The AMA guidance to local authorities states that the local authority should set out clear requirements in relation to staff recruitment, qualifications, experience, use of agency and part-time staff and volunteers. However, the guidance warns that local authorities 'should be careful to avoid over prescription and should not, in most cases, be involved directly in staff recruitment. The local authority should, however, reserve the right to approve significant management appointments' (AMA 1990: 20).

The AMA document goes on to point out that all public supply contracts, including those for social care, are subject to the requirements of Part II of the Local Government Act 1988. Although this stipulates that local authorities may not specify non-commercial considerations in contracts, the local authority must be confident that a voluntary organisation is able to provide the services required in an acceptable fashion and has the managerial, financial and staffing resources required to maintain standards. Local authorities may therefore want to take into account the following considerations: staff qualifications and experience; ability to recruit and retain staff; use of part-time staff and volunteers; management track record (including senior management CVs); suitability to work with children or elderly people; past health and safety record; genuine occupational qualifications (e.g. requiring black and minority ethnic staff in day centres for black and minority elders); financial standing; ability to meet the terms of the contract; previous contract performance; understanding of relevant legislation (AMA 1990). Interestingly, the AMA document also states:

> It is important that local authorities should not opt for detailed involvement in matters of operational detail on the basis of concern about how the organisation would act if left alone. *If an organisation cannot be trusted in relation to such matters, it is questionable whether local authorities should be contracting with it.*
>
> (AMA 1990; emphasis added)

Again, the importance of trust, a critical concept in theories of the voluntary sector's *raison d' être*, arises (see, for example, Hansmann 1987).

Contracting may affect the independence of voluntary organisations in more subtle ways:

> The actual process of specification in writing can have a subtle effect: instead of affecting autonomy and independence directly, it may promote a preference for easily achievable change rather than long-term or risky innovation. It may promote change and activities which will earn fees and subsidy now rather than a change which will require the employment of, for example, a development officer.
>
> (Mocroft and Thomason 1993: 105)

There is some debate as to how real a threat increased dependence on statutory funding poses to voluntary organisation independence and autonomy. Kramer has suggested that the threat may be exaggerated. In practice, Kramer argues, the form and purpose of funding emphasises the mutual interdependency of the parties; and the costs of monitoring and control by statutory funders are too great, both fiscally and politically. Furthermore, the term 'statutory funding' conceals a multiplicity of allocating bodies, thus reducing dependence on any one source (Kramer 1990). Similarly, Forder and Knapp conclude that, in reality, the interdependencies between voluntary organisation suppliers and local authority purchasers will mean that 'the scope for coercive isomorphism is not so much limited, but perhaps of relatively little value to the local authority' (Forder and Knapp 1993: 139; see also Brager and Holloway 1978; Kramer and Grossman 1987; Kramer 1990; Salamon 1987; Ware 1989; Gutch and Young 1989; Saidel 1989).

Despite the doubts about real threats to independence, some voluntary organisations may choose not to become involved in contracts. The notion that:

> Voluntary organisations exist solely to provide services and are simply one of a number of potential providers waiting in the wings of a pluralistic market . . . is a gross and dangerous over-simplification. However, we have an important role in influencing the purchasers, identifying needs, ensuring sensitive assessment procedures, helping draw up specifications, monitoring provision, and influencing future plans.
>
> (Gutch 1993: iv)

This approach will be crucial to the future role of the voluntary sector and the welfare of those voluntary organisations represent. But it may be an option open only to organisations of a size or nature which enables them to attract funding from other sources.

FUNDING FROM THE CORPORATE SECTOR

At present corporate giving provides only a small proportion of total sector income, but it is nevertheless an important source for some, especially larger, organisations in certain fields. It was suggested above that government would like to encourage a much higher level of corporate giving. To what extent may voluntary organisations look to funding from the corporate sector, and what might be the effects of dependence upon this source of income?

It is generally agreed that business priorities in community investment are the priorities of business, not necessarily those of government or the voluntary sector (Saxon-Harrold 1991; Fogarty 1992). The precise nature of these priorities is unclear and 70 per cent of companies have no written policies (Fogarty 1992; Fogarty and Christie 1990).

We know, however, that overall, whether as a result of *ad hoc*ery or implicit policies, the largest beneficiaries of company giving are education, medicine and health; general welfare and the arts are the only other two categories receiving more than £3 million in 1990/1 (Saxon-Harrold 1991). It is possible that these aggregate figures conceal important differences between subsectors. For example, in the United States there are significant differences between banks and chemical firms in the direction of their giving, with the latter giving more to education and the former more to health and human services (Troy 1983, 1984). Nevertheless, even if some industries have different priorities, it remains the case that most money goes to voluntary organisations concerned with education, medicine and health, general welfare and the arts. These are the areas of work most likely to be funded by corporate givers. What sort of organisations are most likely to attract corporate donations?

It has been suggested that corporate givers are most likely to fund organisations which they can 'recognise' and which display organisational structures and procedures with which they can identify (Wilson 1989); similar points emerge from the US literature (Useem 1987). It is, of course, debatable whether this similarity between donors and funders is a cause or an effect of giving. Corporate funders may prefer to fund those they 'recognise' or this may be another example of isomorphism as voluntary organisations come more closely to resemble their funders (see DiMaggio and Powell 1983; Useem 1987).

Available data on corporate giving suggests that reliance on this source of income is an option open only to larger organisations operating in particular industries or subsectors. Furthermore, in order to obtain, or possibly as a result of, corporate funding, voluntary organisations may need to be managed in ways with which for-profit organisations can identify. A survey in the United States found that half of the organisations studied believed that corporate givers did not support their type of work: 'This was particularly true of social service and advocacy organisations serving minorities and the poor. In the absence of government support, these agencies might be forced to alter their programmes to fit the funding priorities of private funders' (Salamon 1987).

What type of funding are corporate givers most likely to provide? The available data suggest that corporate donors appear generally to give relatively small contributions to large numbers of organisations. Research also suggests that corporate givers generally prefer to give short-term funding for specific projects; they prefer projects to organisations, they want something to happen and they do not generally like to become involved in longer-term commitments (Fogarty and Christie 1990; Christie *et al.* 1991). Reluctance to provide on-going core revenue funding or to undertake longer-term commitments may be related to the precarious status of corporate community investment budgets from year to year.

These findings are of fundamental importance to the future of the voluntary sector, given that one of the increasing 'gaps' in available funding is core revenue funding for organisations without which project work and longer-term planning are likely to be jeopardized. Thus corporate giving may do little to reduce the uncertainties created by competitive contracting and may further encourage short-term 'innovation' rather than continuing, secure provision. Furthermore, small-scale, short-term and often partial funding by corporate givers may actually increase demands on trusts and other grant-givers as recipients look for further funding to make up the balance and/or to continue their work (Leat 1993a).

Corporate givers may avoid giving support which may be seen as filling in for statutory responsibilities (Fogarty and Christie 1990; Christie *et al.* 1991). Again this suggests that voluntary organisations cannot look to corporate givers to make good any loss of funding from local authorities. However, the level of giving to education and to medicine and health may suggest that statutory responsibilities are fairly narrowly defined or, as in some charitable trusts, that practice is not entirely consistent with principle (Leat 1992).

Determinants of corporate giving suggested in the literature in Britain and the United States include: level of government spending, level of pre-tax profit, size of the work-force, tax incentives, peer company comparisons, personal contacts and over-lapping memberships of boards of for-profit and non-profit organisations, level of organisation and demands of the voluntary sector itself, absence of old families of wealth in the locality (Fogarty and Christie 1990; Useem 1987).

One assumption of particular importance in this context is that corporate giving is crowded-out by 'big government' and encouraged by a reduction in the role of the state. There is, perhaps unsurprisingly, little evidence to support this view. Indeed, it has been argued that low or reduced government spending is likely to lead to a reduction in corporate giving in so far as it sets a low(er) standard of public responsibility. In the US a comparison of government and corporate giving in fourteen metropolitan areas found that those areas with a lower level of local government expenditure on health and human services were also those with lower levels of corporate giving (Siegfried and McElroy 1981; see also Useem 1987). The same might also be true in Britain but it would be necessary to explore factors such as level of employment and economic development, presence of company headquarters, community charge levels and rate-capping, central government programme and other funding, political complexion of the authority and so on.

The general conclusion from this brief discussion of corporate giving is that it is a relatively low, uncertain source of funding for short-term, one-off projects in larger organisations which resemble for-profit organisations working in particular fields of activity. Organisations and work which do not fit this description may expect relatively little income from the corporate sector. There are, of course, exceptions to this, with some companies giving to small, local projects which look very unlike for-profit businesses. One way in which corporate donations have been channelled to such organisations in recent years has been via the various ITV telethons, charity projects and Comic Relief and (in a slightly different way) the BBC Children in Need appeal. Although these appeals increase the range of recipients of corporate largess, for various reasons they too tend to give large numbers of small and short-term grants; they are not, in general, a source of long-term revenue funding for the voluntary sector (Leat 1990b).

INVESTMENT INCOME

Many larger charities derive significant amounts of income from investment in the corporate sector and some (endowed trusts, for example) derive all, or most, of their income from this source. In many respects investment income raises many of the same dilemmas as fundraising from the corporate sector. Just as charities vary in their style of fundraising so they vary in their approach to managing their investments (see, for example, Salamon 1993).

It would be reasonable to suppose that charities attempt to maximise their income from investments but, in reality, their approaches are more complicated. In particular, and especially of late, many charities are constrained by a desire to pursue an ethical investment policy in keeping with the charity's mission. This in turn raises difficult legal, and organisational, issues if ethical investment reduces the charity's return on its money. Recent legal cases have somewhat clarified the position of charities in this regard. If trustees are satisfied that an investment would conflict with the objects of the charity they should not invest even if there is a risk of financial loss; trustees may avoid investments that deter donors even at the risk of loss, but the greater the potential loss the more sure they should be about the damage to their work caused by the investments. Trustees can accommodate the investment concerns of donors or those the charity exists to help even if it does not relate to their work but 'they should not risk significant financial detriment by doing so'. Trustees may also invest ethically if they would bring the charity into disrepute by not doing so (Webster 1992).

Although these judgements help clarify the position, there is still a range of practical issues for the charity wishing to pursue an ethical investment policy. For example, what business activities might be thought by some, or all, donors to conflict with its mission and/or deter donations? Does it know what donors think and do all donors feel the same? How much will the charity lose, if anything, by investing ethically? How much can it afford to lose? Will the benefit of ethical investment outweigh any loss in activity from the viewpoint of beneficiaries? Furthermore, given the complex structure of modern corporations, how much research at what cost will be required to ensure that the charity is making only ethnical investments?

Consideration of investment income raises another wider issue concerning equity accumulation. All organisations need reserves, not least to keep going through difficult times, to meet obligations to staff and clients and to deal with cash-flow problems often brought about by purchasers and funders. Charities may, however, face special dilemmas in relation to reserves because large reserves may raise questions about the organisation's active pursuit of its mission. Large reserves may also deter donors. As noted above, equity accumulation may also raise questions about pricing and competition within the voluntary sector and with commercial organisations (see, for example, Tuckman and Chang 1993).

FUNDRAISING FROM THE GENERAL PUBLIC

In view of the popular notion that voluntary organisations live on the contents of collecting tins and the proceeds of jumble sales and coffee mornings, fundraising from the general public provides a surprisingly small part of total sector income. But, as noted above, aggregate figures are misleading in that many, especially smaller, organisations are likely to be completely dependent upon income from the general public. What are the advantages and disadvantages of income raised from the general public?

The first disadvantage is that such income is inherently uncertain both for individual organisations and for the sector as a whole. Although the data are difficult to interpret, there is some evidence that individual giving over the last five years has fluctuated, if not actually declined in real terms.

Apart from being uncertain in amount, most types of income from the general public must be raised afresh each year. For many organisations this may seem all too much like painting the Forth Bridge. The vast majority (91 per cent) of charitable giving in Britain is prompted giving, i.e. people give if and when they are asked, if they give at all. Planned giving, which generally gives a charity slightly more security, accounts for only 9 per cent of the total amount given (Pettipher and Halfpenny 1993). Thus dependence upon fundraising from the general public does not generally foster security or longer-term planning in voluntary organisations.

The second difficulty is that it is generally highly labour intensive and, if costed, is likely to be expensive relative to the amount raised. In part, the high labour intensity of fundraising stems from the fact, noted above, that 91 per cent of giving is prompted. Furthermore, the most commonly used methods of giving are not the ones that produce the highest yield. The most common method of giving is through purchasing raffle tickets but this method yielded only 9 per cent of the total; the second most frequent method of giving, door to door collections, yielded only 5 per cent of the total. As Pettipher and Halfpenny conclude: 'individual charitable giving in Britain is characterised by large proportions of the population donating by methods which have low yields' (Pettipher and Halfpenny 1993:16).

In the past, and still today in many organisations, fundraising was the responsibility of volunteers and much of its real cost was therefore hidden. New methods and approaches to fundraising have led to the employment of more highly paid, professional fundraisers, especially in larger organisations. In addition, new methods of fundraising, such as direct mail, are more costly to administer. However, assessing the costs and benefits of fundraising is not as simple as it might appear. For example, any one method of fundraising may appear cost-ineffective, perhaps raising little more than it costs the organisation. But one method combined with a second method may produce much greater effect in money raised. Should the sum raised be attributed to the second method alone or would the second method have had little effect without the first? Another problem in assessing the costs of fundraising is that, for many charities, fundraising, public education and more generally raising the profile of the charity are difficult to separate. Thus a charity may argue that if a poster campaign appears to raise little money directly it is still worthwhile either as a means of educating the public regarding the cause of the charity or as a foundation for future fundraising. Despite these difficulties there has been little, if any, research in Britain into how fundraising costs and benefits are defined and measured.

The third difficulty in fundraising from the general public is that the sorts of expenditure for which the organisation may most need money may not be those most appealing to the general public. So, for example, every charity must find money to pay the electricity bill and many need money to pay staff. But the general public are more likely to give if the charity appeals for money to buy aids for disabled people, food for starving children or a piece of medical equipment. This creates three problems. First, the charity may be unable to raise money for the basic everyday things it needs. Second, the money it raises for direct services may be less effectively and efficiently spent without money for administration and overheads. Third, equipment and buildings, for example, donated directly or indirectly by public fundraising actually cost money to staff, run and maintain and therefore increase the organisation's need for such funding (on this last point see, for example, Romo 1993).

But there is a further twist in the tail of fundraising. The harder an organisation works at fundraising the more it spends; this may not only reduce the net gain but, perhaps equally important, will raise its administrative costs and this in turn may reduce the amount it can raise from the general public. Although the general public tend to have inflated ideas of what charities spend on administration the fact remains that they dislike giving to charities displaying what are perceived to be high administration costs (Halfpenny 1990). There is some British evidence to link higher fundraising costs with lower donations but, yet again, it is important to note that some charities – overseas and social welfare – may be more susceptible to this effect than others – health and religion, for example (Posnett and Sandler 1988).

The fourth disadvantage in fundraising from the general public is that messages and images likely to generate higher levels of giving may be inconsistent with the real mission of the organisation. So, for example, some charities working in the field of disability have been criticised because their fundraising messages play on public pity and sympathy while the mission of the organisation is supposedly to counter public stereotypes of disability by emphasising ability rather than disability. This is one example of the disadvantages of the separation of funding from consumption which supposedly characterises voluntary, as opposed to commercial, organisations (see, for example, Mason 1984; Paton and Cornforth 1992; Leat 1993b).

The fifth disadvantage is that it is not equally available to all organisations. This is not only because different organisations can afford to spend different amounts on fundraising but also because the public have preferences regarding the causes they support. As in the case of corporate givers, individual givers rate medicine and health as most important followed by education. However, in the case of individual givers preservation of the environment comes third, with arts (a top target for corporate givers) coming bottom of the list and rated 'not very important' (Pettipher and Halfpenny 1993: 19). Organisations working in fields which are considered 'not very important' by the general public are obviously likely to have a hard time fundraising (especially if they are also not among the, closely related, fields favoured by corporate givers). The temptation to divert activities into those fields which do appeal to the general public, and are thus more likely to raise money, may be considerable. Both the fourth and fifth disadvantages may all too easily lead to the fundraising tail wagging the organisation/mission dog: promoting fundraising becomes the end rather than a means to the achievement of the organisation's mission.

Thus dependence upon income from fundraising from the general public carries many of the same disadvantages as dependence upon income from corporate donors. It is unreliable in amount, requires considerable effort to raise often small amounts, is likely to be for particular purposes and is not equally available to all types of organisations. Like corporate donations, fundraising from the general public may lead to goal diversion as organisations chase money rather than mission. The dilemma, of course, is that without money principles are difficult to put into practice.

Dependence upon corporate and general public giving may have other more subtle but equally profound effects on individual organisations and on the wider voluntary sector:

Changes towards a more tripartite system of funding will make sustaining and relying on the gift relationship less tenable for many organisations. In particular, those organisations which currently engage in little or no marketing will be forced to think more 'proactively' towards their funding sources. These organisations which rely on money coming to them without actively seeking it will stand a good chance of not receiving enough to secure a future for the organisation.

(Wilson 1989: 64)

Increasing competition for funds between charities will lead, Wilson argues, to far-reaching ideological and practical problems for charities. Charities will need to adopt a different approach to each other ranging from outright competition to complete co-operation in order to secure a greater level of funding for joint or common causes. In addition, they will need to 'rationalise, to streamline, to secure distinctive competence and professionalism in management' (Wilson 1989: 65). This in turn will lead to voluntary organisations adopting much of the strategy and structure of for-profit commercial organisations:

The conflict of cultures is thus one in which the demands of the tripartite funding system create an organisational environment which favours competitive, distinctive service provision, from a tightly controlled, 'lean and fit' organisation. Individuals in these organisations, however, favour an environment which is flexible, open to re-definition and essentially ambiguous. It is difficult to see how the two cultures might be reconciled.

(Wilson 1989: 74)

The end result of further encouragement of tripartitism, Wilson argues, is that voluntary organisations will 'effectively operate only along commercial lines, exploiting the provision of services which will accrue income and avoiding those which will not' (Wilson 1989: 78; see also Ware 1989; Wilson 1992).

FUNDING FROM CHARITABLE TRUSTS AND FOUNDATIONS

Grant-giving charitable trusts and foundations are both part of the voluntary sector and a source of funding for other voluntary organisations. Some trusts have substantial endowments on which they rely for income, others have no income of their own and must fundraise in much the same way as their grant-recipients (Leat 1992). Fundraising trusts face many of the dilemmas and difficulties in raising funds discussed above. Non-fundraising, endowed trusts do not need to engage in fundraising in the conventional sense but must nevertheless 'raise' or protect their funds by sound investment policies. Dependence upon investment income raises two issues. First, income from investment is susceptible to wider changes in the economy and may fluctuate significantly, creating difficulties in planning and practice. Second, as noted above, all voluntary organisations which rely heavily on investment income may have to make difficult choices between maximising their income and ensuring that their investments do not run counter to their missions.

Grant-giving charitable trusts and foundations provide only a very small proportion of total sector income. The amount given by trusts rose in the early 1990s but in a recession may fall again. Thus trust funding always carries the disadvantage that it is, in total, inherently uncertain. Furthermore, the size of trust income tends to follow the cycle of the wider economy whereas the demands of voluntary organisations (and on trusts for grant-aid) are counter-cyclical, i.e. demand rises when there is least money around.

In the past, charitable trusts have tended to favour small, one-off, short-term, capital grants for 'innovation' and 'pump-priming'. They have given grants on the assumption that some other funder would step in to cover the longer-term bill and keep the organisation or the work going. The typical approach to grant-giving has been one of giving 'gifts' rather than acting as an investor or a 'collaborative entrepreneur' (Leat 1992). Recently, however, some trusts have begun to question this gift-giving approach, not least because it was no longer clear that any other funder would step in to keep the work going once the trust grant ended. Some trusts are now looking at their grant-giving in terms of efficiency and effectiveness and questioning the value of giving large numbers of small, short-term grants. Some are becoming investors and collaborative entrepreneurs, rather than gift-givers, in some of their grant-making.

From the viewpoint of grant recipients, the major disadvantages of trust funding are that it is small, in total and usually in size of each grant, and short-term. Furthermore, it is usually only available for certain types of purpose (e.g. capital rather than revenue needs) and is not equally available in all parts of the country or in all fields of work. Precise data on the distribution of trust giving by industry and by geographical region are hard to come by and estimates vary significantly (Leat 1991). It would probably be fair to say, however, that medicine and health and education receive a large proportion of trust funds while organisations working in housing or the environment or with, say, the elderly receive much less. The dominance of medicine and education is by now a familiar theme in this discussion. In terms of geographical distribution it appears that the southern half of Britain receives the lion's share (two-thirds) of trust funding with very little going to organisations in Wales, Scotland and Northern Ireland (Fitzherbert and Forrester 1991). Some part of this concentration of giving in the south may stem from the fact that many trusts give money to head offices in London for distribution to the regions (Leat 1991).

The major advantage of trust funding from the viewpoint of recipients is probably that it usually has few strings attached. Remarkably few trusts appear to have any direct contact with recipients either before or after grant-giving. Unlike some other forms of funding, trust giving generally carries few risks of goal diversion or isomorphism. Trust giving may also encourage diversity in the voluntary sector and provide opportunities to experiment with new ideas and approaches. However, the nature of trust funding may do little to assist voluntary organisations with their core revenue needs and, more generally, may do little to encourage the longer-term survival of smaller voluntary organisations.

Trust giving is neither large enough nor sufficiently stable to provide a secure basis for voluntary sector funding or to cover short-falls in statutory funding. In any case, trusts, like corporate givers and individuals, are reluctant to fund those organisations and areas of work which are seen as statutory responsibilities (Leat 1992). As yet it is unclear what approach trusts will adopt to funding organisations which engage in contracting with local authorities. There is already anecdotal evidence that some trusts refuse to fund organisations with large professional fundraising departments and, for different reasons, trusts may also be reluctant to fund organisations engaged in contracting. In future some organisations may have to make choices in fundraising strategies not previously necessary.

CONCLUSION

This chapter has discussed various sources of, and trends in, funding of the voluntary sector. It has suggested that there are pressures on voluntary organisations to become more cost-conscious and competitive in relation to securing resources. These pressures include increasing demands requiring more resources; rising costs due to inflation, expansion, legislation, regulation and higher standards; loss or diversion of statutory funding; pressures from government departments, legislation, contracting and general public expectations to become more efficient and to be able to demonstrate that.

Increasing cost-consciousness and competition for funding may in various direct and indirect ways divert organisations' goals, shifting attention from mission to income generation (Butler and Wilson 1990; Saxon-Harrold 1990). Indeed, some see the increasing use of the term 'non-profit' to describe voluntary organisations as a reflection of this shift (Perlmutter and Adams 1990; Taylor 1991).

Increasing cost-consciousness and competition for funds may have a range of effects on the voluntary sector and individual voluntary organisations in future. For the reasons discussed above, volunteers may become marginalised; there is likely to be increasing emphasis on the recruitment of well-qualified staff and managers, often recruited from the commercial for-profit sector (Bruce and Raymer 1992). Staff and managers are likely to require higher salaries (Romo 1993). Higher salaries, as well as other costs such as consultancy, management training and so on, will lead to rising costs. Furthermore, higher staff salaries may lead to questions about the definition of voluntary organisations as non-profit distributing (Taylor 1991). Increasing cost-consciousness and competitiveness may lead to changes in organisational structures and processes which may radically transform the style and ethos of voluntary organisations and create what Handy has referred to as a clash of cultures within the organisations (Handy 1988; Wilson 1989; Leat 1993b). This in turn may lead to loss of satisfaction for both volunteers and paid staff and may in turn increase costs further as money (a higher salary) becomes a more important inducement.

It is worth emphasising here that the growth of formalisation, bureaucratisation and professionalism in the voluntary sector cannot simply be attributed to increased dependence on statutory funding (Kramer 1990). As noted above, there may be a tendency to exaggerate the effects of statutory funding on organisational structure and practice and 'pressures for improved agency management, tighter financial control and the use of professionals in service delivery do not, after all, come solely from government' (Salamon 1987: 115). Returning to the approaches briefly discussed at the beginning of this chapter, the growth of managerialism within the voluntary sector may be better explained by institutional theory than by resource dependency. As Kramer puts it: 'These changes were influenced by the growth of "managerialism" in their external environment – in the economy and in the public sector – as well as by a process of institutionalisation within each agency' (Kramer 1990: 50).

Cost-consciousness, competitiveness, contracting and corporatism are likely to alter the role and requirements of board members. Indeed democratic structures of control and accountability may come to be seen as irrelevant, if not counter-productive, and expensive luxuries.

The chart below, based upon experience of boards in the United States, highlights not merely changes in board approaches but also many of the wider organisational changes touched on above.

In future many voluntary organisations may be in competition not merely with each other but also with for-profit commercial organisations. This in turn will raise questions about the definition, and the legal and fiscal privileges, of voluntary organisations (Ware 1989; Rose-Ackerman 1990). In so far as voluntary organisations increasingly put income generation before public benefit mission in their priorities and adopt the language, structure and style of commercial organisations, the non-profit/for-profit distinction will become increasingly tenuous. This in turn may raise questions in the minds of corporate and individual donors regarding the logic of giving and volunteering. Reduced donations and volunteering would further erode any cost advantage voluntary organisations may have.

Contracting with local authorities may complicate further many of the trends noted above. On the one hand, voluntary organisations may find themselves in increasing competition with each other and with for-profit organisations; on the other hand, they run the risk of becoming a second tier of government (see, for example, Wolch 1990). A further danger of contracting in a time of inadequate resources is that, as voluntary organisations become the major front-line service providers, they, rather than the local

The shape of change

Traditional	New wave
Enterprise co-operates with others	Entrepreneurial/competitive
Broad knowledge of organisation's work	Specialised
Generous with time	Pressed for time
Housewives, retired, human service professionals, small business	Large corporations, decision-makers
Mission-oriented	Results-oriented, bored with philosophy
Concerned with quality of performance	Concerned with efficiency, effectiveness and tools to measure them
Contracts with government and limited fundraising	Wary of government restrictions, so board fundraising and capital campaigns
Fearful of market place	Contracts with business, etc.
Good employers	Hire on contracts
Resist merger	Merge and seek to merge
New programmes ancillary	No programme core
Decries competition	Relishes competition
Single entity	Joint ventures
Social work training	Interdisciplinary
Altruistic	Business
Do good	Do well
Mission determines product	Market determines product
Not-for-profit and deficit finance	Some programmes income centres for agency
Serves poor through government grants and voluntary work	Serves through third-party payments, uses surplus for poor

Source: based on presentation by Geneva Johnson, President and Chief Executive Officer, Family Services America (quoted in Taylor 1991: 47)

authority, will be seen as responsible for any short-comings in provision. At the same time voluntary organisations will be hard-pressed to serve the growing number of people who fall outside the statutory welfare net. The effect on the sector's role, reputation and ultimately its survival may be incalculable.

As we approach the end of the twentieth century the voluntary sector is caught on the horns of a dilemma. It needs to enter the market and to become leaner and fitter, more efficient and effective, if it is to survive in the new 'post welfare state' mixed economy. But entering the market, with all its knock-on effects, may reduce the sector to a second tier of government or transform it into a rather ineffective part of the for-profit, commercial sector.

It is, of course, possible that the voluntary sector will, as it has in the past, re-shape itself to fit into the gaps left by the statutory and for-profit sectors and, by that means, retain some separate, distinctive existence (see, for example, Knight 1993). The only certainty is the truism that in the year 2000 the voluntary sector will be very different from that we know today.

REFERENCES

Aldrich, H.E. and Pfeffer, J. (1976) 'Environments of organisations', *Annual Review of Sociology* 2: 79–106.

Association of Metropolitan Authorities (1990) *Contracts for Social Care: The Local Authority View*, London: AMA.

Austin, M. and Posnett, J. (1979) 'The charity sector in England and Wales – characteristics and public accountability', *National Westminster Bank Quarterly*, August.

Batsleer, J., Cornforth, C. and Paton, R. (eds) (1992) *Issues in Voluntary and Non-profit Management*, Wokingham: Addison-Wesley.

Bernstein, S. (1991) *Managing Contracted Services in the Nonprofit Agency*, Philadelphia: Temple University Press.

Bielefeld, W. (1992) 'Non-profit funding environment relations: theory and application', *Voluntas*, 3(1): 48–71.

Booth, T. and Phillips, D. (1990) *Contracting Arrangements in Domiciliary Care*, University of Sheffield.

Brager, G. and Holloway, S. (1978) *Changing Human Service Organisations: Politics and Practice*, New York: The Free Press.

Bruce, I. and Raymer, A. (1992) 'Managing and staffing Britain's largest charities', London: VOLPROF, City University Business School.

Bulmer, M. (1986) *Neighbours: The Work of Philip Abrams*, Cambridge: Cambridge University Press.

Butler, R.J. and Wilson, D.C. (1990) *Managing Voluntary and Non-profit Organisations*, London: Routledge.

Charities Aid Foundation (1993) *Charities in Recession: The Survey Report*, Tonbridge: Charities Aid Foundation.

Christie, I., Carley, M., Fogarty, M. and Legard, R. (1991) *Profitable Partnerships: A Report on Business Involvement in the Community*, London: Policy Studies Institute.

Common, R. and Flynn, N. (1992) *Contracting for Care*, York: Joseph Rowntree Foundation.

Davies, A. and Edwards, K. (1990) *Twelve Charity Contracts*, London: Directory of Social Change.

DiMaggio, P. and Powell, W.W. (1983) 'The iron cage revisited: institutional isomorphism and collective rationality in organizational fields', *American Sociological Review*, 48: 147–60.

Eastwood, M. and Casson, D. (1991) *The Major Companies Guide*, London: Directory of Social Change.

Fitzherbert, L. and Forrester, S. (1991) *A Guide to the Major Trusts, 1991 Edition*, London: Directory of Social Change.

Fogarty, M. (1992) *Company Giving: The Way Forward*, RSU Research Seminar no. 5, Tonbridge: Charities Aid Foundation.

Fogarty, M. and Christie, I. (1990) *Companies and Communities, Promoting Business Involvement in the Community*, London: Policy Studies Institute.

Forder, J. and Knapp, M. (1993) 'Social care markets: the voluntary sector and residential care for elderly people in England', in S. Saxon-Harrold and J. Kendall (eds) *Researching the Voluntary Sector*, Tonbridge: Charities Aid Foundation.

Gutch, R. (1992) *Contracting: Lessons from the US*, London: National Council for Voluntary Organisations/Bedford Square Press.

Gutch, R. (1993) 'A mission to survive', *Community Care*, 29 January: v–vi.

Gutch, R. and Young, K. (1989) *Partners or Rivals? Developing the Relationships between Voluntary Organisations*, London: National Council for Voluntary Organisations.

Haffenden, S. (1991) *Getting It Right for Carers*, London: Department of Health/ Social Services Inspectorate.

Halfpenny, P. (1990) *Charity Household Survey 1988/89*, Tonbridge: Charities Aid Foundation.

Handy, C. (1988) *Understanding Voluntary Organisations*, Harmondsworth: Penguin.

Hansmann, H. (1987) 'Economic theories of non-profit organization', in W.W. Powell (ed.) *The Nonprofit Sector: A Research Handbook*, New Haven, CT: Yale University Press.

Hazel, R. (1991) 'Role reversal', *Trust Monitor*, February/March: 14–15.

Hedley, R. and Rochester, C. (1992) *Contracts at the Crossroads*, Rugby: Association of Crossroads Care Attendant Schemes.

Hills, D. (1991) *Carer Support in the Community*, London: Department of Health/ Social Services Inspectorate.

JAGDCA (1993) *Standards for Registration for Domiciliary Care*, London: Joint Advisory Group of Domiciliary Care Associations.

James, E. (1989) 'Sources of charity finance and policy implications: a comparative analysis', in N. Lee (ed.) *Sources of Charity Finance*, Tonbridge: Charities Aid Foundation.

James, E. (1987) 'The nonprofit sector in comparative perspective', in W.W. Powell (ed.) *The Nonprofit Sector: A Research Handbook*, New Haven, CT: Yale University Press.

Kestenbaum, A. (1992) *Cash for Care: The Experience of ILF Clients*, Nottingham: Independent Living Fund.

KPMG (1992) *Improving Independent Sector Involvement in Community Care Planning*, London: Department of Health.

Knapp, M. and Kendall, J. (1991) *Barriers to Giving: The Economics of Charitable Donations in Britain*, Discussion Paper 741/3, Personal Social Services Research Unit: University of Kent at Canterbury.

Knight, B. (1993) *Voluntary Action*, London: Home Office.

Kramer, R. and Grossman, B. (1987) 'Contracting for social services: process management and resource dependencies', *Social Service Review*, 61: 32–5.

Kramer, R. (1990) 'Change and continuity in British voluntary organisations', *Voluntas* 1(2): 33–60.

Kramer, R. (1992) 'Voluntary organisations, contracting and the welfare state', in J. Batsleer, C. Cornforth and R. Paton (eds), *Issues in Voluntary and Non-profit Management*, Wokingham: Addison-Wesley.

Leat, D. (1989a) 'The significance of fees and charges', in N. Lee (ed.) *Sources of Charity Finance*, Tonbridge: Charities Aid Foundation.

Leat, D. (1989b) *Charities and Charging: Who Pays?*, Tonbridge: Charities Aid Foundation.

Leat, D. (1990a) *For Love and Money: The Role of Payment in Encouraging the Provision of Care*, York: Joseph Rowntree Foundation.

Leat, D. (1990b) *Fundraising and Grantmaking – A Case Study of ITV Telethon '88*, Tonbridge: Charities Aid Foundation.

Leat, D. (1991) 'Grant making trusts in Britain', *Charity Trends*, 14th edition, Tonbridge: Charities Aid Foundation.

Leat, D. (1992) *Trusts in Transition: The Policy and Practice of Grant-Giving Trusts*, York: Joseph Rowntree Foundation.

Leat, D. (1993a) 'Increasing demands on charitable foundations – understanding the ecology of funding', in S. Saxon-Harrold and J. Kendall (eds), *Researching the Voluntary Sector*, Tonbridge: Charities Aid Foundation.

Leat, D. (1993b) *Managing Across Sectors: Similarities and Differences Between For-profit and Voluntary Non-profit Organisations*, London: VOLPROF, City University Business School.

Leat, D. (1993c) *Creating Care at the Boundaries: Issues in the Supply and Management of Domiciliary Care*, Canterbury: University of Kent at Canterbury.

Leat, D. and Gay, P. (1987) *Paying for Care: An Exploratory Study of the Issues Raised by Paid Care Schemes*, London: Policy Studies Institute.

Lee, N. (1989) *Sources of Charity Finance*, Tonbridge: Charities Aid Foundation.

Marchant, C. (1993) 'Stuck in the middle', *Community Care*, 25 February: 24–5.

Mason, D. (1984) *Voluntary Nonprofit Enterprise Management*, New York: Plenum Press.

Menchik, P.L. and Weisbrod, B.A. (1987) 'Volunteer labour supply', *Journal of Public Economics*, 32: 159–83.

Mocroft, I. (1989) Discussant's comments, in N. Lee (ed.) *Sources of Charity Finance*, Tonbridge: Charities Aid Foundation.

Mocroft, I. and Doyle, M. (1991) *Opportunities for Volunteering, 1981–1990*, CRSP working paper No 131, Loughborough: CRSP.

Mocroft, I. and Thomason, C. (1993) 'The evolution of community care and voluntary organisations', in S. Saxon-Harrold and J. Kendall (eds), *Researching the Voluntary Sector*, Tonbridge: Charities Aid Foundation.

Parker, R. (1990) 'Care and the private sector', in I. Sinclair *et al. The Kaleidoscope of Care: A Review of Research on Welfare Provision for Elderly People*, London: HMSO.

Paton, R. and Cornforth, C. (1992) 'What's different about managing in voluntary and non-profit organizations?', in J. Batsleer *et al.* (eds) *Issues in Voluntary and Non-profit Management*, Wokingham: Addison–Wesley.

Perlmutter, F.D. and Adams, C.T. (1990) 'The voluntary sector and for-profit ventures: the transformation of American welfare', *Administration in Social Work*, 14(1).

Pettipher, C. and Halfpenny, P. (1993) 'The 1990/91 individual giving survey', in S. Saxon-Harrold and J. Kendall (eds) *Researching the Voluntary Sector*, Tonbridge: Charities Aid Foundation.

Pfeffer, J. (1992) *Organizations and Organization Theory*, Boston MA: Pitman.

Pfeffer, J. and Salanick, G.R. (1978) *The External Control of Organisations: A Resource Dependence Perspective*, New York: Harper.

Posnett, J. (1987) 'Trends in the income of registered charities 1950–85', *Charity Trends 1986/87*, Tonbridge: Charities Aid Foundation.

Posnett, J. and Sandler, T. (1988) 'Transfers, transaction costs and charitable intermediaries', *Institutional Review of Law and Economics*, 8: 145–60.

Powell, W.W. (ed.) (1987) *The Nonprofit Sector: A Research Handbook*, New Haven, CT: Yale University Press.

Powell, W.W. (1991) 'Expanding the scope of institutional arguments', in W.W. Powell and D. DiMaggio (eds) *The New Institutionalization in Organizational Analysis*, Chicago, IL: University of Chicago Press.

Romo, F.D. (1993) 'Institutional constraints on executive greed: stratification systems in American art museums', *Voluntas*, 4(1): 16–54.

Rose-Ackerman, S. (1990) 'Competition between non-profits and for-profits: entry and growth', *Voluntas*, 1(1): 13–25.

Saidel, J. (1989) 'Dimensions of interdependence: the state and voluntary sector relationships', *Nonprofit and Voluntary Sector Quarterly* 18(4): 335–47.

St Leger, M.M. (1993) 'Shops operated by the top 400 charities', in S. Saxon-Harrold and J. Kendall (eds), *Researching the Voluntary Sector*, Tonbridge: Charities Aid Foundation.

Salamon, L.M. (1987) 'Partners in public service: the scope and theory of government-nonprofit relations', in W.W. Powell (ed.) *The Nonprofit Sector: A Research Handbook*, New Haven, CT: Yale University Press.

Salamon, L.M. (1993) 'Foundations as investment managers, Part II: the performance', *Nonprofit Management & Leadership*, 3(3): 239–53.

Saxon-Harrold, S. (1990) 'Competition, resources and strategy in the British nonprofit sector', in H.K. Anheier and W. Seibel (eds) *The Third Sector: Comparative Studies of Nonprofit Organizations*, Berlin and New York: de Gruyter.

Saxon-Harrold, S. (1991) 'Corporate support of the voluntary sector', *Charity Trends*, 14th edition, Tonbridge: Charities Aid Foundation.

Saxon-Harrold, S. and Kendall, J. (eds) (1993) *Researching the Voluntary Sector*, Tonbridge: Charities Aid Foundation.

Scott, W.R. (1991) 'Unpacking institutional arguments', in W.W. Powell and P. DiMaggio (eds) *The New Institutionalization in Organizational Analysis*, Chicago, IL: University of Chicago Press.

Siegfried, J.J. and McElroy, R.M. (1981) *Corporate Philanthropy in America in 1980*, unpublished paper, Vanderbilt University.

Sinclair, I., Parker, R., Leat, D. and Williams, J. (1990) *The Kaleidoscope of Care: A Review of Research on Welfare Provision for Elderly People*, London: HMSO.

Smith, S.R. (1992) 'Nonprofit organizations in the age of contracting', paper presented to NCVO conference, London.

Smith, S.R. and Lipsky, M. (1992) 'Privatization in health and human services', *Journal of Health Politics, Policy and Law*, 17(2).

Taylor, M. (1991) *New Times, New Challenges, Voluntary Organisations Facing 1990*, London: National Council for Voluntary Organisations.

Troy, K. (1983) *Annual Survey of Corporate Contributions*, 1983 edition, New York: Conference Board.

Troy, K. (1984) *Annual Survey of Corporate Contributions*, 1984 edition, New York: Conference Board.

Tuckman, H.P. and Chang, C.F. (1993) 'Accumulating financial surpluses in nonprofit organisations', in D.R. Young *et al.* (eds) *Governing, Leading and Managing Non-Profit Organizations*, San Francisco: Jossey Bass.

Useem, M. (1987) 'Corporate philanthropy', in W.W. Powell (ed.) *The Nonprofit Sector: A Research Handbook*, New Haven, CT: Yale University Press.

Ware, A. (1989) *Between Profit and State: Intermediate Organisations in Britain and the United States*, Cambridge: Polity Press.

Webster, P. (1992) 'Investing with a conscience', *Trust Monitor*, February/March: 12–13.

Weisbrod, B.A. (1988) *The Nonprofit Economy*, Cambridge MA: Harvard University Press.

Wilson, D.C. (1989) 'New trends in the funding of charities: the tripartite system of funding', in A. Ware (ed.) *Charities and Government*, Manchester: Manchester University Press.

Wilson, D.C. (1992) 'Co-operation and competition in the voluntary sector: the strategic challenge of the 1990s and beyond', in J. Batsleer, C. Cornforth and R. Paton (eds) *Issues in Voluntary and Non-profit Management*, Wokingham: Addison-Wesley.

Wistow, G., Knapp, M., Hardy, B. and Allen, C. (1992) 'From providing to enabling: local authorities and the mixed economy of social care', *Public Administration*, 70: 25–45.

Wolch, J.R. (1990) *The Shadow State: Government and the Voluntary Sector in Transition*, New York: The Foundation Center.

8 Voluntary agencies and accountability

Colin Rochester

INTRODUCTION

This chapter is based on the proposition that demands for accountability pose more difficult and complex issues and problems for voluntary agencies than for their counterparts in the private and statutory sectors.

The real world is generally a lot less tidy than our descriptions of it and the organisation of welfare in particular has become more complex with the introduction by the Conservative government of the values and practices of commerce into the statutory sector. But we can, in broad terms, describe the arrangements for accountability in the private and statutory sector in fairly simple terms.

Private for-profit organisations can be characterised as being accountable to their owners – the shareholders – and regulated by the market (although markets may be 'managed' to a greater or lesser extent by government). Furthermore there is a simple test of their performance – the 'bottom line' in their accounts.

For their part, statutory agencies operate within clear and explicit terms of reference and with duties and powers which are defined in law. They are organised hierarchically both internally and in relation to one another. Ultimately, they are accountable to an electorate for the discharge of their responsibilities. A number of regulatory bodies and mechanisms have been established over the years – such as the audit commission; the district auditor; the education inspectorate. These have had two main functions. In the first place they provide the means by which the superior institution can assert control over the inferior – parliament over the executive arm; central over local government. Second, their reports are intended to provide information which assists the electorate to assess the performance of local and central government and vote accordingly.

The predominant organisational form in private company and public agency alike has been bureaucratic. The clear-cut division in a commercial venture between the owners, the work-force and the customers has been mirrored in the public sector's distinction between elected members, officers

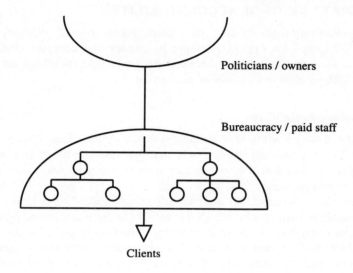

Politicians / owners

Bureaucracy / paid staff

Clients

Figure 8.1 :   The ABC Division

and beneficiaries of services. Billis (1992, 1993) presents this 'ABC division' in diagram form.

The paid staff who produce the goods or provide the services are organised as a hierarchy; there are clear boundaries to their activities and authority and clear lines of managerial accountability.

By contrast voluntary agencies are held to be accountable for their activities in a number of different ways by a variety of constituents or stakeholders – members, beneficiaries, paid and unpaid staff, donors and supporters, government and other funding bodies, the 'community' and the taxpayer. They do not conform to the simple ABC division and their staff are rarely organised as a straightforward bureaucracy.

As a result, their internal structures of accountability are often confused (Harris and Billis 1987: 3). Furthermore, the demands of major funders for accountability may have significant and often unforeseen impacts on voluntary organisations (Billis and Harris 1992; Lewis 1994). Many of them also have to operate within a framework of regulation based on sixteenth-century concepts of charity, administered by a nineteenth-century institution – the Charity Commission – which has been given important additional powers by the 1992 Charities Act.

The bulk of the chapter looks in turn at the problems of internal accountability; the impact of external accountability; and the appropriateness and adequacy of the regulatory framework. But, before turning to those issues, it will consider the different kinds of accountability to be discussed.

DIFFERENT KINDS OF ACCOUNTABILITY

In her pioneering study of multiple accountability in local voluntary organisations, Diana Leat (1988) attempts to unpack the complex concept of accountability and distinguish between its 'variety of meanings and applications'. She makes three kinds of distinction.

Types of accountability

Rejecting Simey's view that accountability can be equated with control (Simey 1984), Leat suggests not only that the term implies a *lack* of direct oversight but also that it is commonly used to describe what may be very different arrangements.

At one end of the spectrum we find 'full accountability' or, in Leat's phrase, 'accountability with sanctions'. This involves the right to demand an account and impose penalties if the account or the actions reported in it are deemed unsatisfactory. The sanctions available are usually powerful – loss or reduction of funding; dismissal or disciplinary action; loss of elected office.

Explanatory accountability is a weaker form which confers the right to require an account – a report and an explanation – but not to impose sanctions – other than expressing disapproval or making criticisms. This is the kind of accountability exercised by Community Health Councils.

A third form is the weakest of the three main types. Here, those seeking accountability do not have any clear rights and are dependent on the willingness of those who are accountable to take their views into account. This 'responsive' accountability is the form in which agencies typically claim to be accountable to the local community. It involves no formal right to an explanation or sanctions, but the fear of losing the support of the community, for example, may be a powerful informal sanction in some cases.

Sources of the right to require accountability

Leat distinguishes three sources of the right to require accountability. Structural accountability is derived from social or organisational structures – parents and children; managers and workers. Delegate accountability is created by specific acts of delegation as a result of which A acts on behalf of B and is accountable to B for what he or she does in his or her name. Communal accountability arises from a feeling on the part of those who are accountable that they owe accountability to some 'community' of others with whom they identify.

Different areas over which accountability is exercised

The set of categories which complete Leat's framework distinguish between the different kinds of activity for which accountability may be required. An organisation may be held accountable:

- for the proper use of money (fiscal accountability);
- for following proper procedures (process accountability);
- for the quality of the work (programme accountability);
- for the relevance and appropriateness of the work (accountability for priorities).

PROBLEMS OF INTERNAL ACCOUNTABILITY

Clarifying the different meanings attached to 'accountability' may help us to disentangle the problems associated with internal accountability in voluntary agencies but we also need to develop our understanding of the distinctive nature of these organisations. During the 1980s Billis found that the traditional ABC model provided an inadequate explanation for the central concerns of voluntary sector managers (Billis 1989a), such as the tensions between the idea of unbounded commitment (the expectation that people would work 24 hours a day) and contracts which spelled out terms and conditions of employment or the desire to work collectively or democratically rather than bureaucratically. Nor could it explain the ambiguity of roles within voluntary agencies, the lack, for example, of clear-cut differentiation between employee and member or between governing body and staff (Billis 1989a).

The theory he began to construct in response to the inadequacies of the existing organisational models characterised voluntary agencies (those voluntary bodies that employed staff) as hybrid or 'blurred' organisations. They combined the characteristics of two different kinds of organisations – membership associations with authority vested in democratically elected officers, on the one hand, and, on the other, bureaucracies with their managerial hierarchies. Many of the tensions could be seen as the result of the organisations' location in an ambiguous zone between the two 'worlds' (Billis 1984, 1989a).

Voluntary agencies can therefore be seen as wrestling with two very different kinds of structural accountability (to use Leat's phrase) which coexist within the organisation. It is small wonder that internal structures for accountability commonly lack clarity and that there are difficult issues about staff accountability to the governing body and of the organisation's accountability to its members or users.

The members of staff interviewed by Leat for her study described their accountability to their management committees as explanatory, although they also recognised that the committee did have the authority to use sanctions. She suggests that the accountability of staff to governing bodies is confused 'because the real capacity of management committees to manage is unclear'. This, she says, arises from a lack of clarity about the circumstances in which 'the initial act of delegation to (paid) staff' took place. In the absence of such clarity it is not possible to define 'the respective areas of competence' of staff and committee.

This lack of clarity about the role of the management committee and doubts and disagreements about where the boundaries lie between staff and committee functions and powers is a common thread which runs through the research literature on both sides of the Atlantic (see, for example, Middleton 1987; Herman 1989; Batsleer *et al.* 1991). There is ample evidence that the roles of committee and staff are interdependent and that the relationship between them is unstable (Harris 1991). In order to clarify this relationship, Margaret Harris has developed an analytical tool called total activities analysis which enables organisations to negotiate and re-negotiate the respective roles of staff and committee (this is described more fully in Chapter 9). Teasing out the nature and extent of the accountability to be required of staff thus needs more than Leat's clarity about the 'initial act of delegation': it requires continuing attention.

Effective accountability assumes that governing bodies possess real authority, that is the 'the ability and the right to influence, direct and control the actions of staff' (Harris 1993: 1). Such authority is generally described as being conferred by the organisation's structure and rules and qualified by the knowledge and expertise possessed by the individuals who make up the governing body. Harris (1993) suggests that this description is based on a 'traditional' model of governance in which the interaction between four key elements in an organisation can be seen as 'a chain which begins with a vision of need and ends with the provision of a service which responds to that need' (ibid.: 6).

While three of the elements in this equation – the governing body, staff and beneficiaries – need no introduction, the fourth – what Harris terms the 'guardians' of the agency – is less familiar. The guardians are a mixture of people unique to each agency and drawn from its founders, members, funders and/or former clients who 'have, or had, a positive concern for the long term survival of the agency and its purposes' (ibid.: 5). The traditional model assumes that this group of sponsors or owners confers on the governing body the authority to employ and manage staff who deliver services to the agency's beneficiaries, clients or users. Accountability is also linear: the staff are held responsible by the committee who in turn are accountable to the 'guardians'.

The reality, however, does not always match the traditional model. Harris distinguishes two other patterns of interaction between the four key groups. The first of these is the 'membership model' in which the agency's sponsors are identical with its members or beneficiaries. In a voluntary membership association the members typically elect or appoint a committee which employs staff not to provide services to third parties but to the members themselves. Accountability in this kind of agency is less straightforward than in the traditional model. Regular and close contact between the staff and the members may well reduce the power of the committee to hold the staff to account.

In the second of the non-traditional models accountability is even more problematic. In this – the 'entrepreneur model' – the guardians or sponsors of the agency are also the organisation's staff. In the traditional philanthropic voluntary organisation the people with the vision of social need set up an organisation as the means of employing others to address the problem: in this newer form those with the founding vision and 'the credibility, funding-potential and root enthusiasm for the survival of the agency' are the staff themselves. While their governing bodies have the formal responsibilities and powers of employers and service providers, they are in effect powerless.

Harris has also described the phenomenon of the 'phantom governing body'. There are agencies where the committee seems to have no clear relationship with the other key elements of guardians, staff and beneficiaries and no real connection with the day-to-day work of the organisation. 'In practice staff are appointed by an *ad hoc* group of guardians, by other staff, or by staff at another organisational level (in a national agency). Once in post they are managed and controlled, if at all, by other staff' (ibid.: 10).

The accountability of staff to the governing body is thus a complex and problematic area. The difficulties associated with lack of clarity about the boundaries of the respective roles of board and staff are multiplied and deepened where those involved may be working to very different models of governance. But what of the second aspect of internal accountability – the organisation's relationship with its constituency of members or users?

It may be useful to make some distinctions at this stage. The great majority of voluntary organisations have members. In many cases membership is purely a matter of expressing support for the organisation's aims; it brings no entitlement to use or benefit from the services provided and, while formally the members possess accountability with sanctions, few of them take part in the democratic processes available to them and it is rare for their power to be exercised in any meaningful way, by for example the voting out of office of the governing body. The active minority may be equated with Harris's 'guardians' while the rest are a paper army. Accountability to this constituency is generally regarded as unproblematic and operates at the level of Leat's explanatory accountability, often in the form of an annual report or more frequent newsletter.

These members form a quite distinct constituency from the users of the agency's services. But, as we have noted, there are other organisations in which the users and members are the same. In the brief discussion that follows 'member' is used to describe such a member/user.

Accountability to users has been part of the rhetoric of the voluntary sector rather than its practice for much of its history. The predominance of organisations whose task is seen as providing an efficient service to others rather than for mutual benefit has restricted participation in decision-making by 'clients' (Rowe 1978). Leat's informants described their practice in terms of 'responsive accountability' – the weakest in her lexicon – and pointed to serious difficulties of implementation. In the first place there was a problem of principle: if the needs of current users were to determine the nature of the services provided this might well involve neglect of the wider constituency of potential beneficiaries. Second, user demands might conflict with the staff views of their professional responsibilities. On the practical level, the problems were to devise an appropriate means of accountability to users on the one hand and the reconciliation of this with external demands, particularly from funders.

Where the user and the member are one and the same we might expect a stronger form of accountability. The evidence is, however, that the problems remain. We have already noted that in the 'membership model' of governance described by Harris the direct relationship of the members with staff on a day-to-day basis may disempower the management committee. In any case, governing bodies may face opposition from trained staff (like counsellors, social workers or lawyers) who will assert their right to make 'professional' judgements and resist what they might see as interference from the clients who happen also to be their employers (Harris 1993). If member participation and user accountability are two sides of the same coin (Rowe 1978), then significant accountability to users may well be restricted to small self-help groups who have yet to grow (or who have resisted growth) and have avoided a process in which increased specialisation and bureaucracy concentrate power in fewer hands (Chapin and Tsouderos 1956). This is probably an over-simplification. While clearly problematic in principle and practice, account-ability to users and members remains a powerful thread in the collection of values and shared meanings that hold voluntary organisations together and give them their individual identity. In any agency with a history of user involvement their coexistence with other demands for accountability will be both a source of tension and a buttress for the assertion of autonomy against the encroachments of funding bodies.

EXTERNAL DEMANDS FOR ACCOUNTABILITY

The problems of internal accountability for voluntary agencies, complex as they are, have been compounded by a rising tide of demands for account-ability from external sources – notably those who provide their funding. Much of the pressure has come from government – both central and local – although other corporate funders have also developed more demanding funding regimes. These changing demands are associated not only with a significant increase in the amount of funding provided, but also with changes in the kinds of activities and items funded and with a changing social policy context.

The 1980s saw a substantial increase in the activities of local voluntary organisations funded both by central government programmes (employment and training schemes; the Urban Programme; and a number of special programmes like Opportunities for Volunteering and the Local Development Agencies Development Fund) and by local authorities of all political hues (although the Labour administrations in the Metropolitan Counties were especially active). New organisations were formed and older established bodies developed new activities in response to changing views of social need, the encouragement of governmental agencies and the availability of funding.

As a result, the local voluntary sector changed quite significantly – although the extent of the changes varied from area to area – in the nature of its 'business' and its use of human resources. Increasingly, the provision of services took precedence over self-help, community development or advocacy and campaigning activities. Many organisations shifted the focus of their attention to more dependent clients and provided more intensive forms of care. And paid staff were employed alongside – or instead of – volunteers (Billis and Harris 1992).

Such radical changes brought new relationships between funders and funded and new forms of accountability. The basis of the transaction was no longer the award of a general grant towards the organisation's total expenses subject only to 'fiscal' accountability – the need for the authority to be satisfied (a) that the organisation and its officers were fit to be trusted with public money, and (b) that the money had been spent in accordance with the purposes for which it had been voted. Instead, grants were made for projects or programmes with specified aims and objectives and detailed budgets of the expenditure to be incurred. At the same time as tightening up and specifying more closely the requirements for 'fiscal' accountability, the new relationship introduced 'programme' accountability – the requirement that the activities funded should be shown to have reached a specified level and quality of provision. Finally, the growing army of monitoring officers and proliferating local authority grants units developed conditions of grant-aid which included 'process' requirements. Funding was dependent on satisfying the officers that the organisation had equal opportunities, health and safety and associated policies and procedures necessary for the proper discharge of its responsibilities to its clients and its employees.

At the end of the decade the team of civil servants who undertook an 'Efficiency Scrutiny' of Government Funding of the Voluntary Sector (HMSO 1990) found a wide variation in the demands for accountability made by different departments and for various programmes. The overriding consideration – to ensure that the government got value for money – required not only that funded bodies could show that they had produced services of a high quality as well as quantity for their 'customers', but also that departments were clear and explicit about their overall aims and restricted their grants to voluntary organisations to activities which directly served those objectives. Departments should no longer 'respond to ideas from voluntary bodies in an *ad hoc* way'. To return to Diana Leat's categories, the report's authors suggested that programme accountability needed to be administered more systematically and rigorously and added a requirement for accountability for priorities.

The Scrutiny report did not look at the funding of housing associations even though they accounted for half the £2.1 billion of government spending on the voluntary sector in 1988/9. This was not, however, surprising: the Housing Corporation and its Scottish and Welsh counterparts were already established as by far the most developed set of instruments for monitoring voluntary sector funding (Ashby 1990; Billis *et al.* 1994).

All housing associations which receive capital funding for housing development are subject to intensive monitoring visits, normally at two- to four-year intervals, as well as more frequent follow-up contacts. The major inspections may last several days and involve both a study of documents and interviews with senior staff and committee members. They are geared to the rating of the association's performance on a scale from A to D in two areas. One 'is concerned with issues of conduct and. . .geared to making a rounded judgement as to whether the activities. . .are consistent with the objects of a non-profit making housing body in receipt of public funds'. The other 'is concerned with whether the committee of management is in effective control of the organisation'. Associations graded C will receive follow-up attention from the Corporation's officers with a view to assisting it to make good its shortcoming. A grade D may well signal such serious failings that the association's capital funding – and its whole future – is at risk (Ashby 1990).

Ashby suggests that the extent of the monitoring carried out by the Corporation combines all four of Leat's types of accountability – 'fiscal', 'programme', 'process' *and* 'priorities' – with a fifth element. He characterises this additional component as an 'organisational health check' which checks that the association possesses 'the staff structure, committee structure and managerial mechanisms appropriate to its role'.

Is the Housing Corporation model of monitoring and accountability of wider relevance? Ashby suggests that the development of markets or 'quasi markets' in the provision of social welfare will accentuate the need for monitoring because of the 'inability of market mechanisms alone to reward good performance and eliminate unacceptable standards'. Left to local authorities with scant resources the mechanisms of accountability, he argues, will lack the sophistication of the systems established in the field of social housing.

Empirical evidence of the impact of the 'contract culture' on voluntary organisations in Britain is very limited – in marked contrast to the wealth of American research literature (Lewis 1994). The development of contracting as the predominant funding relationship for many voluntary agencies is an explicit policy adopted by government as a logical development of the 'value for money' approach which informed the Scrutiny report. It also underlines the tendency for government to treat voluntary organisations as instruments for implementing policy 'rather than social institutions that can make distinctive and different contributions' (Billis 1993).

The introduction of contracting can also be seen as a significant development in the replacement of the dying culture of grant aid with a more formalised financial relationship (Lewis 1994). And it represents a substantial shift of emphasis away from accountability to the user and towards accountability to the purchaser. A senior officer of a social services department interviewed for one of the few empirical studies to date (Hedley and Rochester 1991) viewed the tripartite relationship between funder, voluntary agency and user in terms of 'an owner taking his pet to the vet. The vet provides the service; the pet is in need of it; but the owner pays the bill and is the client' (ibid.: 16).

Accountability is exercised in two ways. Monitoring of the standard of care provided is the responsibility of the new inspection units established by social services departments as a result of the Community Care and NHS Act 1990 and backed by the sanctions of the Registered Homes Act 1984. But the key mechanism is the contract between the purchasing arm of the social services department and the providing agency. On the face of it, this is a mechanism for stringent accountability requirements with clear sanctions.

Contracts typically involve all four of the kinds of accountability listed by Leat – they will specify the services to be delivered (programme accountability); the ways in which they will be staffed and organised (process accountability); the proper heads of expenditure (fiscal accountability); and, increasingly, the arrangements by which the funder can be assured that the services are provided to those clients deemed to be in greatest need (accountability for priorities). The award of a contract may also be conditional on the organisation's ability to pass the kind of 'organisational health check' identified by Ashby. This may not be a formal part of the negotiation of a contract but considerations of organisational strength and professional orientation may well affect the choice of potential contractor (Forder and Knapp 1993; Goulding 1993).

There is evidence which suggests that, in practice, the operation of contractual arrangements of this kind is characterised by a high level of trust (Common and Flynn 1992; Hedley and Rochester 1991; Goulding 1993). Purchasers have either accepted contracts which lack detailed prescriptions or have not put in place sophisticated monitoring arrangements, either through lack of experience or capacity or as a matter of choice. Many of the organisations that have been awarded contracts in the earliest stages of the implementation of the major changes in welfare provision are well-respected and long-established bodies serving well-defined client groups (Forder and Knapp 1993). They have used these assets to limit the degree to which their accountability to the funder removes from them the ability to remain to some extent accountable to their users.

The increased formality of the relationship between voluntary agencies and their central and local government funders and the associated growth of the demands for accountability has been paralleled by similar developments in their dealings with charitable trusts or foundations and with companies. Leat (1992) has explored the complex new problems faced by trusts and foundations as they experienced rising demands for funding from an expanding voluntary sector at a time when governmental sources of funding were in decline. Increasingly, they have doubted the adequacy of the traditional set of assumptions about their role – that they funded activities the state would not or could not support; that they were in the business of priming the pump rather than providing longer-term support; and that their priorities were innovation, unpopular causes and rapid responses to emergencies.

Alongside this re-evaluation of their role trusts have reconsidered their methods of spending their money. Leat distinguishes three models of grant-making. She describes the traditional approach as the 'gift-giver role' – 'giving presents to others to spend on chosen items but otherwise without strings and without any responsibility to give further gifts'. As well as limiting the responsibilities of the funder, this approach requires little if any accountability on the part of the recipient and, given the lack of commitment to further funding, no incentive for it.

By contrast, the roles of 'investor' and 'collaborative entrepreneur' involve very different relationships with the recipient bodies. 'Investing' the trust's money means 'choosing certain areas for investment and putting in the amount of money, over a specified number of years, necessary to produce a return', while the 'collaborative entrepreneur' will work with selected organisations 'to achieve certain mutually agreed and relatively clearly defined objectives' (Leat 1992: 30). Continuing investment will be contingent on the satisfactory demonstration by the beneficiary that the funding has not only been used as agreed between the parties but also to good effect. For its part, collaboration implies the most fully developed form of accountability – that between partners.

The movement away from 'giving presents' to more thoughtful funding with accountability in the trust and foundation world has found echoes in the private sector's corporate giving. *Ad hoc* decisions by an appeals committee or senior manager once a year have been superseded by corporate affairs departments who have developed policies and procedures including formal requirements for accountability. And, increasingly, donations are being replaced by sponsorship as the pattern of corporate support for the voluntary sector. Where donations are essentially altruistic and 'one-way' transactions, sponsorship is seen as a two-sided relationship which is rewarding for both sides. Companies enter into sponsorship arrangements in order to get a return in the form of publicity or public relations for the company or its brands, entertainment opportunities for its staff, access to well-known and important people already associated with a cause and opportunities for the involvement of current or former employees (Directory of Social Change 1987). In this kind of relationship – which is an extension of the business community's patronage of sport and the arts – the voluntary organisations concerned are accountable for the achievement of the sponsor's objectives which may not be entirely congruent with the realisation of the original aims of the activities funded.

External demands for accountability are not exclusive to funders. Many local organisations are either branches or affiliates of national bodies which have responded to the changing social policy climate by intervening to a greater extent in the affairs of their local organisations (Billis and

Harris 1992). This is the case even with the many organisations (such as Age Concern, MIND and the Association of Crossroads Care Attendant Schemes) where the local affiliates, charities in their own right, appear to have a good deal of autonomy (Hedley and Rochester 1991). Increasingly, headquarters staff are monitoring the activities of their local groups, offering written guidelines and direct support, and, in some cases, providing project funding (Billis and Harris 1992). In doing so they are asserting their right to require process accountability and accountability for priorities. While it does not seem likely that the ultimate sanction of disaffiliation will be invoked, national bodies are able to exercise considerable influence by their demands for explanatory accountability.

As well as seeking resources from governmental sources, trusts and foundations and corporate donors in the private sector, many voluntary organisations solicit funds from the public at large. There are significant problems in principle and in practice of accountability to large numbers of individual funders. There is some evidence that those who give expect a measure of accountability. A recent survey (Golding *et al.* 1993) found that just over half the respondents preferred to donate to charities operating either locally or within Britain on the grounds that it was easier to get information about their activities and ensure that the donation was not being wasted. But there can be a great deal of tension between the organisation's sense of responsibility towards its beneficiaries on the one hand and its donors on the other (MacKeith 1992). These tensions typically affect the design or choice of programmes and the extent to which these should be driven by client need as defined by the service-providers within the agency or donor preference as gauged by those responsible for raising funds.

But there are also important issues of fiscal accountability. Golding and his colleagues (1993) found that more than half those who gave to charity were not satisfied that donations actually reached those for whom they were intended and felt that charities were to some extent corrupt. This finding underlines recent concern about the public accountability of voluntary bodies and the adequacy of the regulatory framework.

PUBLIC ACCOUNTABILITY AND THE REGULATORY FRAMEWORK

While there are other mechanisms for regulating voluntary bodies – many of them are companies limited by guarantee and have to meet the requirements of the Companies Acts, while others are accountable to the Registrar of Friendly Societies – the essential framework for the public accountability of voluntary organisations is provided by charity law. Unfortunately, the concept of a charity is not coterminous with the idea of a voluntary or non-profit organisation. A number of voluntary organisations are not eligible for charitable status, while many charities would not conform to any widely accepted definition of a voluntary body.

To qualify for charitable status an organisation needs (1) to be independent; (2) to be controlled and managed by a committee or body of trustees who receive no remuneration; and (3) to exist solely to pursue charitable purposes. The definition of charitable purposes is a matter of common law established by a series of judicial decisions. At its core are the categories used by Lord Macnaghten in a landmark case in 1891:

- the relief of poverty
- the advancement of religion
- the advancement of education
- other purposes beneficial to the community.

As a former Chief Charity Commissioner has pointed out (Guthrie 1988), this is a classification rather than a definition 'and there is scope within them for further development and refinement of the concept of charity in each generation'. This flexibility has made it possible for a wide range of voluntary bodies to gain charitable status; these have included agencies concerned to improve race relations and to promote activities in the field of employment as well as health and social care organisations, environmental bodies and those concerned with the welfare of animals.

Others, however, are excluded from the charitable sector by virtue of two further principles of charity law. The first of these is that, except in the case of organisations set up to relieve poverty, the activities of a charity must benefit either the public as a whole or a significant section of it. This provision will disqualify the great majority of self-help or mutual aid groups. The second principle is that overt political activities are not charitable in law. While charities may use a proportion of their resources to influence or effect changes in public policy which are directly related to their objects and the needs of their beneficiaries (Guthrie 1988), organisations whose principal purpose is political change will be excluded from the charitable sector. Other notable absentees are the majority of housing associations and tenants' and residents' associations. By contrast, the ranks of charities include the universities, the Church Commissioners and Eton and the other public schools, none of whom would figure in any conception of a voluntary sector.

It is also noteworthy that a number of organisations which appear to be eligible to seek charitable status have not done so. Some of these may be unaware that they could register if they chose, but others do not feel that the benefits outweigh the effort involved. They are increasingly in the minority; the Charity Commission estimates the number of registrations in 1993 at 'close to 17,000' rather than the 4,000 average of previous years (*Charity* 1993).

What then are the benefits of registration? There are, first of all, a number of fiscal privileges. Charities do not pay direct taxation (income, corporation and capital gains tax) although – with a very few narrow exceptions – they do pay VAT. Their liability for the business rate raised by local authorities is automatically reduced by 80 per cent. And their donors receive tax concessions to encourage giving under deed of covenant, by payroll deduction and in one-off 'Gift Aid'. It has been calculated that these privileges were worth £1.2 billion in 1991/2. Second, charitable status is a constitutional privilege, conferring on an organisation the protection of the law. And, third, registration is seen, despite the Commission's disclaimers, as a 'seal of approval' or a badge of respectability.

The extent to which the seal of approval will continue to have any currency depends on the effectiveness with which charities are regulated. In England and Wales responsibility for monitoring and regulating charities rests with the Charity Commission; since 1990 similar powers have been granted to the Lord Advocate in Scotland; while in Northern Ireland the Department of Finance has rather more limited powers. The Charity Commission is a curious creation of the nineteenth century which has a dual role. It has judicial or quasi-judicial powers: its decisions to register organisations as charities have the force of law and it can make regulations for the modernisation or amalgamation of charities. It also has administrative functions – such as the maintenance of the register of charities.

Rising concern about the public accountability of the growing charity sector during the 1980s led to a reappraisal of the role and duties of the Commission (Woodfield 1987; National Audit Office 1987; Public Accounts Committee 1988). A new Chief Charity Commissioner spelled out his plans in a public lecture (Guthrie 1988), the register of charities was computerised and a new Charities Act reached the statute book in 1992. In *Charity and the Nation*, Robin Guthrie set out his vision of the responsibilities of the Commission:

> I would describe the aim in these terms: that what people give and do in the name of charity should be directed to the intended purposes and beneficiaries – not only for their sakes but to honour the gift and to promote the common good.
>
> (Guthrie 1988: 6)

The central means of carrying out that mission was to be the creation of an effective monitoring device in place of a register which was known to be out-of-date and inaccurate. The transfer of records to a new computerised system would provide the opportunity to make a fresh start and to keep track of charities that failed to provide information about their accounts and activities. An up-to-date register would be the first step in enabling the Commission 'to identify individual charities which may need advice or assistance. . .or which may be at risk of maladministration or abuse' (Charity Commission 1992).

Such a system of monitoring depends on a regular flow of appropriate and adequate information and some of the central provisions of the 1992 Act are designed to ensure that this is provided. The Act places a clear responsibility on the trustees of a charity to provide annual accounts in a form to be specified in regulations made by the Home Secretary. The requirements will vary according to the size of the charity, but will in all cases involve the production of a report of the year's activities and details about the people administering the charity as well as financial information. Charities will also be required to make an annual return to the Commission. Failure to meet these requirements 'without good reason' is a criminal offence and may lead to prosecution.

A second intention of the Act is to improve the direct accountability of charities to the public. This has two elements. The first is a requirement that members of the public have a right to receive copies of the charity's annual accounts on payment of a reasonable fee. The second requires charities with an annual income of £5,000 or more to identify themselves as a registered charity on key official documents and distinguish themselves from private individuals or commercial companies. Again, failure to carry out these responsibilities without a reasonable excuse can lead to the prosecution of trustees or employees.

As well as providing the basis for an effective monitoring system the Act also sets out to improve the regulation of the ways in which charities solicit funds from the public – in terms both of street collections and of the methods and conduct of professional fundraisers.

'Fundraising abuse' was one of the five types of problem identified by Guthrie as requiring action by the Commission 'to pursue, prevent and bring to book those who abuse the good name of charity' (1988: 11). The others were: 'misapplication of funds by trustees, whether by negligence, incompetence or with intent to defraud; internal disputes, carried to the point where they. . .render the charity incapable of fulfilling its objects; undue political activity; and tax evasion'. As well as assisting the Commission and the public to identify abuses of these kinds, the Act does add to the Commission's powers. Where the Commissioners believe that a charity's property is at risk of misuse or fraud they can intervene to protect the property even where they have not been able to uncover misconduct or maladministration.

The extent to which the strengthening of the regulatory framework will deliver a more adequate system of public accountability remains to be seen. Some of the detailed regulations which will specify the accounting and reporting conventions required are yet to be published. The establishment of a government task force aimed at sweeping away unnecessary restrictions and regulations affecting the voluntary sector, as in other areas of concern, will delay implementation further while the clash between diametrically opposed government policies is resolved. While few will share the view of Perri 6 (1993) that the Charity Commission is a slow and toothless Victorian relic there are serious question marks about the present system.

If we leave to one side the problem of coterminosity, the main shortcomings of the current arrangements seem to be, first, that the scope of the definition and the methods of accountability are limited and, second, that even within those limits the machinery is not likely to be effective. The key task is seen as the prevention or detection of abuse rather than the promotion of effectiveness. The approach is essentially to adopt 'a narrow (casework) role' rather than a 'broader (policy) role' – to focus, that is, on the 'individual errant charity' rather than looking to make a 'contribution to better management in the sector as a whole' (Billis 1989b). The key data required by the monitors remain essentially information about finance. It is true that the 1992 Act adds an obligation to provide a narrative account of the charity's activities, but this is at heart an adjunct to the accounts not a requirement for accountability in its own right.

The narrowness of the Commission's ambition as a monitor and regulator is highlighted by a comparison with the approach of the Housing Corporation (Ashby 1990). The Corporation not only requires fiscal, programme and process accountabilities as well as accountability for priorities, but also submits housing associations to a comprehensive organisational health check. With the exception of its concern about political activity, the Charity Commission by contrast, concentrates its attention on the narrow requirements of fiscal accountability. While the definition of charitable activity has been developed and enlarged over the years, there has not been a corresponding development in the Commission's thinking about its role as monitor and regulator. But even its capacity to fulfil the restricted role it has accepted must be in doubt. Even if it is able to clear from the register the dead and moribund and acquire regularly updated information on those that remain, how, ask its critics, will it find the resources to review the data from the 130,000 charities estimated to be active in 1991/2 let alone the 20,000 that have been added in the meantime?

CONCLUSION

While there are grounds for doubting the effectiveness of the demands for public accountability imposed on voluntary organisations by the 1992 Charities Act, there is little doubt that they will add to the pressures experienced by voluntary sector managers and leaders. As Leat (1988) pointed out, one cost of multiple accountability common to all the organisations she studied (and many more) was that of time. Staff in particular 'were required to produce different reports and different figures at different times for different groups'. There were compensating benefits: for them accountability was a means of gaining support; the sharing or offloading of responsibility; a means of ensuring some interest in their activities; and a source of legitimacy. These benefits were conferred in various measure by different groups.

But the costs of accountability can be very high indeed. Lack of clarity about the often conflicting internal pressures for accountability exacerbated by a range of demands from outside bodies can reveal conflicts and tension over values, purpose and welfare ideologies that can paralyse or disrupt a voluntary agency. Leat's interviewees were able to manage or 'contain' the problems of multiple accountability largely because those making demands for accountability – principally local government funders – did not have the time or knowledge to pursue the matter effectively. After all, the sums of money involved were comparatively trivial. But as the voluntary sector moves onto the centre of the stage – as it has done in the social housing field – the paymasters will not be so easily satisfied. Voluntary agencies will then face extremely difficult choices. One choice is to give precedence to accountability to the funders over all the other demands on them and effectively become 'instruments for the implementation of government policy' (Billis 1993). Another is to make the brave decision not to take the money on those terms; such a course will depend on the strength of the organisation's root structure. A third course of action – to learn to manage the tension between the competing demands for accountability – may also be available to agencies with clear-sighted and effective leaders as well as deep roots.

REFERENCES

Ashby, J. (1990) 'An account of the monitoring of voluntary organisations by a governmental agency', in *Towards the 21st Century: Challenges for the Voluntary Sector*, Proceedings of the 1990 Conference of the Association of Voluntary Action Scholars, London, Centre for Voluntary Organisation, London School of Economics.

Batsleer, J., Cornforth C. and Paton, R. (eds) (1991) *Issues in Voluntary and Nonprofit Management*, Wokingham: Addison-Wesley.

Billis, D. (1984) 'The missing link: some challenges for research and practice in voluntary sector management', in B. Knight (ed.) *Management in Voluntary Organisations*, London: Association of Researchers in Voluntary Action and Community Involvement.

Billis, D. (1989a) *A Theory of the Voluntary Sector: Implications for Policy and Practice*, London: Centre for Voluntary Organisation, London School of Economics.

Billis, D. (ed.) (1989b) *Public Accountability and the Charity Commission's Database*, London: Centre for Voluntary Organisation, London School of Economics.

Billis, D. (1992) *Organising Public and Voluntary Agencies*, London: Routledge.

Billis, D. (1993) *Sliding Into Change: The Future of the Voluntary Sector in the Mixed Organisation of Welfare*, London: Centre for Voluntary Organisation, London School of Economics.

Billis, D. and Harris, M. (1992) *The Challenge of Change in Local Voluntary Agencies*, London: Centre for Voluntary Organisation, London School of Economics.

Billis, D., Ashby. J., Ewart, C. and Rochester, C. (1994) *Taking Stock: The Shifting Foundations of Housing Associations*, London: Centre for Voluntary Organisation, London School of Economics.

Chapin, F.S. and Tsouderos, J.E. (1956) 'The formalization process in voluntary organisations', *Social Forces*, 34: 342–4.

Charity (1993) December.

Charity Commission (1992) *Charities the New Law: A trustees' guide to the Charities Act 1992*, London: HMSO.

Common, R. and Flynn, N. (1992) *Contracting for Care*, York: Joseph Rowntree Foundation.

Directory of Social Change (1987) *Company Charitable Giving*, London: Directory of Social Change.

Forder, J. and Knapp, M. (1993) 'Social care markets: the voluntary sector and residential care for elderly people in England', in S. Saxon-Harrold and J. Kendall (eds) *Researching the Voluntary Sector*, Tonbridge: Charities Aid Foundation.

Golding, P., Radley, A. and Fenton, N. (1993) *Charities, Media and Public Opinion*, Loughborough University.

Goulding, J. (1993) *A Contract State?*, London: Centre for Voluntary Organisation, London School of Economics.

Guthrie, R. (1988) *Charity and the Nation*, Tonbridge: Charities Aid Foundation.

Harris, M. (1991) *Exploring the Role of Management Committees: A New Approach*, London: Centre for Voluntary Organisation, London School of Economics.

Harris, M. (1993) *The Power and Authority of Governing Bodies*, London: Centre for Voluntary Organisation, London School of Economics.

Harris, M. and Billis, D. (1987) *Organising Voluntary Agencies: A Guide Through the Literature*, London: Bedford Square Press.

Hedley, R. and Rochester, C. (1991) *Contracts at the Crossroads*, Rugby: National Association of Crossroads Care Attendant Schemes.

Herman, R. (1989) 'Board functions and board–staff relations in nonprofit organizations: an introduction', in R. Herman and J. Van Tyl *Nonprofit Boards of Directors*, New Jersey: Transaction.

Home Office (1990) *Profiting from Partnership: Efficiency Scrutiny of Government Funding of the Voluntary Sector*, London: HMSO.

Leat, D. (1988) *Voluntary Organisations and Accountability*, London: National Council for Voluntary Organisations.

Leat, D. (1992) *Trusts in Transition: The Policy and Practice of Grant-Giving Trusts*, York: Joseph Rowntree Foundation.

Lewis, J. (1994) 'What does contracting do to voluntary agencies?', *Theory Meets Practice: Proceedings of the Fifteenth Anniversary Conference*, London: Centre for Voluntary Organisation, London School of Economics.

MacKeith, J. (1992) *Raising Money or Raising Awareness: Issues and Tensions in the Relationship Between Fund-Raisers and Service Providers*, London: Centre for Voluntary Organisation, London School of Economics.

Middleton, M. (1987) 'Nonprofit boards of directors: beyond the governance function', in W. Powell (ed.) *The Nonprofit Sector: A Research Handbook*, New Haven, CT: Yale University Press.

National Audit Office (1987) *Monitoring and Control of Charities in England and Wales*, London: HMSO.

Public Accounts Committee (1988) *Monitoring and Control of Charities in England and Wales*, London: HMSO.

Rowe, A. (1978) 'Participation and the voluntary sector: the independent contribution', *Journal of Social Policy*, 7(1): 41–56.

Simey, M. (1984) *Government by Consent: The Principles and Practice of Accountability in Local Government*, London: Bedford Square Press.

Woodfield, P. (1987) *Efficiency Scrutiny of the Supervision of Charities*, London: HMSO.

6, P. (1993) 'Who needs a Charity Commission', *Third Sector*, 25, 7 October.

9 Trustees, committees and boards

Tim Dartington

INTRODUCTION – WHAT IS GOVERNANCE?

This chapter looks at governance as the essential but little understood aspect of the way voluntary organisations are managed. Every voluntary organisation has a governing body – a management committee or board of trustees – which has ultimate responsibility for what the organisation does. This group of people are unpaid volunteers: they must not directly benefit from their position as members of the governing body. For many organisations which employ staff they provide the justification for their 'voluntary' status. They may be the people who set up the organisation, friends or associates of the founders or, in a sense, representatives of those who founded the organisation a hundred or more years before. They may be professional people recruited for their skills or experience. They may be elected because they are thought to represent the kinds of people the organisation is there to serve. If asked, they may not even know why they are on the committee! But in every case they are responsible for the organisation; and, if it is a charitable organisation, they are the trustees, whether they call themselves that or not.

The role of management committee members and trustees is difficult to define. It is more than advisory, but it is not exactly management. Governance is the term used to describe the oversight and guidance which committee members provide, ensuring that the charity or voluntary organisation acts in accordance with its constitution and legal identity.

This chapter looks at the different elements of governance, drawing on the 1992 report of the *On Trust* working party, convened by the National Council for Voluntary Organisations with the Charity Commission. This working party reviewed the widespread need for greater understanding of the role of trustees and looked at ways of strengthening their effectiveness. The publication of the *On Trust* report can be seen as part of a wider concern about the management of charities which produced the Charities Act 1992. There are estimated to be about a million charity trustees and another six million who serve on non-charitable management committees in Britain (Hedley and Rochester 1994). Although *On Trust* was the product of a concern about the management of charities and the specific legal responsibilities of charity trustees its authors addressed their recommendations to the wider audience of management committee members, charitable and non-charitable, whose general roles and responsibilities were essentially the same. In a similar spirit this chapter will treat the terms 'trustee' and 'management committee member' as interchangeable.

'Governance is governance' is the resounding title of Kenneth Dayton's article on the subject.

> 'It's a conviction first of all that governance is not management, and second that governance in the independent sector (the not-for-profit sector) is absolutely identical to governance in the for-profit sector – with one added dimension. . . .No one should be invited to serve on such a board unless he/she is totally willing to undertake the volunteer as well as the governance side of a trustee's responsibility.
>
> (Dayton 1987)

The *On Trust* report defines governance as 'the overall guidance, direction and supervision of the organisation'(*On Trust* 1992).

The language of governance is in reality terribly confused. Trustee, board member, director, member of management or executive committee, these may each indicate subtle differences, but mostly they obfuscate a commonality, which the Charity Commission would like to clarify. 'The charity trustees are the people responsible under the charity's governing document for controlling the management and administration of the charity, regardless of what they are called' (Charity Commissioners for England and Wales 1992).

It is important, in considering catch-all definitions of the governing body role, to recognise, as Dayton argued, that trustees are very often acting as volunteer managers in addition to carrying out their trustee responsibilities. As trustees they represent and safeguard the independence of action that is characteristic of voluntary organisations: not being driven by the urgency to make a profit (though they often make profits in order to survive) nor by the demands of statutory obligation (though they often survive by helping national and local government to carry out their obligations). Ralf Dahrendorf makes this vital link, often understated, with the characteristics of a civil society. 'Liberty needs the manifold associations of civil society, including the voluntary organisations through which citizens express their interests and concerns without calling in the state' (Dahrendorf 1992).

ROLES AND RESPONSIBILITIES

The responsibilities of committee members and trustees are considerably greater than many themselves realise. It was an unsettling finding of the *On Trust* working party that many people were unaware of these responsibilities which the report summarises under three heads:

– legal responsibilities to see that the charity is abiding by its objects and constitution and operating within the constraints of law;

– financial responsibilities to see that any monies and property are held in trust for the beneficiaries of the charity and that all financial matters are properly and effectively managed and;

– all managerial responsibilities, including the appointment of, and contractual relationships with, staff (including volunteers); ensuring accountability to funders, users and members; representing the views of the organisation; and strategic planning, including the identification of the mission of the organisation, maintenance of values and evaluation of the organisation's activities.

In one of the most widely used voluntary sector management handbooks, Sandy Adirondack (1989) provides a rather different emphasis by summarising the main responsibilities of the voluntary organisation committee as: maintaining a long-term overview of the organisation and all its work; making strategic and major decisions about the organisation's objectives, policies and procedures; ensuring that the needs and interests of relevant people and bodies are taken into account when making decisions; ensuring that there are adequate resources (especially people and money) to carry out the organisation's activities; and monitoring the organisation and all its actions (or inaction).

She does, however, also acknowledge the committee's responsibilities for ensuring that the organisation operates according to its constitution and legal requirements and for financial accountability.

Commentators and those who write manuals for trustees emphasise two major strands in the role of the governing body. As well as the importance of a strategic vision they stress the need to manage external relations for the organisation. Issues of this kind faced by trustees include public awareness of the organisation; fundraising and grant-giving; campaigning and advocacy; charity trading; and contracting.

The importance of these external relations has been set out by Evers (1992):

Much of the influence and effectiveness of any voluntary organisation depends on its relationship to the community, locally and at large. A great deal can be done through quietly contacting influential people, interest groups and institutions such as local authorities and government departments.

Relations with national and local government have become increasingly important in the emerging contract culture:

An important part of management's public relations task is to enlist the participation or at least the support of local politicians so that policies may be informed with the best advice. This is particularly true if the organisation provides services funded by local or central government.

(Allen and Houghton 1990)

Governing bodies thus have extensive and onerous financial, legal and managerial responsibilities as well as key roles in developing and maintaining a strategic vision for the organisation and conducting its relations with the outside world. What kinds of competencies and skills do they need to meet these expectations?

COMPETENCIES AND SKILLS

Clarifying the nature of the skills and competencies required of trustees and management committees has two purposes. In the first place it will assist in the identification of potential trustees who would bring to the organisation appropriate skills and expertise gained in other aspects of their lives. Second, it will indicate the kinds of training and support needed by committee members who have been elected or appointed for reasons other than their experience of management in other contexts.

In a perfect world trustees would score heavily on all of the factors suggested by the *On Trust* working party for consideration by those thinking of joining a management committee. In the first place they would need to have a commitment to the mission of the organisation concerned and an understanding of the voluntary sector. They would also be in a position to commit enough time to the committee's work. Then they would need to bring to the tasks a number of individual personal qualities – judgement, strategic vision and leadership potential. And, finally but not least, potential trustees should possess the ability to work with other people and as part of a team.

The skills and competencies required can also be deduced from the list of characteristics of a good board – from the point of view of the director or chief executive who wants more than a rubber stamp for his or her activities – provided by Kathleen Fletcher (1992):

1 The board understands its legal responsibilities as the governing body of the organisation.
2 The board president runs meetings in an effective and efficient manner.
3 The board actively promotes the organisation to the community.
4 The board takes an active part in long-range strategic planning for the organisation.
5 The board chooses new members with regard to the specific skills or connections they can offer.
6 Board members prepare for meetings by reading material sent to them before the meeting.
7 Board members are willing to accept positions of leadership on the board (officer, committee, chairs).

8   Board members review financial statements carefully and ask for explanations of anything they do not understand.

9   The board opens doors to possible funding sources for staff to pursue.

10   The board stays out of administration, which is the executive's job.

A study commissioned for the government's Inner Cities Initiative, established in 1986 to promote the regeneration of disadvantaged neighbourhood by the use of task forces, looked at training needs of the trustees and management committees of small inner-city organisations. While these included professionals and local officials, and on occasion representatives of the private sector, the emphasis was on the involvement of local people, often drawn from the social groups at which the organisation targeted its services.

A survey of thirty such voluntary bodies undertaken in the inner city of Nottingham identified the skills which management committee members wished to develop. These included general aspects of organisation and management such as decision making and conflict resolution; forward planning, target setting and performance review; and running meetings. They also highlighted specific areas of managerial competence such as personnel and employment skills (e.g. recruitment, supervision and discipline); financial control; and the implementation of equal opportunities policies. And they looked to develop skills in external relations including public speaking; fundraising; and liaison with community/voluntary organisations, statutory agencies and the business sector (Geoff Fordham Associates undated). Those experienced in this work will not be surprised to see conflict resolution in the list!

CHARACTERISTICS AND MOTIVATION

The motives of people who join boards may include a mix of reasons. Some are genuinely altruistic, prompted by their support for the organisation's principles and goals. Other motives are personal; the impulse to join may be an interest in learning new skills and acquiring expertise or simply a need to 'get out of the house'. Some are driven by considerations of status such as a desire to acquire a high profile in the community. Others join in the hope of expanding their social circle.

Shirley Otto (1992) has described the motivation of chairs of management committees. The positive comments she records are based on altruism – 'didn't want to see a good thing stop'; on self-improvement – 'learnt a lot', 'gained confidence', 'cv transformed' and 'feel well used'; and the social – 'mixing with people'. The disadvantages and problems expressed ranged from feelings of unsuitability for the task – 'dislike using authority, dislike challenging people' – through disenchantment with colleagues – 'committee don't understand their responsibilities' and 'staff moan a lot' – to more general difficulties in the role – 'constant problems' and (of course) 'too little money'.

There is little evidence that service on a management committee is seen as an honour. Rodney Hedley and Colin Rochester describe how committee members 'saw committee participation as an essential part of the group's work and something that had to be done; as a necessary chore'. They found that committee work was one of the most unpopular types of volunteering. However, they also record positive aspects of being a committee member. 'Committee work took me into a new world of experience. . . . I learnt I had a voice.' Although there is increasingly some talk of job descriptions for trustees, Hedley and Rochester found that 'it was only for treasurer posts, that committee had some sort of "person specification" in mind' (Hedley and Rochester 1992).

Research for the *On Trust* report confirms a generally held view that trustees are more likely to be white, male, professional and elderly than would be representative of society as a whole. Men outnumber women by three to two at both national and local level. Nearly one in five is over 65. The research suggested that traditional blue-collar occupations are almost entirely excluded (Ford 1992).

In the *On Trust* survey, just under half the trustees interviewed described themselves as elected but the majority of these would appear to have been elected without opposition. The survey concluded that the dominant method of recruitment was word of mouth. The *On Trust* working party favoured a more purposeful recruitment of trustees.

> Some trustees, having been recruited by friends or colleagues, are reluctant to offer firm direction to the organisation. They come on to the Committee because they want to be involved, not because they want to manage the organisation.

There are also instances where the staff want to make use of the professional management skills of volunteers but those involved want simply to stuff envelopes (Puffer 1992).

A survey by Charity Recruitment in 1989 quoted in *On Trust* found that 21 per cent of trustees were recruited because they 'knew someone on the board'. Of those surveyed 46 per cent gave more than 20 hours a month to work with the charity; 29 per cent gave more than 30 hours a month. It was suggested that a small number of committed individuals was providing the backbone of voluntary leadership, and that charities needed to devise new approaches to the management of their organisations and voluntary board members. It was suggested that charities faced great difficulties in identifying and keeping committed volunteers, particularly at the trustee level.

PROBLEMS OF IMPLEMENTING THE TRUSTEES' ROLE

It has been suggested that trustees tend to pass through a life-cycle of three stages:

1 start as an energetic ignoramus

2 make every conceivable mistake for five years
3 leave as an exhausted expert.

(from a 1989 Charity Recruitment survey quoted in *On Trust*)

If this experience is to be avoided, organisations have to take active steps to make their governing bodies effective. Peter Drucker, in his work with not-for-profit organisations, has underlined the significance of the board for the effectiveness of such organisations.

> Good boards don't descend from heaven. It requires continuing work to find the right people and to train them. They come in knowing what you expect of them and they have very tough expectations in terms of time and money and work responsibilities. You take a great deal of time to keep the board informed but to also have a two way flow of information.
>
> (Drucker 1990)

This, though, is likely to be more the ideal than the reality. Governance is defined by John Argenti as setting standards of corporate performance and of corporate conduct and ensuring that these are attained. He emphasises that deciding on corporate objectives is the aspect of governance that most non-profit organisations get wrong, and argues that there are not sufficient checks on managers. 'We have empowered managers to determine these things for us; if we let them do that we must not be astonished when they resolve them to their own advantage rather than in favour of their organisation' (Argenti 1993).

However, business skills are not easily transferable to non-profit boards, as has been observed in several *Harvard Business Review* articles, asking, 'Why do astute executives toss out the principles of good management when they become trustees?' (Fenn 1971; Chart and Taylor 1989).

Failure of entrepreneurial will in the transfer to charity leadership has been described as the stunned rabbit syndrome (MDU 1985). There is also some evidence that it is not only private sector managers who suffer from it: health and social services managers can also fail to deploy their managerial skills and nous when they join voluntary agency committees (Hedley and Rochester 1991).

Another key problem is that the apparently straightforward distinction between policy and management or administration is in practice subjectively defined. Richard Chait (1993), while agreeing that the widely held common-sense position that boards should primarily govern and staff should primarily manage offers a reasonable rule of thumb, also quotes an apocryphal chair of a board: 'Whatever a trustee wants to discuss is policy and the rest is administration.' Rather than argue semantic differences he suggests actions to shift the attention of boards from management to governance.

First, he addresses the questions why boards in practice attend more to management than to governance. After discussing managerial responsibilities that legitimately belong with the board, he comments on what he describes as less mature or thinly staffed organisations which 'depend on trustees to manage the organisation's affairs and sometimes to perform hands-on tasks because the staff lacks both the specialised skills to manage the organisation and the resources to retain outside experts'.

There are pressures, at times irresistible, to distort the trustee role, so that it becomes overbearing or ineffective. Chait (1993) gives three reasons why boards are involved as much or more in management as in governance: disillusionment with staff, the emergency issues that come in crisis management and the personal satisfactions that trustees may be looking for.

Management, more than governance, creates an immediate sense of accomplishment and gratification in part because managerial issues are frequently more amenable to decisions and actions. Matters of strategy and policy, by comparison, often require extended discussions, indepth analyses, and a considerable knowledge of the organisation's context – conditions not easily fulfilled by a trustee committee or board that meets intermittently and relatively briefly.

Competence and role can become paradoxically confused. It may be necessary to recognise that individuals on the board will be more competent in areas of fiscal management than any of the staff. John Carver, a prominent consultant on the US non-profit scene, comments that budgets include much that is trivial. 'For those board members fascinated by minutiae or those given to painstakingly plodding through all items regardless of their relative significance, budget approval is a feast' (Carver 1991). He observes that, once a board has approved a budget, it also has to approve any changes, dragging it into the detail of fiscal management.

Carver explores further issues relating to confusion of role in terms of policy-making, delegation and criteria for decision making. He puts forward a range of arguments that boards are ineffective, concluding that they are more honoured for their potential than for their performance. Stimulating boards to become involved therefore has its dangers. He quotes with approval a commentator's description of 'replacing the judgement of the experienced and committed by the sometimes allergic reaction of the previously somnolent' (Riesman 1985).

Having expressed such vehement dissatisfaction and got it out of his system, Carver – like many a chief executive – argues for a policy governance model in which:

the board is foremost a guardian of values on behalf of ownership or stockholder – equivalents. . . .The visionary aspects of deciding public benefit and the need to assure organisational capability to produce in the future compel a long term bias in the board's work. Without becoming managers, then, the board controls the long term environment in which managers produce and plan. Proper governance is not administration writ large so much as it is ownership in microcosm.

(Carver 1991)

However, as is the case with many other commentators, the policy governance model is, as Carver himself says, a prescriptive rather than a descriptive model of what a board does and of the board–executive relationship.

Geoff Poulton, in his study of the management of voluntary organisations, gives little emphasis to trustees and committees, but recognises that the way committees work is related to the dynamics of the organisation.

> Crucially it depends upon whether the organisation is run on the basis of benign dictatorship or by democratic processes. The former is not uncommon in voluntary organisations and, depending upon the judgement and communication skills of the leader, may be very time/energy effective. The latter is undoubtedly much more problematic but can be a means of ensuring that the membership is effectively understanding and pursuing the policy objectives which it has set itself.
>
> (Poulton 1988)

DEALING WITH CRISES

An effective board can be seen as the primary distinctive characteristic of a voluntary organisation. A US handbook (O'Connell 1985) emphasises the voluntary element.

> If a board is relatively inactive, and if most of the money comes from and accountability is owed to government and third party sources, then the organisation is not really functioning as a voluntary institution.

The *On Trust* working party report outlines some of the dangers of over-dependence of trustees on staff.

> It is essential that committee members have the necessary background information and knowledge of the organisation to make their own judgements . . . .one of the problems of being a trustee, particularly a new trustee, concerns a sense of 'impostership'. Organisations are easily dominated by the professional staff; trustees are lay members who find themselves directing such organisations. . .staff often underestimate how much power they have in relation to their trustees – through controlling the flow of information to them. . .if the committee becomes an endorsing body, leaving staff to decide policies and run the organisation, the charity may go into decline when key staff leave, and the committee become vulnerable.

The effectiveness of the board may be related to its ability to adapt to the life-cycle of the organisation. Wood (1992) has suggested that the behaviour of the board is itself cyclical. Following a unique founding period, when the trustees may be the true representatives of the organisation while supporting the first staff, there is likely to be a restructuring, where 'the rhetoric of goals, objectives and results supersedes the notion of mission'.

At this stage, middle-aged professionals recruited on to the board conceive of the agency as a business in a competitive environment in which the best strategy is to have a distinctive product. A period of *over-managing*, likely to drive the chief executive to despair, follows.

In time this develops into a *corporate phase*, and the executive reasserts its authority. Eventually inertia sets in during a phase in which the board is reduced to a '*ratifying*' role until something is perceived to have 'gone wrong' and the lack of board control is revealed. The perception of a crisis triggers an energetic response by the board who embark on a further period of over-managing and restart the cycle.

> Because the group dynamic of the supermanaging phase seems to require a crisis upon which to exercise itself, a powerful executive director's proprietary administrative style may suddenly be perceived by a revived board to be counterproductive, and the executive's resignation may be the unintended consequence.

The responsiveness of trustees to a crisis is even more crucial in small organisations. A study of a voluntary organisation that closed down pointed to the importance of the committee to its lack of effectiveness.

> Most members of the first committee had resigned quite rapidly. . .the committee was consistently short of members, which meant that a lot of work was left undone. . .by 1985 there was poor attendance at committee meetings with the organisation described as 'clearly going down hill'. The inexperience of the committee meant that more of the work was falling on the shoulders of the three officers. . .individual members on the committee were well suited for the work but they were not 'working together'. The committee members had no clear 'job description'. The committee, it was claimed, became anxious about the mounting range of responsibilities it had taken on. It was described as 'naive and daunted by responsibility' which was emphasised by the declining and changing membership and support. It was further described as a 'worried committee' with members 'struggling as employers' and looking for a way out of their responsibilities; '. . . eventually members actually dreaded the monthly committee meetings.'
>
> (Humphrey 1991)

The experience of governance is hugely varied, and the extremes of boredom/ frustration and commitment/enthusiasm are hardly described by commentators. Static models of normative behaviour do not describe the dynamics of what really is going on.

An interesting analysis which throws light on board behaviour is suggested by Margaret Harris, who distinguishes traditional, membership and entrepreneurial models of governance. The traditional element is clearer on authority, with a linear progression from those who are guardians of the mission to those who do the work; the membership model is circular, where the guardians are also the beneficiaries (the clearest example being the self-help group); while the entrepreneurial model recognises the common experience of the staff-led organisation, where those who do the work are also the guardians of the mission. Some serious problems of governance arise where different elements in an organisation are using different models (Harris 1993b).

The membership model is consistent with the work of many campaigning movements. It also introduces the complexity as to whether users of services are thereby automatically beneficiaries of the organisation and excluded from the possibility of being themselves trustees. Many charities make a point of having 'users' on their committees and this is consistent with a general policy direction across all sectors to ensure accountability and local control of services.

THE BOARD–STAFF RELATIONSHIP

The NCVO working party on *Effectiveness in the Voluntary Sector* (1990) stated that there was no single blueprint for the board–staff relationship.

> Problems over such relationships and clashes of personality occur in all organisations, voluntary or otherwise. In a voluntary body, the perceptions and perspectives of the trustees and their concern to maintain a mission of the organisation, may sometimes differ from the perceptions and perspectives of staff preoccupied with their day to day problems.

The *Board Members Book* (O'Connell 1985) also attempts to distinguish the roles of the board and the staff.

> The worst illusion ever perpetrated in the non profit field is that the board of directors makes policy and the staff carries it out. This is just not so. The board, with the help of the staff, make policy and the board, with the help of the staff, carries it out.

Nevertheless, this same resource book recognises how common is the conflict between the chair of the board and the chief executive officer and how often this is a difference of personality. If there is a breakdown of trust and respect, clarity of roles and job description are hardly going to resolve the issue.

Constant reference to lack of clarity or creative tension still leaves uncertain the reasons why chronic tensions between boards and their organisations are seemingly the only consistent finding about voluntary organisation dynamics. In an attempt to 'find another way' of addressing this key issue, Margaret Harris (1993a) has developed a total activities analysis, which places the board's role within the context of all the activities carried out by a voluntary agency as well as recognising that board and staff are interdependent. Over a number of years in projects and workshops involving voluntary organisations of different kinds Harris and colleagues developed a list of activities they had in common. These are:

1 Providing services (direct provision and/or advocacy work).
2 Designing and developing services and structures (including setting policies and priorities, planning and monitoring).
3 Developing and maintaining an understanding of need and demand (for example, in the field of housing, human services or the arts).
4 Maintaining good public relations (including publicity and making links with key people and agencies in the field).
5 Fundraising (from a range of sources and using a variety of arrangements, including donations, grants and contracts).
6 Finance work (including collection and dispersement of cash, accounting, budgeting and budgetary control).
7 Staffing and training (including recruitment, induction and staff welfare work).
8 Managerial and co-ordinative work (including selection and induction of staff, prescription of work, co-ordination of work, appraisal).
9 Logistical work (including providing premises and equipment, materials and other supporting services).
10 Clerical and secretarial work (including recording and communication of decisions, actions and events).

This analysis of functions allows organisations to explore the role of the governing body in relation to that of the staff. Who is doing what? Who should be doing it? If activities are the province of both board and staff, what is the balance or distribution of responsibility? Thus, it helps not only to clarify who does what but also to identify where there are areas of uncertainty, which could be an even more serious issue than staff and board fighting over the dominant role in personnel matters and managerial supervision.

The approach has the advantage of recognising that what is right for one organisation is not the same for another. The avoidance of prescriptive solutions is one of the issues for those who are trying to work with the real-life dilemmas of voluntary agencies.

It also allows for the fact that the balance between the board and staff may be re-negotiated at different stages in the history of the organisation, its growth and organisational development.

Harris also comes to an optimistic conclusion that the governing body–staff relationships in voluntary organisations, often thought to be inherently unbalanced and tense and doomed to dominance by one party or the other, could still benefit from a collaborative approach.

A research study conducted using a collaborative, participative research methodology might reveal that the tensions and inequalities between governing bodies and staff noted by earlier researchers mask an underlying drive towards a co-operative approach to voluntary sector leadership – a drive that can come to provision within the context of an appropriate framework as total activities analysis.

(Harris 1993a)

Chait takes seriously the paradox that in voluntary organisations the staff have to educate their bosses. He suggests that it is the executive's role to articulate an institutional strategy for careful periodic review by the board, to structure board materials to direct trustees' attention to issues of policy and strategy and to equip trustees with the capacity to monitor organisational performance and progress. In turn he also expects the board to manage its own affairs, creating clear expectations for the board as well as clear expectations for the chief executive, and also working to structure meetings to direct the board's attention to matters of policy and strategy, while collecting feedback on the board's performance. All such proposals are dependent on Chait's final proposition that 'in the long run, the organisation will be healthier'.

> Informed, engaged boards attentive to the core components of governance are typically associated with successful, effective organisations.
>
> (Harris 1993a)

Ralph Kramer, distancing himself from the pervasive espoused theory of partnership, proposes a contingency approach involving power-dependency and conflict. He discusses relations between staff and board in terms of status, behavioural norms, role and responsibilities, authority and power. Larger complex professional and bureaucratic organisations, for example, have conditions favourable to staff domination over the board.

> Board members and executive are conceived as interest groups with distinctive resources to influence decision-making and who – depending principally on the nature of the issue – may collaborate or engage in political manoeuvring or conflict.
>
> (Kramer 1985)

But it is worth remembering that a strong executive is not the only threat to an effective board. It may also be dominated by its chair, fragmented into fractions, resistant to any leadership and demanding consensus at all times or aimless and uncertain (Murray, Bradshaw and Wolpin 1992).

CONCLUSION

The impact of contracts or service-level agreements is predicted to influence changes to the boards of trustees of organisations providing services.

> Moving into the contractual process could require important processes of staff and management training and/or the appointment of more expert staff and the recruitment of professional expertise to voluntary management boards.
>
> (Macfarlane 1990)

The contract culture has also drawn attention to conflicts of interest at board level. The *On Trust* report commented:

Many local authority councillors or officers on Committees are unaware that their prime duty is to the charity or voluntary organisation rather than their local authority. Conflicts of interest can arise and the potential legal implications of their involvement are becoming more complex as a result of recent local government legislation.

There are other examples of trustees who see themselves as representing other organisations.

If Committees are filled with representatives of other organisations, and there is a lack of clarity whether they are there to represent the interests of another agency or as members in their own right, they are unlikely to offer the leadership that the organisation needs for itself.

(*On Trust* 1992)

The accountability of boards is under scrutiny as contracting with government agencies becomes the norm. Steven Rathgeb Smith and Michael Lipsky have seen the transformation, in the US, of private charities into state agencies. Their title – *Nonprofits for Hire* – is unequivocal about their message.

The concept of the voluntary agency fuelled entirely by a neighbour-helping-neighbour altruism. . .masks the increasing dependence of non-profit service organisations on government funding. This has the effect of weakening governance. Power is centralised in the chief executive, volunteers are replaced by paid workers, and boards have a limited role in maintaining the philanthropic base of the organisation.

(Smith and Lipsky 1993)

Comparisons with the non-executive director role in companies are part of the debate about what is distinctive about not-for-profit management. Too often the comparison is assumed to be with a known quantity, as if voluntary organisations are the only ones that experience ambiguity and lack of clarity in their management. And what of the boardroom battles that are reported in the financial press – and even reach the sports pages?

It is appropriate that this paper should end on a questioning note. The essential structure of voluntary organisations and the whole question of the effectiveness of boards is increasingly under question. Are we asking too much of the trustee body?

Professionalism and voluntarism sit uneasily together and are both found wanting when charity is understood in terms of a multi-million business, while those who seek to regulate charities argue for further controls. Following the Charities Act 1992 the liabilities of trustees are a subject of interest and debate.

Ultimately, the concept of trusteeship will live or die, depending on the extent to which this form of accountability is seen to guarantee the public good arguments for having a charitable sector at all. The US commentators have been stronger in arguing the significance of voluntarism in the govern-ance of charities and non-profit organisations. The *On Trust* report argued, lacking statistics and resorting to rough-and-ready estimates, that a million people are trustees of voluntary organisations in the United Kingdom. If this is the case, it indicates both the potential and the seeming invisibility of a powerful example of active citizenship.

REFERENCES

Adirondack, S. (1989) *Just About Managing?*, London: London Council of Voluntary Service.
Allen, G. and Houghton, P. (1990) *The Fifth Estate: People and Power in Associations*, European Society of Association Executives.
Argenti, J. (1993) *Your Organisation, What Is It For?*, Maidenhead: McGraw-Hill.
Carver, J. (1991) 'Redefining the board's role in fiscal planning', *Nonprofit Management and Leadership*, 2(2): 177–92.
Chait, R.P. (1993) *How To Help Your Board Govern More and Manage Less*, National Center For Nonprofit Boards.
Charity Commissioners for England and Wales (1992) *Responsibilities of Charity Trustees*, London: Charity Commission.
Chart, R.P. and Taylor. B.E. (1989) 'Charting the new territory of nonprofit boards', *Harvard Business Review*, 67: 44–54.
Dahrendorf, R. (1992) *Introduction to On Trust*, London: National Council for Voluntary Organisations.
Dayton, K.N. (1987) *Governance is Governance*, The Independent Sector.
Drucker, P.F. (1990) *Managing the Nonprofit Organisation*, London: HarperCollins.
Evers, S. (1992) *Managing a Voluntary Organisation: Guidelines for Trustees and Committees*, London: British Institute of Management.
Fenn, D.H. Jr. (1971) 'Executives as community volunteers', *Harvard Business Review*, 49(2): 4–16, 156–7.
Fletcher, K.B. (1992) 'Effective boards: how executive directors define and develop them', *Nonprofit Management & Leadership*, 2(3): 282–93.
Ford, K. (1992) *Trustee Training and Support Needs: Research Report for the NCVO/ Charity Commission Working Party on Trustee Training*, London: National Council for Voluntary Organisations.
Geoff Fordham Associates (undated) *The Training Needs of Trustees: An Inner City Perspective*.
Harris, M. (1993a) 'Exploring the role of boards using total activities analysis', *Nonprofit Management & Leadership*, 3(3): 269–81.
Harris, M. (1993b) *The Power and Authority of Governing Bodies: Three Models of Practice in Service-Providing Agencies*, Working Paper 13, Centre for Voluntary Organisation, London School of Economics.
Hedley, R. and Rochester, C. (1991) *Contracts at the Crossroads*, Rugby: National Association of Crossroads Care Attendance Schemes.
Hedley, R. and Rochester, C. (1992) *Understanding Management Committees: A Look at Voluntary Management Committee Members*, Berkhamsted: The Volunteer Centre UK.
Hedley, R. and Rochester, C. (1994) *Volunteers on Management Committees: A Good Practice Guide*, Berkhamsted: The Volunteer Centre UK.
Humphrey, R. (1991) *Closed Down Case Study 4*, London: Centre for Voluntary Organisation, London School of Economics.

Kramer, R.M. (1985) 'Toward a contingency model of board–executive relations', *Administration in Social Work*, 9(3).

Macfarlane, R. (1990) *Contracting In or Out? The Impact on Management and Organisation*, London: National Council for Voluntary Organisations.

Management Development Unit, NCVO (1985) *MDU Bulletin*, Management Committees Issue.

Murray, V., Bradshaw, P. and Wolpin, J. (1992) 'Power in and around nonprofit boards: a neglected dimension of governance', *Nonprofit Management & Leadership*, 3(2): 165–82.

National Council for Voluntary Organisations (1990) *Effectiveness in the Voluntary Sector*, London: NCVO Publications.

National Council for Voluntary Organisations (1992) *On Trust: Increasing the Effectiveness of Charity Trustees and Management Committees*, London: NCVO Publications.

O'Connell, B. (1985) *The Board Members Book*, New York: The Foundation Center.

Otto, S. (1992) *Evidence to the On Trust Working Party*, London: National Council for Voluntary Organisations.

Poulton, G. (1988) *Managing Voluntary Organisations*, Chichester: Wiley.

Puffer, S.M. (1992) 'Professionals who volunteer: should their motives be accepted or managed?', *Nonprofit Management & Leadership*, 2(2): 107–24.

Riesman, D. (1985) Foreword in M.M. Wood (ed.) *Trusteeship in the Private College*, Baltimore, MD: Johns Hopkins University Press.

Smith, S.R. and Lipsky, M. (1993) *Nonprofits for Hire: The Welfare State in the Age of Contracting*, Boston, MA: Harvard University Press.

Unterman, I. and Davis, R.H. (1982) 'The strategy gap in not-for-profits', *Harvard Business Review*, 60(3): 30–40.

Wood, M.M. (1992) 'Is governing board behaviour cyclical?', *Nonprofit Management & Leadership*, 3(2): 139–63.

10 Management and organisation

Julian Batsleer

In the wake of the Wolfenden Report, the National Council for Voluntary Organisations (NCVO) invited Professor Charles Handy, the doyen of British management education, to chair a working party on *Improving Effectiveness in Voluntary Organisations*. The subsequent 'Handy Report' (NCVO 1981) gave notice that voluntary organisations could not escape the management revolution which had begun to permeate British institutions since the late-1970s. Established service organisations were finding the classic conventions of charity administration ill-suited to the demands of an increasingly turbulent social and resource environment. Structures and procedures inherited from earlier eras of philanthropic endeavour no longer sufficed. In a similar vein, newer groups involved in issue-based advocacy and community self-activity were discovering that principled commitment to empowerment, collective working and grass-roots democracy did not, in itself, guarantee success in the changing circumstances of the 1970s and 1980s (Landry *et al.* 1985).

The encounter between management and the post-Wolfenden voluntary sector has been a turbulent affair. 'Should the salt of the earth be managed?' was the question posed in NCVO's first *Management Development Unit Bulletin* (NCVO 1983). It neatly captures the ambiguity that has characterised much of the language and the practice of management in the voluntary sector. There has been a pervasive worry that management would be a Trojan horse, infiltrating alien systems and practices and undermining the perceived autonomy, cherished values, core identities and distinctive working methods of individual organisations and the sector as a whole. The issue of voluntary sector management has often been at the heart of fierce debates over the shifting boundaries between commercial, public and voluntary agencies since the mid-1970s.

Behind the *angst*, there have been two major dimensions to 'the management question'. One is the emergence of a recognisable *management discourse*; the other is the search for appropriate forms of *management practice*. The first part of this chapter considers factors which have shaped the discourse about the management of voluntary and non-profit organisations in the UK and identifies ways in which that discourse has been elaborated throughout the sector. The chapter then looks at aspects of management practice developed in voluntary organisations since the late 1970s, either to cope with particular problems or to give effect to specific values and choices. The chapter ends with a brief reflection on a few general issues raised by the encounter between management and voluntary organisations.[1]

CREATING A LANGUAGE

On the face of it, greater attention to issues of management offered voluntary organisations a common-sense way of coping with pressures and changes outlined in earlier chapters. In practice, several factors have weighed against a straightforward adoption of mainstream management thinking. Most obviously, the sheer diversity of organisations sheltering under the voluntary sector umbrella means that it has been impossible to define or prescribe a generally applicable set of management procedures or organisational systems. Moreover, suspicions of management have been compounded by a fear that devoting more energy to organisational processes would be a distraction from the 'real business' of working with clients and communities. In an era of financial stringency, voluntary organisations have been sensitive to the charge, however unfounded, of spending too high a proportion of their time and money on such matters as administration, staff development or internal communications.

The major barrier, however, to a serious engagement with management issues was the almost total absence in the UK of a ready-made or generally accepted *management discourse* for voluntary organisations. In the United States, the operation of voluntary and non-profit enterprises has attracted serious attention from major thinkers (Kanter 1972; Kotler 1975; Drucker 1990) and begun to make an acknowledged contribution to the general theory and practice of organisation and management. By contrast, the UK has a less well-formed tradition of management thinking. Moreover, the perceived social and economic marginality of the voluntary sector means that British voluntary organisations have received scant consideration from mainstream management theorists. (There are, of course, a few notable exceptions such as Handy (1988) and Butler and Wilson (1990).)

The upshot is that those involved in voluntary sector management during the 1980s and 1990s – practitioners, policy-makers, trustees, consultants, trainers, researchers – have all been obliged to develop an acceptable language (or languages) with which to articulate their concerns. There have been two broad aspects to the process. The first has been the search for an appropriate framework of ideas and theories. The second has been the fostering of a 'culture of management' in the voluntary sector through the creation of an accessible body of management literature and the growth of programmes and opportunities for management education and organisational development.

Perspectives and theories

Voluntary sector researchers and managers have been highly eclectic in their search for suitable tools of analysis. They have drawn on a staggeringly diverse and often conflicting array of approaches, theories and bodies of knowledge. This has given rise to an abundance of potentially very fruitful ways of making sense of the complexities of voluntary sector management. It has also resulted in a persistent lack of common ground in discussions and debates about voluntary sector management (Paton 1993).

Broadly speaking, 'the management question' has been approached from three directions:

* social policy and public administration;
* organisational theory and management studies;
* community development and 'alternative organisations'.

Although there are overlaps, the pursuit of these separate routes has led to some very different maps of the management terrain, and hence some markedly divergent perceptions and definitions of the management agenda for voluntary organisations.

Approached from the hinterland of social policy and public administration, voluntary sector management is primarily a strategic matter of enabling voluntary organisations to make a distinctive and effective contribution to the overall organisation and provision of human and social services. For individual organisations and the sector as a whole, the management agenda has been inextricably bound up with the wider policy agenda set by the restructuring of the post-war welfare state. Maintaining the independence, integrity and plurality of values of an essentially welfare-oriented voluntary sector is a key management priority; it involves the elaboration of distinctive organisational cultures and processes.

The social policy approach has been reflected in official surveys and reports (NCVO 1984; URBED 1988; Home Office 1989); in debates about how to respond to key shifts in public funding such as the Manpower Services Commission's (MSC) Special Programmes in the 1980s (Addy and Scott 1988) or the 'contract culture' in the 1990s (Gutch 1992); in thinking about how to negotiate the political and institutional transformation of central and local government (Flynn 1990; Stewart 1986; Gutch and Young 1988). The social policy approach to management has sought to steer voluntary organisations along their own unique road, keeping clear of the dangerous highways of state bureaucracy or market opportunism (Billis 1993).

An extension of this essentially strategic perspective has been provided by wider political, economic and sociological debates about 'The Third Sector'. Drawing on the European experience, for instance, a fruitful source of insights and analysis has been the location of voluntary sector management within traditions of association and the politics of civil society (Streeck and Schmitter 1985).

Things have looked somewhat different through the lens of organisational and management theory. With sectoral boundaries and organisational identities in a state of flux, many of the most significant ideas have emerged by stepping aside from the framework of social policy and formal sectoral divisions. Cross-sectoral commonalities have often been more illuminating than stereotypical differences. Assumed distinctions between voluntary sector management and management in other sectors are much less clear-cut on the ground (Paton and Cornforth 1992; Leat 1993). Cherished voluntary sector beliefs and self-perceptions, such as characteristically high levels of staff and volunteer motivation and commitment, may not prove to be as well founded as they are often assumed to be (Hooker and Mabey 1992).

An organisational focus has revealed a plurality of management systems and procedures *within* voluntary organisations which have been overlooked in the quest for unitary processes and common commitments and characteristics. The 'Third Sector' takes on a very different appearance, for instance, if one considers the organisational and management tasks and choices faced by medium-sized welfare agencies alongside those encountered in similarly volatile organisations in operating in other areas – the arts, worker co-operatives (Cornforth *et al.* 1988), environmental groups, trade unions (Watson 1988), churches (Reed and Palmer 1976), decentralised social service departments (Miller 1989; Young 1991). As far as the management of resource acquisition, public relations and marketing are concerned, the problems and dilemmas confronting voluntary organisations are not significantly different from those facing schools, NHS Trusts or universities (Burnett 1992; Cornforth *et al.* 1993). By the same token, many large voluntary organisations are more akin to quangos or private corporations than to other voluntary organisations; many small, self-help groups can best be understood, not as organisations needing management, but as part of an informal economy of clubs and social networks (Paton 1992; Bishop and Hoggett 1986).

The key motifs to emerge from this second approach cluster round such issues as the management of conflict and change and negotiating the diverse demands of internal and external stakeholders – clients, professional staff, trustees, funders, suppliers, partners (Paton and Batsleer 1992). It has contributed to thinking about organisational structures and strategies in ways which do not simply echo debates about social policy or public resource allocation (Butler and Wilson 1990). Drawing on the various disciplines of management studies, it has helped to generate suitable languages for both the softer, human resource end of management and the harder, more technical end of evaluation, financial and information systems and performance measurement. (The emergence of a flourishing Community Operations Research network is an interesting indicator of the creative ways in which one of the more technical disciplines of management science can inform the work of one of the more informal and fragmentary corners of the voluntary sector (Ritchie 1992).) By exploring the diversity and complexity of the management task, this approach has, perhaps surprisingly, also drawn attention to a strong element of contingency and some inescapable contradictions and ambiguities in voluntary sector management.

Between them, the social policy and the organisational theory schools have sung the loudest arias in the voluntary sector management opera. They have been accompanied, however, by a chorus of singers who have been singing a somewhat different medley of songs described here as the community development and 'alternative organisations' perspective.

The various strands of this third perspective are distinguished, not by a common body of theory or a shared organisational agenda, but by a preoccupation with forging alternative, non-conventional answers to the question 'What's voluntary sector management all about?'. For instance, the last two decades have seen attempts to build a management discourse out of the 'Getting Organised' traditions of community development in the UK (Smith 1981; Ward 1984) and the US (Alinsky 1972). Another focus of attention has been the experience of collective working (Stanton 1989). Insights and approaches have been drawn from the organising principles of social movements – the women's movement (Brown 1992), the black movement (Bhatt 1986) – from oppositional and cultural politics (Cockburn *et al.* 1980; Hall 1989) and from a concern for empowerment and alternative modes of leadership (Hosking 1988).

The three broad perspectives outlined here are not, of course, watertight compartments; those starting from any one position have happily plundered from the other two. There are, however, some very real tensions between them; they have not blended comfortably together into a single tapestry of management ideas. Their different orientations have given rise to a persistent lack of agreed focus or shared terms of reference in the quest for a suitable management language.

Dissemination and development

Notwithstanding the fragmentation of the underpinning ideas and theories, the last two decades have seen the emergence of a recognisable 'culture of management' in the voluntary sector. Even small community projects have begun to use the language of business plans, strategic choice, quality outcomes, mission statements and competing stakeholders. There has been much 'dancing with the enemy', despite the persistent anxiety that too large a dose of managerialism might lead to the loss rather than the enhancement of core values and identities. Indeed, there have been signs that too much may have been expected of management. There have been ill-advised hopes and promises that effective management would automatically guarantee growth or somehow transcend the ineluctable messiness and hazards of organisational life in the voluntary sector.

Several vehicles have contributed to the dissemination of management thinking. The first has been the burgeoning literature dealing with various aspects of organisation and management. It has taken a variety of forms. Most prolific have been the 'how to do it' handbooks and the practical advice and information published by such bodies as the Directory of Social Change (DSC) and NCVO. They have been a means of sharing 'practitioner knowledge' in a variety of fields such as general management (Adirondack 1989; Holloway and Otto 1985); volunteer management (Hedley 1992; Willis 1992); evaluation (Ball 1988). They have also introduced new ideas in an acceptable way – marketing (MacIntosh and MacIntosh 1984); governance (Harris 1992); fundraising (Burnett 1992); management development (Paton and Hooker 1990). General information has been bolstered by specialist journals like *NGO Finance* and *Professional Fundraising* and technical reference material such as Croner's (1990) *Management of Voluntary Organisations*. Importantly, however, the management advice literature has been elaborated in countless informal ways through locally produced booklets, information sheets, newsletters and briefings.

A less prolific stream of literature has served to generate a more discursive and, at times, polemical dimension to management thinking. 'Think pieces' such as Landry *et al.* (1985), Handy (1988), Batsleer *et al.* (1992) and Gutch and Young (1988) have all helped to nurture a general management awareness. The short-lived *MDU Bulletin* provided a unique and as yet unreplaced forum for discussion and debate in the sector. To some extent the gap has been filled in other ways – through conference reports, the Working Paper Series of the Centre for Voluntary Organisation (CVO) or the course material emanating from the Open University Business School's Voluntary Sector Management Programme (Paton *et al.* 1991; Cornforth *et al.* 1993). Similarly, a practitioner orientation in journals such as *Nonprofit Management & Leadership* or *Nonprofit and Voluntary Sector Quarterly* has enabled them to begin to extend access to management thinking.

Interestingly, the thinnest literature is the systematic research literature, perhaps reflecting the fact that research resource is overwhelmingly directed towards discipline-based work on policy rather than the essentially interdisciplinary analysis of organisation and management. Centres such as CVO have promoted a growing number of action-research projects; the work of Diana Leat (1988, 1989, 1993, for example) and David Billis (1993, for example) has often contained a strong organisational dimension; Butler and Wilson (1990) remains a rather lonely research landmark in the area of charity structure and strategy. Official reports (Charity Commission 1991, 1992, for example) and individual accounts of particular organisations (Poulton 1988, for example) have also been a source of some useful, if less theoretically rooted, management insights.

Running alongside the literature, the second vehicle for grounding management in the sector has been a growing number of initiatives in the area of management education and organisational development. These have been reinforced by the emergence of a group of agencies, associations and support networks with special interests in voluntary sector management.

Within the sector, the establishment of NCVO's Management Development Unit (MDU) in 1982 was an important catalyst. Building on earlier training offered through such bodies as the Industrial Society, the MDU – and its successor the Management Unit and its partner for ethnic minority groups the Organisation Development Unit (now an independent agency, SIA) – generated a mixture of training courses and consultancy work throughout the sector. It provided a strong 'do-it-yourself' flavour to management development in the sector. Management training became an integral feature of large organisations' in-house staff development. Organisational and management issues also came to feature prominently in the training and information work of local development agencies such as councils for voluntary service, rural community councils and community work training groups (Batsleer 1988). The grass-roots end of management development has been further nurtured by networking and cascading initiatives like Advancing Good Management in the 1990s. Bodies such as DSC, the Charities Aid Foundation (CAF) and the Institute of Charity Fundraising Managers (ICFM) have all mounted a growing number of seminars, conferences and training courses with the aim of extending effective management in the sector.

The post-Handy era has also seen an expansion of management and organisational development activity originating from outside the sector. The 1980s saw a mushrooming of freelance trainers and consultants giving their attention to voluntary organisations. Newer training agencies such as the Management Centre emerged with an explicit emphasis on voluntary and non-profit management; established firms of management consultants began to seek and secure regular business from the voluntary sector. CVO at the London School of Economics had raised the standard of organisational practice before Handy's intervention. Since its original establishment as the Programme of Research and Training in Voluntary Action (PORTVAC) at Brunel University in 1978, CVO has lovingly tended the flame of welfare pluralism and provided a distinctive programme of teaching and research, particularly in the area of human and social service agencies. More recently, the Open University's Voluntary Sector Management Programme has been a source of complementary research and teaching from the management studies perspective and has opened up a route to recognised management qualifications for hundreds of voluntary sector staff each year.

Bodies such as the Charity Evaluation Service or the Charities Effectiveness Review Trust provide management-related advice and support and, of course, management has begun to feature prominently in the programmes and syllabuses of a growing number of training and educational institutions in the social work, youth and community work and health care fields. By the mid-1990s, some organisations were exploring the feasibility of linking voluntary sector management to the national standards of management competence set down by the Management Charter Initiative.

It is very important, however, not to overstate the scale, scope or impact of these various initiatives and agencies. Notwithstanding their energy, they do not amount to a sustained or coherent programme of management and organisational development for the voluntary sector. Much of it has been reactive, opportunistic and short-term; some of it has been of questionable quality. With the exception of the Association of Chief Executives of National Voluntary Organisations, no broad-based forum or recognised network has emerged for managers in the voluntary sector. The bodies which have been most effective are those with a specialist remit such as the Charity Finance Directors' Group or the ICFM which was set up in 1983 and now has 1700 members. Interestingly, it is the latter which has made the most progress in formulating recognised standards and codes of practice for its area of management, even though fundraising, marketing and public relations have until very recently occupied a decidedly lowly and somewhat suspect place within the sprawling pantheon of voluntary sector management!

What has been created, then, is not a normative model of voluntary sector management, but an environment and a broad discourse which have made it possible – at least in principle – for voluntary organisations to look critically at their *modus operandi*. Training courses, consultancies, advice and information have not ushered in an era of organisational homogeneity or a unity of management practice. In many respects they have made the multiplicity of choices and possibilities facing voluntary organisations much more visible. Far from binding voluntary organisations into a straitjacket, the best of the emerging management discourse has nurtured a creative plurality and enabled voluntary organisations to explore and pursue quite radically divergent ends in quite radically different ways.

DEVELOPING PRACTICE

Management in practice is not just a matter of applying instrumental techniques or formulae to a given range of situations and choices. It involves the creation of shared meanings and the exercise of judgement about what is feasible and appropriate in often ambiguous circumstances. Moreover, notwithstanding the assertions of some writers and practitioners, there is neither a correct nor a unique array of management practices for voluntary and non-profit organisations. The aspects of practice considered here are not instances of an emergent 'management line' in the voluntary sector. They merely highlight ways in which some voluntary organisations have responded to distinctive problems and opportunities encountered in four key areas:

• management competences, roles and values;
• human resource management;
• resource acquisition, marketing and trading;
• organisational structures and strategic management.

Management competences, roles and values

A noticeable feature of changes in the size, scope and staffing of the sector has been the growth in the number of paid staff with management responsibilities. For many organisations an abiding cluster of issues has revolved around the roles which paid management staff have to perform, the extent and the limits of their responsibilities and the values and commitments they are expected to bring to their work.

Defining the work and roles of paid managers is, of course, just one aspect of a wider process of professionalisation, with all the concomitant problems of recruitment, salary levels, conditions of employment, training, career paths and so forth. In the case of management, the process has been complicated by the lack of clear boundaries to the roles and responsibilities expected of paid managers.

The process of embedding professional management in voluntary organisations has not been just a matter of replacing old-style charity administrators and general secretaries with new-style chief executives, directors, area organisers or project co-ordinators. Equally significant has been the elaboration of management roles and responsibilities at functional levels – departmental and section heads, marketing managers, team leaders or senior policy officers. Voluntary organisations have also had to take account of the fact that broadly defined management skills and competences have, during the 1980s and 1990s, come to shape professional practice throughout the human and social services: health workers, care workers, youth workers and social workers all now undertake management tasks as a routine part of their jobs.

Inevitably, voluntary organisations and their managers have adopted a range of approaches in tackling these issues. There have, however, been some recurring preoccupations.

In the first place, management tasks and roles in the voluntary sector cannot, for the most part, be designed or undertaken on the basis of a conventional classification of junior, middle and senior management. With the possible exception of a handful of large, national organisations, formal frameworks of functionally defined management competences and levels of responsibility, such as those drawn up by the Management Charter Initiative, are not readily applicable to the actual tasks most voluntary sector managers have to perform. For instance, a newly appointed co-ordinator of a community centre with one full-time and two part-time colleagues and a dozen volunteers has to exercise judgements and responsibilities no less taxing, in management terms, than those facing the long-standing chief executive of an international relief agency. Moreover, unlike the chief executive, she also has to deal with the day-to-day nuts and bolts of management – staffing, operations, monitoring, budgeting and so forth. In most small and medium-sized voluntary organisations, an individual manager tends to cope with the entire gamut of management tasks and discharge a multiplicity of roles and responsibilities, internally as well as externally.

The question of management styles and values has been a second recurring preoccupation (Cornforth and Hooker 1990). The search for management processes deemed to be consonant with the broader social values and purposes of voluntary organisations has led some to make a conscious effort to exercise management authority and responsibility in ways which stress notions of distributed leadership and empowerment (Brown and Hosking 1986; Hosking 1988), the facilitation of learning (Dartington 1992) or participation and co-operation (Stanton 1992). The culture of many voluntary organisations is such that their managers are not expected to disport themselves as old-fashioned bosses.

Expectations that managers will be self-effacing enablers have not always sat easily alongside other expectations that they will give clear – even charismatic – moral leadership to their organisation and strive to maintain the integrity and vitality of its value-base. The exercise of management in value-based organisations is fraught with dilemmas and pitfalls. Given that effective and sensitive management usually involves bargains and compromises which do not always square with principled commitment or missionary rectitude, how should an organisation's core values be reflected in its management practice? The trustees of many established Christian charities, for instance, have had to address the issue not just of a multi-faith environment but of how far they can legitimately expect and require managers, appointed primarily for their professional expertise, to subscribe personally to a specified set of values and beliefs.

A third area of concern has already been touched on in Chapters 8 and 9. Competing demands of external and internal stakeholders and distinctive forms of organisational governance have both shaped the working routines and relationships of voluntary sector managers. Complex patterns of multiple accountability at an organisational level often result in an ambiguous and contradictory agenda for individual managers. Similarly, the scope of and the limits to what paid managers can and cannot do, formally and informally, are shaped by the ways in which an organisation handles the permutations and ramifications of board–executive relationships (Harris 1992; Kramer 1985). Living with the resulting role conflict and role ambiguity is the unavoidable lot of the vast majority of voluntary sector managers.

Broadly speaking, the definition and insertion of professional management roles into voluntary organisations has been sensitive to the circumstances in which they have evolved. For the most part, the arrival of paid managers who have opted for a career in the voluntary sector has not been accompanied by the trappings of 'career management'. The absence of a professional body has already been noted. Indeed, there has been a continuing aura of tentativeness and understatement about professional management. The primary professional identities and allegiances of most paid managers still centre round the social concerns of their organisations rather than their roles and status as managers. Asked what they do for a living, most voluntary sector managers are likely to respond along the lines of

'I work in special needs housing/community development/advice/drug abuse', rather than 'I am a manager working in a voluntary organisation.'

Human resource management

Being responsible employers of paid staff or sensitive and caring co-ordinators of volunteers should, on the face of it, be consonant with the core values and commitments of organisations which are pre-eminently in 'the people business'. In reality, the attempt to develop 'good practice' in the human resource area has required voluntary organisations, large and small alike, to face up to some pervasive tensions and incompatibilities. It has not always been easy to shift deep-seated assumptions that paid staff should be treated as volunteers with an honorarium whose principle reward is the joy and privilege of working for the clients or the cause 24 hours a day and 7 days a week.

Circumstances have not favoured the development of coherent human resource strategies and practices which acknowledge a diversity of motivations and agendas on the part of staff and volunteers. Conflicts of interest and value have been exacerbated by the funding insecurity and resource limitations of many organisations. Voluntary trustees and management committee members have rarely been competent to handle quite complex roles and responsibilities as employers or supervisors. The vagaries and short-term nature of much funding has meant that many small and medium-sized organisations have lacked the capacity to develop the personnel functions which have begun to emerge in larger organisations. They have not infrequently been pitched into the management of severance and redundancy at exactly the same time as they are struggling to make a decent pass at issues of job design, contracts of employment, recruitment practice, salary scales, staff development, leave arrangements or pensions. Not surprisingly, the working environment in many organisations has been far from ideal: isolation, stress and burn-out have been the not uncommon experience of staff in the voluntary sector (Orlans 1992).

The record of voluntary organisations as employers has been patchy. More has been promised and claimed rhetorically than has been delivered – or even deliverable – on the ground (Ball 1992; MSF 1993). A significant proportion of organisations, old and new, have continued to be lax and cavalier about basic matters of contracts and terms and conditions of employment, notwithstanding the role of intermediary bodies in promulgating models of good practice or a gradual growth of trade union membership and representation in the voluntary sector.

As far as salary levels are concerned, many organisations have followed the 'pay analogue' route, i.e. adopting some form of linkage or comparability with scales determined in other sectors, typically the Civil Service or local authorities. Such linkages have not, however, overcome the fact that overall levels of pay in the voluntary sector have been persistently lower than those in other sectors. In some respects, it is simply a reflection of the level of available resources and an unease about being seen to devote a growing proportion of income to staff remuneration rather than direct services to clients. It also reflects, in some organisations, a conscious decision not to allow large pay differentials. Christian Aid, for instance, has agreed a differential of no more than 1:3 between the lowest and highest paid posts. There is, inevitably, a balance in such decisions between a sense of what is fair and appropriate and the need to attract and reward suitably qualified and skilled staff from outside the sector.

To some extent, voluntary organisations have sought to offset low pay by benefits such as maternity and paternity leave, child-care arrangements or access to training and staff development. In practice, aspiration has tended to exceed capacity. Only a very few large voluntary organisations are in a position to provide a meaningful framework for personal and career development. Career progression in the voluntary sector entails moving *between* organisations not within them. Moreover, although many small and medium-sized organisations have felt impelled to offer lots of 'best practice' facilities to staff, they have proved difficult to implement or sustain in practice. Innumerable small projects have been ground down by trying to square the circle of providing flexible and accessible levels of service while, at the same time, enabling a handful of paid staff to enjoy a sensible working week, take time off in lieu for 'unsocial hours', have access to proper leave arrangements, appropriate levels of support and supervision, exercise enhanced rights to maternity leave, attend courses and look forward to a pension. (As more and more staff approach retirement age after years of work in the voluntary sector, the distinct absence of suitable pension arrangements is an emerging crisis for many organisations in the 1990s.)

Another important dimension of human resource management has been the attention given to forms of team work, support and supervision which are 'non-hierarchical' and rooted in notions of co-operation and empowerment. Such developments have undoubtedly helped to generate very creative and satisfying working environments for some voluntary sector staff and very distinctive organisational cultures. For professional staff, innovative and quite attractive styles of work have often provided the major compensation for the lack of underlying security, the volatility and the impermanence of much paid work in the voluntary sector. Indeed, the 'professionalisation' of the voluntary sector has not really been a process of infiltrating a single-minded cohort of highly paid, career-oriented staff. It has been a conscientious attempt to create flexible, responsive and entrepreneurial patterns of work in circumstances which have often borne the hallmarks of casual labour rather than classic professionalism.

The risk, however, has been that moves towards the empowerment of paid staff and enhancing the quality of their working life have not always been in harmony with, or translated themselves into, parallel concerns to empower volunteers, clients, members and users. Nor has the emergence of suitable 'volunteer management' strategies wholly allayed anxieties (Willis 1992; Hedley 1992). Closer attention to volunteer recruitment and selection, training and accreditation, 'contracts', codes of conduct and plans for development has been a contradictory phenomenon. It has resulted in volunteers being constituted much more explicitly as part of an organisation's work-force and a growing demarcation between their roles in effectively and efficiently discharging a range of tasks and functions on behalf of the organisation and their roles in defining its identity and contributing to its overall management.

Throughout the voluntary sector, the issue of equal opportunities has been a consistent preoccupation in the human resource area. Drawing up and implementing an equal opportunities policy (EOP) has been one of the principle devices since the early 1980s for trying to create a coherent, organisation-wide framework for the various dimensions of human resource management. For many organisations, the pursuit of equal opportunities has been seen as the most appropriate way of giving practical expression – in terms of employment systems and procedures, access, working practices, modes of service delivery and general culture and orientation – to the distinctive value-base of the voluntary sector. 'Equal opportunities is good management' has been the oft-heard rationale of what has been expected of EOPs, and for many organisations it was the decision – often a political rather than a management decision – to develop an EOP which first led them to a serious engagement with the practicalities and the detail of human resource management.

Whether a decade and a half of equal opportunities has significantly altered the profile of the voluntary sector is a matter of considerable debate (Nadeau and Sanders 1992). There has been much turmoil and acrimony, some spectacular conflicts (Sivanandan *et al.* 1986, for instance) and persistent claims of thoroughly bad and inappropriate practice and procedures masquerading as 'good practice'. There has been a pervasive confusion about what is achievable through EOPs. Are they about rectifying inequities and injustices in the labour market, about forms of organisational behaviour and culture or about the allegiances of voluntary organisations in wider processes of anti-discriminatory politics? The fact that women form a high proportion of the voluntary sector work-force may be attributable to the normal operation of the dual labour market in which low-paid, short-term, part-time caring jobs have long been defined as 'women's work'. Similarly, the fact that a significant number of prominent and senior managers in national voluntary organisations are women may be due, not to the operation of equal opportunities, but to the historic tendency of leading philanthropists since the time of Elizabeth Fry or Octavia Hill to be women and leaders of industry, commerce and the state to be men – and hardly any of them to be black.

One important outcome of work on equal opportunities has been an emerging recognition of the limits of applying formulaic 'good practice' in human resource management. Indeed, the most significant upshot of trying to develop acceptable human resource procedures and strategies has been the acknowledgement that handling conflict is an inherent and integral feature of voluntary sector management. Voluntary organisations are no less prone than organisations in other sectors to fierce conflicts of interest and identity. The belief that voluntary sector values should somehow prevent conflicts between the different groups of people who work for a voluntary organisation is misplaced. If anything, the turbulence of the last twenty years suggests the opposite. The wide-ranging personal and sectional values, aspirations and interests which different groups of staff and volunteers bring to their work add a singularly intractable edge to all the customary layers of conflict with which managers have to cope.

Resource acquisition, marketing and trading

Voluntary organisations tend to separate their service delivery and resource acquisition functions (Gronbjerg 1993). Clients and users are often quite distinct from funders and donors; staff and volunteers who work with one group of external stakeholders tend not to work with the other. There are, of course, crucial linkages. Indeed, in very broad terms, the overall function of any voluntary organisation is to secure inputs from one group of people and institutions in order to produce outputs for another group of people and institutions.

Although resource acquisition and service delivery are inextricably bound up, the 'real work' of an organisation is usually defined in terms of the clients, users and communities with whom it works in particular aspects of service delivery, campaigning, advocacy or whatever. The outputs end of the process furnishes an organisation's main *raison d'être*. Not suprisingly, therefore, it has been the dominant focus in thinking about management. The upshot has been a rather lopsided perception of the scope of the organisational processes requiring management attention. Work on the inputs end has often been marginalised. Staff involved in fundraising, marketing, charity trading, promotions, public relations and the like have been held at arms length from the rest of the organisation and not infrequently treated with a mixture of suspicion and disdain.

Hidden from view, however, growing numbers of organisations, large and small, have begun to re-define their thinking and their practice in this area. There has been a gradual move away from a fairly static reliance on a handful of reasonably discrete operations and sources of support – grants from statutory authorities and trusts; flag days, fetes and annual appeals; private donations; charity shops and Christmas cards – towards much more comprehensive strategies pursued within a complex and dynamic resource environment. There have been quite major and creative developments at the practical level of technique and skill and at the general level of organisation and co-ordination.

At the level of skills and techniques, more attention has been given to processes of communication. Large organisations have created public re-lations and promotions departments; small organisations have learnt to be more focused in such matters as audience and market research, the con-struction of images and messages, the use of a variety of media and channels of publicity. The use of advertising, direct mail, telemarketing and their associated information management systems and technologies has enabled voluntary organisations to become more sophisticated in the relationships they build with their various publics, donors, 'armchair supporters', occa-sional volunteers and subscribers (Burnett 1992). Securing resources and support from other organisations and institutions is no longer defined primarily in terms of voluntary–statutory grant relationships but in terms of a much wider array of possible corporate resource arrangements with agencies across all sectors – contracts, sponsorships, joint promotions, employee volunteering schemes, secondments and so forth. Charity trading has not been restricted to the well-known shops. More and more organisations are beginning to engage in trading activity to generate income, whether in the form of publications, catalogue sales, cafés, bookstalls and so forth or, more contentiously, in the form of fees and charges for the provision of direct and indirect services (Leat 1989).

Managing and integrating such practices and developments has inevitably been a source of dilemmas and tensions. Charging fees for service raises fears that the adoption of practices and principles of marketing may reduce the richness and diversity of an organisation's relationships with its clients, volunteers, members and users to a single, all-encompassing, cash-based customer relationship. Images and messages effective in securing resources from the public at large or particular individual and institutional donors may well be in conflict with those promoted in other areas of an organisation's work. Being effective in winning resources and support requires an acknowl-edgement of the mixed motivations of individual donors and corporate funders; philanthropic altruism is invariably tempered by elements of ex-change and the calculation of mutual benefit. Risks of goal displacement arise not just from the deals made with corporate funders but from the need to sustain and extend the contribution and involvement of individual donors and active supporters. Time and attention devoted to servicing donors, subscribers and fundraising volunteers with newsletters, meetings and opportunities to shape an organisation's affairs cannot be sealed off from the focus and development of work with clients, trustees, formal members or service-provision volunteers.

As with other dimensions of organisational and management development, enhancing the resource acquisition function has undoubtedly been a signifi-cant shift in voluntary sector operations. To date, the impact is hard to gauge and may well differ between large and small organisations and between those operating in different non-profit markets. It has not, however, been a straightforward matter of surrendering before the onslaught of commer-cialism. It has not simply been the doorway for market forces to enter and contaminate the sacred precincts of voluntary endeavour. There is a consonance between the value-based, client-centred practices and commitments of many voluntary organisations and the orientation of some of the more sensitive, modern thinking about marketing in general. The encounter between them has been a characteristic mixture of ambiguity, fruitful insight and critical adaptation. It has been instrumental in creating a much more grounded and mature appreciation of the overall management agenda of voluntary organisations. It has helped to nurture the potential ability of voluntary organisations to operate more confidently and independently in a variety of modes and across a range of environments and constituencies.

Organisational structures and strategic management

The search for suitable structures has been driven by the need to accommodate increasingly disparate demands. On the one hand, there has been a task orientation in decisions about organisational structure, i.e. arranging internal structures and procedures in such a way that an organisation's primarily external tasks and purposes can be most efficiently and effectively undertaken. The conventional wisdom has been that this disposes voluntary organisations towards loose, flat, non-hierarchical structures which should, at least in principle, enable them to act flexibly and responsively.

On the other hand, there has been an equally marked process orientation. Structures should not simply be instrumental; they should be open and accessible, facilitate learning throughout an organisation, foster user involvement and democratic control and ensure that distinctive styles and cultures of work are supported. In these ways, issues of structure have been informed by wider questions of changing organisational identities and values.

Legal requirements and forms of voluntary governance (Chapters 8 and 9) have affected how voluntary organisations co-ordinate their affairs, as have concerns for adequate financial procedures and controls. More generally, the growing use of monitoring, evaluation and performance measurement as routine management practices and as mechanisms for external accountability has necessitated closer attention to underlying systems and procedures of information management. Similarly, in the mid-1990s, the pursuit of such initiatives as Total Quality Management, National and Scottish Vocational Qualifications, Investors in People and the BS5750 'kitemark' has affected the balance in some organisations between formalism and flexibility.

To date, the goal of simple, responsive *and sustainable* ways of ordering their affairs has proved depressingly elusive for groups and organisations at the small and medium-sized end of the sector. For them, issues of structure essentially revolve around such basic matters as project integration and effective communication within and between a readily identifiable set of groups and teams. As with many small businesses, however, a commitment to 'keep things simple in the interests of our clients/members/users' is blown off course by the sorts of external pressures towards formalisation just mentioned. Complexity also arises from trying to meld into some sort of organisational coherence a bundle of projects and programmes based on quite disparate resource-bases and time-scales.

There are other, internally generated, pressures towards an over-elaboration of structures and procedures. Giving effect to values of participation, democracy or user involvement often results in more and more meetings, working groups, users' forums, internal newsletters and so forth. Commitments to particular methods of working call for a conscious and monitored adherence to agreed (or imposed) procedures and systems. Concerns for the greater involvement of secretarial and administrative staff mean that their jobs are enriched and other staff have to give more time and attention to being self-servicing. In countless, well-intentioned ways small organisations can easily drift towards being cumbersome and 'over-structured' and, indeed, generally over-managed as a growing proportion of their time and resources is absorbed in sustaining internal processes rather than 'getting on with the job'. Losing sight of 'the task' is an endemic danger for voluntary organisations which place a high premium on matters of process and style. Stanton's (1989, 1992) work on collective and non-hierarchical ways of working highlights just how intensely time-consuming they can be.

For larger organisations, the problems associated with structures and decision-making procedures have presented themselves somewhat differently. For the most part, they have been confronted with the standard problems of co-ordinating the work of departments and sections with different functions, rationales and practices in such a way that the overall tasks of the organisation are efficiently performed. As Wilson (1992) has demonstrated, there is no single 'voluntary sector solution' to this time-honoured organisational conundrum. Large charities have successfully operated with structures ranging from the classic functional bureaucracy to ostensibly looser matrix systems and federations.

The experience of growth and change at the larger end of the sector has, however, raised seminal questions about coping with diversity and plurality within an organisation. The problem is not simply a function of size. It is about handling the different and relatively autonomous systems which inevitably operate in any complex organisation. The formal systems of authority, decision-making and work allocation are only one dimension of an organisation's structure. As more specialist staff and departments have become involved, voluntary organisations have also been faced with what Burns and Stalker (1961) described as *career systems* and *political systems*.

Administrators, for instance, not unreasonably wish to develop themselves, their departments and their work in ways which promote 'best practice' in their particular areas of expertise. Journalists, librarians, sales staff, researchers, fundraisers, secretaries, print and design staff, trainers, lawyers and other specialist staff in voluntary organisations all construct their careers, allegiances, standards of practice and formal and informal working relationships around what is appropriate in their respective constituencies and areas of operation. They cannot function effectively on the basis of practices or criteria of excellence which are derived from the work of carers, social workers, health workers, community workers and others involved in direct service provision, campaigning and relationships with clients and communities. Large organisations need, therefore, to acknowledge in their systems and procedures the divergent ways in which different groups and sections operate and the plurality of career loyalties and commitments which staff – and volunteers – seek to express and fulfil through their work.

Relationships between national offices, regions and local branches highlight another aspect of the problems associated with diversity. Loyalty to the parent organisation and loyalty to a particular locality do not neatly coincide. Regional offices and local groups face real dilemmas between developing their work on the basis of common cause with other colleagues and organisations in their area and acting as an efficient and expanding 'delivery point' for their own organisation's particular services. Structures and procedures designed to maintain nationally agreed standards of service, working methods and an overall coherence of identity and image cannot easily serve the equally laudable purposes of supporting and empowering service users and grassroots activists and extending their autonomous control over their own affairs.

Internal conflict and negotiation over the allocation of resources, styles of work, general policy or particular projects is the hallmark of relationships between branches, regions and central departments. Such politicking is an inescapable feature of organisational life and development. But for organisations whose identities have been deeply rooted in notions of a unity of practice, a common purpose and a unique shared vision, it has sometimes been painful to acknowledge such internal diversity and plurality. Operating politically as coalitions of diverse and shifting interests has been a steep learning curve for organisations which have traditionally seen themselves as bands of simple-hearted missionaries.

Structural issues of unity and diversity are, of course, closely related to strategic issues of autonomy and dependence. A major block on the development of thinking and practice in the area of strategic management has been the fact that the relevant issues have tended to be defined and addressed at the level of the sector rather than the organisation. The resulting confusion has manifested itself in several ways.

There are, for instance, substantial problems inherent in trying to translate a policy commitment to 'partnership' on the part of the sector into a meaningful set of strategic and operational choices at the level of individual organisations (Billis 1993: Chapter 13). Ever since Wolfenden, strategic debates about how to respond to welfare pluralism, MSC funding or contracting have faltered on the often unrecognised and unacknowledged disjunction between management options facing individual organisations and public policy options facing the sector. How an individual organisation makes strategic decisions about its interests and balances up issues of autonomy and dependence in such matters as contracting does not map directly on to the wider determination of sectoral interests, autonomy or dependence (Batsleer and Paton 1993). Approaches to strategic management which uncouple organisational and sectoral interests, identities and options have been thin on the ground (Macfarlane 1990; Butler and Wilson 1990; Batsleer and Randall 1992).

The upshot is that much of what has passed as strategic management has been either reactive or defensive. There has been a lack of analytic sensitivity in distinguishing between environmental turbulence and environmental hostility and little attempt by organisations to appraise their positioning within key environments critically. In the case of small organisations, work on strategy has often ended up, not as a process of creative adaptation, but as a *no passeran* affirmation of inviolable commitments and policies to be pursued come what may. Indeed, there is a latent paradox for many value-led groups in the very notion of strategic management. Strategy necessarily implies adaptation and change, a certain amount of ducking and weaving in the face of altered circumstances. Giving faithful expression to core values, by contrast, often implies quite the opposite; it implies standing by one's beliefs and practices irrespective of what is happening in the world around – a position which is strongly reinforced by the enduring edifice of charity law and its tendency to perpetuate an organisation's status quo. For many small groups, strategy has often ended up as rigid and prescriptive plans rather than a more sensitive framework for flexibility and principled opportunism.

In the case of larger organisations, the identification and competitive defence of particular niches has tended to be the dominant strategic orientation, by default if not design (Butler and Wilson 1990). Despite a rhetoric of co-operation and some experience of work on joint projects, attempts to explore the possibilities of collaborative advantage and collaborative capability (Huxham 1991, 1992) have been strictly limited. Large organisations remain locked into their particularity and a sustained approach to external relations involving alliances, coalitions and mergers has yet to get off the ground (Wilson 1990). Networking and regular cross-agency work at the level of the personal and professional practice of staff and volunteers have not, as yet, been extended into strategic management at the organisational level. Membership of national and local associations and federations has been little more than an assertion of shared aspirations; it has rarely been the basis for systematically negotiating and defining organisational strategy.

REFLECTION

The experience of the last fifteen years has confounded both the hopes and the fears that management would tidy up the post-Wolfenden voluntary sector. The development of management thinking and practice in the voluntary sector has been exploratory and multi-faceted. Far from leading to neatness and homogeneity, it has begun to place issues of diversity and ambiguity much more centrally on the agenda of voluntary organisations.

The encounter with management is gradually leading to a reassessment of some of the accumulated folklore which surrounds the operations and identities of voluntary organisations. Take, for instance, the much proclaimed voluntary sector characteristics of flexibility, innovation, cost-effectiveness and a culture of participation. Critical reflection on actual management experience suggests that such taken-for-granted views about the distinctive features of voluntary organisations can be seriously misleading. Some successful voluntary organisations are admirably flexible and empowering; others lurch aimlessly round without restraint. Some tight-knit oligarchies very successfully provide the same set of much needed and valued services with great efficiency year in and year out; others are remarkably cumbersome, introspective and ineffectual. Characteristics and ideals of the sector in general should not be construed as necessary or essential features of the organisation and management of individual agencies. It is the task of voluntary sector management to explore what is appropriate for a given organisation in a given situation, not to rehearse stereotypes, however laudable, or to ignore the functioning of complex and contradictory contingencies.

Voluntary organisations inhabit a value-laden and normatively charged universe. What management has begun to provide is an appropriate language and practice with which to negotiate the inevitable tensions between aspiration in an ideal world and feasibility in the given world. Those tensions are not just between the voluntary sector and other sectors and institutions. They inform the internal operations of each and every organisation. At one and the same time, voluntary organisations are pragmatic coalitions as well as principled missions. The best of management assists voluntary organisations to operate in the twilight zone 'beyond good practice', where what is desirable has to jostle with what is possible. (Conversely, of course, the worst of management lapses into prescription and systematically ignores the fact that living with such ambiguity and imperfection is a crucial element of the management role.)

Critical attention to management has highlighted the substantial differences and discontinuities within the voluntary sector. The interests and values of individual organisations do not necessarily coincide with those of the sector as a whole. Indeed, from the perspective of organisation and management, notions of distinct sectoral values, shared purposes and common allegiances may well act as a barrier to the capacity of individual organisations to determine their own future. A sense of loyalty to and membership of 'the voluntary sector' can prevent individual organisations faced with specific choices in particular circumstances from thinking creatively about ways of developing alliances and coalitions which cut across conventional and current boundaries (Dluhy 1990). The creation – and management – of solidarity and 'common cause' among voluntary organisations may well lead them in quite different social and political directions, towards a radical reordering rather than a reaffirmation of the integrity of the voluntary sector (Batsleer and Randall 1992).

More generally, the experience of management and organisation suggests that an essentially welfare-oriented voluntary sector will be only one component of any emergent 'Third Sector'. Changes in the institutions and practices of the market and the state are such that what may lie between or beyond them will be much more heterogeneous. As more and more voluntary organisations develop the capacity to operate in complex and shifting circumstances, the air of beleaguered parochial piety which still lingers round the voluntary sector may give way to a more self-confident and radical pluralism. In such circumstances, the language and practice of voluntary sector management may become a valuable adjunct to a wider and renewed politics of civil society.

Finally, the contribution of voluntary sector management to the development of management thinking and practice in general needs to be noted. There is a dawning realisation that managing in voluntary and non-profit enterprises may provide useful insights into the definition of generic management roles and competences. Most immediately, the experience of voluntary sector managers is particularly relevant to managers operating in sections of the erstwhile public sector – in schools, colleges, hospitals and so forth – for whom simple private sector models of management are woefully inappropriate and of no more use than the tenets of classic public service administration.

In other words, management may not always be something imported into voluntary organisations. In the fullness of time, the experience of organisational and management development in the voluntary sector may prove to be a valuable export. 'Learning from the non-profits' is not a wholly fanciful dream for the wider world of management and organisation. The long-term social significance of voluntary organisations may lie not just in what they do but equally importantly in how they do it.

NOTE

1 This chapter draws heavily on work developed by the Open University's Voluntary Sector Management Programme. It is important, therefore, to acknowledge the contribution to the ideas presented here of colleagues in the programme, in particular Rob Paton and Chris Cornforth.

REFERENCES

Addy, T. and Scott, D. (1988) *Fatal Impacts? The MSC and Voluntary Action*, Manchester: William Temple Foundation.
Adirondack, S. (1989) *Just About Managing?*, London: London Voluntary Service Council.
Alinsky, S.D. (1972) *Rules for Radicals*, New York: Random House.
Ball, C. (1992) 'Remuneration policies and employment practices: some dilemmas in

the voluntary sector', in J. Batsleer, C. Cornforth and R. Paton (eds) *Issues in Voluntary and Non-profit Management*, Wokingham: Addison-Wesley.

Ball, M. (1988) *Evaluation in the Voluntary Sector*, London: The Forbes Trust.

Batsleer, J. (1988) 'Adult education, management training and the voluntary sector', *Adult Education*, 61(3): 227–33.

Batsleer, J. and Paton, R. (1993) 'Managing voluntary organizations in the contract culture: continuity or change?', paper for conference on *Contracting – Selling or Shrinking?*, London: South Bank University.

Batsleer, J. and Randall, S. (1992) 'Creating common cause: issues in the management of inter-agency relationships', in J. Batsleer, C. Cornforth and R. Paton (eds) *Issues in Voluntary and Non-profit Management*, Wokingham: Addison-Wesley.

Batsleer, J., Cornforth, C. and Paton, R. (eds) (1992) *Issues in Voluntary and Non-profit Management*, Wokingham: Addison-Wesley.

Bhatt, C. (1986) 'Funding the flames: the creation of black crisis managers', *Emergency*, 43–7.

Billis, D. (1993) *Organising Public and Voluntary Agencies*, London: Routledge.

Bishop, J. and Hoggett, P. (1986) *Organising around Enthusiasms: Mutual Aid in Leisure*, London: Comedia.

Brown, H. (1992) *Women Organising*, London: Routledge.

Brown, H. and Hosking, D-M. (1986) 'Distributed leadership and skilled performance as successful organisation in social movements', *Human Relations* 39(1): 65–79.

Burnett, K. (1992) *Relationship Fundraising: A Donor-based Approach to the Business of Raising Money*, London: The White Lion Press.

Burns, T. and Stalker, G.M. (1961) *The Management of Innovation*, London: Tavistock.

Butler, R.J. and Wilson, D.C. (1990) *Managing Voluntary and Non-profit Organizations: Strategy and Structure*, London: Routledge.

Charity Commission (1991) *War on Want: Report of an Inquiry Submitted to the Commissioners*, London: HMSO.

Charity Commission (1992) *Royal British Legion: Report of an Inquiry Submitted to the Commissioners*, London: HMSO.

Cockburn, C. *et al.* (1980) *In and Against the State*, London: Pluto Press.

Cornforth, C. and Hooker, C. (1990) 'Conceptions of management in voluntary and non-profit organisations: values, structures and management style', in *Proceedings of the 1990 Conference of the Association of Voluntary Action Scholars*, London: London School of Economics, Centre for Voluntary Organisation.

Cornforth, C., Thomas, A., Lewis, J. and Spear, R. (1988) *Developing Successful Worker Co-operatives*, London: Sage.

Cornforth, C. *et al.* (1993) *Winning Resources and Support*, 6 Open University Course Books, Milton Keynes: The Open University.

Croner (1991 onwards) *Management of Voluntary Organisations*, Kingston on Thames: Croner.

Dartington, T. (1992) 'Professional management in voluntary organizations: some cautionary notes', in J. Batsleer, C. Cornforth and R. Paton (eds) *Issues in Voluntary and Non-profit Management*, Wokingham: Addison-Wesley.

Dluhy, M. J. (1990) *Building Coalitions in the Human Services*, London: Sage.

Drucker, P.F. (1990) *Managing the Nonprofit Organisation: Principles and Practices*, New York: HarperCollins.

Flynn, N. (1990) *Public Sector Management*, London: Harvester Wheatsheaf.

Gronbjerg, K. (1993) *Understanding Nonprofit Funding*, San Francisco: Jossey Bass.

Gutch, R. (1992) *Contracting Lessons from the US*, London: National Council for Voluntary Organisations.

Gutch, R. and Young, K. (1988) *Partners or Rivals? The Changing Relationship between Local Government and the Voluntary Sector*, Luton: Local Government Training Board.

Hall, S. (1989) *The Voluntary Sector Under Attack. . .?*, London: Islington Voluntary Action Council.

Handy, C. (1988) *Understanding Voluntary Organisations*, Harmondsworth: Pelican.

Harris, M. (1992) 'The role of voluntary management committees', in J. Batsleer, C. Cornforth and R. Paton (eds) *Issues in Voluntary and Non-profit Management*, Wokingham: Addison-Wesley.

Hedley, R. (1992) 'Organising and managing volunteers', in R. Hedley, and J. Davis Smith (eds) *Volunteering and Society: Principles and Practice*, London: Bedford Square Press.

Holloway, C. and Otto, S. (1985) *Getting Organised: A Handbook for Non-statutory Organisations*, London: Bedford Square Press.

Home Office (1989) *Charities: A Framework for the Future*, Cm 694, London: HMSO.

Hooker, C. and Mabey, C. (1992) 'What more is there to learn about organizational commitment?', paper for the British Academy of Management Conference, Bradford.

Hosking, D-M. (1988) 'Organising, leadership and skillful process', *Journal of Management Studies*, 25(2): 147–66.

Huxham, C. (1991) 'Facilitating collaboration: issues in multi-organizational groups', *Journal of the Operational Research Society*, 42(12): 1037–46.

Huxham, C. (1992) *Collaborative Capability: An Intra-organizational Perspective on Collaborative Advantage*, Glasgow: Strathclyde Business School.

Kanter, R.M. (1972) *Commitment and Community: Communes and Utopias in Sociological Perspective*, Cambridge, MA: Harvard University Press.

Kotler, P. (1975) *Marketing for Non-profit Organizations*, Englewood Cliffs, NJ: Prentice-Hall.

Kramer, R. (1985) 'Towards a contingency model of board–executive relations', *Administration in Social Work*, 9(3): 15–33.

Landry, C., Morley, D., Southwood, R. and Wright, P. (1985) *What a Way to Run a Railroad: An Analysis of Radical Failure*, London: Comedia.

Leat, D. (1988) *Voluntary Organisations and Accountability*, London: National Council for Voluntary Organisations.

Leat, D. (1989) *Charities and Charging: Who Pays?*, Tonbridge: Charities Aid Foundation.

Leat, D. (1993) *Managing Across Sectors: Similarities and Differences Between For-profit and Voluntary Non-profit Organisations*, London: VOLPROF, City University.

MacFarlane, R. (1990) *Contracting: In or Out? The Impact on Management and Organisation*, NCVO Guidance Notes on Contracting for Voluntary Organisations No. 3, London: NCVO.

MacIntosh, D. and MacIntosh, A. (1984) *Marketing: A Handbook for Charities*, London: Directory of Social Change.

MSF (1993) *Working in the Voluntary Sector: An MSF Pay and Conditions Survey*, London: Manufacturing, Science and Finance.

Miller, C. (1989) 'Social services departments and community care', *Public Money and Management*, Winter: 27–34.

Nadeau, J. and Sanders, S. (1992) 'Equal opportunities policies: the cuckoo in the nest or the goose that laid the golden egg? Problems encountered and lessons learned', in J. Batsleer, C. Cornforth and R. Paton (eds) *Issues in Voluntary and Non-profit Management*, Wokingham: Addison-Wesley.

NCVO (1981) *Improving Effectiveness in Voluntary Organisations*, Report of the Charles Handy Working Party, London: National Council for Voluntary Organisations.

NCVO (1983) *MDU Bulletin 1*, May, London: National Council for Voluntary Organisations.

NCVO (1984) *The Management and Effectiveness of Voluntary Organisations*, London: National Council for Voluntary Organisations.

Orlans, V. (1992) 'Stress in voluntary and non-profit organizations', in J. Batsleer, C. Cornforth and R. Paton (eds) *Issues in Voluntary and Non-profit Management*, Wokingham: Addison-Wesley.

Paton, R. (1992) 'The social economy: value-based organizations in the wider society', in J. Batsleer, C. Cornforth and R. Paton (eds) *Issues in Voluntary and Non-profit Management*, Wokingham: Addison-Wesley.

Paton, R. (1993) 'Organization and management studies on voluntary and non-profit organizations in the UK: achievements and prospects', paper for symposium on *Researching Voluntary and Non-profit Organisations in the UK: The State of the Art*, London: South Bank University.

Paton, R. and Batsleer, J. (1992) 'A stakeholder typology and approach to voluntary and non-profit organisations', paper for the British Academy of Management Conference, Bradford.

Paton, R. and Cornforth, C. (1992) 'What's different about managing in voluntary and non-profit organizations?', in J. Batsleer, C. Cornforth and R. Paton (eds) *Issues in Voluntary and Non-profit Management*, Wokingham: Addison-Wesley.

Paton, R. and Hooker, C. (1990) *Developing Managers in Voluntary Organisations: A Handbook*, Sheffield: Employment Department.

Paton, R. *et al.* (1991) *Managing Voluntary and Non-profit Enterprises*, 12 Open University Course Books, Milton Keynes: The Open University.

Poulton, G. (1988) *Managing Voluntary Organisations*, Chichester: Wiley.

Reed, B. and Palmer, B. (1976) *The Local Church and its Environment*, Chichester: Wiley.

Ritchie, C. (1992) 'Using analytical methods in the community sector: experiences and developments', paper for the British Academy of Management Conference, Bradford.

Sivanandan, A. *et al.* (1986) *In the Eye of the Needle*, Report of the Independent Enquiry into Greater London Arts, London: Greater London Arts Association.

Smith, M. (1981) *Organise! A Guide to Practical Politics for Youth and Community Groups*, Leicester: National Association of Youth Clubs.

Stanton, A. (1989) *Invitation to Self-Management*, London: Dab Hand Press.

Stanton, A. (1992) 'Learning from the experience of collective teamwork', in J. Batsleer, C. Cornforth and R. Paton (eds) *Issues in Voluntary and Non-profit Management*, Wokingham: Addison-Wesley.

Stewart, J. (1986) *The New Management of Local Government*, London: Allen & Unwin.

Streeck, W. and Schmitter, P.C. (eds) (1985) *Private Interest Government: Beyond Market and State*, London: Sage.

URBED (1988) *Managing Urban Change*, Urban and Economic Development Group, London: HMSO.

Ward, S. (1984) *Organising Things: A Guide to Successful Political Action*, London: Pluto Press.

Watson, D. (1988) *Managers of Discontent*, London: Routledge.

Willis, E. (1992) 'Managing volunteers', in J. Batsleer, C. Cornforth and R. Paton (eds) *Issues in Voluntary and Non-profit Management*, Wokingham: Addison-Wesley.

Wilson, D.C. (1990) 'Co-operation and competition in the voluntary sector: the strategic challenges of the 1990s', in *Proceedings of the 1990 Conference of the Association of Voluntary Action Scholars*, London: London School of Economics, Centre for Voluntary Organisation.

Wilson, D.C. (1992) 'Organizational structure in the voluntary sector: a theoretical overview', in J. Batsleer, C. Cornforth and R. Paton (eds) *Issues in Voluntary and Non-profit Management*, Wokingham: Addison-Wesley.

Young, K. (1991) 'Consumer-centred approaches in the public/voluntary/personal services', *Public Money and Management*, Summer: 33–9.

Select bibliography

Addy, T. and Scott, D. (1988) *Fatal Impacts? The MSC and Voluntary Action*, Manchester: William Temple Foundation.

Adirondack, S. (1989) *Just About Managing?*, London: London Voluntary Service Council.

ADVANCE (1988) *Black People and Volunteering*, London: ADVANCE.

Anheier, H.K. and Seibel, W. (eds) (1990) *The Third Sector: Comparative Studies of Nonprofit Organisations*, Berlin and New York: de Gruyter.

Aves, G.M. (1969) *The Voluntary Worker in the Social Services*, London: Allen & Unwin.

Baine, S., Bennington, J. and Russell, J. (1992) *Changing Europe: Challenges Facing the Voluntary and Community Sectors in the 1990s*, London: National Council for Voluntary Organisations/Community Development Foundation.

Beveridge, W. (1948) *Voluntary Action: A Report on Methods of Social Advance*, London: Allen & Unwin.

Batsleer, J., Cornforth, C. and Paton, R. (eds) (1992) *Issues in Voluntary and Non-profit Management*, Wokingham: Addison-Wesley.

Billis, D. (1993) *Organising Public and Voluntary Agencies*, London: Routledge.

Billis, D. and Harris, M. (1992) *The Challenge of Change in Local Voluntary Agencies*, CVO Working Paper 11, London: London School of Economics.

Bourdillon, A.F.C. (ed.) (1945) *Voluntary Social Services: Their Place in the Modern State*, London: Methuen.

Brenton, M. (1985) *The Voluntary Sector in British Social Services*, London: Longman.

Butler, R.J. and Wilson, D.C. (1990) *Managing Voluntary and Non-profit Organizations: Strategy and Structure*, London: Routledge.

CAF (1990) *Charity Household Survey*, London: Charities Aid Foundation.

Charities Aid Foundation (1992) *Charity Trends 1991*, Tonbridge: CAF.

Chapin, F.S. and Tsouderos, J.E. (1956) 'The formalization process in voluntary organisations', *Social Forces*, 34: 342–4.

Chesterman, M. (1979) *Charities, Trusts and Social Welfare*, London: Weidenfeld & Nicolson.

Common, R. and Flynn, N. (1992) *Contracting for Care*, York: Joseph Rowntree Foundation.

DiMaggio, P. and Powell, W.W. (1983) 'The iron cage revisited: institutional isomorphism and collective rationality in organizational fields', *American Sociological Review*, 48: 147–60.

Drucker, P.F. (1990) *Managing the Nonprofit Organisation: Principles and Practices*, New York: HarperCollins.

Field, J. and Hedges, B. (1984) *A National Survey of Volunteering*, London: Social and Planning Research.

Finlayson, G. (1990) 'A moving frontier: voluntarism and the state in British social welfare 1911–1949', *Twentieth Century British History*, 1(2):183–206.

Gerard, D. (1983) *Charities in Britain: Conservatism or Change?*, London: Bedford Square Press.

Gladstone, F. (1979) *Voluntary Action in a Changing World*, London: Bedford Square Press.

Gosden, P.H.J.H. (1961) *The Friendly Societies in England 1815–1875*, Manchester: Manchester University Press.

Gosden, P.H.J.H. (1973) *Self Help: Voluntary Associations in Nineteenth Century Britain*, London: Batsford.

Golding, P., Radley, A. and Fenton, N. (1993) *Charities, Media and Public Opinion*, Loughborough: Loughborough University.

Gutch, R. (1992) *Contracting Lessons from the US*, London: National Council for Voluntary Organisations.

Guthrie, R. (1988) *Charity and the Nation*, Tonbridge: Charities Aid Foundation.

Hadley, R. and Hatch, S. (1982) *Social Welfare and the Failure of the State*, London: Allen & Unwin.

Handy, C. (1988) *Understanding Voluntary Organisations*, Harmondsworth: Pelican.

Harris, M. and Billis, D. (1986) *Organising Voluntary Agencies: A Guide through the Literature*, London: Bedford Square Press.

Harrison, B. (1966) 'Philanthropy and the Victorians', *Victorian Studies*, IX: 353–74.

Hatch, S. (1980) *Outside the State*, London: Croom Helm.

Hedley, R. and Davis Smith, J. (eds) (1992) *Volunteering and Society: Principles and Practice*, London: Bedford Square Press.

Hedley, R. and Rochester, C. (1991) *Contracts at the Crossroads*, Rugby: Association of Crossroads Care Attendant Schemes.

Home Office (1989) *Charities: A Framework for the Future*, Cm 694, London: HMSO.

Home Office (1990) *Profiting from Partnership: Efficiency Scrutiny of Government Funding of the Voluntary Sector*, London: HMSO.

Home Office (1992) *The Individual and the Community: The Role of the Voluntary Sector*, London: HMSO.

James, E. (1987) 'The nonprofit sector in comparative perspective', in W.W. Powell (ed.) (1987) *The Nonprofit Sector: A Research Handbook*, New Haven, CT: Yale University Press.

Jordan, W.K. (1959) *Philanthropy in England 1480–1660*, London: Russell Sage Foundation.

Knapp, M. *et al.* (1987) *Public Money, Voluntary Action: Whose Welfare?*, Kent: Personal Social Services Unit, University of Kent.

Knight, B. (1993) *Voluntary Action*, London: Home Office.

Kramer, R.M. (1981) *Voluntary Agencies in the Welfare State*, Berkeley: University of California Press.

Kramer, R.M. (1985) 'Toward a contingency model of board–executive relations', *Administration in Social Work*, 9(3): 15–33.

Leat, D. (1988) *Voluntary Organisations and Accountability*, London: National Council for Voluntary Organisations.

Leat, D. (1989) *Charities and Charging: Who Pays?*, Tonbridge: Charities Aid Foundation.

Leat, D. (1992) *Trusts in Transition: The Policy and Practice of Grant-Giving Trusts*, York: Joseph Rowntree Foundation.

Leat, D. (1993) *Managing across Sectors: Similarities and Differences between*

For-profit and Voluntary Non-profit Organisations, London: VOLPROF, City University.

Lynn, P. and Davis Smith, J. (1991) *The 1991 National Survey of Voluntary Activity in the UK*, Berkhamsted: The Volunteer Centre UK.

Macadam, E. (1934) *The New Philanthropy*, London: Allen & Unwin.

Macfarlane, R. (1990) *Contracting In or Out? The Impact on Management and Organisation*, London: National Council for Voluntary Organisations.

Mess, A.A. (1947) *Voluntary Social Services Since 1918*, London: Kegan Paul.

Lord Nathan (1990) *Effectiveness and the Voluntary Sector*, London: National Council for Voluntary Organisations.

NCVO (1981) *Improving Effectiveness in Voluntary Organisations*, Report of the Charles Handy Working Party, London: National Council for Voluntary Organisations.

NCVO (1992) *On Trust: Increasing the Effectiveness of Charity Trustees and Management Committees*, London: National Council for Voluntary Organisations.

Owen, D. (1964) *English Philanthropy 1660–1960*, London: Oxford University Press.

Poulton, G. (1988) *Managing Voluntary Organisations*, Chichester: Wiley.

Powell, W.W. (ed.) (1987) *The Nonprofit Sector: A Research Handbook*, New Haven, CT: Yale University Press.

Prochaska, F. (1980) *Women and Philanthropy in Nineteenth Century England*, Oxford: Clarendon Press.

Prochaska, F. (1988) *The Voluntary Impulse: Philanthropy in Modern Britain*, London: Faber.

Prochaska, F. (1990) 'Philanthropy', in F.M.L. Thompson (ed.) *The Cambridge Social History of England 1750–1950*, Volume 3, Cambridge: Cambridge University Press, pp. 357–93.

Rooff, M. (1955) *Voluntary Societies and Social Policy*, London: Routledge & Kegan Paul.

Saxon-Harrold, S.K.E. and Kendall, J. (eds) (1993) *Researching the Voluntary Sector: A National, Local and International Perspective*, Tonbridge: Charities Aid Foundation.

SCPR (1990) *On Volunteering: A Qualitative Research Study of Images, Motivations and Experiences*, Berkhamsted: The Volunteer Centre UK.

Sheard, J. (1986) *The Politics of Volunteering*, London: ADVANCE.

Simey, M.B. (1992) *Charity Rediscovered: A Study of Philanthropic Effort in Nineteenth Century Liverpool*, Liverpool: Liverpool University Press.

Stedman Jones, G. (1971) *Outcast London: A Study in the Relationship between Classes in Victorian Society*, Oxford: Oxford University Press.

Streeck, W. and Schmitter, P.C. (eds) (1985) *Private Interest Government: Beyond Market and State*, London: Sage.

Van Til, J. (1988) *Mapping the Third Sector: Voluntarism in a Changing Social Economy*, New York: The Foundation Center.

Williams, I. (1989) *The Alms Trade: Charities, Past, Present and Future*, London: Unwin Hyman.

Wolch, J.R. (1990) *The Shadow State: Government and Voluntary Sector in Transition*, New York: The Foundation Center.

Wolfenden Committee (1978) *The Future for Voluntary Organisations*, London: Croom Helm.

Woodfield, P. (1987) *Efficiency Scrutiny of the Supervision of Charities*, London: HMSO.

Younghusband, E. (1978) *Social Work in Britain 1950–1975*, London: Allen & Unwin.

6, P. (1993) *What is a Voluntary Organisation? Defining the Voluntary and Non-profit Sectors* (republication of 1991 paper), London: National Council for Voluntary Organisations.

6, P. and Fieldgrass, J. (1992) *Snapshots of the Voluntary Sector*, London: National-Council for Voluntary Organisations.

Index